• HALSGROVE DISCOVER SERIES ➤

WILD LAKELAND

MARTIN VARLEY

HALSGROVE

First published in Great Britain in 2005

Copyright words and pictures (unless otherwise stated) © 2005 Martin Varley

British Library Cataloguing-in-Publication Data
A CIP record for this title is available from the British Library

ISBN 1 84114 475 4

HALSGROVE
Halsgrove House
Lower Moor Way
Tiverton, Devon EX16 6SS
Tel: 01884 243242
Fax: 01884 243325
email: sales@halsgrove.com
website: www.halsgrove.com

Printed and bound by D'Auria Industrie Grafiche Spa, Italy

CONTENTS

Red deer above Mardale GRAHAM UNEY

ACKNOWLEDGEMENTS

This book has been less a work of my wisdom and more one of the collected wisdom of others, to whom I am grateful. Many people have great stories to tell, if you are prepared to listen. Thanks are due to Alistair Brock and Rob Petley-Jones of English Nature and Frank Mawby who helped me with the coastlands chapter. Staff at the Centre for Ecology and Hydrology at Lancaster University helped with scientific research, particularly Ian Winfield on the water chapter. Juliet Frankland was very helpful with the meadows chapter, letting me see the meadows at Bowber Head, records relating to the farm, and sharing her family's history with me.

The woodlands chapter would not have been possible without the help of Maurice Pankhurst, the National Trust property manager for Borrowdale and Dave Shackleton of the RSPB was invaluable during the writing of fells chapter. Steve Hewitt, the Keeper of Natural Sciences at Tullie House, Simon Webb and Jean Johnston were expert sounding boards during the planning stage. I would also like to thank all the photographers who contributed pictures. All unattributed photographs are by the author.

On the production side thanks are due to Georgia Laval, who volunteered to proof read the text without having even met me and to Roly Smith, Editorial Manager for Halsgrove, for making sure everything ran smoothly.

It is to my family that I owe the biggest debt of gratitude: my wife Joanna, who for six months became a writer's widow managing the household single-handedly in my absence, and my children who patiently accepted the phrase 'We'll do that when daddy finishes his book'. Now that I have, I am free to help them explore Wild Lakeland for themselves.

Borrowdale KEITH WOOD

FOREWORD

by Chris Bonington, mountaineer and Vice-President of Friends of the Lake District

Despite spending much of my time exploring other parts of the world, I never cease to be amazed by the diversity of land-scapes and wildlife Lakeland offers, literally on my doorstep. From my home on the edge of the Lake District National Park, I can look out over the smooth, whaleback fells of the 'Back o' Skiddaw'. The Caldbeck Fells may lack the impact of Scafell or Helvellyn, but with fewer visitors they have a wilder feel.

Although, of course, nowhere is really wild in Lakeland anymore. People have left their mark on these mountains, as they have done throughout the region. The ancient hill fort on Carrock Fell tells us that people lived on these heights long before tourists started coming to Keswick and the streams are rich in rare minerals, which were mined for centuries. The rasping ravens and soaring peregrines echo the upland feel of this landscape.

Yet if I travel twenty minutes north I can be standing on the shores of the Solway Firth listening to the call of a hundred barnacle geese, or looking out over a landscape of ancient lowland bogs. Here, in contrast to the fells, the horizons are wide and skies open. The ground is dominated by soggy sphagnum mosses, which will swallow you up to your waist if you a put a foot wrong.

One of my most memorable encounters with this diversity was when we lived in the Sixties for three years just below Kirkland at the foot of Ennerdale. From our cottage we could see Pillar Rock in the distance, towering above the dark forest of the valley. I could wander through fields guarded by lush hedgerows, past old mine workings, relics of the start of the Industrial Revolution, and up on to Kelton Fell. This gentle rolling hillside is seldom visited, but from here you can look out over the coast to the west and the hills to the north and east.

Wild Lakeland provides a refreshing account of Lakeland's natural history. It tells the story of how it has been influenced and affected by our activities in the past and what hope there is for its future. Through its prose and pictures it sheds new light on a region traditionally known for its lakes and fells. The true variety of its wonderful landscapes, from the sea to the mountain tops, is revealed, its fragility explained and the importance of protecting this special place firmly reinforced.

CHRIS BONNINGTON

Scafell Pike (centre left), the highest mountain in England and the destination for James Backhouse's expedition to discover the Scawfell pink.

1
WILD LAKELAND
Made by nature, shaped by Man

Few people today would set out to climb Scafell Pike from Shap, but in August 1847 that is exactly what James Backhouse did. As the son of a York nurseryman, botany was in his blood, and like his father before him he followed the Victorian craze of plant collecting. There had been talk of a new plant, the Scawfell pink, growing amid England's highest mountains, and Backhouse was on his way to track it down.

Today you could drive from York to the Lake District, scale Scafell Pike and be safely tucked up in bed with a cup of cocoa in the time it took Backhouse to walk from Shap to Patterdale on his first day out. Yet it would be two more days before he would arrive at Wasdale Head. It wasn't until the morning of his fourth day that he set out for his big climb. On a clear day it is claimed you can see four countries from the summit, but Backhouse had a poor day, with the mountains blanketed in cloud; he was lucky to see one country.

Sea pink, the discovery of which on Scafell Pike caused a stir during Victorian times.

It did not get any better during his party's ascent as the wind almost blew them from the summit ridge. In their anxiety not to get sucked into Mickledore, the great ravine which separates the two peaks of Scafell, they strayed north of the summit losing themselves in the boulder field above Skew Gill. On retracing their steps they faced violent waves of squally winds and heavy rain.

Such treatment of visitors to the highest peak in England is not uncommon, but few will have made an ascent in those conditions armed only with an umbrella for protection. Backhouse's record of the trip notes that not only did the storm render their rain guards redundant, but that one was torn apart by the storm, leaving only an iron rod walking stick. Exposed to the ferocity of the elements the party were soon soaked and forced to bid a hasty retreat. The perilousness of their plight did not lend itself to genteel pastimes like plant collecting; the Scawfell pink would have to wait for another day.

That other day dawned the following morning. After the previous day's tribulations, this time Backhouse had fair weather with glimpses of the sun. On Scafell he finally encountered the fabled Scawfell pink, but this telling event merits barely a mention in his notes; he remarks dismissively that it is 'nothing more than an ordinary sea pink', and gives it no further mention.

What does this tale of the antics of an eccentric Victorian tell us about Wild Lakeland today? James Backhouse's discovery is more than simply a curious nineteenth-century adventure. We can use it to explore the foundations of wildlife and landscape in Lakeland.

The high brown fritillary butterfly, a high priority species for conservation in Lakeland. ROB PETLEY-JONES

The natural history of the area is a drama written by three authors, who all come together in Backhouse's story: geology, climate and Man. They form the fabric of Wild Lakeland, providing the tapestry on which the life and places described in this book are woven. Their variety gives it diversity. These three elements explain conundrums like why bird's eye primroses grow near Kirkby Stephen but not around Keswick; why eagles no longer fly over Eagle Crag; how ash trees in Borrowdale have lived twice as long as their counterparts elsewhere and how one plant, like the sea pink, could grow in such diverse locations that it could be mistaken for two separate species.

Cumbria, the county in which Lakeland lies, is England's second largest and it is a country of contrasts. The climb from the coast to the summit of its highest peak, Scafell Pike, gives it the greatest altitudinal range of any county in England. Take a journey between Kendal and Cockermouth and you'll cross a landscape sculptured from four different main types of rock, each leaving its own distinctive signature on the scenery. Lakeland has been described as many things over the centuries, but one accusation which can't be levelled at it is that it is monotonous.

The main aim in life for plants and animals is survival. The countryside may look like a quiet place, but it is a plant-eat-plant world out there, as species compete with each other for space to live and food to eat. The primary weapon in this wildlife warfare is adaption. Those plants and animals which adjust most easily to particular conditions will be those which thrive: if you want to get on in the world of nature, adapt and rule.

Nature loves contrast. Differences in climate and geology from place to place mean there are more opportunities for species which can adapt to that change and rule, even if it is only over a small empire. If a county's nature was a house and its biodiversity the number of rooms, then Cumbria would be Buckingham Palace.

And one of those rooms is just right for James Backhouse's sea pink. The distribution of sea pink in Lakeland shows you those places where its particular adaptive skill has allowed it to fight off competition from other plants. It does not grow everywhere because in most places other plants have figured out better ways of holding territory. However, there are two contrasting locations where the sea pink grows, one is on the coast and the other is on the top of Lakeland's highest peaks. What connects them ecologically is that they are both hard places to live, where only the toughest plants survive, but where the sea pink has adapted to make its own.

A raft spider at Roudsea Moss. Raft spiders can commonly be seen hunting for prey on vegetation next to pools of water, often with the first two pairs of legs held together at an angle and resting on the surface of the water. This allows them to sense the presence of tadpoles, insects and even small fish, which they then haul out of the water. ROB PETLEY-JONES

The earth's surface is a place of constant turmoil; it is a battleground between immense tectonic and atmospheric forces. Rock is forever restless: folding and faulting, boiling and bursting, perpetually exposing fresh material to the eternal elements of water and weather. Today's landscape is simply the latest manifestation of this conflict of nature. None of us is likely to be around long enough to witness this environmental hostility on a large scale and see a mountain form or a lake disappear. However, we can all experience being blown off our feet by the wind, soaked to the skin by the rain or having our fingers frozen by the cold. Imagine how this would feel over thousands of years and this is what it is like to be Lakeland rock.

You don't need to be a geologist to understand the geology of Lakeland, but if you want to piece together the landscape and ecological jigsaw which is Wild Lakeland, knowing about geology helps. Geology shapes the scenery. It also leaves its signature on life: it influences the soil, which dictates which plants grow where. These provide the food for insects, which form the basis of virtually all the food chains for Lakeland wildlife. If you know the geology of a place you can have a good guess at which plants and animals you might find there. Likewise, if you are standing on top of one of its highest

Borrowdale volcanic rock on Bowfell. This hard, resistant rock has given rise Lakeland's highest mountains.

mountains looking at a clump of sea pink, this tells you something about the geology under your feet.

A simple law of landscape is the harder the rock the higher the scenery. Scafell Pike is the highest peak in Lakeland because it is made from the hardest rock, and hardness is one defence against the relentless onslaught of the erosive elements whose mission is to flatten the mountains until all that remains is a featureless plain. Once Scafell Pike was part of a range of volcanoes, which spewed out hot ash and molten lava from within the earth through their vents. Time has solidified these lavas and ashes into volcanic rock, known locally as the Borrowdale volcanics. The more compact lavas and harder ashes have formed the most resistant rocks which stand out as the crags and cliffs of the high peaks of Lakeland. Where weaknesses occur these have been attacked by weathering, resulting in gullies and hollows, adding fine detail to the landscape.

The impact of geology on scenery is well seen from a viewpoint like Gummer's Howe, a small, easily-climbed fell at the southern end of Windermere, with a fine panorama of south Lakeland. Looking north, a skyline of classic Lakeland fells is drawn before you. It stretches from the Duddon valley in the west, through the Coniston fells, the Scafells, the Langdale fells, Helvellyn, Fairfield and across to High Street and the Kentmere fells in the east, and is all hewn from a broad band of Borrowdale volcanic rock which sweeps across the land the breadth of the distance between Ambleside to Keswick.

The sharp change between the bold summits of central Lakeland and the rolling landscape of Windermere and Coniston Water is the telltale sign of contrasting geology. These two great lakes lie on rocks known as Silurian slate. Its fragmented structure makes it more vulnerable to assault from weathering and gives south Lakeland a more pastoral feel, with undulating low, wooded fells.

The Buttermere fells and the mountains of Skiddaw and Blencathra are carved from a further belt of slate that runs from Egremont to Mungrisdale. Their rounded forms and

Bluebells at Witherslack Woods. Southern Lakeland has a more wooded, pastoral feel to it than the central fells.

The smooth shape of Skiddaw reflects its contrasting geology compared to the central fells. GRAHAM UNEY

smooth shapes set them apart from their rough volcanic neighbours to the south. These Skiddaw slates are the oldest rock in Lakeland. Beginning their life as muddy sediments laid down in an ancient sea, aeons of uplifting, crumpling and squeezing by the earth's crust has metamorphosed them into slate. They are not soft rocks, but they are much less resistant to erosion than the Borrowdale volcanic rocks and Skiddaw, despite its current height, is being worn away much faster than Scafell Pike.

Limestone at Great Asby Scar.

Looking south from Gummer's Howe, around Kendal and bordering Morecambe Bay, the Silurian slate is intersected by islands of limestone forming the whale-backed ridges of Whitbarrow Scar and Scout Scar. Limestone is made of calcium carbonate, which over time can be dissolved by rainwater. Underground, this process results in spectacular cave formations, but on the surface the same process literally washes away the hills. This limestone scenery runs like a ring around the edge of Lakeland.

This handful of rock types has been a prime mover in shaping the Cumbrian countryside, but it has not done it alone, and the geological map of the county is splashed with all the colours of the rainbow. While the detailed picture of Lakeland geology is a complex one, its most important impact on Lakeland wildlife is summed up in a single word: soil.

Soil is a by-product of the war of attrition between those forces seeking to build up mountains and those which would destroy them. If you have ever wondered what the soil you are walking on is made up of, look no further than the local geology, as up to half of any soil is made up of weathered material from the underlying rock. This rock can make or break a soil; it contributes to its depth, texture, drainage and colour. Its chemical composition influences which minerals are available for soil nutrients. Potassium helps builds proteins, calcium is an essential component of cell walls, magnesium forms part of chlorophyll and phosporus aids photosynthesis.

Plants are anchored in the soil by their roots and nutrients are essential for their growth. So deep, fertile soils make popular places for plants, in the same way that easy access to services make cities attractive to humans. Plants, like humans, prefer an easy life; scratching out an existence somewhere with thin soils and few nutrients is the botanical equivalent of living on a farm in the middle of nowhere. To find a niche here a plant has to develop a degree of self-sufficiency, reinforcing the importance of adaption for species survival. Take an ecological 'crofter' like the sundew. It survives in boggy, damp places, where a lack of nutrients means most other plants are unable to live. But it can only do this because it learnt to adapt, augmenting its nutrient supply by trapping and ingesting insects on sticky pads on its leaves.

Above left: Rigid buckler fern at Hutton Roof. Lakeland is a stronghold for this balsam-scented fern that only occurs on rocks and limestone pavements.

Above right: Sundew has adapted to grow in places with a lack of nutrients that few plants can tolerate.

If anywhere in Lakeland is out in the floral sticks then it is Scafell Pike. The resistance to erosion which has made it England's highest peak has also left it virtually devoid of soil. But sea pink is used to harsh living. It has adapted to Britain coasts, where it may be inundated by sea water, and thrives on lead-rich soils like those found on mine spoil tips. James Backhouse's sea pink would be well-prepared to survive in the meagrest sliver of earth that covers the summit.

Rock that does not weather will not provide the basic building blocks for soil. Victory in the war of attrition against erosion by the Borrowdale volcanic rocks may have kept

The Langdale Pikes form one of Lakeland's classic skylines. They are made from Borrowdale volcanic rocks that yield thin, poor soils, where only a limited variety of flowers such as foxgloves thrive.

The fertility of Lakeland's limestone soils gives rise to flower rich meadows. VAL CORBETT

the mountains of central Lakeland high, but the price paid for outstanding scenery has been poor soils, limiting the range of plants and flowers which can grow there, and the associated wildlife. Only where a weakness in the rock has allowed weathering to take hold, such as in a gill or gully, or where water that has soaked through mineral-rich rock beds comes to the surface, such as at a spring or flush, are the vital nutrients which allow plants to flourish readily available.

By contrast the limestone which encompasses Lakeland is home to the area's most vibrant flora. Calcium is an essential part of plant cell wall structure, and it is probably the single most important mineral influencing the nature of Lakeland vegetation. Rocks where calcium is able to form part of the soil will be where the richest flora is

found. Many of the county's special plants need calcium-rich soil and, since water dissolves the calcium carbonate of which limestone is composed, calcium is readily available in the soils of Lakeland's limestone country. If you want to see flowers, and the insects, butterflies and birds which feed upon them, go to Hutton Roof, Humphrey Head or Smardale, unsung corners of Lakeland.

This picture of Lakeland geology shows a perfect balance in nature as it means no one landscape can boast all of her wild beauties. The high fells have grandeur and majesty, they are the irresistible, bold line on the horizon, which draws people to them. And yet that very quality has deprived them of the subtlety of detail supplied by a carpet of flowers. The limestone on the other hand is overlooked by many. It does not appeal to the visitor by shouting at them from a distance; yet its riches are more intimate and reward those who seek them out.

The second player in the drama of Wild Lakeland is climate. Asked to sum up the climate of Lakeland in one word, a popular answer would be 'wet'. Yet surprisingly, the number of rainy days is similar to the rest of the country. It is just that when it rains in Lakeland, it really *does* rain.

On the evening of August 13, 1966, at the end of a day which had already seen 12 hours of incessant rain, a violent thunderstorm of tropical intensity raged over the Langdale Pikes. A further 100 mm of rain was deposited into already swollen mountain streams causing them to burst their banks. Flood waters swept away drystone walls and cars off roads; two cows were washed down Langdale Beck before being recovered alive and well four miles away at Chapel Stile. Drinkers at the Dungeon Ghyll Hotel found themselves wading to the bar after the ground floor was transformed into a swimming pool in a matter of minutes, and at the National Trust campsite, tents were washed away when a wall collapsed under pressure and swept a metre of water across the site. Huge boulders crashed down the fellsides scouring sections of Dungeon Ghyll down to bare rock.

Had James Backhouse been out in this storm he would have lost more than his umbrella. But not all Lakeland rain falls like this. However, the rapid rise of air over the fells does tend to lead to an increased intensity of precipitation. It is as if the

Common blue butterflies roosting on cocksfoot grass. RON BAINES

Lakeland is the northern limit for the bog bush-cricket, a speciality of the mosses around Morecambe Bay. STEVE HEWITT

Main: *Sand dunes at North Walney National Nature Reserve.* GRAHAM UNEY
Inset: *The sea holly with its distinctive grey-green spiny leaves is a common plant of the shingle and dunes.*

mountains are squeezing every last drop from the clouds. The prevailing wind is from the west and so, laden with moisture from its passage over the Irish Sea, the heavens open most frequently on the central fells. During 1954, more than 6.5m of rainfall was recorded at Sprinkling Tarn, between Esk Hause and Sty Head, five times the amount which fell on Kendal that same year. Backhouse, and anyone else climbing Scafell Pike, Bowfell or Great Gable, should expect to get rained on; on average more than 10 mm falls each day on the tight cluster fells surrounding the tarn, making it seven times wetter than London.

Rainfall of such intensity and volume is not only unpleasant to be out in, it affects the vegetation too. As the water moves downwards through the soil it washes out the all important minerals vegetation depends upon. As if life wasn't already hard enough for plants eking out an existence in central Lakeland, where mean volcanic rock barely weathers sufficiently to produce soil, to then have this hard-won fertility leached away is a double blow and means only the hardiest species survive in the harsh, acid earth. Where rainwater cannot drain, perhaps in a hollow, or where the slope is not steep enough, colonising plants face a new challenge. The ground soon becomes waterlogged and over time, another distinctive mountain habitat which plagues walkers may start to form: bog.

Wet woodland at Glasson Moss, part of the South Solway Mosses National Nature Reserve.

The hen harrier not longer regularly breeds in Lakeland, but winters in the low-lying and coastal areas, particularly around the Solway RICHARD SAUNDERS

19

Yet it is unfair to tar all of Lakeland with the same brush. It may feel like it, but it does not rain all the time here. The high fells bear the brunt. Being on the receiving end of more than three metres of rain a year, Seathwaite's boast may be as the wettest place in England. Yet just 10 km down the Borrowdale valley, Keswick has less than half this amount. Twenty five miles further east at Penrith, the rainfall drops to one quarter of that at Seathwaite. Penrith lies on sandstone. The lower rainfall is an additional bonus, reducing leaching and further improving growing conditions for plants compared with their high fell counterparts.

Stanley Ghyll, Eskdale.

With so much rain it is surprising that Lakeland receives so little snow. Although originally shaped by glaciers, the area has less than twenty days a year when snow falls in the valleys. It is too close to the sea to ever get really cold, but its large altitudinal range means that it experiences extremes, including some of England's coldest weather. The lack of vegetation on these severe summits reflects the harshness of a climate which has more in common with Greenland than Greenwich. And this is despite them not being high hills compared to other parts of the world. In the Alps the climate is hospitable enough for communities to have lived for centuries at altitudes twice the height of Scafell Pike. In the Rocky Mountains all you would see from the top of a peak the height of Helvellyn is trees, a sharp contrast to Lakeland where it is unlikely that the tree line has ever extended much above 800m.

Temperature as much as geology defines what grows where. As a general rule plants can't grow in temperatures less than 5 degrees C. Lakeland's highest mountains have never been tree-covered simply because their summits have never been warm enough for long enough. The growing season on top of Scafell Pike may be as short as three months, too short for trees to survive. Although colder in the winter, the Alps and the Rockies are warmer in the summer for longer, allowing plants to grow at much higher altitudes.

Places with extremes of temperature like these are often found far from the sea, which tends to have a moderating effect on climate, bringing cool summers and mild winters. July in Keswick, the hottest month of the year, is about 12 degrees C warmer than January, the coldest. This difference is roughly half of what you would expect in Denver east of the Rockies. We may curse the wet weather Lakeland's oceanic

The last decade has seen a revival in the fortunes of the osprey in Lakeland, with activity centred on Bassenthwaite Lake. In 1998 two birds spent the summer there, one of them a chick known to have fledged from a site on Speyside. In 2000, at another site, a pair bred in Lakeland for the time in about 170 years. A chick fledged at Bassenthwaite achieved celebrity status the following year when 25,000 people viewed its first ten weeks from a video link at nearby Whinlatter Forest. Since then ospreys and osprey watching has become a regular feature in Lakeland's wildlife calendar. MARK HAMBLIN

Woodland at Roudsea Wood and Mosses National Nature Reserve, where the absence of grazing animals has allowed a ground cover of bilberry to form.

climate brings, but it could be much worse. Ambleside is at roughly the same latitude as Moscow, where in January the temperature regularly drops to −15 degrees C. It is only its closeness to the sea, and the the associated warming influence of the Gulf Stream, that rescues Lakeland from the same icy fate.

The unique combination of latitude, altitude, temperature and rainfall has produced an ecology delicately balanced between pine forests and permafrost; we can enjoy breathtaking views from the mountain tops without freezing our feet. It contributes to the great diversity of Lakeland's landscapes, compressing a whole host of habitats ranging from seashore to sub-Arctic into less than a 1000m of height. In a day's walk you can watch seabirds skimming the waves for fish at dawn and see purple saxifrage clinging to life on ledges by dusk. Topography adds a further dimension. Different slopes facing different directions provide new opportunities for plants and animals. Round every corner this fusion of elements throws up a new surprise.

Geology and climate may have formed the clay of Wild Lakeland, but Man has been the potter, shaping the landscape with his activities and in turn constraining the wildlife which can thrive there. On that stormy day in 1847 James Backhouse may have felt like the first person to have climbed Scafell Pike, but he was probably 4500 years too late to claim that accolade. Here, and on similar sites on Scafell, the Langdale Pikes and Glaramara, Lakeland's first industry grew up as Neolithic man exploited the hardness of the volcanic rock for the manufacture of axe heads. Tonnes of fist-sized pieces of loose scree were excavated and transported to settlements on the coast to be ground and polished into thin-butted, narrow-faced axes.

Until then, since the retreat of the glaciers at the end of the last Ice Age, nature had been slowly making herself at home, little troubled by man. Tree species had come and gone like guests at a fashionable party as ecological phases ebbed and flowed. First birch, then pine, then oak. Ash and small-leaved lime were the late arrivals. It is likely

Castlerigg stone circle, just one of many reminders of how far back in time Man's connection with Lakeland stretches.

that only the high peaks remained treeless with unbroken forests covering the valleys and lower hills, where bears, wolves and wild boar roamed.

The stone axe changed all that. It spelled the beginning of the end for the upland forest. Any woodland which existed around the factories would have soon been cleared as these areas were converted into industrial sites and summer pastures. It wasn't only Lakeland trees which were chopped down with these new weapons. Langdale axes were market leaders, traded up and down the country in centres as far apart as Argyll and Dorset. Major commercial routes also criss-crossed the Irish Sea. As many as a third of stone axes found on the Isle of Man came from workings on and around Pike o'Stickle; it was big business. Man's exploitation of Lakeland had begun and it would never be truly wild again.

By the time the Romans arrived, a highly developed agricultural economy was already in place, which must have been one of its attractions. Large areas had already been deforested and the need to feed an occupying force would have only accelerated this process. The Romans too, did their bit to tame the landscape, forging roads across the high fells between Ravenglass and Ambleside and over High Street to Penrith.

Each subsequent power that settled made deeper inroads into Lakeland's wild heart. The land had become simply a place of raw materials ripe for exploitation. The

How much different would Lakeland have looked when Roman soldiers were stationed, at Hardknott Fort, Eskdale? RONNY MITCHELL

For many centuries farming has shaped the landscape of Lakeland. The irregular shapes of the walls at Wasdale Head suggest that agriculture has been carried out here since medieval times. RONNY MITCHELL

Vikings, mainly arriving by sea from Ireland to the west, penetrated deep inland to farm fells that must have reminded them of home. Their legacy is the language of the landscape. Features which define the topography, like tarn, fell, beck, gill and dale, were given to us by the Norsemen. Other names tell us about what they did. Ambleside was Amul's summer grazing, Grizedale was the valley where pigs were kept. It was the Vikings who gave the treeless Scafell its name – 'bald mountain'.

But it was during medieval times that Man began to truly dominate Wild Lakeland. The Normans arrived late to this distant corner of England – there are no Cumbrian names in the Domesday Book – but soon made up for lost time, carving the region up and handing vast chunks of land to feudal overlords. The remote daleheads became commercial enterprises in the hands of money-minded barons living in lowland castles in places like Kendal, Millom, Egremont and Cockermouth. Remote holdings, like Gillerthwaite in Ennerdale, became dairy farms or 'vaccaries'. In the late thirteenth century, Gatesgarth at the head of Buttermere supported a herd of 60 cows and their offspring. By the 1300s, Lakeland was a busy place. Even Wasdale Head boasted four vaccaries, part of what was becoming an increasing industrial landscape offering livelihoods for wood-turners, charcoal burners, iron smelters, tanners, miners, fishermen and weavers.

What land the barons didn't own, the church did. Furness Abbey alone owned the Furness fells, between Coniston Water, Windermere and the Leven Estuary, Upper Eskdale and Borrowdale. The Cistercians of Furness were more than monks, they were shrewd businessmen who transformed farming from being a hard, subsistence livelihood into being profitable big business. Their prosperity came from an animal which would shape the future of Wild Lakeland: sheep.

From medieval times onwards sheep farming, using native breeds like the Herdwick, was the hub the of the rural economy. But the wealth of the wool trade came at a price. Forest was cleared to make way for sheep grazing and where it remained grazing stifled woodland regeneration. Heath was transformed to grassland. Variety gradually drained from the landscape. Remaining predators who had once ruled the woodlands were now the enemy, praying on prized but vulnerable stock: the wolf and the eagle were hunted to extinction. By the time James Backhouse made his way up Scafell Pike, the wholesale conversion of the valleys to sheep holdings was almost complete. The mile upon mile of drystone wall, constructed after the Parliamentary Enclosure Acts of the seventeenth and eighteenth centuries, had divided the land up into convenient units for agricultural improvement. Burning, liming and draining enabled all but the poorest acid soils to be reclaimed, turning lower Lakeland into an increasingly managed landscape.

Wildness retreated into the mind. Lakeland's landowners may have treated it as a place for profit, but by the eighteenth century a new dawn of enlightenment was breaking. Early travellers – the 'Lakers' – inspired by journeys to the Alps or the Apennines, were reinventing Lakeland. No longer was it simply a place of work, it became somewhere to stretch your senses, a place to enjoy, a landscape of aesthetics to instill fear and to thrill you. It was a classic landscape: in its farmed pastures the Lakers saw not the taming hand of Man, but pastoral beauty, which contrasted with the sublime force of uncontrollable nature expressed in the hard lines of the high fells.

Not only did the first Lakers bring a fresh eye to view the landscape, they proclaimed its virtues through the written word. They described a place half-imagined, half-real, a landscape of stupendous cliffs rising in grotesque grandeur to dreadful heights where birds of prey built their nests. Reality or a dream, their writings drew more tourists seeking out the Picturesque landscape they portrayed.

Writers even told visitors how best to see the landscape. The Claude glass was standard equipment for the Picturesque tourist. This slightly-convex tinted mirror produced tonal images that supposedly resembled works by French landscape painter Claude Lorrain, whose romanticised landscapes had helped to define the Picturesque. Its use for the tourist was in producing an easy-to-view, soundbite landscape, the composition of which could be seen at a glance and its wild horrors pared down to postcard size.

By the time Backhouse set out to climb Scafell Pike, the reputation of Lakeland's landscape had already made it a top tourism destination. After his sea pink excursion Backhouse thought nothing of returning home to York on foot, but he could have opted for a more comfortable trip via the Kendal to Windermere railway. It had just opened and in its first year carried 120,000 passengers, quadrupling the number of visitors to the town: mass tourism had arrived.

It was not only the scenery which the Victorians coveted. The rarities of the fells also caught their eye. Backhouse was one of a generation of Victorian plant hunters. It was they who first catalogued Cumbria's mountain plants, but many of them, particularly the ferns of its woodlands and the flora of its fells, found their way into collectors' greenhouses and gardens. By this time too, many plants were being used for medicinal purposes. Backhouse may have been disappointed that the fabled Scawfell pink turned out to be plain old sea pink, but in the eighteenth century, Scottish Highlanders survived for days in the mountains nourished by the roots of sea pink. Had he been caught in another storm, Backhouse might have been grateful for this natural snack.

Both Man and nature have helped to shape Wild Lakeland. Above left, at Castle Crag, Thirlmere, the wall builders have used the rock outcrop as part of the field boundary. Above right, in Eskdale, lichen has colonised the man-made habitat of a dry stone wall.

Man's activities in Lakeland has continued unabated until today. However firmly its history may be rooted in geology and climate, its present is uncompromisingly Man's. Look down on any Lakeland valley and the dominant controlling hand is ours. This is perhaps why we still come in our millions to see this dynamic, awe-inspiring blend of Man and nature. The Lakers sought sanctuary in the manicured landscapes of the lakes and low fells and yet were irresistibly drawn by fear and wonder to the high fells, aroused by a wilder Lakeland. Don't we feel the same way today?

Despite nearly 5000 years of Man working this land, Lakeland still retains the imprint of the wild. Its wildness is in its contrast to the increasingly urbanised landscapes of the rest of England's heavily populated and over-managed countryside. It is a place to experience adventure that takes us away from the ordinary of the everyday and where we can discover habitats and animals not seen in such variety elsewhere. It may no longer be wilderness, but this is Wild Lakeland.

Bog asphodel at Roudsea Wood and Mosses National Nature Reserve.

2
COASTLANDS
Bogs, beaches and barnacle geese

Wedholme Flow is an unlikely place to attract the attention of eco-warriors. It is not a nuclear reprocessing plant, the proposed site of a new airport or bypass, or a redundant oil rig. It is a lowland raised bog: an open, flat, damp land of peat, tucked away in north Lakeland, a stone's throw from the Solway Coast. Yet, in February 2002, it was the scene of direct action by the campaign group Peat Alert as part of its National Day of Action against the Scotts Company, the largest supplier of horticultural products in the world.

Along with similar raised bogs at Hatfield and Thorne Moors, near Doncaster, Scotts were extracting Wedholme Flow peat to feed the insatiable appetite of Britain's gardeners, who consume 70 per cent of all peat used in the UK. Easy to access, the deep peat of lowland raised bogs has made them prime targets for commercial extraction. Peat Alert's action was intended to highlight the plight of Britain's raised bogs, a rare habitat. Only 6 per cent of the UK's lowland raised bogs remains.

Wedholme Flow is a Site of Special Scientific Interest and has been designated a candidate Special Area of Conservation under the European Union's Habitats and Species Directive, underlining its international significance. However, such designations have not saved sites like Wedholme Flow, where consent for extracting peat had been given before their nature conservation value was recognised. So common was this anomaly that by the early 1990s, the majority of Britain's peat was being taken from protected sites.

In February 2002, 10 volunteers descended on Wedholme Flow, commited to the cause. But it turned out not to be a high-octane encounter, more a day of direct inaction. There

Peat extraction at Wedholme Flow.
RONNY MITCHELL

The Duddon estuary is internationally important for birds. More than 20,000 waders winter on the estuary including redshank, oystercatcher, ringed plover, curlew and dunlin. The estuary also supports 5000 wintering wildfowl including pintail, shelduck and red-breasted merganser, as well as being home to half of Cumbria's natterjack toads, almost 25 per cent of the entire UK population.

was not much work to disrupt, and the activists had to settle for damming drains and hampering preparations for the spring's peat harvest. Perhaps workers had already got wind of the change that was in the air, as less than a fortnight later came the announcement that commercial peat extraction at the three sites would cease, following an agreement between Scotts and English Nature, the Government's conservation advisors. Lakeland's endangered bog had been saved, but at a price. Permission to cut peat at Wedholme Flow had been granted until 2040 and compensation to Scotts for the loss of earnings there and at the other two sites would cost £17.3m.

Raised bogs, like the other unsung habitats of Lakeland's coasts — its sand dunes, shingle banks, salt marshes and estuaries — are often overlooked in favour of the more dramatic scenery of its lakes and fells. But they are just as important; Wild Lakeland stretches from the sea to the summits. The wildlife and natural habitats which stretch from the Kent to the Solway are equally spectacular to those encountered further inland: the Duddon estuary is home to almost one in four of the UK's natterjack toads, more than 14,000 pairs of lesser black-backed and herring gulls breed every summer at South Walney and nearly a third of England's remaining raised bog is found in Lakeland's coastal hinterland.

Vipers bugloss at South Walney. With 14,000 pairs of lesser black-backed and herring gulls breeding there, South Walney Nature reserve is well-known for its birds, but it is also the best out of only a handful of places in Cumbria to see vipers bugloss. CUMBRIA WILDLIFE TRUST/ KERRY MILLIGAN Inset: *Herring gull.* ROB PETLEY-JONES

In the south, the Duddon Mosses, Roudsea Moss, Meathop Moss and Foulshaw Moss fringe the Duddon, Leven and Kent estuaries and in the north, more raised bog fringes the Solway Firth. Together with Bowness Common and Glasson Moss, Wedholme Flow is part of the South Solway Mosses National Nature Reserve, three of the best remaining examples of raised bogs in Europe, and once part of a bigger area which extended from the coast at Cardurnock in the west across to Drumburgh in the east. 'Moss' is a good descriptive name, as these are the plants most likely to be found in these habitats. Ten varieties can be seen on the South Solway Mosses alone.

The South Solway Mosses began to develop about 7,000 years ago. Melting ice at the end of the last Ice Age caused sea level to rise, inundating low-lying hollows. As the centuries passed, sea level changed and the climate became cooler and wetter, turning the hollows into shallow freshwater pools. As vegetation in these wet areas grew and died back, the dead matter became compressed to form peat, which changed the chemistry of the water turning it more acidic, slowly making it harder and harder for plants to survive.

Waterlogged, highly acidic and deficient in essential nutrients, these wet areas would not be a first choice habitat for most plants. But then sphagnum mosses are not like most plants, and it is these plants which are the key to the development of a raised bog. Sphagnum mosses are experts in colonising hostile environments, and they thrive under acidic conditions. These rootless plants grow from a bud at the tip of their stem, and are able to survive solely by absorbing nutrients from rainfall through the surface of their leaves.

Foulshaw Moss, now a Cumbria Wildlife Trust nature reserve, and one of number of lowland raised bogs found on Lakeland's coastland fringe.

With sphagnum species capable of absorbing up to 20 times their own weight in water, it is little wonder that bogs are so wet underfoot. Once a sphagnum carpet takes hold, it customises the bog chemistry by releasing hydrogen ions, further increasing the acidity of the water and keeping most competitors at bay. Moreover, there are 30 species of sphagnum in Britain, each one adapted to slightly different conditions, giving it the flexibility to succeed in a wide range of environments.

As the sphagnum expands other plants are overwhelmed by the moss and absorbed into the growing mass of peat. Like a rice pudding, the bog now has two separate parts: the skin and the pudding beneath. The surface is the skin. It is clothed in a dense green, gold or reddish coat of damp sphagnum. Only where mosses form hummocks do bogs get dry enough to allow a handful of other plants, such as heather, cotton grass, bilberry, cranberry, crowberry and bog rosemary, or specialised species like sundew, butterwort and bog asphodel, to find a foothold. Even at their most diverse, raised bogs are lean habitats.

Sphagnum mosses are the dominant vegetation on lowland raised bogs.

Beneath the skin is the pudding, the deep, dark, damp depths of peat, which, over time, can accumulate to great depths. Between 13 and 14 metres of peat lies beneath

Wedholme Flow. Peat accumulates at the rate of about 1m per millennium, suggesting that the first peat at Wedholme was laid down soon after the ice sheets had retreated into the Solway Firth. In the cold, acidic environment of a peat bog, things rot much slower. It acts like a giant pickling jar. From the tiniest pollen grain to the skin and bones of a man, raised bogs have locked up a record of the past in an organic time capsule. The only tool needed to begin exploring their history is a spade.

Man's introduction to Lakeland came at a time when the main highway was the sea. Much has happened to the landscape since that time, perhaps as long ago as 4000BC, but faint images of these distant times remain embedded in the memory of Wild Lakeland's coastlands, and from these archeologists have pieced together a picture of the first Cumbrians.

In the summers of 1965 and 1966 an area of rough heather-covered coastland, south of the Ministry of Defence range at Eskmeals and a stone's throw from the beach, was ploughed to form two fields. There were no signs that the land had ever been ploughed previously. After ploughing, it soon became clear that not only was it near the beach, but it once had *been* the beach, as on the western side, pebbles and sand came easily to the surface. To the east the land fell away to a boggy hollow containing several metres of peat. And that was not all the ploughing revealed: fragments of flint were dragged up, which on closer inspection showed signs of having been sharpened and shaped. Further investigation exposed flakes, scrapers, arrowheads, and fragments of pot. Subsequent archeological excavations retrieved an incredible 34,000 artefacts, including 600 tools.

Cranberries on the Duddon Mosses.

This was Williamson Moss, one of several areas in Lakeland that would have once been raised bog, but which had since been improved and turned over to agriculture, leaving the peat just below the surface. Around 6000 years ago it would have been a shallow lagoon, the beginnings of a raised bog, only separated from the sea by a sand bar. The forest here would have been less dense, giving it immediate appeal to any passing travellers. There would have been plenty of fish and shellfish in the sea, waterfowl on the lagoon, trout and salmon in the River Esk and inland, game, nuts, berries and other edible plants. This oasis of sand and water, surrounded by a mixture of open grassland and woods, would have been a truly Mesolithic paradise. So rich was the potential food

Eskmeals Nature Reserve, Ravenglass. Like many of Lakeland's coastal features, the reserve is a dynamic environment. Most of it is a shingle peninsula over which the sea once flowed. Wave action piled the shingle into parallel ridges, forcing the River Esk to change its course. Sand, blown in from the shore, gradually collected on the shingle and has formed into dunes, the highest of which is over 20m high. The dune formation has allowed salt marsh, grassland and seashore habitats to form.

RONNY MITCHELL

Limpet shells.

supply that the settlers need never have moved, which would make Eskmeals one of the earliest recorded permanently occupied sites in England.

Landforms like sand dunes act as a buffer, dispersing the immense power of the sea and shielding the land behind. This makes them dynamic, energetic places, always on the move, always changing and not conducive to agriculture. It is this reluctance to be tamed that has protected their wildness and helped to preserve the imprint of Man over the intervening millennia. Evidence of a coastal kingdom had already been uncovered in the 1930s, when flints where discovered nearby in the dunes at Eskmeals, and further south on a beach on Walney Island.

Both sites showed signs of flint production on a large scale, suggesting that it was a highly developed industry, which included the export of stone axes from factories in the Lakeland fells. Similar sites had already been discovered off the coast of south-west

Coastal grassland at Eskmeals, dotted with bird's foot trefoil.

Scotland. This evidence, combined with the finds at Williamson Moss, shone a spotlight on Lakeland's prehistoric coastlands. Walney Island and Eskmeals were reinvented as important ports of call in an ancient world where the sea offered the easiest means of communication and the people of Anglesey, the Isle of Man, Northern Ireland and Scotland were Cumbria's most accessible neighbours.

The pickling properties of acidic bogs have preserved more macabre artefacts than the cast-offs from Neolithic production lines. A male body was recovered from Seascale Moss, now farmland, in the early part of the nineteenth century. Only the skin, nails and hair remained, which, according to *The Cumberland Pacquet* of June 3, 1834, 'gave the hands an appearance of fine leather gloves, the nails still continuing to the fingers'. The best guess at dating the body estimated it to be at least 2000 years old. Similar bodies from other wetlands in northwest Europe – for example Lindow Man from Cheshire – show signs of rutual killing and it seems likely that the 'Seascale Moss Man' suffered the same fate.

Pyramidal orchid at Eskmeals. Lakeland is almost as far north as this clove-scented orchid is found. It is uncommon and found in only a handful of places on the coast.

One day in July 1991, the driver of a commercial peat extracting machine on one of the raised bogs on the Solway Coast in northern Lakeland was taken by surprise when he noticed a cattle horn protruding from the levelled surface. It proved to be part of a cow's skull, still with considerable amounts of skin and hair intact. Widespread excavations unearthed the additional remains of a few feet bones. Extensive scientific research described a limited biography for the 'Solway Cow', as it became known. The tan-coloured beast dated to the early medieval period and met its end in an area of open water some distance from the edge of the bog, possibly as part of some local ritual. A year later the body of a sheep was found on the same moss. It had died more recently and more mundanely, some time in the last 500 years, having strayed onto the moss and starved to death.

Analysis of pollen captured in the peat throws a different kind of light on the past. Pollen is nature's calling card. Designed to facilitate reproduction by trees and plants, it is also a vegetative fingerprint, which, when stamped into the peat, paints a contemporary picture of the local landscape. But interpreting these tiny clues trapped in sediment deep underground for hundreds or thousands of years is like reading a history when there is only a handful of words on every page. In the South Solway Mosses, scien-

March cinquefoil at Sandscale Haws, its dull reddy-purple colour sets it apart from any other native flower.

tists have used the pollen record to chart the expansion of the forests and their subsequent conversion to grassland as Man arrived there about 5000 years ago. There is even evidence that Neolithic farmers were cultivating cereals long before the Romans came.

One of the most interesting discoveries of pollen analysis comes from Glasson Moss, close to Wedholme Flow. In the early 1990s several circular and linear features were noticed on the surface of the moss, prompting archaeologists to investigate further. Studies of cores taken from the peat revealed the presence of hemp pollen. Cultivation of hemp was widespread in medieval Lakeland. It was so important that in the sixteenth century, farmers were compelled to grow hemp by law. Anyone who owned more than 24 hectares of farmland could receive a fine for failing to turn a proportion of their land over to hemp production.

Fleswick Bay, St. Bees Head. St Bees Head is one of the largest cliff seabird colonies on the west coast of England. Birds seen nesting include razorbills, kittiwakes, fulmars and puffins and it is the only black guillemot breeding site in England.

Common hawker dragonflies mating. The male is blue-spotted, the female are frequently yellow-spotted. Commonly found in upland and moorland habitats, they are also found on the Solway Solway Mosses. RICHARD SPEIRS

The common darter dragonfly is the most widespread darter dragonfly in Cumbria. The straight-sided, orange-red body of the mature male make it easily recognisable. RON BAINES

Its main use was for making ropes which would have had many uses, from hauling carts and boats, to lashing together scaffolding and lifting building materials. To separate the hemp fibres from the wood of the plant, the hard stems had to be rotted or 'ret' in a pool or river. This was a messy process which polluted the watercourse. The practice was clearly widespread and a source of local friction. In the Glasson area, a Holme Cultram manor custom of 1657 records 'that noe tenant or other inhabitant do water any hemp or flax in any river, running stream, brook, or other common pond where beasts used to be watered upon pain of 6s 8d (38p)'. Studies of the features at Glasson Moss suggested that they were rare examples of hemp retting pools dating back 1000-1400 years. These pools and drains would have had the advantage of being away from settlements, reducing the risk to domestic water supplies during retting, which lasted up to six weeks.

Up until the Agricultural Revolution, much of Lakeland's lowland raised bog seems to have remained relatively intact. At Wedholme Flow, peat would have been cut for fuel rather than timber, which was locally used exclusively to maintain sea defences. But large-scale conversion of bogs into agricultural land had not yet begun. However, there were controls over cutting. In the sixteenth century, Elizabeth I established the Sixteen Men of Wedholme, a group similar to a local parliament. One of their jobs was to prevent the wholesale stripping of the coastal raised bogs. Only after the Enclosure Awards, brought about by Acts of Parliament from the early nineteenth century onwards, did the landscape begin to change significantly. Up until the 1800s, the potential of lowland raised bogs as a resource had never been fully realised; bogs, like the high fells, were seen as 'waste land'.

But the awards changed all that. The mosses were divided into strips or 'stints' and gradually Solway's extensive lowland raised bogs shrank under the rising tide of agriculture. The edges were most susceptible to change as they were the easiest places to access. In a raised bog they are also the regions of greatest diversity, as here the acid water from the moss mixes with water with more nutrients from the drier land. Under a natural system, there would be a succession here from bog to

Woodland would naturally form at the edge of a lowland raised bog similar to that seen here at Glasson Moss, one of the best lowland raised bogs in Lakeland.

LAKELAND'S WINGED WONDERS

Eider duck. GRAHAM UNEY

Arctic tern. GRAHAM UNEY

Greenshank. KEITH TEMPLE

Gannet. GRAHAM UNEY

fen to wet woodland of alder and willows and culminating in woodlands of oak, ash and hazel, depending on geology.

At Wedholme Flow the assault on the moss margins was so great that no traces of this habitat remain. During the time of the enclosures, commoners from Newton Arlosh and Kirkbride set about draining the land for farming, or cutting it for fuel. Grain crops were sown on the best land and poorly drained areas used for pasture.

By the turn of twentieth century, large-scale commercial exploitation of Wedholme Flow began with the British Midland Peat Company selling peat as animal litter. The moss had become an industrial site, with peat being removed first by hand, then horse-drawn machines and finally by precision machinery. *The Cumberland News* of January 1951 told the story of the Cumberland Moss Litter Company, a post-war ecomonic success whose peat bales were even exported to America. Photographs showed the peat train on Glasson Moss, carrying flat-capped men and trucks of sods to the processing mill on the light railway which crossed the common.

Ringed plover. KEITH TEMPLE

Scotts' peat extraction on Wedholme Flow was not the destruction of an untouched corner of Wild Lakeland. It may have been the most intensive exploitation, but it was merely the latest in a chain of uses Man has made of lowland raised bogs stretching back over centuries. This story is best illustrated on a map. Around the fringes of the moss are thick green strips, showing stints that were converted to agriculture during the earliest enclosures and are now farmland. About a quarter of the moss remains relatively natural with few signs of incursions by Man. The rest is marked by a maze of parallel lines, each one representing a drain, where the skin of the moss has been punctured, allowing water to seep away. The short, sometimes broken lines are the Victorian drains and in the east, covering about a quarter of the moss, are the longer, more regimented lines marking the commercial peat stripping of the last fifty years, culminating in the buy-out of Scotts in 2002.

Curlew sandpiper. KEITH TEMPLE

Since then Wild Lakeland has been returning to Wedholme Flow. Nature possesses a remarkable resiliance. The Scotts buy-out was the final stage in the beginning of a restoration programme for Wedholme Flow started by English Nature in 1990. The main task is to dam the drains and begin the process of re-wetting the bog. In many

Salt marsh on the Solway Coast, roosting ground for thousands of wading birds including oystercatchers, knots, grey plovers and bar-tailed godwits. In the winter, wildfowl use the adjacent grassland and open water areas, including over 1000 barnacle geese.
VAL CORBETT   Inset: *Barnacle goose.*
MARTIN CAMPBELL

areas beginnings of a new raised bog are already showing. Loose carpets of spagnum are covering hollows and hummocky mosses are starting to form, but with many miles of drains present it is landscape restoration on an unprecedented scale. Wedholme Flow is on its way to recovery. Where commercial extraction took place it removed about a third of the peat, but the haemorrhaging of a habitat which took place during the years of peat extraction has now been stemmed. The wounds are starting to heal, but a lot of scars still remain and it will be a long time before the moss fully recovers.

The pattern of restoration at Wedholme Flow is being repeated in all the South Solway Mosses, which are now substantially owned and managed by conservation organisations. In 2004, on Drumburgh Moss to the east of Wedholme Flow, Cumbria Wildlife Trust carried out major restoration works to raise the water levels. In the same year on nearby Bowness Common, English Nature and the Royal Society for the Protection of Birds (RSPB) bought two farms. What were previously livestock holdings will now reap a harvest of wildlife. Dams and sluices will be installed on land previously drained for pasture at Biglands Farm and Rogersceugh Farm, near Bowness-on-Solway. Some of the fields will be allowed to flood, restoring the water table. For the first time in many centuries, the area of raised bog is set to expand. Birds such as lapwing, redshank and curlew could return to the area, along with rare plants and dazzling dragonflies.

Perhaps more significantly, the land at Biglands Farm is adjacent to the RSPB's Campfield Marsh Nature Reserve. In winter, as many as 1200 barnacle geese come to the marshes, contributing to the nearly 200 species of birds which have been recorded here. The reserve is on the shores of the Solway Firth, the UK's third largest continuous intertidal habitat, which plays host to thousands of wintering wildfowl and waders. This is quintessential coastland.

After centuries of Wild Lakeland's landscapes gradually being eroded into smaller and smaller pockets and leaving wildlife isolated, different types of habitats are now being brought together, extending opportunites for birds and animals. Oystercatchers and bar-tailed godwits assemble on the sand banks of the estuary while dunlins, ringed plover and redshank feed in its muddy creeks. These habitats link with the salt marsh, fed on by pink-footed geese, and wet grassland of the shore, where wigeon and teal make use of the flooded fields in winter. This latest purchase provides an opportunity to join these habitats to the peatlands of the lowland raised bog favoured by snipe and lapwing. Such natural connectivity is rare, but crucial, if wildlife is to thrive.

Coastlands are Lakeland's forgotten countryside. Their remoteness and unwillingness to yield to the plough has helped them to retain their wildness today, and living under the shadow of the more spectacular landscapes of the central fells has left them overlooked as a destination by the modern visitor. Yet the coastal habitats and lowland raised bogs of Lakeland are some of the finest in England, home to internationally-important colonies of birds, plants and animals. They also hold the key to Man's history in Lakeland, offering clues to help solve the puzzles of the past in their peat and sand.

Pebbles at St Bees.

3
MEADOWS
Nature's apothecary

It was 1940 and the intensifying war in Europe was beginning to bite into the economy back home when Raven Frankland paid £1000 for Bowber Head Farm, a rundown agricultural holding in Ravenstonedale, four miles south of Kirkby Stephen. It had little going for it; it was a high-lying farm and its climate was not in its favour. It had too much rainfall and a short growing season. Moreover, the previous decades had been poor ones for farming and, due to the ill-health of the previous owner, little had been done to improve the land. In fact, none of the farm had received much attention: buildings were in disrepair and walls broken down. Locals described it as the 'rafiest' farm in the district.

That didn't worry Raven. His was from pioneer stock. His great-grandfather had started out as a chemist's assistant, but rose to become a famous water analyst who even once tested water for Queen Victoria. Raven had grown up on nearby Needlehouse Farm, which he farmed for his father and, relieved of war duties on medical grounds, he threw himself into farming, adding the land at Bowber Head. One advantage the farm did have was the local geology: Bowber Head lies on a band of limestone which curves its way round the volcanic and slate rocks of the central fells, stretching north towards Penrith and west towards Kendal and Ulverston.

Plants love lime. The calcium it contains forms a fundamental part of the cell structure, and soils where this mineral is available are always more productive. Farmers had known the value of lime for increasing soil fertility for many years, as the profusion of lime kilns which punctuate Lakeland's limestone belt testify.

As a result, like many other farms in the area, Bowber Head was a riot of colour at haytime, with dozen of varieties of wild flowers swaying in the fields, speckling the

Wild flowers attract insects and butterflies like the small pearl-bordered fritillary butterfly. RON BAINES

Opposite: *A traditional upland hay meadow near Lorton.* RICHARD SPEIRS

Hay meadows near Shap. VAL CORBETT

landscape with blues, pinks, yellows and whites. Raven was able to capitalise on this advantage, gradually increasing the productivity of the farm by liming every field and periodically covering the land with basic slag from steel works, which provided an additional source of calcium and also phosphorus.

Steeped in tradition, Raven recognised the value of his meadows and took to heart the words of experienced farmers who told him to keep his 'erbs'. Herbs were at the heart of the traditional hay meadows; this was the name for the flowering plants which grew and seeded each year, dressing the country scene in nature's hues every summer. Having studied land management at Cambridge, Raven was also no Luddite and was well aware that herbs had a further value beyond aesthetics. Hay contained minerals and trace elements that helped maintain healthy stock.

It was not only animals which benefited from herbs. Even as late as the 1930s, around 90 per cent of medicines prescribed by doctors or sold over the counter were of herbal origin. A typical dressing for battle wounds in the First World War was garlic, a natural antibiotic, and sphagnum moss, a natural, highly-absorbent antiseptic. Most plants

Field scabious.

Melancholy thistle.

Rockrose.

Mountain pansy.

Primrose.

Bird's eye primrose.

FLOWERS OF LAKELAND'S MEADOWS

used in British medicine were imported from countries where they grew more abundantly and could be dried more easily. The onset of the second World War severed the supply from Europe and precipitated a crisis for the nation's health.

The year Raven purchased Bowber Head, Whitechapel Hospital alerted Kew Gardens that it was facing serious shortages of essential drugs from plants and asked for help in finding new sources. Nationwide collections of medicinal plants were begun, led by the National Federation of Women's Institutes. Boy Scouts roamed the countryside armed with specially-produced cigarette cards illustrating the types of plants in greatest need.

In 1941, as the shortage of medicines became increasing acute, the Ministry of Health established the Vegetable Drugs Committee, which took over the organisation of medical plant supplies from Kew. County plant lists were drawn up and collection was organised at a local level through county herb committees. In the first year of the herb committees, children from all over Britain collected 1000 tonnes of plants. This figure doubled in 1943 and quadrupled in 1944.

The chairman of the Lancashire Herb Committee, which covered part of Lakeland, was Lady Tomlinson. She lived in Grange-over-Sands and the grounds of her house were used as a local 'bulking' centre, where plants were collected, packed and dispatched to the drug manufacturers. It was all hands to the meadows and hedgerows as she and her committee mobilised the formidable forces of Girl Guides, Boy Scouts, Young Farmers, local schools and Women's Institutes to collect plants by the sackful.

The challenge was eagerly accepted. On average, between 1942-5, Lakeland's herbal army collected 450kg of wild plants and flowers every year. In 1943, in a true showing of the wartime spirit, a local septuagenarian single-handedly dug and dried out 45kg of dandelion root.

More than 80 species were collected. Widely, but not always wisely, used in folk medicine, foxglove tea was a cure for colds, sore throats and fevers. Its leaves and seeds contain the drug digitalis which affects the heart, and during the war they were collected for use in the treatment of heart conditions. But its prescription was a risky

Wordsworth called the skylark the pilgrim of the sky, but there were probably more of them in his day. Between 1968 and 1996, the number of skylarks on Britain's farmland fell by three-quarters. While intensification of lowland farmland has led to populations plummeting in these habitats, in the uplands increased numbers of livestock grazing the fells have led to more open areas, creating new breeding opportunities for skylarks. GRAHAM UNEY

business: too much and the heart could stop altogether. Children were particularly susceptible, with numerous cases of children dying from drinking an excess of foxglove tea recorded. No wonder in parts of the country its usage in treating scarlet fever in children was limited to wearing the leaves in their shoes for a year.

Among the other plants collected, sphagnum mosses continued to be used for dressing wounds, elderflowers for colds and influenza, dandelion roots as a laxative, stinging nettles as an anti-asthmatic to combat respiratory infections, male fern for the relief of tapeworm infections, wood sage as a diuretic and wild thyme as an antiseptic, while valerian acted as a sedative. Even the leaves of poisonous plants like deadly nightshade were collected, its belladonna powders being an used in sedative and antispasmodic drugs.

Foxgloves, one of many wild flowers collected during the Second World War for use in the pharmaceutical industry.

As well as plants for drugs, others were added for general health. Rosehips were collected as a source of vitamin C and conkers from horse chestnut trees were processed to provide a source of glucose for Lucozade. While Lakeland's collectors were keen on conkers, rosehips proved more problematic, and were a constant course of concern to the Lancashire Herb Committee. By 1944 things were so bad that prizes were offered to the schools which collected the most rosehips. It seemed to have the desired effect as between 1944 and 1945 collection increased sixfold. Cartmell Fell School and Coniston School continually received praise from the committee for their commitment to herb gathering, scooping the prizes and receiving certificates to prove it.

The end of the war spelt the end of the herb committees, as the new National Health Service developed long-term policies for the cultivation of vegetable drugs and gradually, as synthesised medicines became the norm, the value given to wild herbs declined.

War changed agriculture too. It had exposed weaknesses in the UK's traditional farming methods and the desire for self-sufficiency in foodstuffs fuelled an insatiable drive towards increased productivity. The farmland scene was transformed from the pastoral to the industrial. Traditional meadows were ploughed up and reseeded with commercial rye-grass. Nitrogen fertilisers were added to accelerate the production of grass, providing more and more food for the increasing number of stock which modern post-war farming demanded.

Agriculture began eroding diversity, replacing nature's variety with a man-made monoculture. Under intensive farming, production reigned supreme. The delicate balance between the needs of wildlife and agriculture, which traditional farming had sought to maintain, tipped sharply away from Wild Lakeland.

But at Bowber Head, Raven Frankland was able to resist the tide. While modern methods may have been more efficient and created greater productivity, he recognised that they came at a price. Intensifying farming increased its scale: as well as increasing income, keeping more animals requires bigger buildings, more fertilisers and pesticides and increases other overheads. The lack of minerals in the silage now used as animal feed, which had replaced the "'erbs" that Raven had been urged to keep, no doubt contributed to larger vet's bills.

Monkeyflower.   RON BAINES

Lakeland's orchids, from left:
Common spotted orchid.
Northern marsh orchid.
Bee orchid.   RICHARD SPEIRS
Fly orchid.   RICHARD SPEIRS

The pressure to intensify was great. As more and more farmers took advantage of incentives to increase production, it became harder for the few remaining traditional farmers to survive. The old ways were less efficient, requiring more labour. It took twice as long to make hay than silage, which can be cut earlier and can produce two or three crops a year.

Raven only kept going because he had been fortunate enough to acquire cheaply a portion of an estate in Dentdale. The additional income this generated meant he could avoid the escalating economies of intensive agriculture and resist the drive down the production farming road. Without an alternative income to subsidise traditional farming during the post-war decades, it seemed that intensification was inevitable.

Even though he eventually moved away from the day-to-day running of Bowber Head, the principles Raven established remained imprinted on its activities. The men who worked for him respected his wishes and even now after his death, the traditional practices he set in place still go on. No artificial nitrogen-based fertilisers or herbicides has been applied to the land and after sixty-five years of swimming against the farming tide, Bowber Head Farm is now internationally-recognised as an island of diversity in an otherwise monocultural agricultural sea.

So overwhelming was the flood of intensification that virtually all of the UK's traditional herb-rich meadows have been destroyed since the Second World War. It is estimated that only three per cent now remain, a measure of the pricelessness of places like Bowber Head's meadows – which hold more 250 types of flowering plants. Moreover, hay is cut in late June or early July allowing farmland birds like curlew and lapwing to breed, unlike silage which is often cut much earlier.

The meadows read like a multi-coloured, living library of wild flowers. Purples of wood crane's bill, betony, melancholy thistle, common knapweed and devil's-bit scabious, mix with blues of meadow cranesbill, harebell, reds of of great burnet, whites of pignut, cow parsley, oxeye daisy, sweet cicely, yellows of meadow and creeping buttercups, meadow vetchling and yellow rattle, as well as abundant grasses and sedges. On the steeper ground common rock-rose, salad burnet, purging flax, burnet saxifrage, cowslip, limestone bedstraw, and fragrant orchid can be found.

The riches of Bowber Head's traditional meadows extend beyond their floral abundance. They trail a thread back in time, which elsewhere the insatiable appetite of intensification has severed. The farm records go back 400 years and show that although two of the fields were ploughed during the Second World War, many of them have never been agriculturally-improved in the modern sense.

The silence of the land across the centuries holds many secrets. There is still evidence of strip farming from medieval times when farms were communal. Earth drains uncovered in some of the fields date back to monastic times, when Bowber Head was under monastic control and three canons and a handful of laymen were sent from Watton Priory, near York, to farm in Ravenstonedale. There are still two fields called Canon Hole and Far Canon Hole today.

Pignut flowering in a meadow near Staveley.

Piper Hole meadows, still part of Bowber Head Farm despite being slightly detached to the east, holds the darkest secret. Local legend tells how, during the second Jacobite rebellion of 1745, as Bonny Prince Charlie was retreating from the English, one of his Scots pipers got separated from his party and sheltered in a hollow in what is now Piper Hole meadows, but which at the time was part of Lockholme Foot Farm. To console himself he began to play his beloved bagpipes. It turned out to be an unwise move as the sound was heard by the farmer who caught him and murdered him. He was buried under the hearth of the farmhouse and in the same year the name on the deeds was

Lapwing, one of a number of farmland birds that has seen a decline. Between 1987 and 1998 number of breeding pairs in Cumbria fell by more than half.
KEITH TEMPLE

Wild thyme, one of the many flowers that have medicinal or culinary uses.

changed to Piper Hole, adding a chilling authenticity to the story. It is a macabre thought that the meadows may not have been ploughed since the piper piped his last.

It is not only colour, diversity and history which has disappeared from the landscape with the loss of Lakeland's herb-rich meadows; botanical heritage has seeped silently away too. Rye-grass has few cultural associations, but the wild flowers in Lakeland's last remaining meadows have stories to tell that have seldom been heard by a society slowly moving its roots out of the soil and into the city. The technological age is still relatively new and over the millennia of Man's history, plants have been put to a vast range of uses, some more fantastic than others. The use of wild thyme in cooking and as a tea seems very reasonable, but how much success it has had as a moth repellent or cure for alcoholism is unclear.

Several types of bedstraw can be found in Lakeland's meadows, across all geological types. Heath bedstraw is commonest on the acid soils of the central fells. It is almost identical to limestone bedstraw, which as its name suggests prefers limestone areas, where lady's bedstraw and northern bedstraw also occur. They all share the scent of newly-mown hay and their name is derived from the habit of using handfuls of the flower for stuffing mattresses. The roasted seeds of lady's bedstraw are said to be a substitute for coffee, but the claim that a sprig in the shoe prevents blisters, could only be confirmed by a very curious fellwalker.

Yellowhammer, once a common bird of pasture and farmland. KEITH TEMPLE

Oxeye daisies.

Grass of Parnassus, a much-loved flower of upland wet meadows. It was voted Cumberland's county flower in a poll conducted by Plantlife in 2003.
RICHARD SPEIRS

Some wild flowers still share there secrets today. The delicious aniseed taste of sweet cicely leaves can still be enjoyed and can be cooked with tart fruit to reduce their acidity. Thankfully though there are more effective cures for snake and dog bites. Meadowsweet's medicinal past reaches back to the time of the Druids, for whom it was revered as a sacred plant. Like many plants, it was multi-purpose, being widely use for complaints for which today we would employ aspirin. Its flowers sweetened tea, its roots gave a black dye and its plant tops a yellow dye. Unfortunately, the scarcity of most of these plants means that their pleasures can cannot be enjoyed as they used to be, since the picking of many of them has been made illegal.

In the few places where the natural variety of wild flowers once common in Lakeland can be found, a more intimate reading of the landscape can be made. Plants are adapted to respond to the availability of different minerals in the soil. The flora of soil formed where the underlying rocks are alkaline or rich in lime and other plant nutrients are very different from those which grow in acid soils and soils deficient in lime; every meadow displays a signature of the local geology. In central Lakeland, the thin, acid soils are unproductive with few wild flowers. Pasture land is also restricted to the valley bottoms which increase pressure to improve the productivity of what little suitable land there is for grazing.

Remnants of these upland hay meadows can still be found in Langdale, Borrowdale in Westmorland and Bretherdale. Here, the presence of flowers such as betony, foxgloves, sheep's sorrel and heath bedstraw and grasses such as wavy-hair grass and purple moor grass are a sign of the acidic nature of the slates and volcanic rocks from which the soil has been formed. As with penguins and polar bears, these plants would not be found growing beside flowers such as common rock-rose, hairy violet and northern bedstraw and grasses such as blue moor grass and quaking grass. These lime-loving plants are restricted to Lakeland's limestone, which outcrops in an eastern line from Morecambe Bay at Humphrey Head, Whitbarrow Scar, Scout Scar, Hutton Roof Crags and around Orton.

While not strictly meadows, these escarpments are an important part of Wild Lakeland. Farming is difficult on their steeply-sloping, often stony ground and they have maintained much of their diversity. Many areas are now managed for conservation of their rich wildlife, including a number of rare species and habitats. As well as

Whitbarrow Scar, one of several lime-stone outcrops in southern Lakeland.
SIMON WEBB

unusual plants such as angular Solomon's seal and dark red helleborine, Hutton Roof Crags have a rich variety of butterflies, including high brown fritillary, pearl bordered fritillary and Duke of Burgundy. Great and Little Asby Scar, in the Orton Fells, form the second largest area of limestone pavement in the UK.

Lakeland's best meadow flora can now be seen in places like these, which have been least affected by the intensification of agriculture, and include some unlikely locations. In 1857, at the height of the Industrial Revolution, a railway was built from Tebay to Kirkby Stephen to carry fuel from the Durham coalfields for the iron furnaces of Barrow-in-Furness. Coke-laden steam trains racing through the countryside hardly sounds a recipe for Wild Lakeland, but since the railway closed in 1962, the disused line has turned into a haven for nature.

Ironically, the construction of the railway protected a corridor of herb-rich grassland from the agricultural intensification which has affected the surrounding fields. The best sites are now looked after by Cumbria Wildlife Trust as nature reserves. In high summer the banks of Smardale Gill National Nature Reserve, north of Ravenstonedale, are ablaze with common rock-rose and bird's-foot trefoil; bloody cranesbill and

Dark-red helleborine, a flower limited to Lakeland's limestone areas. SIMON WEBB

Scotch argus butterfly, only found in Lakeland at Smardale. It is one of the latest butterflies to fly, with adults not usually taking to the wing until late July. RON BAINES

common wintergreen also grow here. The Scotch argus and northern brown argus are just two of the rarer butterflies which make it their home. At nearby Waitby Greenriggs Nature Reserve, west of Kirkby Stephen, a remarkable 210 species of flowering plant have been recorded.

Lakeland's other unexpected wild flower oases are its roadside verges. Like disused railways, roads have been saved from the worst excesses of production farming, creating a tunnel of wildlife. Insect life, especially bees and butterflies, is particularly abundant in herb-rich verges, which also support small mammals and birds. Lakeland's verges are so important for wildlife that the most important are individually managed, with the timing of the cutting planned to help protect the wild flowers and cuttings removed to prevent fertility increasing. There are nearly 700 km of these special verges in Cumbria. Road users are most likely to see common knapweed and meadowsweet, which occur on over half of the verges, but altogether almost 500 species of wild flowers have been recorded.

Lakeland's meadows are a fragile part of Wild Lakeland. Despite at one time being so common as to be ordinary, today they are extraordinary. After the Second World War, it became virtually impossible for farmers to resist the relentless drive for increased productivity in agriculture which stripped meadows of their value. Only people like

Bluebell and dog's mercury on Great Asby Scar. The channels between blocks of limestone pavements provide a sheltered environment for micro-ecosystem akin to woodland to develop.

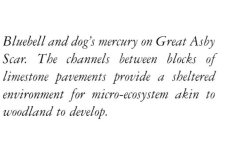

Roadside verges, like this one near Kirkby Stephen, are an important habitat for flowers, insects and butterflies.
Inset: *Six-spot burnet moth.*   RON BAINES

Fieldfare, a common winter visitor to Lakeland's fields and pastures. KEITH TEMPLE

Columbine at Cumbria Wildlife Trust's nature reserve at Latterbarrow. Often a garden escapee on roadside verges and railway lines, the native variety occurs here and at other sites around the Kent estuary.

Raven Frankland, who recognised their worth and could afford to escape the agricultural treadmill, could buck the trend. Their actions may have been seen as anachronistic at the time, but now, as the light that herb-rich meadows shine on the natural world has slowly been recognised, what they did has become visionary.

As the value of the old meadows has once again been recognised, their seed has become a vital store of genetic gold, offering the opportunity to restore past diversity. In summer 2005, Friends of the Lake District took the first steps towards recreating an upland hay meadow in Borrowdale, Westmorland. However, it was only possible because seed from one of the few remaining traditional hay meadows was available locally. It is early days for the project, but if it succeeds it could provide inspiration for others. These refuges of yesterday's flora are both a link with the past and a hope for the future.

Water on oak leaf.

Oak leaf on ice.   RICHARD SPEIRS

Frost on oak leaves.

Oak leaf in autumn.

4
WOODLANDS
Lakeland's rainforest

February 23, 1857 was a busy day for Joseph Flintoff. According to his handwritten notebook, Flintoff set off into Borrowdale where he collected over 800 specimens of more than 40 types of mosses. His grand tour took in Castle Crag, Thornthwaite Gill and Lodore and Great Woods, and his closely-written descriptions of mosses with their unpronounceable Latin names were accompanied by delicately-drawn sketches to aid their identification.

At first glance, mosses may seem like an undifferentiated green mat, but close-up they exhibit an amazing variety of structure, only revealed at a scale usually overlooked by the human eye. Flintoff wanted to capture this diversity in his sketches. Not only did their forms appeal to his artistic nature, but he also needed to be clear about the differences between them because he did more than just collect mosses, he sold them too. The nineteenth century witnessed the rise of the great Victorian craze for collecting. Flintoff's contribution was to compile and sell bound volumes of his mosses, which must have had a ready market as early souvenirs of Lakeland.

Flintoff had time on his hands. Although not from a wealthy background – he was one of six children from a Quaker family in North Yorkshire – he landed on his feet when he married a well-off widow, Mrs Cheetham, and came to live near Keswick. A contemporary directory describes him as 'a gentleman of Lizzick Hall, in the township of Underskiddaw', an imposing mansion off the Keswick-Carlisle road. His life of leisure allowed him plenty of time to explore every nook and cranny of the Lake District on his collecting excursions, but the woodlands of Borrowdale were his favourite haunt.

Now, as then, Borrowdale's woodlands hold a special place in Wild Lakeland. Their

Borrowdale woodland from above Derwent Water.

Troutdale Woods, Borrowdale. RICHARD SPEIRS

distinction is their timelessness. Their names: Great Wood, Johnny Wood, Lodore and Troutdale Woods, Seatoller Wood and Stonethwaite Wood, echo through time, and would have been as familiar to Flintoff and generations before him as they are to us today. They clothe the valley sides like a blanket. They are moist, damp places with a climate of their own. Cross from the closely-cropped pastures of the valley floor into one of these green kingdoms and a different sense of nature is present.

They are Atlantic oakwoods, a rare habitat in the UK confined mostly to the west: Scotland, Lakeland, parts of Northern Ireland, Wales, Devon and Cornwall. They experience high rainfall, making them lush, verdant places. Mosses hang from gnarled trees; splashes of brightly-coloured liverworts and lichens paint nature's graffiti on boulders and bark, and ferns fan out from shady corners.

Atlantic oakwoods are a glimpse of what the first woods must have been like before the arrival of man. Once they would have covered large areas of Lakeland, but now only small patches remain, scattered from Naddle Forest in the east through the woodlands of Ullswater to Scales Wood in Buttermere and Side Wood on the shores of Ennerdale Water. But none are as extensive as those of Borrowdale: this is Lakeland's rainforest.

Atlantic oakwoods at Side Wood, Ennerdale.

Atlantic oakwoods contour the fellside at Scales Wood, Buttermere.

67

It is no wonder, then, that in Flintoff's notebooks the numbers of specimens collected read like cricket scorecards: *Necra crispa* 53, *Bryum capillare* 18, *Bartramia halleriana* 23. There is no record of just how many volumes of his *Mosses in the English Lake District* Flintoff made, but eighty years after his death half a dozen copies were still circulating in the secondhand bookshops of Keswick. The Victorian energy for exploring the natural world and having a piece of it in their homes seemed insatiable. Almost every drawing room had its display of curios: ancient fossils, exotic shells and rare minerals lined walls and windowsills. And Lakeland was no exception to the craze.

In Flintoff's day, Keswick boasted two museums, the fashion for curiosities irresistibly drawing people from across the land. His bound collections of mosses were a shrewd exploitation of the trend, a contemporary equivalent of Kendal Mint Cake. And it was not just mosses. Flintoff's interests spread to another of Lakeland's woodland specialities: ferns, which he collected and sold in similar bound volumes. There is copy at Keswick Museum: 40 pages of thick, heavy paper, each with a carefully pressed and mounted fern with its name and where it was found labelled in Flintoff's meticulous handwriting.

The mosses of Lakeland's Atlantic oakwoods were a focus for Victorian collectors like Joseph Flintoff.

Lakeland's geography makes it ideally suited to ferns. 'The English Lake Country might not inappropriately be called the Land of Ferns,' writes W.J. Linton in his *Ferns of the English Lake Country,* a best-seller going into three editions at the height of the collecting mania during the mid-nineteenth century. According to Linton, Lakeland boasted 35 of Britain's 43 indigenous ferns, exploiting the region's diverse geology, altitude and aspect, and favourable climate. He goes on to intimately describe each fern, where it was found and by whom. Judging by the list of names, Flintoff was not the only enthusiast in the area.

So great was the interest in ferns and their collecting that those early naturalists decided to form a club. In September 1891, the first meeting of the Northern British Pteridological Society was held in Kendal 'for the purpose of forming an association of fern growers and enthusiastic admirers of ferns for the north of England', the minutes record. Subscription was five shillings (25p). In the following years members decided to drop 'Northern' from the society's name to broaden its appeal. The British Pteridological Society remains the country's leading fern organisation today.

Ferns in Naddle Forest. Lakeland's climate makes it ideally suited to the growth of ferns.

The largest survivor of Borrowdale's famous yew trees. It is estimated to be at 1500 years old and one of a number of ancient yews in Lakeland. There is enough room for eight people to squeeze inside its hollow trunk. In 2003 it was named as one of 50 Great British Trees by the Tree Council to mark the Queen's Golden Jubilee.

This obsession with ferns undoubtedly led to their depletion in the wild. In the terraced houses of Keswick, aside from having Flintoff's fern albums and others stacked on their bookshelves, no self-respecting Victorian would be without a selection of ferns in their garden. Many of these plants would have been taken from the local woods. Demand was sufficiently large for there to be a fern nursery established by a local collector, William Askew, at Derwent House on the road between Lodore and Grange. Although the house is now a private residence, the nursery was open until the early decades of the twentieth century.

Despite this assault, many of these viridescent fruits of the forest can still be found in Borrowdale's woodlands today, and this set them apart as Wild Lakeland. It is the longevity of these woodlands and the damp climate which has given rise to this richness. Nature works over a long timescale: the more time it has, the more diverse it becomes.

The redstart, or 'firetail' as it is locally known, builds its nest in holes in trees.
KEITH TEMPLE

However, no-one is too sure about how far back in history Borrowdale's woodlands stretch, or in fact any woodland in Cumbria. We do know that, as in other parts of Britain, Lakeland was once a lot more wooded that it is now. Only about one-tenth of Cumbria is wooded and about half of that figure is made up of conifer plantations, the wildlife interest of which is far less than their broadleaved counterparts. South Lakeland still has glorious stretches of wooded countryside, particularly among the Furness Fells and in the Duddon valley, but, with exception of Borrowdale and Ennerdale, North Lakeland is much less wooded.

Charting past changes to Lakeland's woodland is not straightforward. Its history is like a jigsaw shaped by nature's dynamics, climate change and man's activities, but there are only a few pieces from which to build up the full picture. There is much about it that we can only guess. After the last ice age had wiped the landscape clean, woodland soon arrived on the scene. Pollen from trees, trapped in the sediment which has accumulated on the beds of lakes and tarns, acts like an arboreal footprint and gives us evidence of what trees grew where and when. Scientists analysing these sediments can journey back in time, tracing the rise and fall of individual species of Cumbria's woodland dynasty.

The wood warbler is a slim elegant bird with a shivering trill, which likes woodland with little ground cover. Its Lakeland strongholds are the mature woodlands around Loweswater, Nether Wasdale, Torver and Elterwater. KEITH TEMPLE

Opposite: *Red squirrels have become an icon of Lakeland, still one of their UK strongholds. Genetically distinct from other red squirrels and immortalised by Beatrix Potter, they are under threat from the rising tide of grey squirrels and the parapox virus.* KEITH TEMPLE

Although the last vestiges of ice finally left Cumbria about 10,000 years ago, it had retreated from lower lying areas much earlier than this. Sediment cores extracted from Burnmoor Tarn, above Eskdale, provide a record of local vegetation going back 14,000 years. Records from nearby Devoke Water also extend over the same period allowing dated measurements to be cross-checked. The earliest post-glacial invaders were juniper and birch, followed closely by hazel. The latest arrivals, small-leaved lime and ash, completed Lakeland's native tree inventory about 6000 years ago. These first forests have become known as the 'wildwood'.

The records of the spread of the wildwood reveal that the open fells, such an iconic characteristic of today's Wild Lakeland, have not always been this way. Encouraged by a warmer climate, the wildwood laid a carpet of foliage across the countryside. Sediments cores recovered from Red Tarn beneath Helvellyn, at a height of over 700m, suggest that trees were once widespread locally even at this altitude.

The wildwood landscape would have been dominated by broadleaved woodlands containing oak, elm, hazel, alder, birch, small-leaved lime and ash. This was the golden age for trees, when for a millennium, woodlands reigned supreme in Lakeland. Species' dominance ebbed and flowed on nature's tide, governed by fluctuations in climate and variations in soils. Then, about four and a half thousand years ago, Man began to change the woodlands – and they would never be the same again.

By combining analysis of pollen records with other historical information, a more detailed picture of the fate of Lakeland's wildwood emerges. By about 2500 BC, Neolithic man had begun to venture into the high fells and had discovered the source of a tool capable of large-scale landscape change. Archaeologists have found evidence of stone axe factory sites in the Langdale Pikes dating back to this time. Langdale axes have been discovered throughout the country suggesting that it was a major industry.

Ramsons flower early in spring before the leaves appear on the trees and shade the ground from sunlight.

In nearby Angle Tarn, sediment cores reveal a corresponding decline in tree cover during the period when the sites were being worked. Forests would have been cleared for grazing and for charcoal, which was used in the axe manufacturing process. Charcoal discovered at the sites has been found to contain oak, hazel, alder and birch, just the sorts of trees which would have been growing locally prior to man's arrival. Within 500 years, Langdale's ancient upland woodlands were transformed into heather moorland and grassland.

What began in Langdale was repeated elsewhere, as slowly Lakeland's woodlands retreated. By the time the Romans arrived, agricultural advances had already increased the rate of deforestation, particularly in lowland areas. The presence of a large military infrastructure no doubt acted as a catalyst for further woodland removal. Pollen records show that there were occasional periods when woodlands made a comeback, but they would never again achieve the rule they had over the land before man arrived.

From Norman times onwards, written records make it easier to piece together the story of Lakeland's woodlands. Barons would sometimes sell portions of their land to monasteries in the hope that by gaining favour with the abbots and monks they would ease their passage to heaven. Furness and Fountains Abbeys were the main beneficiaries of this baronial benevolence.

Furness Abbey acquired land between Coniston and Windermere and also in Borrowdale. The charter of Alice de Rumeli to Furness Abbey relating to the transfer of the land in Borrowdale suggests a country wilder than today, but still far removed from the wildwood. It was a land populated by 'hart and hind, wild boar, goshawks and other sharp hooved and horned wild beast', in which the abbots and monk were offered 'all liberties in the hillish and plain ground, in meadows and pasture, in ways and

Pollarded ash trees in Seatoller Wood, Borrowdale. Pollarding of the trees has extended their life and some of them are thought to be as much as 700 years old, more than twice the typical age for ash. Their longevity has allowed them to become a reservoir for lichens with some trees holding 30 species and making Seatoller Wood the most important woodland for lichen in north west England.

75

Bluebells at White Moss Common. KEITH WOOD

paths, waters and standing pools, mosses and turbury land ploughed and to be ploughed, sown and to be sown'.

So where is the wildwood today? This is not an easy question to answer since we cannot tell how old today's woodlands are. Dating woodland is an inexact science. They are like families: unless the cycle of growth, death and regeneration keeps going, a woodland will die in the same way that a family line will cease without children. And just as knowing the age of one family member won't tell you how far back its history goes, so knowing how old a single tree is won't help pinpoint the age of a woodland.

The boldest that conservationists will be is to define an 'ancient semi-natural woodland', that is one which has been in existence since at least 1600. The evidence of pollen records prior to this makes it unlikely that any wildwood remains today. Although the ancient semi-natural woodlands of Borrowdale are a shining example of Wild Lakeland, even with their remarkable diversity they must be only an ecological echo of Lakeland's first forests.

Moreover, being classed as an ancient semi-natural woodland does not imply an absence of Man's intervention over the last 400 years. On the contrary, many woodlands are only here today because the resources they offer have been valued and managed in the past. Their story reads like a social history. Although places for quiet rest and relaxation today, woodlands would have been noisy, bustling places, they were the industrial estates of the Middle Ages.

Coppicing was the most common form of woodland management. A young tree would be cut down to about 30cm above the ground. In spring, the stump, or 'stool' would send up new shoots, which would be left to grow before being cropped again. Coppiced every fifteen years, each stool would provide as many as 20 six-metre poles. There was hardly a contemporary industry which didn't use coppiced wood: tanning, brewing, mining, textiles, agriculture, transport and construction, and charcoal production all depended on it. The value of woodlands couldn't be over-estimated. As well as being a raw material, coppiced wood was converted to charcoal, a multi-purpose industrial fuel. The smelting of iron using charcoal goes back to Roman times, and is captured in local place names like Cinder Hill, Forge Wood and Smithy Beck.

Pollarded oak in Langdale. Woodland products were far more valuable in the past having a variety of uses from brewing to building. Coppicing was widespread, particularly in southern Lakeland. RICHARD SPEIRS

Woodlands were nature's corner shop. Oak supplied timber for ships and houses, oars and tool handles were made from ash, birch was used in wood turning, hazel for withies and laths and alder for clog soles. Industry's appetite was insatiable. In the sixteenth century, a German company gained royal approval to begin working copper and other mines around Keswick. It needed so much wood that local supplies were insufficient and a buyer had to be sent to Ireland to procure additional stocks.

The value of land was measured by the amount of wood which grew there. When Sir James Ratcliff, the second Earl of Derwent Water, was found guilty of treason for his part in the Stuart uprising of 1715, his estates were confiscated and assessed by the number of trees they contained. Men were dispatched onto his land to record individual species fit for cutting. In Keswick's woods, over 6000 oak, more than 5000 ash and nearly 3000 other trees were counted. Many of these were cut down and replanted with native species along with beech, horse chestnut, larch and sycamore.

Once maps start to be published an assessment of changes to individual woods becomes possible. In Joseph Flintoff's time the latest in cartography was the Tithe Map, an eccle-

Autumn colours in Seathwaite Woods.   KEITH WOOD

siastical land survey of Cumbria carried out in 1842. The use of every field in every parish was surveyed and its owner recorded. Its primary purpose was to allow the local church to assess what tithe it could claim from each of its parishioners. However, it coincidentally provides a fascinating contemporary insight into how land was being used.

Unlike today, when most of Borrowdale is given over to sheep farming, the Tithe Map shows a far more diverse, less wooded landscape with many fields turned over to arable. Borrowdale's woods are described not in terms of their nature conservation value, but their use to the Victorian farmer. Johnny Wood, Grange Wood and Great Wood were described as 'woodland'. This meant that animal grazing may have been restricted and the wood used for building and other domestic purposes. However, Seatoller and Stonethwaite Woods are described as 'pasture'. This probably doesn't mean that trees were absent, but that the land was a mixture of wood and pasture. Cover would have been more sparse than today, and they would have been used as shelter for sheep and cattle and winter grazing.

Wood anemones, one of the first signs of spring. RICHARD SPEIRS

Today, if you climb the Bowder Stone you cannot poke your head above the canopy of oak and birch. Yet the Tithe Map illustrates a more revealing history of the woodlands which now grace the Bowder Stone and hang above Lodore. They too are described as pasture. This could also mean wood pasture, but other evidence suggests that there might have been little or no woodland here at this time. On the first edition Ordnance Survey maps, printed twenty years later, trees are conspicuous by their absence from this area.

Furthermore, on the wall of the National Trust's office in Borrowdale is a black and white photograph taken around the turn of the twentieth century looking west from the Bowder Stone and showing a treeless landscape. All of this is tantalising evidence suggesting that things in Borrowdale have not always been as they seem. The primeval feel to the Jaws of Borrowdale may be a more recent return to a far more distant past than might be imagined. While most of the woodlands have been there for centuries, their extent has clearly shifted over time. It may have looked as it does today for less than a hundred years.

However, it is the overall longevity of the woodlands which is the key to their nature conservation value today. And while the international importance of these and the

Lush vegetation typical of Atlantic oakwoods at Lodore Falls, Borrowdale.

other Atlantic oakwoods in Lakeland cannot be overstated, it is easily overlooked. This is because what makes these woodlands so special is not a cute and cuddly mammal like a red squirrel, or a rare and majestic bird like an osprey, it is a group of plants so uncharismatic that even their collective name is enough to send the most budding amateur naturalist scurrying back to Keswick for a cup tea: bryophytes.

Bryophytes is the collective name for primitive non-vascular plants such as mosses, liverworts and hornworts. They form one of the largest groups of land plants in the world, and the 136 species of bryophytes which have been recorded in Borrowdale's woodlands puts them in the same league as the temperate rainforests of North America, New Zealand and Chile. In Johnny Wood they coat the boulder-strewn floor. In the Lodore gorge they hang off trees. Their verdant cloak hushes the sounds of the wood, the atmosphere is close, clouds twist and turn, drifting between trees.

They may not be the wildwood, but they have a primeval feel, reflected in the bryophytes which are primitive plants which do not have tubing to carry sugars, nutrients and water through their tissues like other plants. They depend upon retaining water in their leaves, giving them a crucial role in maintaining woodland humidity and explaining why cracks and crevices on the woodland's slopes drip with moisture.

Despite the abundance, variety and importance of bryophytes, few people's identification skills of them extend further than being able to recognise the characteristically-spongy green cushions of sphagnum moss, which typify Lakeland's bogs. This is not surprising because bryophytes, unlike most other wildlife, have an image problem.

Even people with only limited interest in birds would probably know that the golden eagle was one of Lakeland's rarest avian inhabitants. But there must be only a handful of experts who know that Johnny Wood is home to *Sematophyllum micans,* one of Britain's scarcest mosses. The downfall of bryophytes is that they are most commonly known by their Latin name. As if it wasn't hard enough to try to distinguish between a multitude of species of moist green rock and bark carpets, you need to learn a new language in order to name them! It is no wonder then that bryophyte-spotting has never caught on, which is a shame because they have a beauty and distinction which is wrapped in their detail at a microscopic level.

Plagiochila spinulosa *alias prickly featherwort.*

Lepidozia cupressina *alias rock fingerwort.*

Trichocolea tormentella *alias handsome wollywort.*

Metzgeria conjugata *alias rock veilwort.*

BRILLIANT BRYOPHYTES. ALL JONATHAN SLEATH

83

Greater spotted woodpecker, whose characteristic drumming is one of the sounds of spring in Lakeland's woodlands.
KEITH TEMPLE

But they also have English names. *Sematophyllum micans's* other name is sparkling signal-moss. Many names are also descriptive, bringing the miniature world of bryophytes to life. *Ptilium crista-castrensis* is an unpronounceable rarity of Stonethwaite Wood, whose north-east facing slopes make an ideal home for mosses and lichens. However, its English name is ostrich-plume feather-moss, which suddenly gives it an identity. It was one of Joseph Flintoff's favourite finds, and the thumbnail sketch showing its feather-like features which grace his notebook graphically reveal how it came to get its name. Other English names for mosses and liverworts, like many-fruited bearded-moss and Funck's rustwort, are equally colourful, giving these understated plants a whole new personality.

Lichens are another of Lakeland's Atlantic oakwood specialities in need of a makeover. They are part fungus and part alga, which can form into fantastic shapes on trees and rocks. The alga photosynthesises, while the fungus provides a stable, protective environment. The fungus forms the main body of the lichen and, in most cases, the alga lies sandwiched between upper and lower fungal layers. Its growth rate can be as small as a fraction of a millimetre a year, but undisturbed it can live to a great age.

The longevity of Borrowdale woodlands has proved a stable environment which favours lichen growth. In Seatoller Wood nearly 200 species have been recorded. But like bryophytes, their cause has been hindered by the words used to describe them. Seatoller Wood is the only place in England where *Leptoguim burgessi* has been recorded but this special quality of Wild Lakeland passes most of us by.

Wood sorrel. SIMON WEBB

Given their conservation value, regardless of whether we recognise it, it is not surprising that Borrowdale woodlands are carefully managed. They are looked after by the National Trust whose long-term perspective means that plans can be drawn for the future without worrying about the shifting economy of agriculture. After centuries of use as a resource by Man, nature is now taking centre stage once again. No longer is the wood needed for building, tanning, coppicing or even shelter for sheep. Now it is all about naturalness and the value of the associated increased biodiversity which this brings.

Such a change is also challenging ideas about what woodlands should be like. The most natural woodlands in Europe, in countries like Poland and Romania, are a contrast to

Lakeland's woodlands. Nature is left to get on with it, with very little intervention in their management.

But if a tree falls down in our woods it needs to be tidied up. Dead standing trees are unsightly; a forest cluttered with snagged and fallen timber or with twisted ancient trees are a risk to visitors. Generations of treating woodlands like industrial landscapes has convinced us that a clean forest is a healthy forest, when in fact the opposite is true. Deadwood is the phytoplankton of the forest, underpinning the woodland's wildlife. Beetles, bacteria and fungi love it, bats and birds live in it, and the organic matter into which it decays forms the soil which will nurture the next generation of the woodland. In January 2005, an estimated half a million trees where blown down in gales which swept across Cumbria. Many people saw it as a disaster, scarring Lakeland's picture

Fallen timber in Johnny Wood, Borrowdale. Dead wood like this is a vital component of woodland habitats.

postcard landscapes. But for woodland managers in Borrowdale, it was dream. One act of nature resulted in a massive leap in their quest for naturalness, a fuel injection into the woodlands engine which will ultimately boost biodiversity. In a century's time, if left to their own devices, these areas of deadwood will be indistinguishable from similar habitats in the ancient forests of Europe and eastern North America.

Another sign of increasing naturalness comes from the changing attitude towards sheep. Woods are good for sheep, but sheep are not always good for woods. Too many sheep grazing in woodlands can inhibit regeneration and reduce the biodiversity. Traditionally, sheep have held a higher value than woodlands, which have been seen merely as a source of shelter and winter food.

In recent times, however, the worth of sheep has declined. At the same time the value of the woodland biodiversity has become increasingly recognised. The church commissioners who surveyed the Tithe Map would be in for a shock if they visited today, with sheep now excluded from many areas that they had described as wood pasture back in the 1840s.

Sheep are also being controlled on currently unwooded National Trust land. Around Falcon Crag, sheep have been excluded since 1999. Since then a vast range of wild flowers have returned and juniper, willow, alder, hawthorn, ash and oak are all regenerating. Nature is making a comeback. If nothing else, history teaches that Borrowdale's woodlands are dynamic. There may be more trees now than when Joseph Flintoff set out on his moss and fern collecting excursions, and many more are planned over the next twenty years. A new wildwood is coming to Wild Lakeland.

Herb Paris. JEAN JOHNSTON

5
WATER

Home to the ice fish

The question of how many Arctic charr it takes to make a decent fish pie may not be one to trouble many cooks today, but for those in charge of the kitchens at Rydal Hall in the late seventeenth century, it was of utmost importance. Rydal Hall was owned by Sir Daniel Fleming, a major figure in the public life of Westmorland at the time; he was also an Arctic charr pie fanatic and he knew his fish. His estate included the Brathay and Rothay rivers which feed into Windermere: waters that are still important spawning grounds for Arctic charr today.

The book of accounts he kept shows not only the number of fish bought, but also the size of the pie they made. Fleming's pies frequently weighed up to sixteen kilograms, so they incurred hefty carriage charges when they were to despatched to relatives and influential friends in London. And Arctic charr are not big fish: five good-sized fish might weigh a kilogramme, so if fish made up half of the dish, a Rydal Hall housekeeper needed 40 Arctic charr to satiate his master's penchant for pie.

While it is found across Britain and Ireland, Lakeland is the only place in England where Arctic charr can be found. It resembles a slender trout, with a bluish-grey to greenish-brown skin covered in yellow, cream, pink, red or orange spots. The most striking feature is the colour of its belly, which ranges from dull pink to bright vermillion: in Wales they call it *torgoch* – 'red-belly'.

Arctic charr, one of Lakeland's most elusive fish, which can chart its history back to the last Ice Age. FRESHWATER BIOLOGICAL ASSOCIATION

Opposite: *Buttermere, home to the Arctic charr.* KEITH WOOD

Glaciers formed Lakeland's tarns and lakes during the last Ice Age. Stickle Tarn, Langdale lies in rock hollow carved out by ice.

Of all the freshwater fish, Arctic charr symbolises Wild Lakeland best. Trout, perch, pike and even salmon may be found in its streams, rivers, tarns and lakes, but they do not share the same distinction, character or history. Not for the charr the shallow, convivial waters of Grasmere or Derwent Water. It is at home in the depths. The nine lakes in which it can found are in Lakeland's top ten deepest waters, and it would be in all of them had not the effluent from the Greenside Mines poisoned Ullswater's population.

Arctic charr is a lover of the cold because it came with the ice. Further north where the seas are colder it is a migratory fish, swimming up rivers from the sea to spawn. This is perhaps what the ancestors of Lakeland's charr once did, until the warming climate at the end of the last Ice Age made the seas uninhabitable, leaving communities solitary and landlocked. Throughout the proceeding millennia of isolation, populations have slowly grown apart genetically. So great are the differences that in the UK many were originally described as distinct species. Even in Lakeland, charr in Haweswater and Windermere were thought to be so different that at first they were given different names.

Water boatman are able to float on the water surface. FRESHWATER BIOLOGICAL ASSOCIATION

Records of commercial fishing for Arctic charr on Windermere go back to the thirteenth century, showing that Daniel Fleming was not the only one with a taste for this red-bellied trout, another name by which the charr was known. By the sixteenth century, the lake had been divided up into sections or 'cubbles' for fishery legislation and control. There seemed a voracious appetite for its pinky flesh and between the mid-seventeenth and mid eighteenth century, its price trebled. Instead of making pies however, housewives now baked the fish in decorated pots before dispatching them to London, where, according to Thomas Robinson, rector of Ousby near Penrith, they were a much sought-after delicacy.

'The fourth remarkable Lake is Buttermere, wherein is bred a sought of fish called Charrs, much like the Ullswater Trout,' he writes in his *Essay towards a Natural History of Westmorland and Cumberland,* published in 1709, 'The Male is grey, the Female yellow-bellied; the Flesh upon them is Red, and crisp to the Taste. They are more luscious and delicious than Trout. They are in this country baked in pots well seasoned with spices, and sent up to London where they are a great rarity.'

The small patch of dark colour at the mid-front edge of each wing give the four-spotted chaser dragonfly its name. Commonly found by marshy tarns and pools it lays it eggs by dropping them directly into water, where the larvae live in debris at the bottom. RON BAINES

One Coniston inn even kept live charr in a wooden box so visitors could choose the fish they wanted to eat before it was cooked. Overfishing was a recurring problem: in 1768 Arctic charr fishing was banned on the River Rothay for seven years so that stocks could recover. A century later stocks were so depleted on Windermere that netting fish was banned for six years, and in 1884 a bylaw imposing restrictions on mesh sizes and length of net used was introduced. By the end of the nineteenth century, commercial fisheries on Windermere alone were catching 12,000 charr each year, worth an estimated £1200.

In Windermere and Coniston Water, Arctic charr is still caught and sold locally today, but it is now more of an art than an industry. Since charr swim and feed at varying depths, to catch one requires great skill or good fortune. A charr fisherman uses two rods with long weighted lines, one cast over each side of the boat. Sidelines are added at regular intervals on the main plumb line and spinners attached to act as lures. Then the boat is gently rowed through the water until a fish bites, but they do not come easily: six to eight fish is considered as a fair day's catch.

These unusual fish are as old as the lakes in which they live. The landscape may seem as if it has always been there, but 10,000 years ago it was brand new. Like a sculptor unveiling her most recent work, the peeling back of the glaciers at the close of the Ice Age revealed nature's latest creation. Lakeland is a thoroughly modern landscape. It is so new that the marks of the maker can still be seen; evidence of ice scratching, scraping, plucking and ploughing is everywhere.

Once ice reaches a certain thickness it becomes viscous. It moves like honey on bread. A thin layer of honey on a slightly tilted slice of bread moves only slowly, but tilt the bread or add more honey and its flow speeds up. In the same way that, given sufficient momentum, honey sliding down bread will begin to pick up crumbs and add them to its sweet, viscous mass, so sufficient weight of ice will drag stones and boulders along its base. The addition of millions of tonnes of sharp rock makes glaciers a highly effective machine for redesigning countryside. We have no idea how Lakeland looked prior to the Ice Age because, like a bulldozer moving sand, snow and ice has reshaped it at will.

During the last Ice Age, a layer of ice at least 800m thick covered Lakeland. There is evidence of glacial action on the highest summits and ice probably left no peak exposed. It plucked at rocks giving rise to crags and ridges. In hollows at valley heads, small cirque glaciers formed. Over time the pressure of ice deepened these glacial basins, creating steep walled, armchair-shaped cirques. They pockmark the landscape and there are more than 150 scattered across the high fells.

The neatly-carved rock bowls which the melting ice left behind were perfect places for water to collect, forming the tarns which are a hallmark of the hills. Lakeland's mountain tarns are a remarkable testimony of the capability of ice to erode rock. Blea Water, hidden in a steep-sided cirque on the eastern flanks of High Street, is not a place to drop your wedding ring. It is barely 500m across, yet it descends to a remarkable 63m, making it deeper than every other water body in Lakeland, apart from Wast Water and Windermere.

Evidence of the power of ice in sculpturing Lakeland is not restricted to the mountains. Glaciers, moving as fast as half a metre a day and armed with rocks and boulders, scooped out material and exploited geological weaknesses to create much larger basins in the valleys. These filled with water to form the lakes from which the area takes its name.

The work of glaciers in shaping Lakeland's valleys is well-illustrated in Windermere. At just over 10 miles, it is England's longest lake. Yet it is almost two lakes. The water around Belle Isle is much shallower than the rest and sandwiched between two deep basins, one to the north and one to the south. To the north, glaciers flowing from Grasmere and Langdale combined, excavating deep into the softer rocks on which the lake lies. By the time the glacier reached Belle Isle, it was clearly running out of erosive steam. Only after a new glacier, which had already gouged out Blelham Tarn and Esthwaithe Water, joined the flow from the west did the ice have sufficient push to carve out the deep basin in the south.

Water mint is common around ponds and tarns and in ditches throughout lowland Lakeland. FRESHWATER BIOLOGICAL ASSOCIATION

So intense was the work of the ice that Windermere's lowest point lies 25m below sea level; the true rock bed is even lower, as many metres of sediment have accumulated since the lake was formed. Parts of Wast Water and Coniston Water are also below sea level. Arctic charr live in all of these lakes, whose waters are so deep that even the warmest summers have little impact on their temperatures. Once the Ice Age had finished creating its final landscape, it is easy to see why it would have preferred to stay in these deep, cool waters as the seas around Britain slowly warmed up.

These lakes and other waters (Buttermere, Crummock Water, Haweswater, Thirlmere, Ennerdale Water and Loweswater) which are home to Lakeland's most charismatic fish share other qualities which set them apart. They tend to be harsh, remote places. Not only are their beds barren and stony, reflecting the hard, mean rocks from which the mountains that sweep up around them are carved, but their waters yield little life too. As soils provide food for terrestrial life, so water feeds aquatic life.

Lakes, tarns and rivers take ingredients from their surroundings – salt from seas spray, dust and gases rinsed by rain, minerals weathered from rocks, and water flushing through the soils – and mix them like a soup. The 'flavour' of the soup controls the richness of life. Diatoms, tiny algae-like creatures, make their skeletons from silica, and calcium is an essential ingredient of fish bones and snail shells. Without magnesium there would be no chlorophyll (the green pigment which allows plants to photosynthesise), and without oxygen, there would be virtually no under-water life at all.

The majestic figure of a heron standing motionless by the riverside is one of the enduring images of Lakeland. Heronries can be found on most of the major rivers with almost 40 throughout the area.
MARTIN CAMPBELL

Lakeland's wildest lakes make thin, flavourless soups. The miserly volcanic rocks and sedimentary slates on which the lakes lie don't easily give up their minerals. Any nutrients that might once have been washed from the soils have been leached away by persistant rain and falls of acid precipitation have further increased the paucity of their waters. The land around Wast Water, England's wildest lake, is the least fertile in Lakeland. Only scattered gorse, bracken and solitary oak, rowan and hawthorn punctuate its stark nothern shoreline, while its southern shore is almost totally bare, just a continuation of the broken screes which tower above it. Having fewer nutrients and being less affected by Man, the purity of Lakeland's remoter lakes and tarns, and the specialised wildlife which lives there, sets them apart.

Wast Water, England's wildest lake: remote and rocky, clean and clear it typifies Lakeland nutrient poor lakes. KEITH WOOD

Bassenthwaite Lake, one of Lakeland's most diverse lakes. A haven for aquatic life and with a richly vegetated shoreline, it is an internationally important place for wildlife. VAL CORBETT

Mayfly nymph, one of the many creatures lurking beneath Lakeland's waters.
FRESHWATER BIOLOGICAL ASSOCIATION

In contrast to the bleakness of wild lakes like Wast Water are waters like Bassenthwaite Lake and Blelham Tarn. With cultivated shorelines and backdrops of rolling, wooded hills and fertile fields, they also have a more pastoral setting. And what they lack in wildness they make up for in wildlife: their waters are richer in nutrients and sustain millions of phytoplankton, microscopic floating aquatic plants, including algae.

They may only contain a handful of cells, carried along on the currents, photosynthesising as they go, but more than 1000 bizarrely-shaped and unpronounceably-named species of algae have been identified in Lakeland's waters. They fuel the food chain and are the foundations on which the complex house of the life of a lake is built. On the ground floor phytoplankton feed a whole raft of molluscs, crustaceans, worms and invertebrates. Above them come species like mayflies and dragonfly nymphs, toads and newts. In the attic are fish, although even they can become dinner for otters and ospreys.

These lakes and tarns may be peaceful places for a picnic, but in summer productive waters like these are a frenzy of aquatic activity. Water boatmen, with long oar-like hind legs, scurry across the surface. Water fleas jerk and jump in the lake. Their bodies are transparent, so it is possible to see their hearts beating, food passing down their gut and blood circulating round their tiny bodies. Dragonfly nymphs lurk menacingly. The underside of a nymph's mouth can flex like an arm, shooting out under blood pressure.

A mayfly emerges from its 'dun' form, the first stage in its life-cycle, which lasts for less than twenty-four hours.
RON BAINES

In the 1950s otters were commonplace in the UK, but their numbers declined sharply reaching their lowest point in the 1970s. In recent times the otter has fared better in Lakeland. Between 1998 and 2002 sightings in West Cumbria increased by almost a third. There are now well-established populations in River Leven and Eden catchments and around the Solway, which appear to be spreading into parts of Cumbria where otter numbers are lower. GRAHAM UNEY

With several local names such as water ouzel, bessy ducker and water pye, dippers must have been a common bird in Lakeland for a long time. Although the population has declined over the last thirty years, current estimates suggest that there may be as many as 6000 in Cumbria, mostly on upland water-courses. KEITH TEMPLE

Spines then unfold and grab an unsuspecting prey, holding it until the mouth part retracts and the nymph gobbles down its dinner. The brightly-coloured dragonflies and damselflies into which they transform and which dart over the water, are no less ruthless. They are both carnivorous and predacious, devouring not only large numbers of insects, but even their own kind.

If biodiversity were colour, then Lakeland's waters would cover all shades of the spectrum, with Wast Water at one end and Bassenthwaite Lake at the other. But the emptiness which saturates Lakeland's wild waters also furnishes them with other qualities. They may resist life, but they embrace light. The water flowing through the pools and rills of Lingcove Beck, Langstrath Beck or any of the mountain gills which cut through the volcanic rocks of the central fells is so clear you could toss in a 10p coin and see it shining among the pebbles in the bed from the banks.

Nutrient rich waters lack such transparency. They are crammed with clouds of micro-scopic plants and animals absorbing light as they photosynthesise, casting darkness below. If you built a house in Ennerdale Water, you could sit on the chimney and still see the foundations; if you stood in Bassenthwaite Lake, you would be lucky to see your feet.

Water clarity is crucial to creatures like the Arctic charr. Light penetration diminishes almost logarithmically with depth. In clear water, the intensity of light at 20m is one ten-thousandth of that at the surface. Imagine what fraction remains at 60m, depths where charr are known to live, and what impact a small reduction in light passing through the water might have on Lakeland's last Ice Age survivor.

Not only does the clarity of the wild water allow light to illuminate its depths, but it changes its colour too, since different wavelengths of light penetrate to different depths. Wild water is greeny-blue, as in clear waters these shorter wavelength colours travel deepest; in shallower, cloudier lakes, long wavelength colours like red penetrate more effectively, subtly changing the water colour.

One major advantage for the specialist wildlife which inhabits Lakeland's loneliest waters is that there is plenty of oxygen to go round. Even though they may spend all of their lives submerged, aquatic plants and animals from phytoplankton to fish still depend on oxygen, which is dissolved from the atmosphere and mixes into the water. Demand for oxygen is much greater in productive lakes and tarns, where vast numbers of creatures of all levels of sophistication are competing for survival.

In summer, the warm nutrient-rich layers close to the surface become jam-packed with phytoplankton. They make the most of the long days for photosynthesis and utilise the higher levels of oxygen near the surface. They also shade the deeper water, which in turn restricts the mixing of water between the surface and the bottom, limiting the amount of oxygen available for life in the depths. Moreover, dead and decaying matter falls to the lake bed and its decomposition increases the demand for oxygen. So it is not all good news for productive but shallow lakes like Rydal and Grasmere. Their bottom waters may become completely devoid of oxygen by the end of the summer, making them uninhabitable.

Lakeland's richest waters have to perform the delicate task of making the most of their food source, without using up all of their vital oxygen in the process. The scales of this difficult balancing act can be completely thrown by the actions of Man, whose exploitation of lakes, tarns and rivers extends to more insidious activities than fishing for Arctic charr. During the late twentieth century, sewage treatment and agricultural pollution began to have a serious impact on Lakeland waters.

Butterbur often forms dense stands especially in damp riverside woodlands and scrub. It reproduces in an unusual way having male and female flowers on separate plants. RICHARD SPEIRS

Stanley Force, Eskdale, where the water plunges 20m over what early guide-books described as 'the finest waterfall in Lakeland'.

The turquoise and gold flash of a kingfisher may be seen on many Lakeland rivers, particular in the north. During the nineteenth century many birds were killed and their plumage used for fishing flies and fashion accessories. KEITH TEMPLE

Derwent Water. KEITH WOOD

To counter rising populations and increasing tourism, sewage works were built in towns and villages adjacent to several of Lakeland's most productive lakes. While this was good for human health, it was a disaster for aquatic life. Treated sewage effluent, high in phosphorus, was discharged directly into already nutrient-rich water. Grasmere, Elter Water, Esthwaite Water, Windermere and Bassenthwaite Lake all received a huge boost in their food supply.

Increased use of fertilisers on nearby agricultural land added more phosphates and nitrates to lakes and tarns, as run-off seeped through the soil, exacerbating the problem. The result was a bonanza time for algae, which gorged themselves on this windfall. Rocky shores were coated in a slimy blanket of weed, and signs warning of the dangers of swimming became a common sight as algal blooms sprang up in late summer and early autumn. Oxygen depletion in lower levels of shallower lakes became more common, creating lifeless zones of unpleasant and often foul-smelling mud and slime.

Mountain tarn on Pavey Ark. There are so many tarns and pools like this in Lakeland that some do not have a name.
GRAHAM UNEY

The little grebe favours lowland waters, with most birds being found towards the coast or in southern Lakeland.
KEITH TEMPLE

By the late 1980s, the problem was encroaching on the jewel in Lakeland's crown: Windermere. Concentrations of phosphorus in its south basin were now between fifteen and twenty times those measured thirty years previously. In 1988, even its deep waters became devoid of oxygen, impacting for the first time on its precious Arctic charr. The symptoms of a catastrophe were there for all to see. Echo-sounding revealed charrless waters, fisherman reported declining catches, and the number of its spawning sites hit an all-time low. There was a chance that the charr would disappear from the lake altogether.

The threat of the loss of this Ice Age survivor prompted swift action. In the early 1990s, equipment to remove phosphorus from waste water was installed at sewage works. The impact was almost immediate. Oxygen levels returned to normal, nutrient levels dropped, and amounts of algae decreased by half. Windermere was brought back from the brink and the Arctic charr lived to fight another day. Ten years later estimates

River Derwent, Borrowdale.   KEITH WOOD

Sunbiggin Tarn is a rare example of a lake on limestone, making it important for wildlife. It is surrounded by fen and swamp which makes it an important place for breeding birds. As well as being home to a large colony of black-headed gulls, many other waterfowl and wildfowl use the tarn, such as wigeon, teal, little grebe, goldeneye, pochard and whooper swan.

The vendace is a fish unique to Lakeland, found only in Derwent Water and Bassenthwaite Lake. FRESHWATER BIOLOGICAL ASSOCIATION

suggested that there were as many as several hundred thousand Arctic charr in Windermere.

The Arctic charr may be Lakeland's best-known celebrity fish, but it is not the only one that has survived since the Ice Age. Two further glacial cousins inhabit our waters: the schelly and the vendace. Both are whitefish and look similar to herrings. The schelly can be found in a few places elsewhere in Britain and lives in Ullswater, Brothers Water, Haweswater and Red Tarn, beneath Helvellyn. The vendace is unique to Lakeland. It is found in Derwent Water and Bassenthwaite Lake and nowhere else in the UK.

Lakeland's waters remain a battleground for these ancient species. Changing conditions in Bassenthwaite Lake have made the future for vendace there precarious, and all three species face a new threat from fish that have been introduced into their waters. In recent years ruffe, dace and roach have been recorded for the first time in a number of lakes, and the impact of this is only now beginning to be realised.

Alien species like this tend to bully their way into the local ecosystem, upsetting the natural balance by competing for food, colonising spawning grounds and acting as

River Esk, one of Lakeland's clear-running mountain rivers.

predators. Once they are in it is hard to get rid of them. In spring 2005, Ratherheath Tarn, near Staveley, was emptied of fish in an attempt to eradicate one such alien, the top-mouthed gudgeon, a carp-like invader which had been introduced. Such drastic measures are impossible in larger lakes where little can be done.

These non-native fish are thought to have been introduced by anglers, who use them as bait. As a measure of the seriousness of the problem, the Environment Agency has now banned this activity in the 14 waters which are home to Lakeland Ice Age fish. Time will tell how well the Arctic charr and its glacial neighbours survive this latest assault. They will certainly fair better in the wilder lakes, where remoteness and inhospitability has diluted Man's impact.

It is hard to escape water in Lakeland. Lakes, tarns, rivers and streams flow like veins across the landscape. But while water may be everywhere, it is not all the same. Some lakes are laid out like postcards, their water-lily spotted surfaces set within a picturesque frame of farmland and trees. It is a comfortable scene and one which lends itself to a life of ease for both Man and wildlife. But it is not one without struggle, with species battling for superiority among themselves and for survival alongside Man.

Icicles in Hopegill Beck KEITH WOOD

There are also more desolate waters in Lakeland, which have qualities that both disturb and compel. Although not always instantly recognisable, their sense of place is more than just a feeling. Their wildness can be captured: the hostility of their setting, their comparative lifelessness, the colour, depth and clarity of their water all set them apart and brand them as special. They do not welcome wildlife, but for some species like the Arctic charr, which has outlasted the ice sheets, been baked in pies, potted in jars, swamped by sewage and attacked by aliens, they are home.

6

FELLS

Empire of the skies

William Hobson is not a name many people associate with Lakeland, yet his story marked a watershed for the natural history of its fells. A doctor from Leeds, he was an enthusiastic ornithologist who made regular trips to Lakeland. He even called his house The Langdales. But Dr Hobson liked to do more than just watch birds; he collected their eggs too.

The Lakeland fells are famous for their birds. The variable hardness of the Borrowdale volcanic rocks from which the central fells are formed has given rise to an uneven and rugged topography, which has helped to produce the highest inland cliffs in England. And where there are crags and coves, there will be birds which nest there.

Lakeland's birds of prey punctuate the life of the high fells. They are at home in the wildness of the mountains. Yet despite the remote solitude of their haunts, they have long attracted the attention of Man and none more so than the three great predators of the precipices: the peregrine falcon, the raven and, the noblest of them all, the eagle. So deep has the impact of these three birds been on the culture of Lakeland that they have been immortalised in the names of the vertiginous rocks which they make their own. There are at least 33 Raven Crags in Lakeland as well as many Eagle Crags and other derivatives, such as Iron Crag, Erne Crag and Heron Crag.

However, Dr Hobson was not interested in ravens, and eagles had long since left the crags which bare their name above Langstrath Beck or overlooking Easedale. Instead, he went in search of peregrine falcon eggs. In the spring of 1939, he and two friends set out for the crags above Thirlmere. Taking eggs was illegal, but enforcing the law was almost impossible. Thefts were commonplace; in 1938 only one nest belonging to

Opposite: *Eagle Crag, Borrowdale, but the eagles that once lived here have long gone. Commenting on their demise in 1819, William Green wrote that they were 'so destructive to the lambs and consequently injurious to the interests of the shepherds that their extermination became absolutely necessary; but their breeding places being inaccessible, by footsteps, a hazardous experiment was embarked upon. A man, at hazard of his life, was lowered down the face of the rock, about sixty yards. A piked staff, such as is used by the shepherds when they travel the mountains, was the weapon with which the man defended himself against the attack of the parent bird while he robbed their nest of the eggs or eaglets. If birds, their possession was his renumeration, if eggs then every neighbouring shepherd gave five shillings'.*
KEITH WOOD

The peregrine falcon has nested for centuries on Lakeland's crags, but it has often been under threat KEITH TEMPLE

peregrines, buzzards or ravens had escaped being robbed, and this only because it had been watched night and day for 11 weeks. Eggs were taken either by private collectors, like Dr Hobson, or for commercial sale.

In 1939 there was only a handful of nesting peregrines. Fearful for the future of these iconic species, Friends of the Lake District had spent the princely sum of £60 to pay for watchers to protect breeding birds in Lakeland's high fells. In April of that year, a local forester had watched Hobson and his accomplices climb onto Nab Crag where the peregrines were nesting. One of the men was then lowered down the crag on a rope and placed the eggs into his pocket. By the time the three men had climbed down the police were there to welcome them. They were caught red-handed and hauled before magistrates in Keswick. On May 12 they became the first people to be successfully prosecuted for robbing a peregrine's nest in Lakeland and were given the maximum possible fine of £1 for each of the four eggs they had taken.

The fine may not have been great, but importantly a message had been sent out to other would-be collectors. Up until then it had been open season for peregrine persecution. Collectors targeted their eggs, falconers wanted their young and the adult birds were killed by pigeon-fanciers and the game-rearing fraternity, who blamed them for killing their own birds. In 1892 the Rev. H. A. MacPherson published his book

A Vertebrate Fauna of Lakeland, which was a comprehensive study of the state of wildlife at the end of the nineteenth century. In it he describes the overwhelming onslaught which the peregrine was facing, their nests plundered by visitors guided by local men or by locals themselves.

'One pair nested annually from 1883 to 1889, either at Iron Crag or Falcon Crag,' he writes. 'The Rev. H.D. Rawnsley informed me that in 1883 this pair nested at Falcon Crag, and their two young ones were taken. In 1884 they nested at Iron Crag and one young was taken. In 1885 the old birds returned to Falcon Crag and were robbed of their eggs on the 3rd of April. They bred in another locality the following year, but their young were taken. In 1887 they nested at Iron Crag, and their eggs were taken. In 1888 they nested in the old place, and the young were removed.'

Elsewhere he describes the shooting of a pair of peregrines in Swindale by two game-keepers of the Earl of Lonsdale who were 'very anxious to have them killed in conse-quence of them being so destructive amongst the Grouse'. The female was shot on their first outing, but they had to return a second time the kill the male, which they then had stuffed by a taxidermist in Shap. It was the eighteenth victim of the gamekeeper's gun. MacPherson concludes the story with the disturbing observation that 'No species could increase in the face of such destructive measures'. It is not surprising then that the first recorded prosecution was seen as such a significant breakthrough.

The raven suffered similar emnity. Local parishioners even paid a reward to those who killed a raven and brought its head to the churchwarden. Wordsworth recalls the practice of hanging dead ravens in churchyards in his *Description of the Scenery of the Lakes*. 'This carnivorous fowl is a great enemy to the lambs of these solitures', he writes. Two pence (0.75p) was the going rate for 'head-money'. It was sufficient incentive to bring in 18 ravens in Hawkshead Parish in 1769, and between June 1766 and August 1767, 48 birds were killed. So successful was the custom in Cartmell that one commentator wrote 'There are

The raven is a bird indelibly stamped on Lakeland, with over 30 Raven Crags marked on maps. Current population levels are now perhaps at their highest in recorded history. KEITH TEMPLE

no ravens now in the parish, 1883. The last I saw was about thirty years ago, flying and croaking near the foot of Windermere'.

But the story of the extinction of eagles from Wild Lakeland is perhaps the most poignant, for these giant predators of the skies symbolise the essence of wildness. They prey upon anything from a red deer calf to a field vole. It was their reputation as killers which ultimately led to their demise in Lakeland, where their taste for lambs was sufficient for them to be branded a scourge by shepherds who sought out eyries, however precarious their location.

It is likely that both golden and white-tailed eagles were both once widespread in Lakeland. Earliest references to eagles reach back to the thirteenth century. Similarities between the two birds may make records of sightings hard to differentiate, but they both suffered the same fate. This contemporary account by the Rev W. Richardson describes what must have been a common fate for this majestic bird. 'A pair of the Golden Eagles had an aerie in Martindale two successive years, the first year the female was shot, and the male, after an absence of about three weeks, returned with another female. The next year, 1789, the male was killed, after which the female disappeared'.

Both golden and white-tailed eagles nested in Borrowdale during the eighteenth century. Head-money was one shilling, paid by the churchwarden of the local parish church at Crosthwaite. In 1769, the poet Thomas Gray visited Grange-in-Borrowdale. His journal records a conversation with a local farmer who had plundered an eagle's nest the previous year. 'All the dale are up in arms on such an occasion,' he writes, 'for they lose abundance of lambs yearly, not to mention, hares, partridges, grouse etc. He was let down from the cliff in ropes to the shelf of the rock on which the nest was built, the people above shouting and hollowing to fright the old birds, which flew screaming round, but did not dare attack him. He brought off the Eaglet and an addle egg.'

No birds, even as large and powerful as the eagle, could survive in the face of such hostile persecution. By the end of the eighteenth century, the golden eagle had disappeared from Lakeland and the white-tailed eagle was no longer breeding here. The last white-tailed eagle to be captured was on Black Combe in 1838, and there has only been one sighting of the bird since.

A *lover of Lakeland moorland habitats, the golden ringed dragonfly, easily recognisable by its yellow banding, is one of the largest dragonflies in Britain.*
RICHARD SPEIRS

Sunlight illuminates Honister Pass. SIMON WEBB

Above: *One of the area's best stands of juniper occurs in Little Langdale. Fabled for its use to flavour gin, juniper was once widely used to make charcoal, but is now under threat and measures are being undertaken to conserve it.*

Right: *Upper Eskdale, one of the wildest corners of Lakeland.*

The fells during MacPherson's time were a different place from today. Agriculture had been reborn with the Enclosure Acts of the eighteenth and nineteenth centuries, covering the countryside with the intricate geometry of drystone walls. But outside this new landscape the open fells remained relatively unscathed. Victorian farmers described this land, so sought after by today's outdoor enthusiasts, as 'waste' – land of no value.

It may have held little value to agriculture, but it provided a home to many other upland birds like red and black grouse, buzzard, ring ouzel, hen harrier and even dotterel and ptarmigan. Virtually all of them faced persecution by Man, who zealously sought out virtually anything with wings and their young.

For some it was sport. MacPherson describes how it used to be 'Common practice for parties of gunners to scour High Street and other mountains for Dotterel on their first arrival in the spring. No opportunity was ever neglected of shooting as many as possible, their feathers being in brisk demand for tying flies'. Indeed, despite their sweet flavour, a plucked bird was only sold for four pence (1½p), whereas its gaudy plumage fetched six pence (2½p), so highly-prized were its feathers by anglers. Red grouse were once so common that it was killed in any season. However, the size of the population was so large that this had no serious impact on its numbers. In 1850 black grouse were common in the woods of the Furness fells and as far south as Holker Hall.

For others it was the gamekeeper or the shepherd who precipitated their decline and, in some cases, extinction. The hen harrier was once common on the wild moors around Tebay and in other parts of Lakeland, but according to MacPherson it was 'The ruthless hand of the game-preserver' which 'pressed on the task of extermination'. Hundreds of pairs of hen harrier were shot by gamekeepers in the nineteenth century, and adventurous young men were hailed as heroes for destroying the eggs or nests of birds of prey. In 1827 the *Carlisle Patriot* triumphantly related how Isaac Colebeck of Gosforth scaled Pillar Rock and killed three young buzzards in their eyrie.

These were dark times, when malevolent clouds of human prejudice swirled over the high fells. For centuries sheep had been the currency of the mountains. Managing these

Red grouse. Once too numerous to shoot red grouse are now only found in a few upland areas. KEITH TEMPLE

agricultural assets had created the Picturesque landscapes of the eighteenth and nineteenth centuries. There was no room for raw nature in this land made for livestock. Anything which threatened farming livelihoods was to be eradicated, and these predators became pests. It was a time when the life of a sheep was worth far more than that of a peregrine, a raven or an eagle. These kingly birds of the crags were an expendable part of Wild Lakeland.

The twentieth century brought with it more enlightened times, and now both the raven and the peregrine are enjoying a renaissance. Increasing numbers of sheep on the fells have been good for the raven, as carrion forms a large part of its diet. There are now between 80 and 90 breeding pairs in Cumbria, making it the only large raven population in England outside the West Country and the Welsh Borders. There may be many of them, but this does not necessarily mean that they get on with each other. Research has shown that the average distance between each pair is just under three kilometres. Given that there are only so many cliffs and crags in Lakeland, this means that unless they become a little more friendlier to each other, or find new places to breed, ravens may one day run out of room in Lakeland.

The road to recovery for the peregrine has been more rocky. By the time of Dr Hobson's prosecution there were less than 40 pairs in Lakeland. By the mid 1960s the population had plummeted to just eight pairs. With so few birds rearing young, the peregrine was in danger of being lost from Lakeland completely. But persecution was not to blame. The rapid expansion in the use of pesticides in agriculture after World War II was affecting the food chain. Sitting right at the top, peregrines where being poisoned by toxic residues absorbed from their prey. Not only did the poison kill the adult birds, but it also thinned their eggshells, decreasing the likelihood of hatching and rearing young.

Peregrines are particular about where they nest. Traditionally they preferred cliffs between 350-600 metres in altitude, and after a successful campaign against the pesticides responsible for the rapid reduction of their numbers, peregrines began to return to these old haunts, sometimes even to the same nesting sites as past generations. It was the beginning of a remarkable recovery for this bird, which has come to embody the spirit of Wild Lakeland.

Pillar Rock, ideal territory for Lakeland's birds of prey which have not always been welcomed. In 1827 a local man climbed these crags and killed three young buzzards nesting here.
GRAHAM UNEY

By 1977 peregrine numbers had bounced back to pre-war levels. They did not stop there, but kept on rising and now almost 100 pairs have been recorded in the county. The recovery has been aided by the desire of many people to see it happen. After egg thieves renewed their efforts on Falcon Crag, near Keswick, following the peregrine's reoccupation in 1970, local enthusiasts set up a crag watch to protect the birds. Keswick Mountain Rescue Team even slept beneath the crag at night. The reward of this labour of love have been to see almost 40 young birds born at this one site over the past twenty years.

Cotton grass on Birker Fell.

More than 1000 birds have now fledged since the crisis of the 1960s, giving Lakeland one of the highest densities of peregrines in the world. Crags have become crowded places. As the traditional remote, high cliff territories filled up, so peregrines had to find new nesting sites on less remote crags and abandoned quarries, and have even been recorded on lowland crags and industrial slag banks. The recovery of the peregrine is one of the great success stories of Wild Lakeland and it seems Cumbria is now full. For the peregrine at least, there are no more vacancies.

There is, however, plenty more room for golden eagles. Despite the great joy a glimpse of this majestic bird has given to the many people who have been lucky enough to see it since it reappeared in Lakeland in 1957, the eagles existence among the high fells is as precarious as its perch. Since then breeding has been recorded at three different locations. However, following the disappearance of his mate in February 2004, there is now only one solitary male bird swooping over Lakeland's skies from his nest in the eastern fells.

At best, the eagle population at this site has been fragile. The missing female was only the second recorded and she had not successfully bred for almost ten years. Since the birds here began breeding in 1969, there have only been five adults and 16 young fledged. Scotland is the home of the eagle in Britain and the Lakeland pairs had drifted in from the north. Their numbers are declining in Galloway, but increasing in the

Borders. Lakeland's remaining male is young, perhaps only seven or eight years old, and has time to mate again.

The scene should be set, for with its craggy cliffs and open spaces Lakeland is classic eagle country. But the eagles it yearns for may be unlikely to come. Walkers, climbers, and even hang gliders now crowd the haunts of this solitary bird, which likes to hunt undisturbed. Any prospective mate would be forgiven for taking one look at Lakeland's busy fells, turning tail and following the thermals back north again. The prospects for the eagle hang on a thread.

The landscape has also changed since MacPherson's day, when its diversity favoured the eagle and persecution was the main threat. A more subtle activity of man has subsequently hastened the decline of many upland birds. Changes in agriculture during the twentieth century may have brought about massive improvements to productivity, but they have come at a pace with which nature could not keep up, and Wild Lakeland has paid the price.

Following World War II, national self-sufficiency was the new Utopia, and Lakeland's contribution was to sacrifice its fell lands to increasingly intensive sheep production. Farmers were paid by the Government to improve moorland by draining, liming and reseeding. Supplementary feeding allowed sheep to be kept on the fells all year, instead of being brought down in the winter and allowing the vegetation to recover.

The colourful hay meadows associated with traditional upland farming have been replaced by endless fields of emerald green. Between 1930 and 1970, drainage, the use of fertilisers, and land reclamation destroyed two-thirds of Cumbria's species-rich grassland, taking with it the habitats of yellow wagtail, snipe, grey partridge and corncrake. The texture and vibrancy has seeped away from much of the fell land. The heather moorlands which once clothed the fells and were home to black grouse and even hen harrier in Victorian times, have become grassland. Red grouse, which were once too numerous to shoot, are now confined to parts of Skiddaw, Whinlatter and the Shap and Armboth Fells. Mixed farming, which was once commonplace in valley bottoms and created a more diverse vegetation cover, has gone, taking the habitats for birds such as lapwing and redshank with it.

Scree on Goat Crag, Borrowdale. There are numerous scree slopes on the fells, important habitats for specialist plants like parsley fern.

Opposite page: *Golden eagle, a giant of the skies, but for how much longer will it grace Lakeland's fells?* MARK HAMBLIN

Sheep continued to be the commodity of the mountains, their numbers rising inexorably. In the last half of the last century sheep numbers grazing the Lakeland's fells rose to six million. One out of seven of England's national flock grazed Cumbria's fellsides. Even in the two decades up to 2000, the number of breeding ewes on the hills of England rose by a third.

The insatiable expansion of their upland empire has taken its toll on the wildlife. Too many sheep on the fells leads to overgrazing. This changes variety of species that can grow and affects the wildlife which is found there. The changes which allowed sheep numbers to increase have also led to a decrease in people working the land. With fewer labourers, jobs on the fells get neglected: without cutting, bracken spreads like a green and bronze flame across the fellsides; and without shepherding sheep graze where they will, selecting the choicest plants.

Carrock Fell, highlighting the impact of unsustainable grazing by sheep. The slopes in the foreground are covered in dense heather and juniper, but on the opposite side of the River Caldew intensive grazing has left the fellside bare.

Crummock Water and the Buttermere fells from Loweswater Fell.   RICHARD SPEIRS

All of this happened in some of the most precious countryside which England possesses. Lakeland's fells are priceless. England's prime wildlife sites are called Sites of Special Scientific Interest (SSSIs) and Lakeland is littered with them, particularly on the fells where they cover massive chunks of countryside. Specialised mountain habitats like upland heath, upland grassland, blanket bog, crags and cliffs, screes and gullies and the summits of the highest fells make Lakeland fells some of the most important landscapes in England.

The bilberry heaths of the Buttermere fells are more extensive than on any other site in north west England, and include other species such as heather, cowberry, crowberry and even bearberry. There are also unusual lichens and clubmosses. Here peregrine, raven and occasionally dotterel can be seen. Skiddaw boasts the largest area of heather moorland and blanket bog in Lakeland. The fells north and west of the River Caldew are clothed in purple robes of heather in late summer, blended with the rich greens of dense patches of juniper. In the vast areas of blanket bog around Skiddaw House, cloudberry makes one of its few Lakeland appearances, alongside the bog rosemary.

The fir clubmoss (above) is not related to mosses or ferns and has no flowers. Instead it reproduces by means of spores.

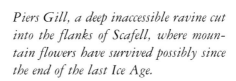

Piers Gill, a deep inaccessible ravine cut into the flanks of Scafell, where mountain flowers have survived possibly since the end of the last Ice Age.

124

These are perfect places for wading birds such as curlew, snipe and golden plover. North of its summit is Skiddaw's most unusual habitat: a carpet of twisting, dry low-lying shrub and ground-hugging vegetation known as montane heath. Strange mosses and dwarf bushes are the plants which have adapted to this hostile place. The Scafell ridge in the closest thing Lakeland has to the moon: a vast plateau strewn with boulders on which nature's paintbrush has daubed splashes of brightly-coloured lichens. These seldom-seen habitats are the true currency of the high places of Lakeland.

Perhaps the brightest jewels are found in the cracks and creases in the landscape; the places where weaknesses in the rock have been exploited by weathering and erosion, etching deep lines of time on the faces of the fells. Lakeland's rock faces and ravines are not only home to its special birds, but are also a haven for its rare mountain plants, some of which are found nowhere else in England. Fed by the minerals released as the rock has been worn away, watered by tumbling gills and trickling seepages and away from the worst excesses of overgrazing, Lakeland ledges drape foliage like hanging gardens in the hills.

They are a more lush, richer world than the closely-cropped grasslands and bald rock of much of the mountains. The eastern coves of the Helvellyn range from Fairfield to Brown Cove, the vertiginous ledges of Honister Crag, the deep incisions of Piers Gill and Skew Gill, beneath Scafell and the bold buttresses of the Screes overlooking Wastwater, are the best places to see this secret green world, but shades of it are present in many of the more inaccessible gills and crags in the fells.

While many of this flora of the fells may also be found at lower altitudes, some are exclusive to the high fells. These mountain flowers and plants are not only unusual because they are uncommon, but also because they have survived here for a long time. Mountain flowers are to Lakeland's fells what the Arctic charr is to its waters. Plants such as mountain sorrel, dwarf willow, purple saxifrage, bearberry and mountain avens may well have survived on the ledges and cliffs of the high fells since the end of the Ice Age. After the glaciers retreated the bare, open ground which was uncovered was ideal for colonisation by these kinds of species. During these cool post-glacial times, when Britain was still joined to Europe, a spider could weave a web from Scotland to Siberia using only mountain flowers like these for support.

The summits of the highest fells are often covered with boulder fields like here on Great End. The green colour between the boulders is not grass, but woolly-hair moss, a characteristic rare mountain plant. SIMON WEBB

Where mineral veins come to the surface, crags can be coated with a mixture of woodland meadow and mountain flowers, like here on the eastern side of Helvellyn.

But their dominance was short-lived, as the changing climate encouraged wave after wave of ecological invaders. Rising temperatures and advancing forests, which reduced the amount of open terrain, drove these plants to higher ground. Their territory was squeezed further under the wet conditions which created Lakeland bogs: damp, hostile habitats where no mountain flora could thrive.

These climatic shifts have squeezed mountain flowers into the last corners of Britain and now they are only found in the highlands of Scotland, Snowdonia and Lakeland. Those few locations where mountain flora still hold out are a monument to the tenacity of these ancient species.

It is remarkable to think that there are still places in Wild Lakeland in which the plants and flowers have survived for more than 10,000 years. They are a botanic thread through time, the last remnants of a vast floral empire. Man's management of the fells for sheep brought a further threat, for sheep have a capacity to graze on all but the most inaccessible places. The decline of Lakeland's mountain flowers rang perhaps the loudest alarm, warning of the slow deterioration over the fells over the last century.

The full extent of the perilous state of nature in the fells was revealed in 2000 when English Nature, the government's nature conservation advisors, carried out research into the condition of the prime nature conservation areas, the Sites of Special Scientific Interest (SSSIs). The results made for unpleasant reading.

The research graded their condition from 'favourable', for sites being managed in a way which would sustain the special qualities for which they had been designated, to 'unfavourable', for sites whose management was actually eroding the reason for which they had been designated. Despite having been recognised for their wildlife value, the research revealed that 90 per cent of upland SSSIs in Cumbria were in unfavourable condition. Lakeland's fells were on the verge of an ecological disaster.

As if this was not sufficient impetus to act, soon afterwards the government decreed that all of England's SSSIs were to be brought up to favourable condition by 2010. Action was urgently needed and tackling the problems of overgrazing by sheep was the first target.

Starry saxifrage.

Mountain sorrel.

Bearberry.

Alpine lady's mantle.

Waterfall rich in mountain flora in Dungeon Ghyll, Langdale.

All this happened at a time when agriculture was also changing, prompted not least by the foot and mouth epidemic of 2001. Nearly half of all farms affected had been in Cumbria and in the aftermath, with falling market prices, many farmers were questioning the wisdom of restocking to pre-epidemic levels of sheep.

English Nature seized on the opportunity this gave to both support the fragile rebirth of agriculture and give benefit for wildlife and the landscape. A quantum shift was happening in the fells as suddenly wildlife had a value. Sheep, the age-old kings of the mountains, had a challenger. Farmers were offered financial incentives to reduce the number of sheep grazing on the fells, money that effectively kept farms going while preventing further deterioration of Lakeland's distinctive mountain habitats.

This change has not only affected individual farms, but also whole mountain areas. Grazing levels on almost the entire Skiddaw, Helvellyn and Scafell massifs have been

Helvellyn from Moor Divock. Changes to how the land is being managed on the massif could help its mountain flowers make a comeback in the future.
KEITH WOOD

reduced to sustainable levels and shepherding has been encouraged in an attempt to keep sheep away from the most sensitive areas, such as the internationally important mountain flora habitats in the eastern coves of Helvellyn.

The impact has been remarkable. In many areas sheep numbers are down to a fraction of their pre-foot and mouth levels. Where monitoring has taken place vegetation has made a strong recovery and the proportion of SSSIs in favourable condition has risen from 10 per cent to over 50 per cent. Prescribing such a drastic shift in how the fells are looked after was perhaps the only cure for their failing health, but what the long-term implications will be for Lakeland remain uncertain. Conservationists have high hopes a more diverse, more colourful future, while farmers fear for the survival of their flocks and their livelihoods.

Lakeland's upland birds and mountain flora are the specialities of the fells. They are passengers in a landscape which is familiar with change and that has set out on a new journey as part of a dynamic nature, continually on the move, shaping winners and losers in every habitat. In post-glacial times natural succession was the driver for change, but more recently Man has had his hand firmly on the wheel, inadvertently steering nature down an uncharted ecological path. The journey, even since MacPherson's time, has been a treacherous one, but perhaps now, at the start of the twenty-first century, Wild Lakeland is returning to the fells once more.

Roseroot, a fabulous flower of the fells.
SIMON WEBB

Inscription on window of St Olaf's Church, Wasdale Head.

A snowy day over Stickle Tarn and the central fells. Such days could become a thing of the past if predictions of milder wetter climate for Lakeland prove to be true RONNY MITCHELL

THE FUTURE OF WILD LAKELAND

Bloom or bust?

It has been a long time since Lakeland has been truly wild in its most natural sense. Initially after the glaciers and ice sheets had finished creating the canvas of the modern countryside, wind and water set to work on the detail, keeping the landscape on the move. For perhaps 6000 years, Lakeland changed only in the way nature intended. Coastlines were drawn and redrawn, woodlands waxed and waned, rivers meandered at will across the landscape. Climates could not stand still: sometimes cold, sometimes warm, sometimes dry, sometimes wet. Every shift in climate bought with it winners and losers as wildlife came and went. Wild Lakeland back then was a very different place to today.

It is not possible to know whether the first humans in Cumbria arrived by chance or design. They could have been Mesolithic ocean traders washed ashore in a storm on Walney Island, or ancient settlers emigrating from Ireland or Scotland, attracted by the bountiful coastal plains of West Cumbria. However they came, they introduced a new tension into the natural system and would become a key force shaping change. Now, there is hardly a square inch of land where the imprint of Man is not apparent.

The habitats – the coastlands, meadows, woodlands, waters and fells – are work in progress, and we should not hold onto our image of them too tightly. As in the past, the future will be shaped by a combination of our actions and the forces of nature, worked out on the raw materials of rocks and soils, which are the building blocks of the landscape. But in this dynamic system, the impact of how the land

South Walney Island. The island was the home to some of the first settlers in Lakeland and it has been shaped by man and nature ever since. RONNY MITCHELL

131

CLIMATE CHANGE WINNERS

Above left: Insects can expect to thrive as temperatures warm: feeding better, living longer and reproducing faster. They are highly mobile and will easily more to new habitats when conditions become suitable. The azure damselfly is expected to do especially well; studies have shown that it can disperse by almost kilometre a year. RICHARD SPEIRS

Above right: Marsh helleborine. Southern Lakeland is currently about as far north as marsh helleborine can grow. It is limited to a handful of sites on the Duddon estuary and in the Orton fells, but warmer temperatures might allow it to spread further north. RICHARD SPEIRS

Left: Upland bogs, like this one at Blea Tarn, could benefit from increasing rainfall, but what grows there will change. There could be more sphagnum and bog myrtle, but cloudberry and bog rosemary could decline or disappear altogether.

Inset: Oystercatchers numbers are already increasing and could rise even more, along with populations of other water birds, if rising sea levels increase the amount of habitat available. KEITH TEMPLE is farmed and the role of climate change will dominate Wild Lakeland over the coming decades.

Forty years ago, Lakeland's climate was markedly different to today. In January 1963, temperatures in Lakeland remained below freezing for twenty-eight days. Snowdrifts up to 6 metres high cut off farms and closed roads. Ice floes choked the Kent estuary. On Windermere, it took a team of 20 firemen, policemen and villagers, using ropes and ladders, nearly two hours to rescue a couple who fell through the ice while walking back to Belle Isle after enjoying a Saturday evening in Bowness. The lake was the focus for numerous weird and wonderful activities. Skating was popular, as was ice hockey. The inability to access the water didn't prevent people enjoying boating: they took up ice-yachting instead. There was even the rare sight of a motorcycle being ridden across the lake.

These stories now sound like fiction. Windermere was ice-covered for more 60 days in 1963, but the lake did not freeze at all between 1988-1996. Climate change is a political hot potato and a great train of scientific endeavour has been set off attempting to track conclusive proof within the complex systems of the world's weather. Driving the train are the climate modellers, whose number-crunching super computers calculate our weather's destiny, telling us how warm and wet we will be in 50 or 100 year's time. Following closely behind them are the field workers, scientists who monitor conditions today and collect data, which can then be used to test how good the predictions are.

According to the climate modellers, Lakeland faces a warmer and wetter future. Winters will be milder and summers warmer, with hot summers increasingly likely. Although annual rainfall is set to increase, the change will vary seasonally, with more rain falling in autumn and winter and less in summer. Sea level is set to rise at twice its current rate. Monitoring by scientists in the field is suggesting that these may be more than just predictions: there is evidence that it is already happening. One of the longest records of changing climate in Cumbria, stretching back to the 1930s, comes from the Moor House meteorological station, high in the north Pennines. Although not truly Lakeland, it is an illustration of what is happening in a similar upland location nearby.

Records over the last seventy years show that temperature at Moor House has significantly increased over the last couple of decades. Six of the warmest years since 1850 have been since 1990. Moreover, this trend varies between seasons, with winters showing the bulk of this increase and little change occurring during the summers. This has had a knock-on effect on the number of frosty days and the amount of snow. By 2000, frost frequency had fallen by almost a quarter compared to the 1953-79 period, a figure which climate models for northern England had predicted would not be reached until 2065. Snowfall shows a similar dramatic decline from an average of 72 days between 1949 and 1970 to 33 days in 2000, 27 days in 1998 and just 25 days in 1997. The picture of rainfall mirrors climate models with the 1990s showing more rainfall in winter and less in summer compared to previous decades. All of this science no doubt reinforces the stories shared in pubs, shops and homes throughout the region.

If this pattern is reflected across Lakeland, wildlife and landscape cannot hope to escape its impact. But guessing who will be the winners and losers is hard, as natural systems are almost as complex as climatic ones. An increase of 1-2 degrees C is estimated to be equivalent to a migration northwards of a species range by 200-300km, the distance from Birmingham to Carlisle. Species currently at their northern limit in the county, such as field maple, dogwood, old man's beard, horseshoe vetch, small-leaved lime and squinancywort, could all exend futher into Lakeland.

The anticipated rise in sea level may alter the shape of the coast, but salt marshes and coastal dunes will form in new places if coastal protection policies allow them. If areas of estuaries increase, then so could the number of birds. Bogs and bryophytes are potential winners, as they are particularly suited to the predicted increase in rainfall, as long as they can withstand the anticipated hotter, drier conditions in summer. The composition of hay meadows will change, but their future is more driven by agriculture than climate.

Rising temperatures will ultimately be reflected in Lakeland's waters, which could make its rare fish losers. The Arctic charr, schelly and vendace, with their links to the last Ice Age, prefer cold conditions. Yet detailed long-term water temperature records from Windermere have shown an increase in recent years, both in terms of annual

While much of wildlife falls victim to changes in its habitat either man-made or natural, the buzzard has proved itself to be master of change. A versatile predator, it is not dependent on one food source and it is an adaptable nester. Its resilience to changes in land use make it less susceptible to short-term trends in agriculture. It is found almost everywhere in Lakeland which with an estimated population of 7000, has steadily risen over the last thirty years. The buzzard is one bird for whom the future seems to hold no fear. KEITH TEMPLE

CLIMATE CHANGE LOSERS

Top right: *Globeflowers could be lost from upland hay meadows as temperature warms, and could also prove susceptible to the accompanying loss of flies that are vital to its pollenation.* RON BAINES

Bottom right: *Ledge vegetation like this on Helvellyn contains plants that are adapted to cold conditions. In a warmer world, the higher the habitat the more likely it is to lose out, as there will be nowhere for its species to migrate.*

Inset: *The mountain ringlet butterfly is Britain's only upland butterfly and is restricted to the hills of Central Scotland and the Lake District. Warming temperatures could lead to its extinction in the UK.* RICHARD SPEIRS

Below: *Moss campion is only found in a few sites in Lakeland today: this cool-loving Ice Age survivor could go if temperatures warm.*

average temperature and, particularly, of milder winters, and there is no reason to suppose that other lakes will not also change in these ways. This presents potential problems both for adults in the cold waters of the deep during the summer, and for their eggs as they incubate over the winter in shallow spawning grounds.

But it is the fells which face the most uncertain future. The expected climate change would be like shifting the tree line 150-200 metres upwards. This may be good news for species such as oak, birch, willow and bell heather, which could all find new areas in which to expand, but there are no winners for the most specialised mountain plants. If you grow on top of a mountain it is difficult to migrate any further upwards. The days of mountain avens, Alpine lady's mantle and various saxifrages and sedges in Lakeland could be numbered.

How successfully Wild Lakeland negotiates the transition to a warmer world will depend on how much room we give it to adjust. The recent renaissance in Wild Lakeland has been directed by the hand of Man, carefully controlling and managing the landscape to maximise opportunities for wildlife. It is very much nature on our terms. If nature was in charge there may not be as many high brown fritillary butterflies, or

Warmer temperatures mean that wild daffodils are flowering much earlier than in the past.

137

The numbers of nuthatch have already
increased throughout Lakeland over the
last twenty years, spreading throughout
the major valleys. It is set to continue
growing as its breeding is related to
winter food supplies that should be secure
as temperatures warm.   KEITH TEMPLE

The southern hawker is one of several
species of dragonfly which has expanded
its range across Lakeland and is now
fairly widespread in Cumbria, except in
the uplands.   RICHARD SPEIRS

138

natterjack toads as there are today. In the future, if we want to maintain and expand current diversity, we will need to be even more careful in our management of land. As rising temperatures shake up nature's distribution map, species and habitats will need to be allowed to respond. Wildlife will be on the move, away from old haunts and into new territories as it adjusts to changing conditions. If we don't ensure that there are suitable habitats to allow this to happen, some species may not survive.

In some cases the change has already begun. Wild daffodils now bloom in mid March, a month earlier than 150 years ago. Birds such as the nuthatch have spread into parts of Lakeland where they never used to occur, while other species, such as blackcaps, are increasingly spending the winter here rather than migrating further south. Dragonfly empires are already expanding, with five new species recorded in Cumbria since 1994. Records of the comma butterfly have increased from five before the 1990s to over 400 since 1991.

The impact of climate is inextricably linked to what we do with the landscape. In Lakeland this means farming, and farming is at a crossroads. The direction it takes will have a profound effect on Wild Lakeland. An indication was given early in 2005 when the National Trust announced that on the retirement of its current tenant at High Yewdale, near Coniston, the farm would be split between four neighbouring farms. The trust is one of the area's largest landowners, looking after almost a quarter of the Lake District National Park.

The decision by the National Trust to split up High Yewdale Farm, near Coniston, may have been precipitated by changes to agricultural policy at a national level, but it has caused controversy among the local community.

It was not a popular decision. High Yewdale was one of 14 farms which had been bequeathed to the trust by Beatrix Potter. In her will she had stipulated that her farms should be let and managed the same way and on the same lines as she had previously let and managed them. Many local people saw the decision to split the farm up as a betrayal of her trust. Even Prince Charles joined the fray. A local action group was set up and more than 400 people signed a petition opposing the break-up and calling on the trust to re-think its decision; the letters pages of *The Westmorland Gazette* raged with indignation.

The trust, however, stayed firm. Their action, they argued, safeguarded the bigger picture. It would help to secure a long-term future for Lakeland agriculture and the Herdwick breed, as well as the landscape, character and culture it has created. Rather than being contrary to Beatrix Potter's will, their decision was consistent with it, the trust claimed. She had herself amalgamated farms, and as a forward-thinking businesswoman, would have understood its position.

The war of words over High Yewdale symbolises the perilous position of farming in Lakeland today. The decision about the splitting-up of the farm was precipitated by political maneouverings many miles from Cumbria, by people who have perhaps never seen a Herdwick sheep. For decades the Lakeland farmers have been subsidised to keep sheep. The more sheep they farmed the more money they got paid, regardless of the demand for the lamb and wool they produced. The result of this policy has been a rise in sheep numbers well above what the land could sustain, which has been responsible for much of the decline in Wild Lakeland since the Second World War.

Lakeland hill farmers face an uncertain future as does the landscape they look after.

This farming support has been funded by the Common Agricultural Policy (CAP), a monolithic system which devours a disproportionate amount of the European Union's budget. In 2003-4, in Cumbria alone, 6000 farmers shared nearly £87m of agricultural subsidy. During the same period the European Union embraced Eastern Europe, taking on board countries like Poland and Hungary, where agriculture is dominant. The increased burden this put on the CAP threatened to cripple the union's finances, and pruning became inevitable.

The knife cut immediately prior to the decision over High Yewdale and the National Trust had seen it coming. In January 2005 the UK's agricultural support system was turned on its head. Farmers would no longer be subsidised to produce food. Instead they would be paid for the amount of land they farmed. This disconnection of agriculture from production would help to heal the damage of the previous decades of over-production. But the National Trust had looked into the crystal ball, and for hill farmers the future looked bleak.

The trust is one of the largest owners of upland in the UK, and research it carried out on 60 of its tenant farms, including 20 in Lakeland, revealed that some hill farmers

could see their incomes cut by half. The separation of support payments from agricultural production has exposed the stark reality that livestock farming in the hills is simply not profitable and in many cases will be a loss-making exercise. There may not be a way forward for some farms, like High Yewdale. Amalgamations could become increasingly common as small farms in particular fail or are unable to adapt to an area-based subsidy system, which by its nature favours the big guy. In some places farming could be removed from the landscape altogether.

So what will be the impact of this fragile farming future on Wild Lakeland? It is too early say. However, one profound implication of the changes to the farming subsidy system is that the arrow on the land management dial for Lakeland, which for the last fifty years has been firmly fixed on food production, is now slowly turning towards wildlife. As the financial rewards for using land for food production have declined, so the value of enhancing its wildlife has increased. Conservation organisations and the Government are now having a much greater influence in the management of the countryside. Even in agriculture, conservation is playing a far more significant role than it was twenty years ago. This is reflected in the new subsidies, which farmers only receive if they comply with environmentally-friendly practices.

The first fruits of this switch are beginning to show. In almost every habitat examined in this book there is a swing towards allowing natural processes a greater role in how the landscape operates. Lowland raised bogs are being restored following years of peat

Ennerdale and Pillar. A remarkable experiment is being undertaken in Ennerdale. The three main landowners – the National Trust, the Forestry Commission and United Utilities have stepped back from managing the valley to let natural processes shape its landscape and wildlife. Wild Ennerdale, as the project is known, is a long-term vision for a more Wild Lakeland over a whole valley that will help conserve its important habitats and inspire those who visit.
VAL CORBETT

Take a good look at the view. Panoramas like this one from King's How looking up Borrowdale to Skiddaw could be very different in fifty years time.

extraction; upland hay meadows are being recreated; the amount of native woodland is now on the increase; our waters are cleaner than they have been for many years and plants and flowers are returning to sustainably-grazed fellsides. However, the transition to an increasingly wilder Lakeland may not suit everyone, as one person's wildness is another person's waste. There are fears that if agriculture retreats from the landscape, nature will take over and there will be a return to the 'waste lands' of the pre-enclosure days.

Perhaps all we can say for certain about what will happen to Wild Lakeland is that we should be prepared for change. Although with our understanding of what has happened in the past, this should come as no surprise. In some ways the future of Wild Lakeland seems very different, but on another level it is all remarkably familiar: climate, geology, and Man, locked in a three-way tussle to shape the landscape of tomorrow.

The timeless Lakeland skyline.

FIND OUT MORE
ABOUT WILD LAKELAND

If you enjoyed this book and want to discover more about Wild Lakeland I recommend the following books, information from which is included in Wild Lakeland. The Collins New Naturalist Series' *The Lake District – A Landscape History* by William Pearsall and Winifred Pennington is still the best general book on landscape and wildlife in the Lake District, despite being more than 30 years old. The companion New Naturalist volume, *Lakeland* by Derek Ratcliffe, is a scholarly exploration of the area focusing mainly on natural history. For a more detailed study of the plants and flowers of Lakeland, Geoffrey Halliday's *A Flora of Cumbria* is unbeatable. Similarly exhaustive on its subject is *The Breeding Birds of Cumbria*, produced by the Cumbria Bird Club.

For those interested in more general wildlife, every year the Cumbria Naturalist Union produces an annual digest of what was seen where in the county in its *Birds and Wildlife in Cumbria*, and if it is history you are interested in the Rev. H.A. MacPherson's *A Vertebrate Fauna of Lakeland* cannot be too highly recommended. Cumbria Wildlife Trust and English Nature also produce some informative leaflets to specific sites. If you are interested in a lighter read you might prefer *Flora of the Fells* and *Tarns of the Fells*, two short general introductions to these aspects of Cumbria's mountain landscapes.

If you are moved to action, you could join one of the two organisations which will benefit from a donation from the proceeds of the sale of this book. Cumbria Wildlife Trust and Friends of the Lake District work to conserve the landscape and wildlife conservation of Lakeland and would appreciate your support.

Cumbria Wildlife Trust
Plumgarths
Crook Road
Kendal
Cumbria
LA8 8LX
Tel: 01539 816300
www.cumbriawildlifetrust.org.uk

Friends of the Lake District
Murley Moss Business Park
Oxenholme Road
Kendal
Cumbria
LA9 7SS
Tel: 01539 720788
www.fld.org.uk

*Feasting
with
Panthers*

Feasting
with
Panthers

Or, The Importance of
Being Famous

BY PETER CONRAD

THAMES AND HUDSON

© 1994 Peter Conrad

British Library Cataloguing-in-Publication Data
A catalogue record for this book is available from
the British Library.

ISBN 0 500 01642 9

Printed and bound in Slovenia

CONTENTS

SUPERSTARS AND OTHERS

I DID NOT EXACTLY FEAST WITH THE PANTHERS IN THIS BOOK. ROBERT Maxwell, exercising the tyrant's privilege, denied me food all day. Jeffrey Archer caused me to be overfed as I ate my way across Cornwall in his wake, but the motive may have been the same: a diet of bleeding beef and clotted cream is as bad for you as starvation. At dinner with Vidal Sassoon in abstinent California, where the new puritanism demands that you shun sweets, I felt quite depraved when I accepted his fiancée's offer of frozen yoghurt. Hungry again in St Petersburg, I gratefully gobbled slices of a wafer cake which circulated around the upper levels of management in the opera house I was visiting. Back in London, I resisted the temptation to raid Tom Jones's uneaten breakfast, sent up from the restaurant known to him as The Grosh.

I did share a bottle of wine with Joan Collins, who signed the rim of her glass with the imprint of her ripe, pouting, painted mouth. I have no doubt that Wim Wenders would have offered me a glass of mineral water, if only he had worked out how to pour liquid from a bottle which still had its cap on. My heartiest meal was a lunch cooked by John Boorman's housekeeper, supplemented by a pint of Guinness which his driver – taking me back to the airport in Dublin after a few hours spent in Ireland – insisted I must drink before I left the country. But I should not forget that, in Sydney on another occasion, I ate Joan Sutherland for dessert.

Of course the food was not the point. For the writers of the 1890s, who used the phrase as a shorthand for decadence, to feast with panthers was to indulge in illicit excitements – the sort of specialized depravity which, in Dorian Gray's case, required a carriage journey to the lower depths of the East End. I did less feasting than Dorian, even though I travelled a good deal further to meet some bad and beautiful people.

For the most part, the panthers behaved as their nature dictated, savagely. Maxwell casually maimed several creatures further down in the financial pecking order. Archer aroused a gathering of senescent seaside Tories into a lynch mob. The prehistoric thugs of the World Wrestling

Federation snapped limbs, cracked skulls, and gloatingly sat on one anothers' faces. Michael Jackson, despite a ticking-off from Oprah Winfrey, continued for a few more months to clutch his groin with his gloved and glittering fist, and Barry Humphries presided over a rowdy Dionysian rite with a bouquet of pronged gladioli. Joan Collins slunk and slithered with a big cat's rippling grace, while Leonora Carrington – a believer in the totemic matriarch whom she calls the Great Crone – planned surreally wicked revenges on her landlady. Joan Sutherland docilely and blamessly embroidered, but I heard Luciano Pavarotti insist that, since he was dying, everyone else should suffer an equivalent torment. Celebrity, I came to suspect, entailed exemption from the rules of good behaviour and benign consideration to which the rest of us meekly subscribe: a famous person is as unsocialized as a baby, or a wild beast.

Thanks to these expeditions, I learned this and a few other important truths about the modern world – or rather I learned that, in the modern world, truth is of no account at all. Maxwell played a game of hide and seek with me, speeding off in fast cars to unknown addresses like a fugitive from justice and cheekily enquiring at the end of the day if I had seen through his grandiose bluff. After reading my report on his sadistic threats and thundering rages, he gave an interview in which he pitied my stupidity. It seemed I had not got the joke: he had been play-acting – he maintained – for my benefit. Of course, in a way, he had. His entire life was an imposture.

From Sir Edward Heath I learned how politicians cope with inconvenient truths which contradict their dogmas. They grunt dismissively, then repeat what they have said before. If old and venerable enough, they affect not to have heard you. From the wrestlers, who bludgeoned Japanese or Iraqi bogys at the behest of their corporate scriptwriters, I learned that the conduct of moral warfare is, like politics, a matter of strutting and posturing, an exchange of ritualized abuse and of blows which do not hurt.

Maxwell kept the intimidated truth-tellers at bay by using the law against them, gagging them with libel writs. One of my other discoveries was that the law is perfectly happy to be used in this way. Richard Golub, declaring his willingness to take on Hermann Goering as a client, put it succinctly. When I asked whether he worried about the truth of the cases he brought to court, he shrugged like jesting Pilate and appealed to the relativity theory and the uncertainty principle: 'Who cares? The truth is the truth in that context.' Then, just as Maxwell pretended that his rages

had been merely histrionic, Golub claimed that his nimbleness at manip-
ulating half-truths and brazen fictions made him an artist.

The other truth I gained from Golub, and confirmed on a trip to the
Universal Studios theme park in Florida, was that everyone in the United
States chooses their life or their hair-style because they have seen someone
living it or wearing it on television. You must have a 'role model', which
assumes that you consciously intend to perform a role and that your glossily fictitious predecessor or mentor is a mannequin whose look asks to be
copied. Life is an affair of imitation. It amused me to read about an
exchange on the White House lawn in September 1993, at the signing of
the accord between Israel and the PLO. Richard Dreyfuss was among
those invited to attend the ceremony. I have no idea why the star of *Close
Encounters of the Third Kind* was considered an appropriate witness,
although President Clinton – a politician of the media age, who chose his
job because he saw Kennedy doing it on television – is partial to the company of film folk. When Arafat and Rabin came out together, Dreyfuss
turned to his neighbour, a journalist from *The New Republic*, and said 'Do
you believe this?' The journalist wondered at Dreyfuss's wonderment:
'And you're the guy who saw those aliens land!' History overlaps with science fiction; reality aspires to the condition of a movie.

This is the state of things ordained by post-modernism. In a society of
simulations, a skyscraper on Madison Avenue pretends to be a
Chippendale tallboy, a young hustler from Buffalo pretends to be Sidney
Poitier's son, *The National Enquirer* pretends that a woman in an
Arkansas trailer park has given birth to ten green Martians, and everything more or less amiably jokes about its own inauthenticity. A superannuated actor is elected President because he looks presidential, while a
master criminal takes to the air in a helicopter emblazoned with both the
Union Jack and the MGM lion. Joan Collins's paintings, commissioned
from an artist who can turn out Fragonards and Bouchers to order, flaunt
the same fakery.

My problem is that I am not sure if the joke is so very amiable, or if
such things ought to be a joke at all. After my experience at the wrestling
match, I looked up the reflections of Roland Barthes on the subject. His
view of it differed from mine. He acclaimed the wrestlers as 'gods' and saw
in their huffing and puffing 'the pure gesture which separates Good from
Evil, and unveils the form of a Justice which is at last intelligible.' If I
derived less metaphysical reassurance from the spectacle, it may have been

because my enjoyment was marred by an old-fashioned concern about the gap between truth and fiction. Justice – Sid Justice to be exact, known to his opponent as Shit Justice – was one of the players at Madison Square Garden, embodied by a swaggering bundle of decorative sinew in bright blue underpants. But unlike Barthes, I could not accept the sign as a substitute for the thing itself. As a matter of principle, it still worries me that Macho Man Randy Savage, who was born in Columbus, Ohio, should have been declared a native of Sarasota, Florida by his minders in the executive suite.

Sometimes the *Zeitgeist* arranges incidents which, trivial in themselves, sum up a segment of social and moral history. In New York before Christmas in 1993, while I was finishing work on this book, one such event occurred: the Trump wedding. As I read about it and watched it on television, it came to seem like a family reunion in which most of the themes and some of the characters in this book were present as guests.

Donald Trump had been one of the heroes of the previous decade in New York, when Mayor Koch bankrolled the city by handing it over to rapacious and self-aggrandizing property developers. Trump raised monuments to himself all over Manhattan and along the boardwalk in Atlantic City; I once found myself, to my annoyance, having to fly to Washington on the airline which he briefly owned. Inflated with self-conceit, Trump offered to hire himself out to the Bush administration as a global negotiator. People touted him as a future presidential candidate.

Punctually, as the 1980s ended, his bubble burst. He squeaked clear of bankruptcy by offloading exorbitant assets, simultaneously divorcing his wife Ivana, a skiing Czech. She solaced herself by lending her name to a kiss-and-tell novel about their marriage. The book was written for her by a surrogate with a trustier command of English than Ivana herself possessed. Trump's own consolation was Marla Maples, who resembled a younger Ivana. This trade-in was at first angrily contested by Ivana: she underwent plastic surgery to make herself look more like her replacement. Even so, Trump did not repent. Marla was allegedly a model, and anyone with a rudimentary knowledge of capitalist culture and its built-in obsolescence is aware that you should invest in the latest model on the market. Besides, he was in love: hadn't Marla told a tabloid that he supplied her with 'the best sex I've ever had'? Having followed the horizontal route to celebrity, Marla took advantage of her new status. She turned herself into a commodity, promoting a brand of jeans which were not discernibly different from any other brand, except for the fact that Marla claimed to have designed them. These jeans, best worn very tight, bore Marla's flagrant motto: the brand name was 'No Excuses'. The celebrity jettisons guilt and shame on the way to the top.

By the summer of 1993 Trump had been reflated by an infusion of Japanese funds, and Marla was big with his child. They named their daughter Tiffany, after the jewellery store on Fifth Avenue whose sale of its air rights made it possible for Trump to build the most overweening of his towers, named of course after himself. Marla, in post-partum mode, saw another marketing opportunity. Alliterating furiously, she dreamed up a collection of maternity wear called Maternal Moods by Marla, which she unveiled – so as not to break the alliterative spell – at Macy's. She simpered sweetly about the baby whose patron saint was a shop: on the advice of the image consultants, the scarlet woman who luxuriated in 'the best sex' had become a Madonna.

Now that she was a virgin again, and once she had signed an agreement limiting her right to the spoils when they divorced, Trump decided to marry her. Questioned about his timing, he displayed the inspired opportunism which the celebrity needs if he is to absorb the accidents of history and the tragedies of others into his personal mystique. A fortnight before the nuptials, a mad gunman had opened fire at random on a Long Island Rail Road commuter train, killing six passengers. It was 'the massacre' which prompted him to legitimize Marla, Trump declared: it had reminded him of fragility and the preciousness of life. Celebrities, especially those who are no longer being regularly celebrated, are often to be found in the vicinity of disasters. Didn't Bianca Jagger soberly don fatigues and have her photograph taken in Bosnia?

Trump's previous marriage had been solemnized by the demagogic preacher Norman Vincent Peale, and Marla worshipped at the Marble Collegiate Church, where Peale used to be pastor. She and Trump had chosen well: Peale's lucrative doctrine of self-puffery, 'the power of positive thinking', gives a gassily religious tinge to the American creed which holds that all dreams will come true if you wish hard enough and promises that each of us is a potential celebrity – a faith devoutly maintained by many characters in the first half of this book. Peale's successor therefore sanctified the union at the Plaza Hotel.

The secular powers in New York also queued up to anoint Trump. When he arrived at City Hall in a limousine with Marla and produced the thirty-dollar fee for their marriage licence (advanced, I suppose, by his Japanese creditors), the document was personally signed by Mayor Dinkins, who then toasted the couple with non-French champagne. Dinkins – not surprisingly, given this craven behaviour – had recently lost an election for a second term. Other politicians gratefully accepted invitations to the wedding (along with a gaggle of gossip columnists and television news readers). Power treats celebrity with due deference, even with envy: the Trumps and Marlas and Ivanas of our time, invented by the force of their positive thinking about themselves, are accountable to no electorate, and need make no excuses.

The wedding, held while Ivana simmered among the Colorado snows, was an enchanted constellation of religion and real estate, salesmanship and sex, bringing together the power of those who hold elected office and the different, less tenuous power bestowed by scandal and shamelessness. The spirit of the age, with Pastor Arthur Caliandro from Marble Collegiate as its deputy, joined the hands of Trump and Marla.

Agape at this festival of false values, I asked myself again why the world was like this, how it had come to pass. The original sin, I think, was Andy Warhol's. In the 1960s he reconfigured society and redefined its beliefs in accordance with the dictates of Pop Art. It was he who invented the superstars, recruited from his entourage of dope fiends and drag queens. For him, this was a malicious joke. He knew that Ultra Violet, Bill Name, Candy Darling and Ingrid Superstar were talentless parasites. However, he also knew, having learned his trade in advertising, that publicity can speedily magic away all inconvenient truths. Selected anonymities therefore became celebrities, but for only fifteen minutes each. They were then discarded, like empty cans of Campbell's soup, to be replaced by newer versions of the same. The economy depended on disposability: why shouldn't people also be treated as consumer items, with a strictly regulated shelf-life?

With sinister wit Warhol called his studio The Factory, because it was in the business of manufacturing fame, as well as art. The superlative in his category of superstardom admitted the inflationary hype of the exercise. These people were not stars at all: fanatical exaggeration was necessary to pretend that they were. Since then the cynicism of the marketers has ruled out such irony: witness the control exerted by the World Wrestling Federation over the humanoid cartoons it has invented. But because superstars are now ten a penny or a dime a dozen, a new and more portentous category has had to be created. In 1993 *The New York Times* decided that Glenn Close's performance in the musical *Sunset Boulevard* merited such a promotion: the paper's critic officially declared her a 'megastar'. Before long, megastardom will be thrust upon every starlet, and another rank will need to be devised. Macrostardom, magnastardom, supercalifragillisticexpialidocioustardom? The language, already overtaxed, may soon expire from flatulence.

All this came to pass because Warhol's cottage industry was only too successful. Having made a fortune from paintings which – pointing the way towards Ivana Trump and other 'virtual' creators – he usually relied on others to produce, and finding that his own instalment of celebrity had outlasted a quarter of an hour, he forgot that the whole thing was intended as a lethal jest. Though still consorting with addicts, call boys and other scuzzy downtown fauna, he moved to the Upper East Side and – in need of customers – began to cultivate the Shah of Iran and Imelda Marcos, Kuwaiti sheiks and Bolivian tin merchants, or tinselly blow-ins like the Baroness de Bodisco, Princess Minnie de Beauvau, 'Princess Polignac who does P.R. for Cardin'. Warhol also reckoned Prince and Princess Michael of Kent to be 'real classy', especially when the Prince aristocratically trod on a wet painting.

Warhol harried dowagers whose cosmetic-surgery scars had not yet healed, wanting fees for sycophantic portraits of them. One of his later portraits, repainting a magazine cover, was of Joan Collins. In the 1960s, silk-screening the face of Elizabeth Taylor to infinity, he had experimentally laughed at the difference between the singularity of beauty and America's mass production of imitators, lookalikes, wannabes. The portrait of Collins – blowsily pretty, applying paint like make-up – allowed for no such scepticism. It could not afford to, because that would have reduced its market value.

Warhol had come to realize that his signature, like the formula the alchemists dreamed of, was an instant source of funds. He once autographed a sick bag during a flight from Miami to New York. The gesture was enough to attach a price tag to it. The auctioneers who control his estate are currently engaged in equally whimsical valuations, as they prepare his leavings for sale. Among other booty, the estate contains bundles of Polaroids – snaps made at parties, meant to be thrown away. These have vexed the valuers, who are caught between two equally compelling financial imperatives: they need to keep prices reasonably low, so as to escape tax on the estate, but they also want to push prices as unreasonably high as they can, in order to maximize profits when the items they assess come up for auction. This has prompted some bewildering reversals. One valuer appraised the Polaroids, which have their own built-in obsolescence because they will inevitably fade, at a few cents each. A second opinion declared this too modest, and immediately proposed one hundred dollars a snap. Value is no longer intrinsic or inherent. You are worth as much as you can get away with making others pay for you. This is the economy of celebrity, where something as intangible as Michael Jordan's 'image', conferred on a sneaker, can generate twenty million dollars a year, and David Hampton is able to claim that his life-story (which consists of the lies he has told) is worth three hundred million dollars.

History ended during the years – 1989 to 1993 – when I was writing these pieces, and I sometimes wondered if the wrong side had not won, or if the right side might have won for the wrong reasons. Can it really have been *Dynasty* and *Dallas* which toppled the Berlin Wall by putting on show the tawdry trophies of affluence? Margaret Thatcher liked to congratulate herself on having vanquished communism; perhaps Joan Collins should have claimed the credit. On Friedrichstrasse in what used to be East Berlin, I found that freedom – as the second of Wim Wenders' fallen angels recognizes – consists of the right to buy Benetton sweaters and Rolls-Royce cars. In Beijing, the counter-revolution had its headquarters in a Kentucky Fried Chicken franchise at the southern edge of Tiananmen Square. In St Petersburg, however, it was different: I felt ashamed of my hunger pangs and my homesickness for hot water when I saw how Valery Gergiev and the Kirov musicians derived moral sustenance from music, hoping that their performances might belatedly do justice to a martyred composer.

After outings with a monster like Maxwell or a huckster like Archer or a shimmying shyster like Golub, my reward was to be sent to visit people I admired like Gergiev or Wenders or David Hockney, and my relief was to find – by contrast with Maxwell's rabid tirades and Archer's barked orders and Oprah's intimate dialogues with America or the Universe – how unpresumptuous they were.

Early in 1994 I saw Ivana, still enthroned among the gilded glitz of the Trump Tower with a tiara of flossy hair on her head, remark in a television interview that she understood and pardoned the importunities of the press, because 'when you have achieved certain things in your life, of course the public will be interested in you.' I longed to know what Ivana's achievements were. To have grown that upswept fringe, as golden as the chair she sat in? To have braved the cosmetic surgeon's knife? To have autographed multiple copies of those novels she did not write? To be giving this interview? Celebrities are spoiled artists, convinced that it is enough to have created themselves. The genuine artists – busy creating other worlds or other people, or else absorbed, like the musicians I met, by the discipline of re-creation – tend not to be especially interested in themselves. Hence Natasha Richardson's dismay when she was recognized during a massage. Stretched out naked, she lacked the means to become someone else. Hence too Ian McKellen's vacant-faced flirtation with non-entity: it is his own lack of a personality which enables him to bring to birth those alternative personae who lurk inside his body. Joan Sutherland scrupulously denies any affinity with the melodious maniacs she played on stage, just as Barry Humphries maintains a superstitious distance from Dame Edna.

The would-be artists I met thought that criminal sleight of hand or legalistic verbal trickery counted as art. At best, they saw art as a means of marketing themselves: what other need could be served by the novels of Jeffrey Archer and Joan Collins? In a society where all men and women can proclaim themselves artists, art can only be defined as whatever it is that the self-proclaimed artist happens to do. Vidal Sassoon fancied that a haircut merited comparison with a sculpture by Modigliani or a building by Mies van der Rohe. The classical notion that art might help us to enjoy life or endure it, and the romantic notion that art trespasses on mysteries beyond life, still bizarrely recur. Oprah Winfrey nodded in agreement when Michael Jackson told her about his intention to heal the suffering nations, and explained that a concert tour is – well, sort of – the Second Coming with some extra help from lasers.

But before I despaired about 'the disease of images', as Wenders calls it, I had some salving reminders of what it truly means to be an artist. It means, among other things, the capacity to alter the world, or our understanding of it. Boorman reimagines the Irish valley he lives in, resurrecting the past or divining the future in the present. The games Hockney plays with his electronic gadgets question our assumptions about space and time, and make us reconsider the physical and mental routines of our existence. To be an artist is not simply a matter of posing for your photograph or attaching your trademark to a perfume bottle, a sick bag, or a novel someone else has written for you. There are professional qualifications, unfair as that may sound: talent, skill, even dizzy virtuosity are required. Artists do things which others cannot do. Sometimes, like Joan Sutherland, they do things which it seems impossible that human beings should be doing at all. Yet many of them – modestly insecure, unlike the self-made superstars – are puzzled by their own abilities. Since they do not know who gave them the genius which controls them, they cannot be sure how long it will be theirs, or even whether the donor might not have made a mistake. I was touched to hear Sir John Gielgud say that he had shied away from the movie camera for fear that he would be 'found out', and saddened to be told about Orson Welles's conviction of his own fraudulence. Maxwell, who was a fraud, surely entertained no such doubts.

This book begins with a very bad man, and ends with a very good woman. On my day with him, Maxwell's conduct was predictably bestial. But my metaphor breaks down in the case of Joan Sutherland, who is quite unlike a panther. Indeed she once described herself, using a phrase I would never have dared to apply to her, as 'just a stolid old cow'. Is it possible that great art and humane virtue might belong in partnership after all?

With two exceptions, earlier versions of these articles appeared in *The Observer Magazine*. I am grateful for the editorial and organizational skills of Angela Palmer, Madeleine Lim, Janet Briggs and especially Andrew Billen. The article on Natasha Richardson and her family was commissioned by *The New York Times Magazine*, and edited by Annette Grant. The interview with Sir John Gielgud also appeared, somewhat neutered, in *The New York Times*. I am glad I now have the opportunity to give Gielgud's bear back his erection, deemed 'unfit for print' on West 43rd Street. Since their first publication, all of these pieces have been extensively rewritten and in most cases considerably lengthened (not only by restoring erections).

ACTION MEN

IN PURSUIT OF MAXWELL

LIKE SOME PORTLY GOD IN A BAROQUE PAINTING, ROBERT MAXWELL descended on us from the sky, accompanied by a temper tantrum of thunder. On the tarmac at Heathrow airport, early one morning in May 1991, a group of attendants scanned the horizon for the helicopter which improbably contained his bulk, his briefcases, his portable phones, and his intimidating persona. An underling passed on the latest bulletin from the helipad above Fleet Street, on top of the newspaper offices which the tycoon – scoffing at any resemblance to a jar of instant coffee, and defying anyone else to share a name which he chose for himself at random when he arrived in England from Czechoslovakia after the war – had rechristened Maxwell House. The message, delivered with a tremor of fear, was that 'He's on the actual chopper.'

A while later, a command was delivered from on high for the benefit of terrestrial employees, who were converging on the airport by road: 'Mr Maxwell will wait for no one.'

Then, with an angry rumble of rotary blades directly above, came the ultimatum: 'The Chairman will land in one minute.'

Two legs lowered themselves uncertainly from the helicopter, lumpily followed by a besuited girth which it seemed they could hardly be responsible for holding up; at length there emerged the jowly, menacingly jolly face of the mogul himself. The chopper disgorged a jumbo. The Chairman had indeed landed.

He did not kiss the tarmac. He had touched down only in order to bounce higher into the air. We were off, apparently, to Brussels. Perhaps we might also be coming back, although Maxwell – for whom power entailed mystification, and the secretive sequestering of information – had indicated that he might whimsically decide to go on to Moscow or New York or whichever world capital turned out to require his presence that day; if so, we would all be swept along by his personal jet stream of affluence and self-importance. His travelling valet, manhandling a regiment of garment bags in case of detours, remembered having recently hopped to Paris for the afternoon with Maxwell only to end up in Bucharest four days later.

Striding towards his private jet, he discovered that this morning he would have to tolerate an air-traffic delay of five minutes. He huffed, puffed, and worked himself up to the day's first explosion. 'What is the reason for this?' he demanded of the flossy stewardess on the jet, whose expertise did not extend beyond making coffee. I suppose he could have barked at the inconsiderate controllers in their tower, who had forgotten to give him priority; he preferred to blame subordinates, whose squirmings gave him pleasure. 'We should have gone last night. You must anticipate these things', he growled at the stewardess.

The cup she was presenting to him shook pleasingly in her hand. She retreated from the force field, only to be summoned back with a shout: he demanded biscuits. He ate and drank with extra relish, enjoying the fact that coffee had been offered to no-one else. Power takes even greater pleasure in witholding food than in reserving information. Having drained his cup, he nodded in my direction. 'You can give him one after we take off', he said to the stewardess. 'Not now. He'll only slop it.'

An American public affairs man – transferred, as Maxwell imperially remarked, 'from another part of the empire' – hurled himself on to the plane in flustered panic as it began to taxi. He had been delayed in passport control. 'Why', Maxwell wished to know, 'do you not have a British passport?' He made it sound like a personal failing, a sackable offence. The American gabbled that his application was in, but to become British you had to spend two years in a queue of documents. 'Let us see', said Maxwell, intimating influence at the highest levels, 'how we can expedite that.'

The public-relations man by now had recovered his breath and his professional jargon. He flicked through a succession of papers, listening for Maxwell's grunts of approbation. 'I tried to address as many sensitivities as they could tell me about. Do you want me to start actioning this now in terms of P. R.? OK, Chairman? Willco. And you're happy with the way we're playing it today?' The Chairman basked in this technocratic babble. It conferred a mystique on the ordinary business of hucksterism and self-advertisement; it transformed existence into a grand and exclusive game.

Then he brushed the public relations man away, temporarily weary of flattery. 'Get Kevin for me', he told a secretary, and thrust at her one of the cellular phones which were his tentacles. Later in the day he introduced me to his son Kevin, whom he described in mock-heroic style as 'the next generation'. Maxwell liked to show off Kevin and his brother Ian as his assurance of surrogate immortality; they also served as vehicles for their father's sins. All they inherited, a year after the day I spent with Maxwell, was his debts, his disgrace, and the possibility of serving on his behalf the prison term for fraud and theft which he had evaded by conveniently dying.

Back at the office in Fleet Street that morning, Kevin might have been entertaining parricidal thoughts. 'You cancelled?' roared his father into the phone. 'That's appalling. Did you do so politely? Then will you please call him now and apologise? Good manners cost nothing.' This edict was compulsory only for the next generation; Maxwell, upbraiding inferiors, had granted himself an exemption. Money endowed him with the savage, unsocialised privilege of childhood: the right to behave exactly as he pleased, and to disbelieve in the feelings of others.

As we were now in the air, pointed towards an undisclosed destination in Brussels, I asked if I might see the day's itinerary. I did so, of course, very politely. Maxwell shot me a suspicious look from beneath eyebrows bristling like barbed wire, and went into conclave with his secretary over a piece of paper. Before it could be handed over, the paper had to be mystified, invested with value by being runically encoded with secrets. Their mutterings gave me to understand that certain things on the paper were forbidden to me. The secretary was instructed to scratch out the name of a certain person with whom Maxwell had an appointment.

She cross-hatched the name and passed the paper on. By turning the sheet over and angling it into the light, I could still read the identity of the top-secret individual, written back to front. It meant nothing to me. This was probably another of Maxwell's bluffs; his entire life was a confidence trick, so why should he not have promoted a nonentity to such arcane status in order to baffle or impress me? Feeling naughty, since I had still not been allowed a coffee, I said 'You needn't have gone to so much trouble. I've never heard of him anyway.'

Maxwell hesitated between relief and incredulity, between anger at the inefficient secretary and annoyance that – because of my ignorance – I would not have appreciated the import of the meeting in any case. 'There', he said with a cannonade of chuckles, 'you have the difference between a man of letters and a man of ACTION. Action is what matters. All else is transitory. That is the secret of success in life.'

Buoyed up by the thermal draughts which were wafting us over the English Channel, borne along on the magic carpet of his power and his money, he sprawled in his seat and, manoeuvring his embonpoint into the aisle between us, became expansive. England had slipped away behind us; Maxwell explained to me his own part in abolishing it. 'When I grew up, I was always reading Sherlock Holmes. I had never seen England, but I imagined it enveloped in fog. Later on, as a Member of Parliament in the Wilson years, I introduced the Clean Air Bill and made smokeless coal mandatory. It was my revenge on romantic England. I did away with its fog! So there's my small footnote to the history of our time.'

Revenge on England may well have been Maxwell's obsession, and the motive for his financial skulduggery. 'Of course the English dislike me. They hate my success. But I just sail on, I suffer no slings and arrows.' The last phrase smugly co-opted Hamlet, and did away with his moody melancholy as briskly as Maxwell had expunged those peasoupers. 'I am not contemplative, I regret nothing. I always tell the English that they live there by accident. I, however, live there by choice. So it is up to them to accommodate themselves to me.'

Maxwell's self-conceit was as indefinitely extensible as his waistline. He banished the English to second-class citizenship in their own land, just as a few months before at the launch of his new daily paper he had declared, 'I am *The European*.' Now he proceeded to tell me, as the fields of Flanders appeared on cue beneath his soaring shadow, that he was Europe.

Speaking in the orotund tones of an editorial, he shook his head over 'the whole malaise of Britain, its metastasizing mental cancer. I had such faith in a Britain which was declining by the time I arrived there after the war. It was a personal disillusionment to me. We have gone from being number one to being number nothing. My Buy British campaign for the Labour government was our last chance to retain an industrial base. Since then we've been overtaken by Italy. Italy! But the other day a former Prime Minister – I won't tell you which one – said to me, "What a tremendous service you are rendering to the nation. Your launch of *The European* shows us the world that Britain still counts for something" '.

Do people, I wondered, really talk like that – even former Prime Ministers, or Maxwell ventriloquistically lending words to some imaginary former Prime Minister?

Meanwhile Maxwell, transforming his life into an allegory, had arrived at the triumphant end of his paragraph. 'You see then that what I am doing today is what I am all about. I am helping Europe to compete on equal terms with America.'

Translated into less world-historical terms, this meant that he was handing over a cheque from one of his spurious charitable foundations to a new laboratory for cancer research in Brussels. His business interests were of course being served by the transaction: Maxwell's Pergamon Press published the institute's journal. Pergamon was the source of his first fortune, after he dreamed up the lucrative wheeze of persuading scientists to submit articles on their research for free which he then sold back to them at extortionate prices in a library of periodicals. Royalty had been suborned to witness Maxwell's gesture, and the Duke of Edinburgh was on his way from London, in a less plushly appointed private plane, to pull a string and unveil a plaque. Maxwell glanced down proprietorially on the barbered pastures and idling windmills of Belgium. The Chairman was descending.

Once on the ground, dispensed from immigration formalities like a head of state, he charged through the outhouse which receives passengers from executive jets and began to organize his motorcade. 'Judy', he ordered, 'you go in front. I'll have you', he added, bestowing an honour, 'in beside me. The rest of you take another car – *une autre voiture*.' The man of power can assume that there will always be another car, though if there is not it hardly matters, so long as he is himself comfortably seated. Maxwell settled into the back of the Jaguar, unpacking his enormous body like luggage.

As we drove off, the organizing continued, interrupted by a call to Kevin to announce 'I have landed' and to check that he had made obsequious amends to whoever it was he had not met. Power is also about placement, the creation of hierarchies and the policing of precedence: our first stop was the diplomatic suite at the Sheraton Airport Hotel, where Maxwell was awaited by a patient group of petitioners for favour. Like his own court chamberlain, he choreographed the occasion in advance on the cellular phone. When bludgeoning unions during strikes or contract negotiations, he had devised a technique for dividing and ruling. The various parties were installed immovably in separate rooms while Maxwell commuted between them, spreading confusion and misinformation, until he achieved their surrender. This is how he was intending to manage his touchdown in the hotel. 'How big is the suite? Where are you keeping them stacked up? Put Grierson in the sitting room, and my two *other* visitors [more world-famous people I had never heard of] in the bedroom.'

Engrossed by the spatial layout of this stop-over, Maxwell did not notice that – on our way presumably from one side of the airport to the other – we had traversed half of suburban Brussels. The driver did not know that he was supposed to go to the Sheraton at the airport, and was on his way to the city centre. 'Monsieur', snarled Maxwell, having found another hireling to bully, 'vous êtes un idiot.' In the rear-view mirror the driver's face, already squeezed beneath his officious cap, folded into itself like that of a frightened rabbit. Maxwell smirked. He had learned a great deal from the tinpot tyrants of Eastern Europe whom he so assiduously cultivated: they gave him lessons in petty terrorism.

When we got back to the right Sheraton, the hotel manager was in attendance, practising genuflections on the front steps. Before permitting himself to be greeted, Maxwell remonstrated with his secretary: 'Judy, will you check when you get into the car that they know where they are going? Make sure they have written instructions. Always book the car from the hotel, not from some outside firm. We are five minutes late because of this. Query their bill when it comes in: we won't pay.' Financial genius, I perceived, entails an infinite capacity for taking pains – or for being a pain. Conjuring with millions, Maxwell quibbled over a few niggardly pence; complaining about the loss of time, he had already lost more of it in order to make sure that his world-encompassing corporation defaulted on that bill. The totalitarian ogre, like God, sees everything, and minutely scrutinizes all accounts.

In the hotel lobby a life-sized model of Mannequin Pis piddled into a pool, its playful trickle gurgling in tune with the muzak. The Chairman ascended in a glass-walled elevator. Up in the diplomatic suite, he shuttled – like Henry Kissinger on a slightly smaller scale – between the sitting room and another, more occult huddle in the bedroom, with as much banging of doors as in a French farce. His secretary despaired because she could not recall the combination to the briefcase with the brass tag labelling it NO. 1. 'And', she whimpered, 'the fax machine isn't operational!' Either lapse might provoke a tirade. But Maxwell contented himself with hammering on the bedroom door: one of his advance tacticians, over-mindful of security, had locked a group of conspirators inside, and Maxwell could not get at them.

I wondered what these meetings could be about. The secretary, tearfully grappling with the clamped briefcase, did not reply. The American public-affairs man, eager to oblige, said 'I'm loose as a goose on that one, I'm afraid I'm out to lunch on that completely', which I took to mean that he didn't know. Later in the day I asked Maxwell what the subject of the bedside conference had been. He looked more than usually self-important and uttered a single word in his cavernous whisper, breathing out a trail of resonant ellipses after it: 'Deutschland...'. Another of his grandiose bluffs, I presume.

Already the next occasion – the opening of the cancer lab and the presentation of Maxwell's cheque – was being frantically choreographed. A Maxwell employee produced a floor plan. 'The only person who's allowed to be mobile is Prince Philip – though of course Mr Maxwell has to be mobile as well, because he meets the Prince in one room and then presents the cheque somewhere else. Everyone else is in set places. And security will be one hundred and fifty per cent. They'll have half the Belgian army around the building.'

I arrived, *dans une autre voiture*, to find that half the Belgian army con-sisted of one bored policeman and a sniffer dog as incontinent as Mannequin Pis. Upstairs, a fierce British lady with a double-barrelled name-tag enforced the embargo on mobility, marshalling people to their colour-coded portion of the floor: 'Will you go to your yellow bit please? and stay there!' She had done her best to ritualize space on the hastily con-verted office floor, organizing a guard of honour of potted shrubs on the grey carpet to mark out the place where the ceremony was to be per-formed; nevertheless guests milled about in an uncourtly chaos, and a paratrooper, elbowing his way through the crowd, knocked down her stunted border of greenery. She had chosen Bach for the soundtrack. She may also have chosen the videotapes of an oncology conference which played for their own amusement in a corner.

The Chairman's arrival was announced by a flurry of flashbulbs. A photographer from *The European* had been ordered to Brussels with instructions to get a picture of the proprietor with Prince Philip; meeting an envoy from one of Maxwell's other newspapers in the scrum, he mut-tered, 'What are they punishing you for?' Another minion had set up a stall among the oncology videos to display the wares of the Pergamon Press.

The scientist in charge of the laboratory bowed low, said to Maxwell, 'Let me introduce you to some dignitaries', and performed some introductions. The vamp with the expensive tan was Signora Cicilitra from Superchannel, the shy pair of mice were His Imperial and Royal Highness the Archduke Christian of Austria and his Archduchess. Trailed by a cub reporter from *The European*, for whom he spelled out the names of the dignitaries, Maxwell worked the crowd. His advice was beseeeched, his intercession besought. 'Write me a letter', he boomed. 'Robert Maxwell, *The European*. That's all the address you need.' He vanished briefly into a huddle with a tiny dapper flunkey: one of his many bankers, he told me, and the possessor of the 'the biggest cash mountain in Belgium'.

The Duke of Edinburgh slipped unostentatiously into the room, and made his way through the crush with no attendant snappers and scribblers. Royalty can no longer afford the despotic prerogatives of celebrity. 'C'est impossible!' muttered one of the laboratory's publicists, contrasting Maxwell's self-promoted media event with the self-effacement of the Duke. 'Vous voyez', said a disgruntled colleague, 'Monsieur Maxwell est stealing le show.'

There was a reason, apparently, for the Duke's astute low profile. Putting down roots in the opposite corner of the room, where he quizzed the researchers about the minutiae of their work, he was determined not to move towards the impending encounter with Maxwell and the photo opportunity which would induct him into the Chairman's scrapbook. Aware of the snub, Maxwell noisily commanded me to attend on him. 'I', he said, 'am supposed to be giving a speech, though no-one appears to know where or when. Of course I am quite happy *not* to give the cheque.' The Duke, having edged towards the ceremonial zone of shrubs, veered away towards the wan Austrians as if the wind had changed.

'Did you invite them? Are they friends of yours?' I asked Maxwell, whom I had seen chatting to the erstwhile imperial couple.

'NO!!!' he roared, as megaphonic as a headline. 'I am a man of the people. I do not mix with aristos'. He aimed the vowels of the last word like a trio of paper darts at the averted back of the Duke. 'When you find me hobnobbing with princes, you will know I am finished.'

I wondered what small talk the Archduke might have had with Maxwell, born a citizen of his defunct empire.

'I asked him', said Maxwell with a smirk of glee, 'how many of the languages of the Austro-Hungarian Empire he spoke. He said there were too many, they divided them up among the members of the famly. I told him that *I* speak them all!' This oneupmanship accomplished a historical revenge: Maxwell's private empire extended further than that of the Archduke's ancestors had ever done.

Meanwhile, other grievances remained unappeased. The royal consort from an obscure offshore island still kept Maxwell waiting. 'I *may*', he loudly grumbled, 'change my mind about the presentation.'

Maxwell's boisterous bad manners appealed to the mischief-maker in me. Keen to see what I could get away with, I asked him how much money he was donating. I was fairly sure he would not accuse me of vulgarity. Indeed he did not. He reached into a pocket, fished for the cheque, unfolded it with a flourish, and held it out for me to look at, hoping to see me drool. It was for 175 thousand dollars.

Taking a further risk, I asked Maxwell if I could hold it. He narrowed his eyes sceptically, then handed it over. The scientist in charge of steering Prince Philip through the crowd must have noticed the exchange and panicked, because within seconds he had delivered his guest to Maxwell, who snatched the cheque back from me. After a long homily citing his own recovery from a cancer declared to be inoperable thirty-five years before, and enjoining everyone present to look upon him as a symbol of hope, he pointed it towards Prince Philip, who was obliged to reach out and tug it, as delicately as possible, from Maxwell's fingers. The Prince mouthed a silent, strangled 'Thank you'.

Downstairs, improvising the order of his motorcade for a dash to the next, still-undisclosed destination, Maxwell reflected sadly on the difference between his magnetic self and the uncharismatic Prince. 'Wasn't it embarrassing? They only wanted photographs of me. And I'm afraid his retinue noticed! The same thing happened to me once in Moscow with the Prime Minister of Belgium. Everyone was lined up at the airport ready to greet him. Then I arrived, and he was left standing. And I don't even have big tits like Elizabeth Taylor. No, you get another car.'

I got one somehow, and told it to follow the already revved-up Chairman. Fifteen minutes later we lost his trail on a building site in the centre of Brussels. A hole in the ground had apparently dilated to swallow him. Maxwell's whole life was a game of hide-and-seek; those Sherlock Holmes stories must have taught him about the master criminal's delight in outrunning and outwitting his pursuers. Eventually we discovered that his car had made an unofficial detour across the building site, scattering hard hats, and vanished through a disused entrance into an underground parking garage. Down below, an attendant remembered him leaving the car at a trot and shoehorning his body into a lift. I followed, and each time the door opened, another receptionist in another ornate ante-room shrugged as I asked about the fugitive. I caught up with him on the top floor, outside the boardroom of a bank.

In a vestibule hung with tapestries of rollicking Flemish peasants who were gutting a pig, Maxwell – on his way to lunch – looked over his shoulder from between a pair of ponderous swing doors. 'You *were* clever to get here', he said, 'but you're not coming to this. This is His Holiness the Pope speaking. If we have a crust left over, we'll send one out to you.' No crust ever made its way through the vault-like doors. I read an ancient copy of *Newsweek*, as if on a visit to the dentist, and reflected that life at court – whether a prince's or a dictator's – is about waiting, about the humiliating business of mere attendance.

Having fatly lunched, Maxwell reappeared, flanked by the delighted banker with the cash mountain, who had no doubt prevailed upon his guest to accept a loan of a few million francs. A photograph was taken to commemorate the occasion. Before allowing it, Maxwell checked on the sheen of his jet-black hair, and dragged a plastic comb through his eyebrows. Along with the details of his financial crimes, the truth about his coiffure emerged after his death: a barber who had sworn an oath of confidentiality was flown by private plane to wherever in the world Maxwell happened to be, carrying a phial of black dye for the Chairman's hair. Megalomania naturally encompasses personal vanity. Even Maxwell's enormous bulk was a source of pride to him: a physical proof of supremacy, as if he carried round within him all the people he had eaten.

He farewelled the banker whose cash mountain he had nibbled at for lunch, raising his fingers in a papal salute: 'Urbi et orbi!' That morning he had enjoyed a small social victory over two monarchies, laughing at the monoglot Archduke and requiring Prince Philip to reach out and prise away a cheque he was supposed to be giving; logically the next step was an impersonation of the Supreme Pontiff.

Down in the garage he decided that he would travel on alone with the lawyer – ordered up from Paris for the day – whom he introduced to me as 'my global counsel'. Maxwell fancied this global conceit. His corporate icon was a spinning planet with a purple M branded on its continents and oceans and a red girdle encircling it like one of his own capacious belts. He was a globular man: like the earth perpetually in motion. Having called the lawyer to heel, he rapped his driver on the shoulder: 'Allons-y!'

he shouted. A wrist flapped vaguely in my direction: 'Another car.'

This time, however, there was no other car. Neither did I know where Maxwell was speeding. Without Belgian francs, I threw myself on the bank's mercy. The officials were no doubt accustomed to forking out, with a fawning smile, the hyperbolic sums Maxwell demanded; supplying me with a taxi driver required much more anxious debate. At last I even extracted the address for which Maxwell was bound: he was due back at the cancer laboratory in the suburbs, where he would explain his charitable impulses to the press and tell them – as he had already told me on the flight that morning – that he had no possessions, did not collect art or antiques, lived in a council house (albeit a baronial one with its own private park, leased to him by the city of Oxford), and thought that the only purpose of great wealth was to assist others, for to give was more blessed than to receive.

The great giver smirked when, huffing and puffing, I staggered into the room where the muted oncological videos were still playing. The press conference was attended by the hacks from Maxwell's London dailies and one or two Belgian newshounds, for whom it must have been a slow day in the Low Countries.

'Order, order', Maxwell unnecessarily ordered. The snapper and scribbler from *The European* set to work with a will. But before Maxwell could recite the moral fable of his charmed, altruistic life, the researchers insisted on describing to him the projects which his cheque would subsidize. The overture went on too long for his liking, and he resorted to the ancient tricks of the upstager. He yawned cavernously, and stretched his legs beneath the table. He rolled his sleeves up, adjusted his cuff-links, then rolled the cuffs down again and readjusted the links. Incapable of a whisper, he talked to his neighbours on the platform and guffawed at a joke he had made. At last he was able to describe once more his private, unremunerated mission for the betterment of mankind.

Then it was time for the Chairman to lift off again. The Pergamon employee who had been staffing the stand which touted Maxwell's scientific journals – and also giving away corkscrews and bottle openers imprinted with the corporate emblem – crept forward: 'May I be presumptuous, sir, and ask for a ride back to England? All the scheduled flights are full.' He had flown over for the day, and if not allowed a seat on the empty jet would have to spend the night in a hotel, at Maxwell's expense.

Maxwell, however, ignored the fact that the young man's motive was to save him money. Like a dog with a nose for fear, he sniffed another victim. 'Why', he barked, 'did you not make arrangements?'

'I wanted to, but I was not allowed out of the building while the Duke was here.'

'Why did you not anticipate that? Let this be a lesson to you.' After a long, skewering pause, he grunted, 'You may come to the airport. You must stand by. I cannot guarantee you a place on the plane.'

Enthroned in the jet, Maxwell summoned the boy, who was dragging two suitcases of Pergamon samples, together with the kit of party favours, across the seething tarmac. 'Where is the hitch-hiker?' The boy peered around the door, looking prematurely grateful. 'You must wait. Put your bags down. Stay there, outside. We will tell you.'

'Yes, sir', said the boy, as if accepting alms, and resumed his position on the molten runway, breathing fuel. Power is also the capacity to degrade those who depend on you.

The pilot assured Maxwell, who already knew it, that there was plenty of room on board. Ignoring the message, he ostentatiously relaxed. He unbuttoned his shirt, unpeeled his socks and hurled them away, ate several apricots. Advised of another air traffic delay, he did not fret or threaten as he had done at Heathrow, because the postponement enabled him to prolong the boy's torture. He pottered off to the plane's lavatory, and returned with his fly gaping open. A mound of fish-net underwear oozed out of captivity. I wondered if you could point this out politely, for his own good, to a man like Maxwell. Yet from the way that he radiated delight in his own cruelty to the boy outside, I guessed that the lapse was deliberate: a primal exhibition of contempt for others, and a small, seamy manifesto of hostility. Occasionally he glanced out at the broiling boy. He might have been peering into the oven to keep an eye on the progress of his dinner. Only when the plane had been cleared to take off did Maxwell send for him.

'You're lucky, mister', he remarked as the stand-by passenger, dragging Maxwell's wares, sidled down the aisle as if skirting a kick.

'Thank you, sir', said the boy, spared the boot only because Maxwell happened to be barefoot.

He was not yet out of danger. Skulking close to the lavatory door, he inadvertently irritated his employer by opening one of the cases and taking inventory of the Pergamon tomes. I suppose he only wanted to demonstrate his industriousness. But the crackle of paper and a scuffling in his peripheral vision enraged Maxwell. 'Mister,' he cried, 'sit still, or I will put you off this plane.' We were at twenty thousand feet, with the placid English Channel beneath. This would surely not have deterred Maxwell from off-loading a victim in mid-air. It was the sort of thing Nero might have done, if he had enjoyed the use of a private plane. The boy shammed death, which he must have thought preferable to his current life, for the rest of the journey.

Back at Heathrow, Maxwell charged through the terminal. His passport remained in his pocket: his famous face, which glowered at the immigration officers, was his ticket of admission to the country. When we got to customs, he suddenly thrust the NO. 1 briefcase at me. I trotted compliantly behind, wondering what leaden weight it contained: boulders carved from the Belgian cash mountain? Once we were out of range of the inspectors, Maxwell grabbed it back with a snarl, assuming that I meant to steal it. I realized that I had served as his bag man, and had probably broken the law on his behalf.

Although his helicopter was throbbing in readiness, he made a detour to a news-stand where – with the omniscience of a malign deity – he intended to check on sales of *The European*. A hapless customer was buying a tabloid published by Maxwell's rival, Rupert Murdoch. Maxwell, his hand descending onto the man's shouder, performed a citizen's arrest. 'Who are you? Where are you from? Why are you buying *The Sun*? Have you read *The European*? You can't get it in Ireland? Ridiculous! Why don't you buy a copy? Can you afford it, or do you want me to pay for it? Good, you pay for it yourself then. Off you go. Now you know not to buy the lying *Sun*.'

The girl at the cash register could not supply the statistics he demanded, and was told to telephone her manager upstairs. She made the call, and reported 'He's a bit tied up.'

Maxwell declared the reply 'unacceptable'.

'He's having', she pleaded, 'his tea.'

Maxwell rolled his eyes and repeated to me his solemn diagnosis of Britain and its metastasized mental cancer.

Two entire minutes drained away, with Maxwell prowling in circles like a corralled steer. Out came the cellular phone, and calls were placed to the editor of *The European* in London, who was made to take the blame for the manager's tardiness ('I have been waiting *five* minutes'), and to the headquarters of the newsagent W.H.Smith in another airport building. 'Tell that man', shouted Maxwell, 'he must get down here now or I shall speak to Mr W. H. Smith personally. Right now, I'll hold on the other line. I've been waiting *ten* minutes'. Power expects the instant gratification of its whims. Maxwell, shaking the phone in his fury, was an obstreperous baby, bludgeoning the world with its rattle. Power can also exaggerate with impunity, since no-one will call its bluff. Did Maxwell really believe that there was a Mr W. H. Smith? It was like imagining you could place a call to Mr Harrod, or to the Kentucky Colonel.

I remembered the incident when Sir Edward Heath, a few months after Maxwell's death, told me of a summons he had received from Maxwell late in 1989. He agreed to stop at Maxwell's office in Fleet Street on his way back to Westminster from a lunch in the City of London. Maxwell, contemplating new worlds in need of conquest as the Berlin wall teetered, wanted advice from Heath about the future economic soundness and political stability of Germany. Heath, rather too optimistically, told him not to worry. Maxwell then picked up the phone and told his secretary to connect him with Chancellor Kohl in Bonn. Her reply, which came suspiciously soon, was that the Chancellor could not be contacted. 'Get me the foreign minister', snapped Maxwell, with a sideways glance to see if Heath was registering appropriate symptoms of awe. Sounding as if she had been coached, the secretary next rang back to say that the Chancellor and the foreign minister were both in Moscow that afternoon for a meeting with President Gorbachev. 'Then call the Kremlin, woman!' cried Maxwell. 'I will speak to all three of them.'

Heath excused himself at this point in the charade. 'I decided then', he said to me, 'that the man was mad'.

At the Heathrow news-stand, the manager arrived while Maxwell continued to make phone calls complaining of his non-arrival, and patiently waited for his presence to be noticed. When Maxwell boomingly asked how *The European* was doing, he replied, to no-one's surprise, 'Very well'.

Maxwell beamed. The paper's sales were actually negligible, as he well knew. But the mad have absolute faith in their own fantasies, and a madman with power can compel others to share their conviction. Prosecuting his advantage, he made a bid for better display of the paper on Sundays.

'Yes,' said the manager, furiously nodding, 'on Sundays we stack it on the floor!'

Maxwell swept on, having added two more nervous breakdowns to the day's quota. The helicopter managed to haul him beyond the reach of gravity. As we bounced back towards Fleet Street, he phoned ahead to his office and discovered that a stenographic minion called Brenda had gone home early. The engines spluttered apopleptically. She had a headache, he was told. He wished to know the precise location of the headache, and would expect a medical certificate to be submitted. As an afterthought,he asked for her number at home so he could telephone to make sure she was there. Perhaps, I thought, he might land the helicopter in her back garden? Her loyal colleague in the office said they had no home number for Brenda, and altruistically endured the inevitable tirade. Another pair of nervous breakdowns could be totted up.

Dispensing terror from on high, Maxwell propped his arm out of the helicopter window. A gold cuff-link the size of my fist hung loose, not properly secured after his fiddling and fussing at the press conference in Brussels. It came perilously close to tumbling down on to suburban Hounslow, where – like a gift from an enemy bombardier – it might have cratered a lawn or concussed a garden gnome. Maxwell's secretary rescued it in time. As we swerved up the Thames and swooped over Westminster, Maxwell surveyed the inner courtyard of Buckingham Palace, the crockets of the House of Commons, and the dozing lions in Trafalgar Square. 'I am', he reminded me, 'the only person in the country permitted to over-fly the centre of London.'

We floated on to the helipad on top of the *Mirror* building, carpeted with fluorescent green Astro-turf. The Chairman, a prince of the air, seemed reluctant to land. He stayed on the roof and did business among the extractor fans, wheeling and dealing in French and German above a din of pneumatic drills from the streets below. Fresh secretaries were ferried up to take dictation. A chef in a starched apron climbed the steep metal stairs with a cup of tea for him. Maxwell sipped, spat, and sent it back: 'It's bags, I won't be fobbed off. How dare you serve me second best?' A second, more authentic cup was produced; Maxwell did not drink it. Power means fanatical fastidiousness, as well as conspicuous waste. The chef stumbled away to have his nervous breakdown in the kitchen.

Told to stay out of earshot while Maxwell trilingually bought and sold countries on several telephones, I studied the heraldry of the parked chopper. It had been emblazoned with red, white and blue stripes, and a banner headline on its underbelly announced that it was travelling FOR-

WARD WITH BRITAIN. Maxwell, warning the British people that they had less right to live in their country than he did, stole the national insignia and flew the Union Jack over their heads as his personal pennant. Inside a circular shield were Maxwell's corporate initials, MGN: Mirror Group Newspapers. Beneath this, poking its head through a hoop, a lion roared, as if one of the dozy big cats in Trafalgar Square had awoken famished. Not content with sky-jacking the British flag, Maxwell had also grandiosely rewritten the trademark of a Hollywood studio: MGN alluded to Metro-Goldwyn-Mayer, kidnapping its lion. FORWARD WITH BRITAIN replaced MGM's motto, *Ars Gratia Artis,* and was equally cynical in its cover-up of commercial profiteering. The merger of patriotism and showbiz had a sinister ingenuity. Didn't it hint – with a riskiness which must have titillated Maxwell, insured against exposure by his team of libel lawyers – at the truth? The great defrauder was himself a fraud, the personification of untruth in advertising.

Below the roof terrace, the next configuration of contacts awaited him. He moved them around by remote control, dividing and ruling. 'Put Sir John in the study', he said into one of the phones. 'And I'll have the man from Tass in the sitting room.' Assured they were where he wanted them, the Chairman descended into what he laughingly called, when pretending to be one of us, his 'flat'. The top floor of the featureless office block had been made over into a cloud-high country house, with stuccoed ceilings, gilded mirrors, and ruched curtains which framed views of a dwarfed, grovelling London far beneath. Some details of the set-dressing needed attention: a varnished side table was piled with dog-eared tabloids, rather than copies of *Horse and Hound* or *The Lady.*

Maxwell, again flirting with danger, pointed out a fireplace flanked by marble columns. As he knew I would, I touched the stone, which felt wrong. I tapped it with a knuckle, and it echoed: tin. I looked at him. He stared back defiantly. After all, he had more or less invited me to discover the imposture. But his gaze said, Go ahead, try to prove it. It added, I'll see you in court.

Though it was not yet evening, I felt quite faint from the denial of food, worn out as well by the sensation of having been absorbed into the exorbitant, exhausting drama of this man's life. Maxwell made no concession to weariness, or to any human weakness. Mobilising that portentous bulk, he converted mass into energy, words into money, the ego into omnipotence. I was desperate to escape, as if from a spell, and to reclaim my own innocuous identity. Before he strode through a door and introduced 'moi sin Kevin' to the man from Tass, I told him I was going home.

There is a formality to the termination of a celebrity interview, which the subjects invariably observe. They always ask if you have got what you wanted, if you have enough. (You always reply that you have, and they always formulaically hope that they will see you again.) Maxwell had his own variant of this concluding flourish. 'Ah,' he said when I admitted that, like Brenda, I had had as much as I could take for one day. 'So tell me then, before you go. Have you deciphered the enigma of Maxwell?'

The question itself summed him up. He could refer to himself as a third person because that is exactly what the monstrous, self-made creature known as Maxwell was. The name was invented at the time of his naturalization; it belonged to a character who had also been made up, a role the devilish pretender was playing. And the enigma? To call himself this announced, with the teasing contempt which counted as his nearest approximation to good humour, that he was a mystery, which he challenged you to solve. Enigma invoked espionage: it was the name applied to the most urgent and potentially damaging of state secrets by professional code-breakers during the last war.

Of course I failed the test he set me. No, I had not found him out. No-one had; not just yet. To guess at his crimes would have required an imagination equal to his own in devising them. A master criminal is a fantasist, even an artist, warping reality until it matches his greedy dreams. Maxwell designed his life as a sardonic, vindictive practical joke on the country which had failed to appreciate the honour he bestowed on it by living there. But his triumph was too easy and automatic: people believed his lies, and entrusted him with their savings. His confidence-trickery only amused him if there was a possibility of being caught. Hence his titanically bad behaviour, provoking subordinates to see if they would rebel and say what they thought of him. None ever did, confirming his scorn for those he victimized. Hence too the clues he scattered before amateur detectives with their notebooks like me, and his motorized hide-and-seek in Brussels. He was a Moriarty in quest of his Sherlock Holmes. The dullards at the Serious Fraud Office, who seized the files which incriminated him only after his death, did not qualify. Neither did I.

'See yourself out, will you?' said Maxwell, superciliously content – or perhaps disappointed? – that he remained, for another day at least, ahead of the game.

EDWARD HEATH IN BRONZE AND LATEX

A PUBLIC MAN IS AN AMBIGUOUS FIGURE. COMPOUNDED FROM THE images others have of him, he shuttles back and forth between honorific likenesses made to line the corridors of power and the cartoons which he keeps in his lavatory. Does he recognize himself in the official portraits or in the scurrilous deformations of the satirists?

Despatched to Salisbury to spend the day with Sir Edward Heath, I expected to encounter a cartoon. Political life transforms people into caricatures of themselves, condemned to eternal self-repetition. Television, the medium on which they eternally repeat their pompous saws and brazen lies, has made them inescapably visible, so much a presence in our homes and lives that we grow to dislike them as intensely as if they were obnoxious neighbours or detested relatives. They become their mannerisms, and scrape at our nerves whenever we watch the news: the whine and whimper of George Bush, the nagging shrillness of Margaret Thatcher or – even worse – that plummy contralto octave which her voice coaches taught her to use when she was affecting sympathy. To be a politician is to suffer from what the media age calls an image problem; the ailment goes with the grubby, self-glorifying trade. Perhaps Heath's front door would be opened by Gerald Scarfe's version of him: a monster with a triangulated face and a nose honed to stiletto sharpness. Or perhaps the definitive version of Heath was his latex alter ego from *Spitting Image*, blustering out denunciations in a self-made patrician voice whose vowels sometimes plummet below stairs.

I had forgotten that public men, of course, do not open their own doors. A policeman let me through the gate, and a housekeeper with a gaoler's clanking collection of keys let me into the house. In the entrance hall, instead of Heath pulled apart by Scarfe or remoulded by the sculptors of *Spitting Image*, a more official tribute stood before me: a copy of a bust made for the Oxford Union, whose president he was in the last year before World War II.

The bust was swaddled in a blanket, like a felon about to be bundled into a police car. The sculptor, who had just delivered it, rushed to and fro attempting to decide about where it should be placed. He was spoiled for choice: Heath's house in the close beside Salisbury Cathedral is a museum commemorating his multiple careers. In the drawing room, photographs of grandees advance across the piano in a military parade. A mirrored alcove exhibits his yachting trophies. His library has the usual dreary shelves of memoirs, but also columns of compact discs, mostly conducted by Heath's friend Karajan. The dining room is walled with moody watercolours of the house by John Piper, another friend. In its owner's absence, the place advertised the completeness of the man: states-man, sailor, musician, connoisseur – a very different Tory animal from the philistine profiteers of the Thatcher era. But this was another image, a scrubbed and polished public façade. Who could live up to such a house? Did anyone even live in it? The entrance hall contained no drip-ping umbrellas or muddy boots.

Unblanketed, the bust looked grumpy. The face sagged, its over-hanging folds set in bronze. A stiff tie, its anchorage, implausibly held up the swelling chest and frowning head. 'We had five three-hour sittings', said the sculptor. 'He slept most of the time, though whenever he woke up he'd deny it.' In cold metal, the sleep could have been eternal: to share your house with an effigy of yourself is an admission that you might as well be dead, because you belong to history. Is this why the public man collects cartoons for the lavatory? Distorting his face, the satirists at least treat it as a living thing. Waiting for Heath to appear, I wondered whether to expect the beaked monster invented by the caricaturists, or a solemn, soporific monument.

When he did come in, I hardly recognized him, even though the house is furnished with images of the man. But images never tell the three-dimensional truth. A political career and regular appearances on the television news add six inches to anyone's height. Could this small figure really have eyeballed Saddam Hussein, as he claims to have done at a meeting in Iraq during preparations for the Gulf War? Heath is bent by age, but his face – paler now than in his yachting days, when it resembled a piece of carved Polynesian teak – remains unlined, and thus looks intimidatingly blank. Keeping watch from behind it, he has taught it to give nothing away. He has grown a formidable set of jowls as extra insula-tion, which make his head look as if, like a bust, it is standing on a man-telpiece. Despite the face's self-control, his clothes have fewer scruples. He was wearing, on the day I visited, a pair of quite violently, seafaringly blue trousers; his shirt struggled to contain a tummy the size of a haggis.

Introduced to the bust, he looked uncomfortable. It cannot be easy to meet your own death mask, with your flesh a mouldering green. 'You have captured', he said to the sculptor, 'the worst aspects of my personality.'

The debate about placement, on a column carved from the heart of a mahogany tree, began. 'Have you tried both loos?' asked Heath. 'We've got another bust by someone else up in the attic, you know.' Eventually this one came to rest in the drawing room, where it reared sternly above the stool of the grand piano. 'It will ruin my playing,' Heath prophesied. In profile, as you come in, the bevelled nose resembles a spinaker; staring down the length of the room, the totem of your host is something of a conversation-killer. The adamantine glare of the thing reduced even its original to silence.

'What it needs,' I said as Heath met its gaze warily and the sculptor adjusted its angle, 'is a seagull to sit on top of it. Sort of a nautical touch'.

The remark, once uttered, slopped on to the immaculate carpet like a spilled drink. I glanced at Heath, whose own face was expressionless marble, as unforthcoming as the bust's. Oh well, I thought, to be shown the door for impertinence will make good copy. Then I noticed a disturbance some way below the alabaster mask. His tummy was heaving, as if the haggis had given itself indigestion. No sound emerged from his mouth, and his face moved no muscle, but this was a symptom of laughter. He was amused! Maybe Heath's centre of gravity has sunk lower over the years, but the journalistic cliché about his shoulder-shaking jollity is anatomically quite misplaced. When he laughs, it is the diaphragm which does so for him. Only much later, if at all, does the eruption travel upwards; the face – even when Heath himself says something funny, which he does surprisingly often – seldom relaxes or relents.

When we retired to the library, Heath disconcertingly turned back into a statue of himself. His sentences resembled plaques, unveiled to imaginary rounds of applause. 'I am now', he casually remarked, 'the second most senior holder of the Charlemagne Prize.' The full import of this honour escaped me, but I could tell from the gravity of Heath's tone that it entailed being written into history, made an immortal, set up on a plinth as a resting place for gulls. Pomposity – the studious care of his own reputation – is the politician's professional duty.

Shakespeare's Caesar, a public man with no private identity left, makes

the vain boast which has became an oath of office for grapplers on the
greasy pole:

> I am constant as the Northern Star,
> Of whose true fixed and resting quality
> There is no fellow in the firmament.

Politics is necessarily a quicksand of contingency, of volatile situations and
unforeseen circumstances. Why then do the temporizers and compromis-
ers who make it their occupation insist on pretending that their sole concern is to keep faith with their principles, even though we can see them
ducking, diving and dodging, betraying one another and themselves, in
order to stay afloat and in power? Heath's obsession at the end of his
career is to defend his record and to insist, like Caesar, on its consistency.
Above all he stands by his decision, when he was Prime Minister during
the 1970s, to make Britain a member of the European Community. No
qualifications could be admitted; disagreements were met with a grunt of
'What?' and a pretence of deafness. This was the repetitiousness of the
public man, who plays an archival tape when he talks. 'You must have
read the books about me', said Heath wearily in answer to one of my
questions. Had he convinced himself that those books contained all the
truth there was? He fortified himself for the ordeal of going through it all
again with a plate of petits-fours left over from his morning coffee.
Standing all day on a pedestal is a hungry business.

One of the arts a politician must possess, which Heath's poker-playing
visage is superbly adept at, is the capacity to outface evidence which
undermines his views. We met in June 1992, between the Danish and Irish
referenda on Maastricht and soon after the assembled European
Community finance ministers dismissed the budgetary proposals of
Jacques Delors. Events appeared to be turning against the goal of
European union which had been the mission of Heath's political life.
Adhering to his faith, he growled at these recent embarrassments like an
Alsatian dealing with intruders, and ordered them to go away. The most
infuriating trait of politicians is their incapacity to admit contradiction
and complexity – everything which makes life interesting and characters
round. Do they realize what inveterate liars – or twisters of the facts –
they are? Mrs Thatcher's technique, when asked awkward questions, was
to go on talking so as to trample the questioner. '*Please,*' she would sometimes pause to say, 'let me finish.' Heath, claiming the privilege of age,
simply pretended not to hear. I asked about the violent recurrence

of nationalism in a Europe supposedly on course to abolish the nation state. Hadn't this tragic irony caused Heath to reconsider his reading of history? What about Bosnia? 'We have got to prevent Europe from tearing its guts out', he said. Having waited for me to get that down, he then added 'And we have.' That was that. I am still not clear what the self-fulfilling second sentence referred to.

Answers were issued like memos.

On the Danish vote, which had refused to ratify the scheme for unification worked out by the politicians at Maastricht: 'We are a nation of fifty million. Why should we take note of twenty-one thousand people? In politics there's a terrible tendency to listen to the minority, just because they bellyache.'

On the anticipated Irish vote against the treaty, engaging in damage control which ultimately was not necessary: 'I wouldn't pay too much attention to the Irish result. It's all so confused with sex.' (Heath's pronunciation of sex is as peculiar as a New Zealander's: he calls it six, and chops off the vowel with testy distaste. The confusion which he feared would warp the Irish vote was a debate on abortion, which got entangled with the argument about Maastricht.)

On Delors, whose proposals for an integrated European state had provoked Mrs Thatcher to screech 'No, no, no, no!!!!' in the House of Commons: 'What is this British mania about him? The man is not a socialist, that's a Thatcherite slur. We are still suffering from 12 years of Thatcher and her bigotry. She had no time for anyone but herself, after all she sacked 29 members of her government.'

On the internal strains of German reunification: 'Another British obsession, just because the British want to break the Community up. You ask the people in Malmö' – this was shortly after a mob of lager louts, visiting for a football game, had run amok in that Swedish city – 'who they'd rather have, our soccer hooligans or the so-called German neo-Nazis. You'd be surprised by what they say. We don't understand the end of communism here, because Thatcher took all the credit for it. She said we saved Eastern Europe, meaning that she thought she did, but the Iron Curtain was first breached by Hungary, and here in this country we are still passing legislation to keep people out.'

In Heath's cosmology, Thatcher functions as the equivalent of original sin: all evils can be attributed to her. She has not been forgiven for deposing him as party leader twenty years ago, or for offering him no worthy job in any of her administrations. During her years as Prime Minister, he seethed on the back benches. When she was manoeuvred out of power in 1990, his official comment simply quoted her triumphal announcement of victory in the Falklands War in 1982: 'Rejoice,' he boomed as if uttering a mortar, 'rejoice.'

The mutual animosity of Heath and Thatcher raises interesting questions about the psychological motives of politicians. Despite all the cant about principle, isn't politics the conduct of personal warfare by other means? Those means, for this pair of august Tory elders, remain those of the school playground: the poked tongue and the raised finger, the sly kick and the unauthorized punch below the belt. No mode of attack was ruled out. Thatcher's snidest assault on Heath was sexual, when she told a journalist that 'I don't feel it is a man looking at a woman, more like a woman looking at another woman.' He retaliated by referring to her as a man. Throughout our talk he called her merely Thatcher, as if she were the cigar-chomping cross-dresser from *Spitting Image*, and conceded her the female pronoun with an audible reluctance. He professed not to mind that ennoblement has given her a new forum in the House of Lords: 'Who's going to take any notice? The Lords have a way of dealing with this. They just politely listen to the maiden speech, then go away. Everyone's deserted her. All her former intimates say openly that she's barmy.'

The antagonism between Heath and Thatcher made them tear the map of the world down the middle. It was her grand ambition to turn moribund Britain into the United States on a somewhat cosier scale. Although she considered Reagan a dunce, she was smoochily devoted to him in public. By the time he left office, she considered herself to be in control of the Atlantic alliance, and before the Gulf War she upbraided George Bush for turning 'wobbly'. Meanwhile she did her best to sabotage European union by haranguing continental colleagues, haggling over British contributions to the communal budget, and counting the change she received back from Brussels as suspiciously as a shopper convinced that her butcher is a crook. Heath's world-view reverses hers. His European agenda makes him hostile to the pretensions of American power. A cheeky self-quotation stated his position: 'I say at my speeches about European affairs in America that only two per cent of Americans have heard of Europe, and only one per cent know where it is – so I'm aware that mine is an uphill campaign.'

He told a revealing story about the imperial American presidency, which derived from the funeral service in Melbourne for Harold Holt, the drowned Australian Prime Minister who was Lyndon Johnson's obsequious helper in Vietnam: 'Johnson arrived at the cathedral with about fifty-two security men, one of whom walked up the aisle beside him carrying the box of nuclear codes, in case he decided to blow the world up while we were in church. Then the Prince of Wales arrived, with just one security man. And Johnson got up from his pew, told the Prince how glad he was to see him, and actually welcomed him to Australia! The Prince said very quietly, "Thank you Mr President, but this is my country, so let me welcome you."' This may have been the sly, ironic victory of English breeding – mock-modest, actually supercilious – over good-natured American crassness, but it also illustrated the mental delusion which prevails in the world of high politics. Australia was no more Prince Charles's country than it was LBJ's; for both the adolescent aristocrat and the grizzled Texan warmonger, the ego had become a territorial imperative.

Heath has refused to learn the timidity appropriate when dealing with superpowers. A BBC film about the Queen in 1992 included a glimpse of him at a Buckingham Palace reception castigating James Baker, George Bush's Secretary of State, for his failure to go to Baghdad to remonstrate with Saddam before the Gulf War. Heath himself ventured there to plead for the release of British hostages, and after three hours with Saddam concluded that he was not an insane aggressor but a cunning critic of Western hypocrisy: 'He said to me, "Remember when I fought Iran. You all supported me then! And it's no good complaining about all these arms I have. Who sold them to me?"' The arrogant standoffishness of the State Department, in Heath's view, precipitated war. On film, Baker looked distinctly sullen at being rebuked. When he mumbled something about not being able to go, Heath harumphed: 'Well, I went.' The Queen made an effort to defuse the situation by giggling at Heath: 'Of course you could go there, you're expendable now.' Peace, however, was not restored, and Heath told the simmering Baker 'I got a message back that Saddam Hussein now rather wishes he'd taken my advice.' Baker then huffily strode off: 'A pity they cut that from the film. But they couldn't show him turning his back on the Queen.'

The anecdote betrayed the bitterness of the unhonoured prophet, the unheeded oracle, but Heath refused to accept that his own journey to Bagdad – from which Thatcher, hoping it would be a one-way trip, withdrew Foreign Office protection – was particularly brave: 'You've got to be a leading British sportsman to think of yourself as a hero every time you fail at something'. The comment puzzled me, until I noticed that Heath's tummy was at its suggestive work. This was a joke. Unfortunately it requires explanation: the tabloids had recently been weeping inky tears over the footballer Gary Lineker, who, for the first time in his career was ordered off the field in Sweden during his last match for England. Such meretricious patriotism disgusts Heath and, having outgrown the need to be diplomatic, he does not mind loudly saying so. 'We love to claim we're heroes when we lose. It's because we feel inferior to the rest of Europe, and that's also why we're so suspicious of the European Community. We're hopeless at languages, for instance'. Heath could be heard in the BBC film replying rather deliberately to Mitterrand's greeting at the Buckingham Palace party, 'Bien, merci, et vous?' The words did not exactly trip off his tongue, but in this mono-glot land it was at least a start.

Although he snorted impatiently at any dissent from the European policies he supports, he talked in a different register – fondly and fer-vently – about Europe itself. An early biographer, George Hutchinson, reported the opinion of Heath's friends that 'he is a romantic, but bottled in'; a romantic, perhaps, in whom the love of persons (given Heath's emo-tional callowness, which has toughened into a forbidding self-enclosure) is sublimated into a love of places. Salzburg, for instance: he remembers staying in the Bavarian Alps in 1937 and walking across the Austrian bor-der in the evening to have a drink in Mozart's home town. Or Rome, where he recalls a dinner at the Villa Madama and the view down across the city: 'It was an August night, the cypresses were somehow glowing'. As Prime Minister, he fancied bridging the Channel so he could drive over from his parliamentary seat in Kent for dinner near Calais, returning safely home before midnight. The fantasy, interestingly, excluded the possibility of spending the night in France; food is a prudent and polit-ically respectable form of pleasure.

Their self-repressed romanticism makes the English yearning interna-tionalists and busy travellers. 'Luxe, calme et volupté' are situated abroad; they cannot be translated into English or brought back in your duty-free allowance. But in Heath's case the journey is its own reward. His imagina-tion does not dwell on the sunny gratifications at its end, because he is already planning the return trip. His dash to Holt's funeral in 1967, sharing a plane with Harold Wilson and Prince Charles, earned him a certificate for the fastest flight ever made between England and Australia. He is still irritated by the waste of a few hours on the way back, when Wilson – who was then Prime Minister and could dictate the flight plan – insisted on touching down in Western Australia, 'so he could see some long-lost great-uncle or other.' He fantasizes about one day being able to circle the earth within twenty-four hours: breakfast in London, a futuristic plane to Australia in time to see the Melbourne Cup being run in the afternoon, back to London for dinner on the same evening. (It is essential, in these science-fiction scenarios, not to miss a meal.) When I commented that he might have to live a good deal longer before aeronautics caught up with him, Heath accepted the challenge: 'The old lady who had this house before me got to 94. That gives me hope'. He then risked a smile of self-congratulation: he has already, like Nixon did, lived long enough to be present at his own rehabilitation. Surviving is also, since he has seen Thatcher out, his revenge.

Sailing and music, his two extra-curricular pleasures, allowed him to indulge a romanticism which his political caution inhibits. He no longer sails – 'Can't afford to under this government', he says with a ruction of the tummy – but he still exploits the reputation for sporty flair it gave him. I asked how he had coped with the heat at his investiture as a Knight of the Garter (yes, there is a garter, and no, the Queen does not slip it over the ankle personally; she retains a page boy to do the bending). There was another deep-down chuckle as he remembered the accidents of the scorching day in the spring of 1992, with perspiring peeresses subsiding inside their ermine and Yeomen of the Guard crumpling. 'No, no,' he said, 'the sun doesn't bother someone who has sailed as much as I have.' Clearly he enjoyed the thought that, at the age of 75, he was made of sturdier stuff than those molten yeomen.

The romantic appeal of music, and his refusal to surrender to it, are illustrated by a story about his first frustrated negotiations over Britain's entry into Europe. At the end of a day spent arguing with de Gaulle on behalf of the Macmillan government, he used to look out of his window at the embassy and overhear a Paris which his duties kept him from visiting. He solaced himself by thinking of Delius's symphonic poem, 'Paris, The Song of a Great City', which begins with a stealthy, opiate dusk and goes on to hurl itself into the erotic frenzy of the night. The reverie of the conscientious Lord Privy Seal may have strayed in that direction, but he could only permit himself to enjoy it at second hand, by silently playing Delius's score inside his head as he toiled away at his papers.

Music and politics have shadowed each other throughout Heath's life, with the former supplying fulfilments denied by the latter. Though he campaigned against the appeasement of Hitler when running for election to the Oxford Union, he went on to invite Sir Thomas Beecham to speak there in a debate on the motion that 'This house would like to appoint a dictator'. Beecham, who cancelled at the last moment, intended to nominate himself for the post. Authoritarianism, disallowed in a politician, is quite proper in a conductor. 'I greatly admired Karajan's perfectionism', said Heath. 'Nowadays it's the fashion to say you must be slovenly, that it's more authentic if there are mistakes in a performance.' I suspect Heath also envied the disciplinary methods of Karajan, which no politician could have got away with. He described Karajan rehearsing the deportment, not the playing, of the European Community Youth Orchestra, which Heath helped to found: 'He told them, "When I come on, you stand. And when I say stand, I mean straight, not wearily dragging yourselves to your feet. At the end of the concert, you may not applaud me. That is the job of the audience." In Salzburg, when he came out for his sixth curtain-call, one of the cellists made the mistake of stamping his feet. Karajan, as he walked past, elbowed him in the ribs rather sharply. I imagine that hurt quite a bit.'

If Karajan was the musician as more-or-less benevolent despot, Leonard Bernstein, another of Heath's friends, was the musician as unpolitical man, a romantic without repressions. A story is told about a reception for Bernstein at Downing Street during the terminal gloom of the three-day week, the low point of Heath's calamitous regime. Trades unions had shut down the country. To ration power, shops closed for half the week. Television was ordered off the air after the evening news. By candlelight, the nation coldly pondered its decline. Bernstein, sweeping in after a concert, greeted Heath by asking 'Ted, how's your tottering government?' In some versions, the flamboyant, not to say flaming conductor calls Heath darling and gives him a kiss. I asked Heath if the story, minus the kiss, was true. 'Sounds like Lenny', he said. Another incident with Bernstein sums up Heath's use of music as a respite from the dreary routine of public life. In New York for the twenty-fifth anniversary celebrations of the United Nations, he decided he could not abide another official dinner, so got his secretary – Sir Robert Armstrong, who as head of the civil service defended the Thatcher government's economies with the truth in the *Spycatcher* trial – to arrange a rendezvous with Bernstein. 'Robert then had the butler interrupt the dinner with a very long face, saying there was an urgent message from Downing Street. I went straight over to Lenny's apartment. I thought I was getting away from politics, but all he wanted to do was argue about Vietnam. At least he wasn't entertaining any Black Panthers that night.'

Often for Heath, the purposes of politics have coincided with those of music. On the first tour undertaken by the European Community Youth Orchestra, he invited the heads of state in each country to attend the concerts, and conducted the relevant national anthems himself when Claudio Abbado refused to raise his baton for such doggerel tunes. 'We started in Holland, and as it happened I knew the Dutch national anthem well. They used to play it on the radio during the war before the news. They played all the Allied anthems, and the more Allies we got, the worse things became musically. Anyway there was enormous applause. Everyone said they had never heard it played so passionately!' Rather a sad outlet for passion, perhaps: why waste it on the Dutch national anthem?

Heath propounds his ecumenical message musically. He is proud to have rescued Elgar's 'Cockaigne' overture from its xenophobia. The piece is a swaggering evocation of Edwardian London, with flags, brass bands and saucy cockneys; Heath took it on the road in the new post-imperial world, conducting it with the Berlin Philharmonic in Paris. This experience prompted a characteristically orotund reflection: 'As I was saying to the Pope, when I was in Rome last week, music is international...' Heath left an interval of silence for me to sound the depths of this thought, and to hear the dropped name reverberate like an echo in the Royal Albert Hall. Politicians, who seldom listen to anyone but themselves, have an endearingly naive tendency to say things like 'Music is international' as if they were minting the phrase there and then; I can imagine the Pope nodding sagely. But the fact that it's a truism does not make it any less true, and it is the recurring theme of Heath's life.

Music is also an agreeable antidote to politics because, when discussing it, Heath happily forgets to censor his thoughts. One perk of age is that there are no more grown-ups to be afraid of: hence Heath's impolitic fury against Thatcher, or the engaging indiscretions of his musical gossip. He dismissed a certain famous conductor (name supplied on request) as 'a monkey with a stick', and relished describing how Abbado, 'my favourite enemy', drilled the ECYO to give him unspontaneous ovations. 'I suppose he's all right in Rossini, or in Mahler. There's so much going on in Mahler, how can you ever tell if it's well conducted? But he tries to pretend he's a big fellow when he's not. And who's that other dreadful man who just took over the Chicago Symphony from Solti? Barenboim, that's the one.'

Earlier the face stayed sober while the tummy chortled: for so reserved a man as Heath, every joke is a gamble. But now he took a mischievous glee in describing how he had teased Plácido Domingo, who as a result – being even more public a man than Heath, and unable to suffer any humorous slight to his dignity – is no longer speaking to him. After much nail-biting anxiety on the part of the organizers, Domingo had sung at the inauguration of a cultural centre somewhere in the north-east of England. Heath, present as a guest of honour, went backstage afterwards and said dismissively 'Pleased to meet you. You sing quite well, and you even look like him.'

'Like who?' asked the stupefied Domingo.

'Like Domingo', said Heath innocently.

'But I am Domingo', Domingo declared.

'Oh no,' said Heath, 'you can't be. Domingo would never come to a place like this. He'd just promise to and not turn up. He does that all the time – but he usually doesn't send a lookalike in his place. Have you been singing long? Where did he find you?'

Retelling the story, Heath roared 'He was furious!', and the hiccups of the haggis for once made it all the way to his face, which flushed pink with sheer naughtiness. Though Heath's seniority at Westminster has made him Father of the House, he is no genial, mellow paterfamilias. He is more like a slightly cranky, scarily frank grandad who has given up mealy-mouthed niceties and feels entitled to tell the truth with impunity.

Showing me around the garden he designed after moving to Salisbury a few years ago, Heath gave a good impersonation of an old man peacefully relegated to pasture. The lawns were mown and rolled in stripes like bespoke cloth, orchids sweltered under glass, and conveniently unembraceable maidens of metal and plaster preened in the shrubbery. Here too, however, there were testimonials to the public man: 'The Dutch have named a tulip after me, and every year they send over 750 for me to plant. But we've been overrun by pheasants here, and this year they ate all the bulbs!' Pheasants have no sense of history, and no respect.

At the bottom of the garden, where the trees stand back to disclose the river and the water meadows from which Constable often painted the cathedral, there lurked another reminder that the tenant was no sedate, pottering squire. While admiring the back of Heath's house, with its cranky Gothick window and its archaeological layers of pebble, stone and brick, I noticed a man loitering in a wooden hut beside the water. A gardener, I thought, having a smoke. Then the man walked out of the hut towards us: he had a sub-machine gun under his arm. Trussed into a bullet-proof vest, he crossed the lawn and entered the barn. The spire of Salisbury Cathedral – for Constable an emblem of permanence and spiritual fortitude, although its symbolic strength was depleted and it was wearing a splint of scaffolding in 1992 – overlooked the incongruous scene.

I gasped, and said to Heath, 'I didn't expect a man with a gun in a cathedral close.'

'I hope', said Heath, 'he's got more than one gun.'

The usual vital sign showed that this was a joke, though of the gallows-humour variety. It was also something of a boast. Proud that the state took such pains to guard him, he relished the thought of danger stalking the perimeter of his rural idyll. The barn housed his personal security force, currently watching our movements on television monitors. A detective accompanies Heath whenever he leaves the grounds; I was warned that, if we went out to lunch, I would also have to feed this taciturn third party.

It seemed irrelevant to ask why anyone might want to harm Heath, two decades after his term as Prime Minister had ended. But the whole embattled, expensive arrangement says something about the esteem in which we hold our elected leaders, who must be protected from us long beyond the retiring age. Do they suspect what we think of them after all? A public man knows that reality is dangerous; guns are arranged around his borders to keep it from trespassing.

What Makes Archer Run?

'T HE COVER? OF THE CHRISTMAS EVE ISSUE?'

The eyelids of Jeffrey Archer, which up to that point had been batting like coquettes' fans in furious self-defence, flicked open and stayed that way. Then, after focusing for a while on the distant prospect of publicity, they fluttered shut again. Their agitation signalled mistrust.

'But why me, on Christmas Eve?'

'Because,' I said, thinking very quickly, 'you bring gaiety to the nation.'

Archer always has a disaster on the go, or a recent gaffe for which he must make amends. That very week, in November 1989, the London tabloids had been nastily exulting in the premature closure of his play *Exclusive*, and also relishing the possibility that his landlords might evict him from his penthouse above the Thames, in which we were talking. He accepts with gallantry his status as an occasion for mostly harmless sport. As if conferring a bequest on the nation, he has made his life a public possession. Its splendours and miseries, his periodic acts of self-destruction and his spectacular recoveries from the loss of fortune or position or reputation, are played out in full view, for our amusement. On the morning when we met he was deliberating over another small donation of himself, sizing me up to see whether I looked trustworthy enough to be taken along on a tour of Cornwall, where he would be rallying the Conservative troops. He feigned hesitation, but the dangled bait of a magazine cover had already persuaded him. Besides, was it not his duty to put himself on show, whether as an exemplar of Tory values or as a character in a cartoon?

The tabloids have adopted Archer as a man we love to hate, because they calculate that we secretly envy him. But his sweet ingenuousness at the same time makes it hard not to be sneakingly fond of him. He has no guile – an endearing deficiency which cost him his parliamentary career and relegated him to the political sidelines as a rabble-rouser – and very little shame. I realized, a little belatedly, that I meant what I had said to him. And he, having taken it in, smiled in appreciation.

'You know, Peter', he said, 'I can't deny it's all rather fun. Being world-famous, I mean – *and* being worth several million pounds'. From anyone else, the remark would have been insufferable. But Archer made it with wonderment, as an entranced spectator of his own life, and even with modesty. He had resolved to allow the little people, with me as their medium, to share at Christmas in the wish-fulfilling bliss of being Jeffrey Archer.

The blinking eyes now gave themselves a rest from me, and panned appraisingly over the view.

Archer's characters favour aerial perspectives, altitudes of domination. The newspaper editor in the doomed play *Exclusive* oversees affairs around the globe from a rotating beige module beneath a perspex dome, with clocks tallying time in all the world's capitals. The assassin on the crane in his thriller *Shall We Tell the President?* can 'see the White House as no one has ever seen it'. The jumped-up immigrant hotelier in *Kane and Abel*, his saga of social mobility, occupies an eyrie on the forty-second floor, with Manhattan twinkling below: a girlfriend remarks, in a line of dialogue which tells as much about Archer's ear as it does his value-system, 'You've learned how to adjust to the style of a multi-millionaire. I've never seen anything more extravagant in my life.'

Archer, though only on the tenth floor, outdoes his own creations. His panopticon in Vauxhall – which he used to unguardedly describe as his 'Westminster flat', overlooking the fact that it is on the low-rent southern embankment – commands central London. The angle of the room points up the river to the Houses of Parliament. Big Ben outside the window rhymes with a grand-father clock in the corner, and on the wall, augmenting the cleaned and quaintly finicky actuality across the water, is an oil painting of the same view by Albert Goodwin, dating from the Edwardian sunset of empire – Westminster aflare in a Turneresque sky, the river clogged with mercantile shipping: power at its florid apex. Archer blinked at the diminished city, which no longer possesses the refulgent pomp of Goodwin's painting. The Thames that November morning was the colour of tea, with beached barges on the shingle. Small twisters of grit blew above the railway line taking tired commuters into Waterloo. No wonder Archer had so readily agreed with me that the nation needed cheering up.

When we met he was still out in the cold, exiled on the wrong side of the river. Margaret Thatcher made an attempt to ennoble him, though his former colleagues in the House of Commons blackballed his nomination; John Major eventually succeeded, sending Archer to the House of Lords in return for his services as a warm-up man at meetings during the 1992 election campaign. In 1989, Archer had not been a member of Parliament for fifteen years: he stood aside in 1974 after a financial embarrassment. Brought back as a publicist, he was forced to resign his position as Deputy Chairman of the Conservative Party in 1986 when a tabloid accused him of consorting with whores. But he had laid in a lifetime's supply of writing paper with the House of Commons crest (a grim descending portcullis), piled beside an assortment of investment brochures on a desk in one of the windows aimed at Westminster.

Around his eyrie were propped brass facsimiles of his bestsellers. The books resemble ingots: since they were created in order to make money, it was appropriate that they should have been remade in metal. Too brashly rich and too scandal-prone for acceptance into the Establishment, Archer has adjusted, as the girl in *Kane and Abel* puts it, to membership of the plutocracy. His penthouse is the kind of place where tycoons used to live in films, with flimsy cardboard skylines outside the window, and it has a cinematic pedigree. Archer took over the apartment from John Barry, who wrote the music for the James Bond films, and the coy digits 007 remain in his telephone number; Sean Connery used to live on a lower floor. The new tenant revised the role to suit himself. Bond the dilettante mutated into Archer the achiever and eager fixer. The bed-sized sofas now host pow-pows with captains of industry, press barons, oil sheiks, film producers and Olympic athletes, definitely not romps with Pussy Galore.

Archer belongs in such glossy, illusory suroundings because his life has been a conscious act of dramatization, working through a scenario as improbable as any of his fictional plots. His biographer Jonathan Mantle (unauthorized, and unmentionable in Archer's presence) fingers him as a phony. Mantle cites a CV Archer drew up at the age of twenty when applying for a job as a gym teacher. In it, he claimed to have been a pupil at Wellington, not specifying whether he meant the School or the College. In fact he attended the humble School not the grand College, but the elision meant that his employers – keen to be deceived, like all snobs – could give him the benefit of the doubt. He also claimed to have graduated from Sandhurst (Army Physical Training Instructor's Course) and Berkeley (Honours Diploma); both qualifications were imaginary. Later, Mantle has him telling a journalist 'My father was a colonel in the Somerset Light Infantry.' His father, an obscure character, seems to have been merely a newspaperman living in the East End.

It would be easy to conclude that Archer in all these cases - and there are others – was fibbing. I would rather say that he is not economical but over-generous with the truth. He decided at an early age to be a hero, a man with a destiny – or with several destinies: to play cricket for England, to be Prime Minister, to win the Nobel Prize for literature. (Robert Maxwell had a similar agenda, and when proposing to his future wife he solemnly promised her, as if such delusions supplemented the marriage vows, that he would one day be Prime Minister.) Along the way, when truth had the temerity to disappoint Archer, he blinked at it and, with his eyes closed, dreamed up some new world-beating ambition. His creativity has proved happily contagious, which is why he is entitled to regard himself as a national asset. Engaging secretaries, he rechristened them if he considered their names to be shop-soiled. A Noreen was told that she would henceforth be Natalie, an Yvonne overnight turned into Jo. Both girls declared themselves to be delighted with the substitution.

Even physically, Archer seems to have engineered himself. Once a champion sprinter, he still has the lean, hungry physique. He perched on the edge of a sofa like an athlete on his mark, and – to illustrate a point about the hard work involved in saga-writing – ran an impromptu marathon on the spot, with some gasping hyperventilation as he finished. Running fast is a triumph of will, training and tuning the body as an engine; Archer is still ready to streak off whenever the pop-gun sounds.

The spry runner's body is accompanied by a brusquely belligerent manner, learned perhaps during that fancied sojourn at Sandhurst. Archer is erect, his enuniciation is clipped, and he struts as if a brass band were playing inside his head. His batman/driver/minder, a burly Scot who served in the army in Belfast and then went to work for the Sultan of Brunei ('I looked after his princesses – quite nice really'), explained to me that Archer 'likes regimental skills'.

Certainly their progress around the country, as Archer stoked up the morale of Tory troops, was planned with a generalissimo's precision. At St Austell on the Cornish coast, hotel pages scurried into formation as Archer vaulted from his Daimler, barking commands before he hit the ground: 'Where are the masses?' Informed that two hundred little old ladies awaited him in the dining room, he snorted like a stallion scenting battle: 'What a turnout? Am I signing books? Are they all £5? Have we got someone competent to collect the money? My, my,' – as he scanned a red carpet, punitively vacuumed for his arrival – '*what* a smartening-up we've had here! Trying to join the real world, are we?' I could almost see the field marshal's baton under his arm; the whole of Tory Britain was his parade-ground. It is his voice which imposes this view of himself on you. Archer has a loud-hailer where lesser mortals stow their tonsils. Only the blink rate hints that it may all be a mask, sustained by unstinting effort.

The *Daily Star* called him a liar when he paid blackmail money to a prostitute whose services, he insisted, he had not used. This cost the paper, when Archer sued, half a million pounds. I prefer to think of him as a dreamer, who designed this dashing, imperious persona and armour-plated it with money, until he could either buy society's attention or afford to ignore its condescension and disbelief. His books are usually described, by himself among others, as a contrivance for raising funds. In 1974, exhibiting his customary naïvety, he was fleeced by some shady Canadian stockbrokers. He promptly set himself to produce a best-selling novel so he could pay off his debts. 'I am not by nature a person who can live off the state,' he righteously told me. 'I had to do something, so I wrote *Not A Penny More, Not A Penny Less.*' Possibly he believes that the problem of dole-dependence in Tory Britain could be solved by the concerted output of pulp fiction.

I don't accept this authorized version of his motives. The novels were not a detour. They are a necesssity to Archer, because they elaborate the life-long agenda he has imagined for himself. Politics is only the art of the possible. Soap opera, Archer's genre, is the overweening art of the impossible. He shies away from expressing literary opinions, but he did admit to me that F. Scott Fitzgerald is one of his favourite writers.

'Of course,' I said, suddenly realizing how inevitable the choice was. 'You're Gatsby.' Gatsby promoted himself to greatness by the ardent force of his wishful thinking. He fancifully sent himself to Oxford, just as Archer beamed himself to Berkeley; in fact Archer's own Oxford connections are almost as tangential as Gatsby's, because he enrolled there in 1963 for a one-year course at the Institute of Education and was not even officially an undergraduate. These, however, are the factual quibbles of a petty mind, which fiction idealizes away.

Archer looked nervous when I mentioned Gatsby, and his eyelids went into overdrive. He let the comment pass, perhaps deciding that I had made it because I thought he resembled Robert Redford, and hurriedly changed the subject by saying that he also liked Kipling: 'I have a lot of him in me. All his values are mine.'

Although he is quick to boast about other achievements – having 'run for my country', or having been the youngest member of the Greater London Council and the House of Commons – I found Archer touchingly bashful on the issue of literary ambition. 'I'm not a writer, I'm a story-teller,' he recurrently said, almost conceding that yarn-spinners are con men. As if to fend off the charge of effeteness, he described writing as manual work: 'Most people of my energy don't write, but I *adore* the hard physical grind of it.' For Archer, even reading is hard labour, for which there ought to be graduated rewards. He once told his publisher that he had read John Fowles's novel *The French Lieutenant's Woman* three times, and earnestly asked – how can you not like him? – 'If I read this book another five times, do you think I will have a chance at the Nobel Prize?' The publisher had to tell him, as delicately as he could, that this outcome could not be guaranteed. Convinced that writing is an athletic activity, an exercise routine, Archer promised me that he would retire at the age of sixty: 'Look at Graham Greene. He's eighty-five and he just can't cut it any more.'

When we met Archer had just put in three hundred hours on a new novel, *As the Crow Flies*. The grind was sweetened somewhat because those hours were distributed over six autumn weeks in the Bahamas. A time-and-motion study had already allowed him to estimate how much of the job remained undone: 'It will take me another six hundred hours to get it right.' Like a proud craftsman, he showed me his tools. His fountain pen is reserved for writing letters: 'I think it's rude not to use one,' he quixotically added. For the books, he trades down to a felt tip: 'I find it glides over the paper that much more easily.' A literary discussion with Archer would consist in the comparison of nibs, not of prose styles. Only the spoils, I think, persuade him that this a serious activity, something a man can do without fear of sissiness: 'There are only *three* of us in this country who make *real* money from writing.'

Still he feels obliged to demonstrate that writing can be an industrial production line by volunteering for marathon autograph sessions. Miffed that Joan Collins had signed seven hundred copies of her first novel at

Harrods in a single sitting, only to be vanquished by Shirley Temple's quota of thirteen hundred, he took himself off to a bookshop in Dublin and kept signing until he had outstripped both authoresses. 'Good Thatcherite competitive stuff', he remarked to me. At his political speeches around the country, Archer acts the travelling salesman, uncrating paperbacks to sell and sign.

Despite these evasive estimations of writing as a navvy's chore, Archer has a more personal investment in his fiction. Like any art, good or bad, his novels document his secret life: they flagrantly fulfil his wishes. He would have preferred a father who was a colonel. Denied that by biological circumstances, he invented one in *A Matter of Honour*, and supplied the colonel who went (as Archer could only pretend to do) to Wellington College and Sandhurst. Abel – the Polish peasant who believes himself to be a baron's heir and whose profit-grubbing when he migrates to America is an assault on niggardly reality – is another of Archer's self-images. Abel, like Archer, 'rose above all his classmates in everything but height', yet learns 'to hold himself so that he looked taller.' Archer too is small, but has a towering, swaggering mien. And if Abel represents how Archer began, his opposite Kane, a patrician Boston banker, is what Archer aspired to become. *As the Crow Flies* conflates the two figures, tracking its hero from poverty in the East End to a peerage at Westminster; John Major, it seems, took the hint. Even the newspaper editor in *Exclusive*, somnabulistically played on stage by Paul Scofield, was another Archer epigone: the know-all who knows everyone, he has Michael Caine's home phone-number, and can wheedle house seats for a Plácido Domingo first night out of a contact at Covent Garden.

Archer planned his move from novels into the theatre as a shrewd entrepreneurial expansion. In 1988 he bought the Playhouse in Northumberland Avenue, off Trafalgar Square, establishing a power base. Though *Exclusive* ignominiously folded, his first play, the courtroom drama *Beyond Reasonable Doubt*, was still trundling lucratively around the provinces – between seventy and eighty thousand pounds a week in the till, he reported to me. But the profit motive covers a psychological attraction. The novelist can only be an observer, like Archer gazing wistfully at Westminster from across the river in Lambeth. The dramatist, however, deals in action and aggression; the theatre, like a parliamentary debating chamber or a court of law, is an arena for self-imposition.

The QC in *Beyond Reasonable Doubt*, accused of murdering his wife, brazenly conducts his own defence. The play coincided with Archer's risky claim for damages from the *Daily Star*, in a trial which entailed the exposure of his personal life and introduced anatomical details into the reckoning. The prostitute, reading the body of the client she alleged to be Archer like Braille with her hands, declared that his skin on his back was rough and scabby. His wife testified that, on the contrary, he had smooth, unblemished skin. The baring of Archer's back was a symbolic transaction. The celebrity buys fame at the cost of privacy; he must reconcile himself to being a public possession.

In a line from *Exclusive*, which Archer could deliver a good deal more authoritatively than Scofield bothered to do, the editor announces a scoop by rounding up the hosts of all the talk shows on television – 'Ring Wogan, Frost *and* Aspel!' Archer also understands that talk shows are the proving grounds for celebrity, and with characteristic daring or ingenuousness he volunteered – as a follow-up to his ordeal in court – to be interrogated by the most ruthless of talk show hosts, Dame Edna Everage.

Edna's programme, supposedly taped in a penthouse even glitzier than Archer's, is a doubly barbed satire on celebrity. Edna herself, the innocuous Melbourne housewife convinced of her own superstardom, enables Barry Humphries to mock the self-delusion of those whose sole purpose in life is to be famous. Celebrity is Edna's vocation, a career open to the talentless. But although she is Humphries' creature, she ignores the strictures of her creator. When he disappears into her spangled gowns and puts on her rhinestone-studded spectacles, he renounces all power over her. She escapes from control, and uses the show to make publicity for herself. Guests are necessarily her rivals, invited in order to be snubbed. Having made themselves comfortable in one of her arm chairs, they find they are in the pillory.

The true celebrity will not flinch, calculating that all publicity is good. Zsa Zsa Gabor did the rounds of the American talk shows at the time of her altercation with a cop in Beverly Hills, using the incident – which led to a prison sentence for disorderly conduct – to remind a forgetful world that she still existed. Phil Donahue asked the elderly, obstreperous harridan with the spun-sugar hair and the peppery accent a potentially lethal question: 'What are you famous *for*, Zsa Zsa? What did you ever *do*?'

Zsa Zsa instantly replied 'Dollink, I hoff had six husbands' – or eight, or whatever. Donahue had missed the point. It's immaterial to ask what a celebrity does: a celebrity just is. If achievements are required, serial polygamy or a breach of the Beverly Hills traffic code will do.

Archer, appearing with Dame Edna, could not quite manage the brazenness of Zsa Zsa. He looked ill at ease as Dame Edna slapped on to his label a sticky badge labelled JEFF, in case she should forget who he was while talking to him. He responded to her raillery with a fixed grin, and once made the mistake of trying to outwit her. Dame Edna had loudly bragged that Mrs Thatcher was among her most closest friends.

'Oh,' said Archer, proprietorial about his patroness, 'I haven't seen you down at Chequers, or at No 10.'

'I go privately,' snapped Edna. 'She invites you with a lot of other people.'

Archer's smile seemed to have been stitched onto his face. When he began his pitch for *Exclusive*, Edna squirmed in an agony of boredom, stifling yawns. Then she summarily ejected Archer, pressing a button which sent his chair skidding offstage while he blinked in consternation.

Humiliation, as Archer understood, was part of the bargain, and no reason for complaint. The celebrity must embrace embarrassment and turn disaster to account, as Zsa Zsa did by merchandising her tiff with the cop. We tolerate celebrities only so long as they agree to destroy themselves periodically (and then amaze us by recovering). If they don't oblige, we are obliged to destroy them.

'We're both players, Barry and I,' commented Archer gamely when I mentioned his disappearance into Dame Edna's garbage chute. 'I'm on the show again next week. Actually, I don't quite get on it. I ring the bell downstairs and you see me on the closed-circuit TV, asking if I can come up to the penthouse. But Edna says she's never heard of me – imagine! She won't let me in.' His eager laughter did not dispel the pathos of the scene. The boyish, bouncy candidate for celebrity is turned away from the door; his fifteen minutes of fame have expired.

Rejected by Dame Edna, Archer remains dear to the Tory party faithful in the sticks. Although he had to resign first as a Member of Parliament and then as Deputy Chairman of the Conservative Party, he maintains his morale-boosting tours of the constituencies. His approach to these occasions is frankly theatrical. In place of an electorate, he now has an audience.

I followed Archer around Cornwall, into which he exploded before noon, having woken up in Scotland. 'I've been on two aeroplanes today already' was his vaunting entry-line. 'A hot Bovril at once please, my throat's a little scratchy.' His chauffeur had driven the Daimler down from London, its trunk loaded with crates of paperbacks, to meet him at the airport in Plymouth and carry him between three gigs up and down the county: lunch at St Austell, mobilizing the faithful in the one Cornish seat the Conservatives did not hold; a clotted-cream tea at Falmouth, where another of Archer's best friends, the runner Sebastian Coe, was to stand at the next election; and dinner in a country club on a golf course, apparently frequented by Mrs Thatcher's husband, at St Meillon. There was a brief crisis when the driver left behind in St Austell the sign saying 'ALL BOOKS £5', needed for Archer's autograph sessions. The party agent in Falmouth sped back to the previous town to fetch it.

At each meal, Archer delivered the same two-part performance to different versions of the same people: red-faced majors, fading widows, bank managers as grey as their suits. By the end of the day, I knew Archer's spiel by heart, and it looped incessantly inside my head all night as I lay awake in an unfriendly bed at the golf club, trying to coax the lunch of rubbery chicken, the tea of cream scones and the dinner of leathery beef through my system.

The first part of Archer's routine each time was solemnly inspirational, cueing applause with its rat-tat-tat ballistic delivery. The climax always came with Archer's announcement that, as he traversed the globe publicizing his books, he was told by assorted heads of state and political bosses that 'in Margaret Thatcher – leader of the Conservative Party, Prime Minister of this country – we have found the greatest leader of our nation since Winston Churchill.' The gouty majors flushed purple, their jowls quivering an endorsement, while the fading ladies hummed in unison. Every time, the room erupted. Archer, bearing down on his *t*s and rolling his *r*s like boulders, proceeded to breathe fire. 'Ittt drrrives mmme mmm-mad!!!' he roared on three separate occasions, with the sonic boom of a departing 747, 'to hear what Mr Kinnockkk' (much mirth at that hollowly reverberating *k*) 'says about the National Health Service' (dying fall on this elegiac organization).

Archer's para-military imagination has informed him that *esprit de corps* is cemented by identifying an enemy. At tea he targeted two waiters, innocently distributing trays of scones. 'Can we *both* stay out now, please?' he requested, the 'we' very definitely not including himself. The wretched waiters hurled themselves through the swing doors, looking as if they hoped the floor would eat them and their pyramids of scones. Archer, after a pause which allowed the two hundred people present to savour the distress of the waiters, then resumed his fulminations against the Labour opposition and Mrs Thatcher's detractors in the press. A neat and flattering trick: you create the illusion of privileged intimacy, even of conspiracy, by expelling the servants.

At dinner, the photographer sent out with me from *The Observer* became Archer's target. Again he halted proceedings, and apologized to his listeners for the impedimenta which his celebrity entailed – one uninvited guest with a notebook, another with a camera, both of them eating meals they had not paid for. 'Go away now, photographer', he yelped, flapping his arm as if at a troublesome fly. Aside, he remarked in a confidential undertone, 'He's from *The Observer* you know, we don't like them anyway.' The majors hissed like a nest of vipers. Archer turned back to the photographer, who was stranded on the floor between dining tables, and spoke very loudly and slowly, as if addressing an idiot or an alien: 'These people have come to *see* me, and you're in the way. Did they feed you, photographer? Go over there then.' Having ensured his own visibility – the celebrity's prime concern – Archer preened for the benefit of a corner table of wilting widows, who reddened beneath their powder: 'Can you see me now, m' dears?'

After his political sermon, Archer proceeded to conduct the inevitable raffle, raising funds for the local party. At this point, he always switched personae. His impersonation of Churchill, or of Olivier's Churchillian Henry V rallying troops for combat, changed to mimicry of Dame Edna Everage – not the Edna of the talk show, patronizing her fellow superstars, but Edna live and dangerously at large in the theatre, hauling members of the audience out of their cowering anonymity and making them describe their bathrooms while her face puckers in disgust.

No longer preaching to a devout congregation, Archer playfully insulted his audience. When he muddled one of his jokes, he instantly passed on the blame: 'Do I have to explain it? I'd forgotten I was in Cornwall.' Ticket-holders were made to stand up and sit down, ordered to pay attention and given extra roads to canvass at the next election if they didn't do as he told them. Ridicule was doled out along with the raffle prizes. To one of the genteel widows, handing her a whisky bottle: 'Fourth one this week, I see. Try and totter back to your table, my love.' To a doddery grandma who won a thermos flask, the third prize: 'Off you go to the building site with that tomorrow, darling.' To a ruddy-faced yokel who won nothing: 'Soon as I saw you, sir, I knew you were a loser.' To a young woman bemused by her potted trophy: 'It's not a *flower*, it's' (eyes rotating heavenward in Ednaesque exasperation) 'a BAY TREE!!' With reference to an old man limping away with a brace of reeking pheasants: 'I've known Jim for a long while. Once on Blackpool pier we both entered a Robert Redford lookalike contest. We lost to a West Indian gentleman, of course.' To the party worker who shyly presented him with her amateur cookery book: 'I shall treasure it, I shall place it next to the pearls given me by the Maharajah and the block of gold from the Shah of Iran.' To his host at the banquet on the golf course: 'Thank you, Chairman, for the wine at the top table. I've never been served Ugandan burgundy before.'

Wasn't this raillery a little harsh? To be sure, it usefully reminded the listeners of their superiority by stigmatizing funny foreigners – West Indians and Ugandans, Shahs and Maharajahs. But shouldn't these good Cornish folk have been spared such pointed contrasts between Archer's fame and wealth and worldliness and their own lowly lot? Archer had a sergeant-major's justification for the routine: 'It's good for them. It makes them strong. It gets them ready for the fight. Why else do you think I do it? What do you think I am, a song-and-dance man?'

That, however, is precisely what I had begun to suspect him of being. His consolation for the loss of office is his discovery that politics is now a matter of image, and that an ultimate, unchallengeable power belongs to the celebrity. The moral rules have been waived: the celebrity's charmed life escapes the usual penalties for bad behaviour. Like Dame Edna deriding those housewives who have bought tickets to her stage show for the privilege of being laughed at by her, Archer can safely assume that the old dear with the thermos or the puzzled recipient of the bay tree will not object. Has he not singled them out and made them briefly famous? Surely their values are the same as his; they must therefore be grateful that he has conferred his magic aura on them for a few seconds. From him an insult is an honour.

A celebrity is dispensed from having to be politic: his mistakes, misfortunes and mis-speakings (as when, during his period as Deputy Chairman, Archer blithely suggested that the Protestant bigot Ian Paisley would make an excellent Premier of a united Ireland) all contribute to his mystique. Political responsibility would compel Archer to be hypocritically cautious and mince his words; it would take away his freedom to be himself, and to make his singing, dancing, suing contribution to the nation's gaiety. Like the gods of classical myth, the celebrity is not expected to be better than us, only bigger or brasher or richer or randier. The superego has been surgically removed from him. He lives with reckless indifference to the opinion of others, asking only that they spell his name correctly.

Before we parted, Archer positively goaded me to write a hostile account of him. He guessed that I did not share his political convictions; he was sure I would never share his literary success. As he pityingly told me while we drove across Cornwall, 'You're at a disadvantage in comparison with me. I'm not hampered by your education.' He had already commented with a forgiving smile, when I asked about the reviews of *Exclusive*, 'Oh, when you make a *very* large amount of money from writing, there will always be others who think they can write better....' It was my function to confirm his world-view: either I admired him (and secretly wanted to be him) or I envied him (which was an even sincerer form of flattery).

'You'll see, Peter', he said as we shook hands. 'No matter what you say about me, I won't protest; I never do.' It was both matey ingratiation, and a dare. I drifted away disabled, reflecting how impossible it is to dislike someone so devious and yet so endearingly, self-confoundingly transparent about it.

Except that this was not quite goodbye. Archer, queueing in a corridor along with the other dignitaries who were about to process into the golf-club banquet, summoned me back. 'He wants you again,' said the chauffeur, rearing over me like the beefeater on the gin bottle. Now what? Was my boot-polish going to be inspected? Archer had already upbraided me in front of the simpering Tory ranks as 'an unkempt colonial scruff'. Being a player, I would naturally not mind.

In the corridor, the procession shuffled sideways until the chauffeur delivered me to Archer. An index finger like Lord Kitchener's on the recruiting poster jabbed me conscriptively in the chest. 'I wanted to tell you', said Archer, 'that I've decided I know who you *are*.' I quaked. Previously denounced as a lefty, was I now to be found out as a back-stabber, another journalist who – after having been allowed a ride in the Daimler and granted, for a day, the status of his new best friend – would now go home and betray him?

'You remind me', he said, turning up the volume and digging into my sternum with his finger, 'of one of my characters.'

Who? I weakly wondered. Probably the hit man in *Shall We Tell the President?*

'You are', announced Archer, 'half Abel and half Kane. Here you are, you've come from nowhere like Abel – from Timbuktu or Tasmania or wherever it is – and you've ended up just like Kane, with your job at Oxford. You may laugh, but that book is about YOU.'

I did not laugh, but shuddered at the power of the man's fantasy. Having invented himself, he could now re-invent me as a version of himself, defying me to pretend that my own dreams and desires were not the same as his. No wonder that reality, abashed, has backed away from the advancing juggernaut which is Jeffrey Archer.

Still prodding, he leaned forward and thrust his face into mine, his eyes wide open. This time it was me who blinked.

BEAUTIES AND BEASTS

SMELLING JOAN COLLINS

WHILE I WAITED FOR JOAN COLLINS TO APPEAR FROM THE ADJOINING bedroom, I studied her décor. It had been a long wait – almost four months. Everything about the lady is studiously eroticized, and the first principle of seduction is to tantalize, to defer surrender in the hope of intensifying expectation.

Four months earlier, at the beginning of 1990, she had promised to talk. She had sound commercial reasons for doing so, of course: she would soon have a second novel to sell, along with a bottled version of herself in the form of a perfume to which she had leased her name; she was also eager to promote her return to the stage in London. But making a date proved more complex, as she juggled projects and whimsically alternated between continents. Once our meeting was due to happen in London, then it jumped overnight to the south of France, where she was allegedly making a television programme with Omar Sharif. When the programme was cancelled, the meeting likewise went – as they say in Hollywood – into turnaround. Having nibbled my nails to the quick, I was advised that the venue would now be Los Angeles, where she was to be filming a miniseries adapted from the novel she published in 1988, *Prime Time*.

Messages were relayed through Judy Bryer, who has been her secretary since the 1960s and who looks enough like her employer – though less glamorous, and therefore no competition – to have done duty as her stand-in on the set of *Dynasty*: Judy sacrificially sweltered under the lights while the real Alexis remained in her dressing room, plumping up her power shoulders or lacquering her mouth. Reassured by Judy, I got as far as New York, where I waited to be summoned the rest of the way. After a week, my patience fraying, I called to request a bulletin. 'Oh,' said Judy, with the excited frisson of one who lives vicariously through the tizzes and tantrums of another, 'didn't you know? Joan walked out of *Prime Time*, the script was rubbish. She'll probably be going back to London in a few days. Take care.'

A few more days passed, during which I took extra care. Then I had a call: 'Joan and I', announced Judy, 'think that next Tuesday would be auspicious.' I speculated about the auspices: did she mean that they had consulted a soothsayer?

I am always early for appointments, allowing myself plenty of time for morale-boosting circuits of the block before ringing the door bell. In this case I was four days early. When I arrived in what Joan Collins liltingly calls 'LaLaLand' on the Saturday afternoon, I rang Judy Bryer at home, as instructed.

'What a coincidence that you should call!' said Judy. 'Joan and I are just off to the airport. Enjoy your stay.'

Hearing my moan of dismay, she quickly added 'No, no, we're only going to Vegas for the weekend. We're going up to see Júlio's show. He's sent his plane for us. Oh yes, of course we'll be back for Tuesday.'

For the next three days I watched the news each evening to make sure that the Iglésias jet had not come to grief in the desert.

On the Tuesday afternoon, however, there was still more waiting to be done. Judy installed me on a sofa in the living room of the house at the top of Coldwater Canyon, then returned to her typing in a backyard cabana. Joan, next door, was preparing a face to meet my inquisitive face. Fidgeting on the sofa, I realized that, with a vamp like Joan Collins, waiting – being dangled in a state of delicious, tremulous suspense – counts as a variety of foreplay. It would be better, I thought, if I had something to occupy me. I therefore took inventory.

Outside, beneath the bleached Californian sky and the sooty blur of Beverly Hills below, the blue filtered water of the swimming pool gently slurped. Inside, a tropical forest flourished in a corner. Colour-coordinated fish lazily circulated in a globular tank above the bar. A metal flamingo spread wings of jagged crystal. I made a tiptoeing tour of the fixtures and fittings. My feet sank through the white rugs as if into sand dunes; when I returned to the sofa, its white over-stuffed cushions closed around me like surfy breakers. The room was decorated with images of its unseen owner, smiling in silver-framed photographs, portrayed in a gallery of prints which made her look as lush as a ripening orchid. Jewel-bordered mirrors waited, more patiently than I was doing, to reflect her face. A white grand piano had its lid propped open, expecting her to slink into position alongside it and moan through a torch song. But the only noise in the room was also white: the distant hum of the air-conditioning.

Having brought me slowly to the boil, Joan Collins opened the bedroom door and sauntered in. I understood at once why the preparations had been so protracted. The entire football team of UCLA must have been enticed up the hill from Westwood to help tighten that belt around her tiny waist. Each black curl on her head had probably been primped by its own elfin hairdresser. Her smile had been rehearsed until it was perfect, and she had surely spent a considerable time memorizing my name. While the footballers tugged and the coiffeurs tonged, she had probably been watching me – through a peephole perhaps, or on closed-circuit television – prowl the room appraising the contents. Not that she minded, because she at once elected to share my incredulity by laughing at her surroundings.

'This whole room is an effect', she declared with a dismisive sweep of her jangling wrist. 'It's a stage. I can see you'd noticed.'

She led me on another circuit, briskly taking the room to pieces. I admired the pouting Joan Collins lookalike in the painting by Tamara de Lempicka. 'Oh, that's a fake', she tittered: 'There's this person who'll copy whatever you like – Tamaras, Fragonards, Bouchers. It helps keep the insurance premiums down.' I tried again with the orchidaceous portraits of her on another wall. 'Isn't it sad?' she said with a grimace. 'The man who did those dropped dead at a Celebrity Aerobics Tournament!' I detected the onset of a giggle, curtailed by a bite of her glossy lip.

The house with its upholstered swank seemed ridiculous to her because it belonged to a previous existence. It was a lair for Alexis Colby to rampage through, chomping a celery stick and plotting devilment while she ran a scarlet talon down the pecs of Dex. 'Yes, this was my *Dynasty* house. One spent all one's life in that very unattractive studio, surrounded by lights and cables, with only a trailer to get dressed in; there was no glamour to the work at all. I wanted to have a house like this, just once. It's very important to me aesthetically to be surrounded by beauty. But there's nothing much to this, after all. These are just ordinary sofas with extra padding, that's just a glass table with a few books on it. I've done this effect, now I need somewhere smaller. The house is on the market, as a matter of fact. No-one has ever been in that pool except my little godson. There's a screening room in there' – she waved towards an alcove across the white Sahara of carpet – 'for whoever wants it; I prefer to watch videos in bed. Now I just want to live in my own reality, even if it isn't the reality of a housewife in Barnes.'

She pointed to the acrobatic Erté mannequins on the wall, and the black porcelain camel with the fern growing from its hump: 'I don't even like this style any more. I've had it with Art Deco. I'm more into the eighteenth century in my flat in London now. All I need is a few bergères and some candlesticks. I also have a place near St Tropez, where I'm *very* Provençal and simple. I really think I should have been born French.' Along with the house, she was divesting herself of her *Dynasty* persona. 'I live very quietly these days, trying to be wiser. It's all part of growing old – gracefully, I hope.' When the series was running, she could not go to the supermarket for fear of being mobbed. Now she was able to shop with impunity once more. 'It's all ephemeral,' she shrugged. 'I bet Ronald Reagan can go to the supermarket these days. Mind you,' she added, perhaps regretting the dispensation Alexis granted her from the chores of daily living, 'I never particularly *liked* going to the supermarket....'

Alexis was a collective creation, the result of a partnership between the actress, the script-writers and – most importantly – the spirit of the age. Her demise, coinciding with the retirement of eighties ideologues like Reagan and Thatcher and the downfall of the decade's moguls like Maxwell or Donald Trump, conceded that the times had altered. With her baubles and her oil wells, the character embodied the mercenariness of her period. The greedy eighties purged its conscience by licensing every greed except that for food, and Alexis also symbolized its narcissistic obsession with looking good, staying lean and hungry. Earlier bad girls like Jean Harlow – a print of whom hung on another of Joan Collins's walls, mainly because her platinum hair matched the decor – munched chocolates in bed. Alexis got the energy for her evil-doing from crudités and vegetarian dips.

The public morality of the eighties revalued ancient vices and transformed them into virtues. 'Greed', as Michael Douglas put it in Oliver Stone's film *Wall Street*, 'is good.' Joan Collins embarked on her own course of special pleading when she played Alexis: 'I wanted to make her likeable, even though she wasn't written that way. So what if she was rich? I don't have the English horror of making money.' For the actress, however, the character's conspicuous consuming mattered less than her sexual wilfulness. 'The people who attacked her were just frightened because she was powerful. Women are still such second-class citizens. Why should we have to walk around covered up, and live in terror of being raped? And here we have President Bush saying that you can't have an abortion, even if you're fifteen and have been gang-banged.' Alexis represented an elegantly lethal backlash against misogyny and male domination. The revenge was personal as well as sisterly. The men in Joan Collins's life have included, by her own reckoning, a sadist, a neurotic, a drug-user, and a gold-digging cad; as she remarked when we ran through the list, adopting a woebegone cockney accent, 'I've 'ad me knocks, Peter.' It gave her belated satisfaction to put on display a woman who used men as they had used her.

Her defence of Alexis the careerist concentrated on the character's exemplary value for women. She avoided discussing the different use made of her by the male imagination, although *Prime Time* acknowledges the squalid business of permitting yourself to be merchandised as a sex symbol. One of the contenders for a role on *Saga*, the novel's version of *Dynasty*, is 'a plumpish, short, pretty woman of thirty-six, who, with the expert application of myriad cosmetic devices, exotic outfits and a number of cleverly arranged postiches and nun's hair wigs, was regularly transformed into the fantasy woman of every truck driver and construction worker from Hoboken to Hollywood.' A certain self-disgust is insinuated here: the character functions like one of the inflatable, ever-compliant ladies sold in Times Square sex shops; as an actress she is available for hire in whatever pornographic playlets her customers devise. *Prime Time* admits the indignity and ugliness of the profession when the woman is slaughtered, then raped by a crazed fan. To make yourself a vessel for so many dreams and desires is certainly soiling, probably dangerous. I mentioned the notorious 1979 film poster which announced 'Joan Collins IS *The Bitch*', and the still from the same tacky shocker in which she preened in a chauffeur's cap, a fur coat, a corset and a garter belt. Wasn't this much the same as advertising your services in a phone booth?

She did try to persuade the film's producer, she said, to substitute 'is' for the less inflammatory 'as', and to get rid of the strident capitals. The still she passed off as 'a bit of a joke'. I'm not sure that the fetishists to whom the image appealed would have shared her sense of humour, but the reply illustrated her instinctive reliance on comedy to circumvent embarrassment and dampen sex. It also hinted at her awareness that the carnality of the characters she plays is itself a joke, a put-on not a come-on. Eroticism like hers depends on exaggeration, which tilts it towards caricature. In 1987 Annie Leibovitz photographed Joan and Jackie Collins on the razzle in the back seat of a limousine, awash with champagne and littered with overblown roses. In the photograph Jackie affects the lofty composure of the traditional Hollywood star, consenting to be looked at but disdaining – behind her outsize shades – to look back. By contrast with her sister's regal deportment, Joan squirms restlessly, even rampantly, on the leather banquette. Her hands are busy shredding one of the white roses, and her mouth sags suggestively open, probably uttering something unrepeatable. The persona is gloriously sluttish, yet as harmless in its comic excess as the swaggering hips and rolling eyes of Mae West. During the session, Joan demanded a roll of gaffer's tape from Leibovitz's assistants; she applied it to her breasts, deepening their cleavage, then planted a rose in the globular cleft. The result is sexuality pushed into a parody of itself. Beside the warily dignified Jackie, Joan resembles a female impersonator, flamboyantly exposing gender as a charade.

Her performance in *Dynasty* had the same wicked excessiveness. The American actors – Linda Evans as Krystle, her aura of saintliness maintained by the camera's kind, soft focus; John Forsythe as Blake, waxily inanimate – toiled through their roles in earnest. Collins always seemed to be mocking the series, naughtily adding winks of complicity as she delivered her lines. My personal favourite was the occasion on which Alexis, languorously weary of the world, sighed, 'I'm still searching for the perfect sunset. I thought I'd found it once in Maui, and then once again in Monte-Carlo....' On film, no one had dared to voice such sentiments since Bette Davis in *Now Voyager* said that we needn't go on longing for the moon, because we have the stars; the difference is that Davis appeared to believe it, whereas Collins spoke her line in full, arch awareness of its fatuity. Proving how unseriously she took the whole thing, she had no memory of this quest for the sunset; but she did quote with venomous glee the remark made by Alexis when reunited with her alienated, abusive daughter Fallon: 'I'm so pleased your father had your teeth fixed. A pity he couldn't do anything about your mouth.'

Once the portentous and unfunny Henry Kissinger agreed to a walk-on in a *Dynasty* episode. He played himself: who else could he get away with being? Alexis, eyeing him, ad-libbed: 'Henry, darling, we haven't met since Portofino – *wasn't* it fun?' Too leaden-witted for the game, Kissinger looked flustered, as if wondering why no one had written something for him to say in response. Beguiled into a fiction by his vanity, he could not find the way back to real life. Joan Collins owned up to her mischief-making: 'I was scurrilous on *Dynasty*. The Americans sometimes didn't get it, irony and sarcasm don't translate here. If you slink around being voluptuous, people think you can't be funny. They didn't see what a good actress Marilyn Monroe was until after she died.' As a girl she adored pin-ups ike Betty Grable; these days, when curled up in bed with a video, she prefers comedians like Rosalind Russell and Carole Lombard. Among contemporary performers she admires those who flaunt their sexuality and simultaneously laugh at it: Madonna with her trashy underwear, or Cher, who turned up at the Oscars in 1988 wearing a cobweb.

She learned her gallant tactic of self-parody the hard way, after suffering through some terrible films. One of her earliest, *Land of the Pharaohs*, was disowned by its director, Howard Hawks. Unlike Lauren Bacall in *To Have and Have Not*, Jean Arthur in *Only Angels Have Wings* or Angie Dickinson in *Rio Bravo*, Collins was hardly the kind of matey woman Hawks envisaged as a companion for his heroes. He bullied her to speak in a more baritonal voice, although her soubrettish chirp kept on reasserting itself; he upbraided her for over-eating, since her stomach was so plump that the umbilical ruby required by the censors repeatedly popped out. 'That film', she remembers, 'was so far over the top it wasn't even in this hemisphere!' Caked in dusky body make-up, she plays Princess Nellifer, sent to Egypt in the lieu of the eight thousand cattle her country owes in tribute. Pharaoh (the stiffly British Jack Hawkins) strips her, sends her off to be flogged, then smacks her face for continued in subordination. After these demonstrations of affection, he promptly marries her. A glimpse of the treasury where Pharaoh hoards gold for his use in the after-life turns Nellifer into an ur-Alexis. She ingratiates with Pharaoh's muscular security guard ('Hold me. Tighter!'), dispatches a cobra to take care of her husband's heir and his previous spouse, then gloats as Pharaoh himself expires on the floor: 'Now I shall rule in Egypt! Soon it will be mine, all mine!' (William Faulkner wrote the dialogue while drunk.) A loyal priest entices her into the pyramid during the burial ceremonies for the Pharaoh, and there, to her irritation, she is buried alive: 'My lord priest,' she miaows ungrammatically, 'I am well aware of your enmity and hostility, and I can assure you that it is mutual.'

She was assigned to another exotic travesty entitled *Esther and the King*, directed (and probably also disowned) by Raoul Walsh. The king in question was the Persian ruler Xerxes, improbably played by the angular-jawed, corn-fed Richard Egan; Joan Collins becomes his consort after winning a beauty contest, thanks to the connivance of an altruistically infatuated eunuch. The film bestowed a heroic mission on the actress who has described herself as 'a quarter-Jewish princess out of Bayswater, by way of Sunset Boulevard'. 'Actually,' she said, 'I don't really feel Jewish – not as much as Judy, she keeps all the holidays – but in that film I saved the entire Jewish nation from extinction. I was never very clear about the plot. Esther was this village girl from Judea, and the king of Persia wanted to kill off all the boy babies. I soon put a stop to that!'

Confused by her combination of sultriness and humour, Hollywood could only cast her as a parody of its older and more sacred monsters. She inherited the role of the gold-digging shop girl played by Joan Crawford in George Cukor's *The Women* when that film was remade – badly, she at once volunteers – as *The Opposite Sex*. She remembers spending days rehearsing a scene of devilment in a bubble bath, sitting in lukewarm detergent which caused her nether parts to puff up. She tested for the part of Cleopatra which the studio awarded to Elizabeth Taylor, and when Taylor fell ill was put on stand-by to take over. She was to be, as she puts it, 'instant Cleopatra, like Nescafé.'

Trollopy queens being her speciality, she had long had designs on this character. She auditioned for drama school in London with a speech of Shaw's kittenish Cleopatra, addressing Caesar as an 'old gentleman'. Eventually she got her chance in 1981, though only in circumstances of ignominious farce. After sizzling to a crisp in the ocean off Hawaii for an instalment of *Starsky and Hutch*, she had vowed to do no more episodic jobs: such shows recruit their 'guest stars' from the limbo where half-forgotten celebrities wait for the phone to ring. Then her agent offered her an appearance on the series *Fantasy Island*, in which the sleek procurer Ricardo Montalban and his attendant dwarf Hervé Villechaise (recalled by Joan Collins as 'a nightmare of a short gentleman') made dreams come true for visitors to their resort. 'I refused straight off, but the agent told me "They want you to play Cleopatra," so I said 'Ah-hah...' My character turned out to be some drab woman was having an affair with Mark Antony. The Antony they gave me was the tallest man I ever worked with – six feet four inches whereas I'm five foot six. There was *quite* a disparity! Basically, it was a dreadful piece of crap.' With the cruel logic of parody, even the clothes she wore were bedraggled hand-me-downs from her illustrious antecedents. 'They took me to the costume warehouse, and one of the dressers said, "Ooh, I think we've still got some of Elizabeth's things from *Cleopatra* here." Then he fished out this green rag net, a bit of tat you wouldn't even give your maid! Some of the other stuff had been worn by Cher at Caesar's Palace in Las Vegas. But I did get Claudette Colbert's jewelled helmet from the old de Mille *Cleopatra* in 1934. Remember her in the tank of milk?' She guffawed at the grandiose folly of it, and at her own cheapened, second-hand imitation.

She loses no chance to ridicule Hollywood's smarmy piety about its past, and the feudal protocols of its caste system – A and B lists for parties; the shuddering dread of banishment to invisibility in restaurants by that all-powerful St Peter, the maître d'. 'I'm too cynical, too incendiary for LA. This is a town you don't dare insult because everyone's so protective of themselves, they take it all so seriously.' Shortly before we met, her unguarded tongue had got her into trouble with those new puritans, the political-correctness police. Wafting out of a party at two in the morning on Oscar night, she was asked by a reporter whether she approved of the awards. 'I said I was glad the old lady won – now, what *is* her name? – yes, Jessica Tandy – and then I said wasn't it amazing that Daniel Day-Lewis, who's really *so* handsome, had made himself look such a fright in *My Left Foot.* Two days later, a letter came from something called Media Services for the Disabled Community of America, rebuking me for being so insensitive about paraplegics and demanding a public apology within twenty-four hours or else they'd send copies of the letter denouncing me to all the media and major publications.... I pointed out that the National Head Injury Association is one of my charities because my daughter nearly died after a car accident, and I reminded them that I'd made myself look pretty frightful to play the Witch in *Hansel and Gretel* – black teeth, hook nose, warts, the lot. But it does no good. You don't dare make jokes here now.'

Prime Time ends on the beach at Malibu with a marital reunion made possible by a sacramental banquet of comfort foods flown in from London: Earl Grey tea drunk from a china teapot bought at Harrods, McVities chocolate digestive biscuits, 'custard creams, ginger snaps and Scottish shortbread from Fortnum's.' But the British delicacy Joan Collins craved most keenly in her Californian exile was irony, which does not travel that far: 'That's why I want to get back to the theatre, where every-one sends everyone else up all the time.'

She returned to London in the summer of 1990 for two plays, both by Noël Coward: *Easy Virtue* on television, and *Private Lives* in the West End. Both Coward heroines were already, like the ersatz Tamara on her wall, developing a resemblance to Joan Collins (and with her usual scurrility she added a new exit line of her own to *Private Lives*, hav-ing Amanda declare, as she walks out on Elyot for a second time, 'I'm going to Dallas' – or did she mean *Dallas*?). 'Larita in *Easy Virtue* is a *femme du monde*, a free spirit, a woman with a past,' she said with a balefully significant glance; 'with Amanda I want to show what it means to have loved a man deeply for ten years – I want to communicate *passion*.' Italics cannot convey the serpentine hiss with which she uttered the word. Faced with such breathy commitment, I did not like to suggest that the two coveted roles might once more be parodies of her man-eating mystique. In Larita's defiance of society and Amanda's illicit resumption of her romance with Elyot, Coward was vindicating his own homosexuality and announcing that all lapses from convention should be forgiven to those who 'behave exquisitely'. Perhaps this news would not have disconcerted her, since she has smiled on the antics of the effeminate comedian Julian Clary, whose early act was called The Joan Collins Fan Club. She is aware of her status as a camp pin-up: an icon of desire who is viewed, by many of her male fans, quite without lust.

She does not mind exploitation, so long as she is permitted to exploit herself: 'Other people have made enough money out of me – why shouldn't I make some?' To this end, she has bestowed her name and her persona on a line of lingerie and a video collection, on jewellery and perfume. A market-leader, she was among the inventors of that intriguing contemporary genre, the celebrity novel. This is the literary equivalent of those perfumes which are sold by using the image and allure of the star who pretends to have autographed the bottle. The celebrity novel is also intended to exude the celebrity's intimate aroma, to confide her secrets in fictionally encoded form. *Prime Time* and its suc-cessor *Love & Desire & Hate* – 'a bit of an epic' as she described it, its title borrowed from a poem about decadence and satiation by Ernest Dowson – play the game expertly, with exactly the blend of candour and slyness which typifies Collins.

Prime Time teasingly purported, after the demise of *Dynasty*, to tell the truth about the early days of a plutocratic television series called *Saga*, in which the role of the expensively over-dressed villainess is awarded – against competition from various washed-up nymphomaniac witches – to a British outsider. Chloe, the victor, is Collins herself; the other characters are the subjects of a naughty guessing game. Can the elderly Emerald, gloatingly reduced at last to pauperdom, be Collins's joke about Krystle, her rival on *Dynasty*, and her revenge on the long-suffering Linda Evans? Both characters are named after brittle, more or less valuable bits of glass. I knew there was no point in asking, because the Mona Lisa would only smile, with perhaps an optional wink.

It puzzled me that someone as professionally gratified as Joan Collins had developed, at a fairly ripe age, a literary vocation. Could sibling rivalry have anything to do with it? A desire perhaps to reclaim her fictional right to the territory co-opted by her sister Jackie – Hollywood and the seamy scandals of the casting couch? I asked what Jackie, a failed actress, thought of Joan's writing. The famous face smiled again. 'I'm having dinner with her tonight. I'll ask her, if you like.'

Out-manoeuvred, I wondered what else could be responsible for the belated compulsion to write.

'Oh, I've been writing for years. I've always kept diaries. I started *Prime Time* on a skiing holiday. I couldn't ski – I still can't – so I started to scribble.'

Really? With her own fair hands? Remembering Jeffrey Archer, I wondered if she would produce a pen with a fourteen-carat nib as evidence.

'Don't think', she said indignantly, 'that I did it like Barbara Cartland, lying on a sofa with three girls taking dictation.'

Of course I was asking the wrong questions. Literary workmanship is hardly the point of a celebrity novel. Ivana Trump has never claimed any involvement in the writing of her contributions to the genre, which mythologize her own life; some people, noting Ivana's unsteady command of English, doubt her capacity even to read them. Joan Collins would not have needed so much help, but the evidence hints that, as a busy lady, she found ways around the time-consuming toil of putting sentences together: *Prime Time* has an acknowledgment to the secretary who deciphered her shorthand. Anyway it's irrelevant to wonder who wrote a celebrity novel. Do we worry about Joan Collins's supervision of the chemists who concocted a fragrance in her name? The relation in both cases is symbolic. What breathes from the bottle is the quintessence of Collins; likewise the book is a souvenir of her, like an autograph. Its authenticity is attested less by her having written it than by the fact that she has already signed it. *Prime Time* comes with her signature engraved in golden scribble on the front cover. Of course we know that celebrities cannot keep up with the industrial demand for remnants or reminiscences of themselves, and (as *Prime Time* cattily intimates about Emerald) they sometimes employ secretaries to sign the photographs they send out to fans. But as her marathon at Harrods demonstrated, Joan Collins was content to prove the signature's veracity by doing it all over again at the point of sale. The purpose of such a book is to justify the book tour, the personal appearance, the signing session. A writer is an invisible voice; celebrities exist only so long as they are visible.

The art lies in the ingenuity of the self-exploitation. In the nineteenth century, hero-worship mimicked the fanaticism of Catholic devotion. The admirers of Garibaldi, gathered outside a hotel where he was staying, begged the servants for his nail clippings, as if grappling for fragments of the true cross. The great man's body was a reliquary. Oscar Wilde pioneered the modern cult of celebrity by recognising that the devotees would be just as satisfied with fakes, simulacra. During his American tour, he was besieged with demands for locks of his lank, aesthetic hair. In fear of imminent baldness, he suborned the hotel employees to donate their own. The change since then lies in the celebrity's realization that nothing needs to be given away. The up-to-date celebrity is in the business of self-marketing. Ivana Trump, boldly showing the way, spends hours at the weekend in a television studio, selling her fashion collection on the Home Shopping Network. It's beautifully appropriate that the scandal-sheets which report on – or invent – the marital calamities and weight crises of celebrities like Ivana or Oprah Winfrey or Joan Collins should be known as supermarket tabloids. Temptingly displayed beside the cashier's desk, they acknowledge that the celebrity is also for sale, along with the canisters of non-dairy Kool Whip cream substitute and the meat-free vegetarian salami.

If capitalism is a culture as well as an economy, then celebrities are essential to it because they translate fame into a trademark and a licence for making money. A celebrity is a brand name, a person who has been tagged with a designer's label indicating that we must pay a special premium. *Prime Time*, which comes complete with Joan Collins's own identifying brand in that gilded signature, is obsessively brand-conscious. Instead of describing things, it tells you who designed them. Chloe at the beginning strides on to a British Airways plane bound for Los Angeles, settles herself in the first-class cabin, and accepts a glass of Evian water; she is wearing a Gianni Versace silk blouse and carrying a crocodile Morabito overnight bag. For her, character is costume. Auditioning, she ponders the choice between impersonating bitchiness in a black-satin Valentino gown and playing the seductress, which calls for her red chiffon number by Ungaro.

This eye for the lucrative names on the labels never goes out of focus, even during scenes of barnstorming hysteria and foul-mouthed vituperation. On one occasion, Chloe comes home to find her husband orally copulating with a teenage girl in their bed. She decides, reasonably enough, to leave him: '"Fuck you, Josh. Fuck you! Fuck you!! *Fuck you!!!*" she screamed, as she snapped the lid shut on the Vuitton case.' The dialogue here, incidentally, is a self-quotation: in her memoir *Past Imperfect* Joan Collins remembers flying to Palm Springs in 1955 in an unsteady two-engine plane to spend the weekend with Sydney Chaplin, Charlie's son. He failed to meet her at the airport; finding him drunk in the bar at a tennis club, she terminated their relationship as follows: '"Fuck you, Sydney", I screamed. "Fuck you. Fuck you. Fuck you. Fuck you!"' The fictional version has one fewer 'Fuck you', but makes amends in its crescendo of exclamation marks and in those screeching climactic italics. Life, raised to a higher intensity, is changed to art. The sign of this sublimation is that Chloe, even while yelling obscenities, retains the composure to choose the Vuitton in which to remove her belongings.

Later in the novel she blunders upon another adulterous tableau in the connubial jacuzzi; now what infuriates her is that Josh and his pick-up have been drinking champagne from her Lalique glasses. Although Chloe sobs 'uncontrollably' as she staggers from the polluted house into the sympathetically lachrymose Malibu night, Joan Collins cannot allow the obligatory brand name to be blurred, either by tears or rain: our heroine climbs into 'her silver Mercedes' and drives away.

The nail clippings and locks of hair coveted by hero-worshippers in the nineteenth century had no negotiable value. Their supply was also drastically limited. Heads cannot sprout hair at will, nor can toes and fingers produce cuticle to order. The modern celebrity has solved both problems, finding ways to sell the chimerical idea of the self without suffering the depletion Wilde feared when he checked on the length of his hair. Hence that most immaterial and notional and over-priced of gift items, the celebrity fragrance. Made of air, its supply is infinite, and will never be unable to meet the demand.

'Yes, there are a lot of "celebrity fragrances" around', said Joan Collins, positioning the inverted commas with a puckering of her mouth. 'Júlio has one; you should try it. And at least I'm more discriminating than that dancer chappie who let them use his name and couldn't care less what the thing smelled like.' (Research next day in a department store on Wilshire Boulevard disclosed a product called Misha, which allegedly contained the essence of Baryshnikov. I did not request a sample, imagining the odour of used ballet slippers.) 'I said I'd only do mine if I could be involved in how it smells. And I insisted on a pretty bottle. They said we would get into skin care later on: we'll do bath products next. I'll only endorse something if it suits who I am. I would *never* get involved with pet food.' It is certainly hard to picture her spooning horse meat into a bowl for some slavering spaniel – although, recalling her brush with the disabled, she superstitiously added, 'Not that I have *anything* against animals.'

She then revealed that she was wearing the perfume now: 'What do you think of it?'

I apologised that my sense of smell was a bit retarded.

'Yes,' she said, tightening her lips petulantly, 'it is very subtle. Perhaps you're out of range.'

I shuffled shyly across the sofa towards her, sniffing as I went. Still nothing. She leaned towards me; I plunged my nose into her neck, and promptly sneezed on her shoulder.

Having been regularly drenched by Leonard Rossiter in the series of Cinzano commercials they made together, she dried herself off like the uncomplaining trouper she is, and said 'It's called Spectacular.'

'Maybe you should call it Subtle?' I suggested, blowing my nose.

'That would not', she replied with the authoritativeness of Alexis, 'be quite so commercial.'

By now it was dusk. Through the smog, Beverly Hills twinkled into light below. Coyotes roam in the canyon above; the gardens of her neighours are planted with signs advertising the security patrol they employ, promising ARMED RESPONSE and spelling out the emergency phone number 1-800-GET HELP. She lowered the metal screens which fortify her windows, shutting out the marble harem girls who pose around her pool. 'When I was on *Dynasty* I had to have guards out front all the time. But that didn't stop two black kids from Watts wandering right into the house one day. I'd just got out of the bath! They told the guard they were friends of mine.' I remembered the Manson gang, scuttling down through the scrub in a canyon like this one to carve up Sharon Tate and her friends.

'This isn't a pretty town,' she said, listening to the sirens which howled along Sunset Boulevard. 'I couldn't live here without working. I even' – the most shocking of her impieties – 'hate the weather. I don't play tennis, I don't like lying in the sun. And the air! It's like inhaling minestrone.'

The rich can afford to lock the city out, or to overlook it. She listened in amazement to my stories of homeless encampments on the beach at Santa Monica, bag ladies berating God beside the freeway, and drunken riots in the backs of buses. 'You mean,' she gasped incredulously, 'you actually travelled on a city bus?' I asked what she liked to do in Los Angeles, since she obviously did not go for walks on the beach or rides in the bus. She thought for a long time, and laughed. 'This afternoon I went to look at a sixty thousand dollar diamond bracelet in a shop on Beverly Drive! No, no, my favourite thing is to go to the Universal City Complex over in the San Fernando Valley. They have fifteen screens there, and you can see three different movies in an afternoon, in the kind of gorgeous, luxurious cinema I remember when I was a girl in London.'

I had to leave. It was time for her – having so laboriously got herself ready for me – to undo all the work and change into someone else for the dinner with her sister. 'I'll be all alone here', she said with a shiver. Suddenly she was more than ever estranged from the uselessly ostentatious house. When I asked her to call me a taxi, she could not find a telephone among her treasury of Art Deco. I, having cased the joint earlier, had to lead her to it. Then there was a hunt for her encyclopaedic Filofax and an anxious debate about whether the number would be under 'taxis' or 'cabs'. By the time the taxi – no, cab – arrived at the spiked iron gate, she had taken her face off and wrapped herself in a bathrobe. 'Now,' she said, lost once more, 'how do I get you out of this fortress?' She padded barefoot into the yard and searched in her beige Rolls-Royce (So *Prime Time* is fiction after all: Chloe drives a silver Mercedes) for the remote control which alone knew how to open the gates. As the gates swung shut, the thin, waving figure in the white bathrobe seemed smaller and frailer than the fantasies about her, imprisoned in a house she had bought with the proceeds of dreams and was finding it difficult to get rid of.

Next day, in the sulphuric lowlands, I went to see the fallen star which is named for her, cemented into the pavement on Hollywood Boulevard. I was told where to find it on the Walk of Fame by Judy Bryer, who proudly said 'The site is prime.' Nearby is the opiate pagoda of Mann's Chinese Theater, bilious green and sanguine red. Joan Collins shares the block with a few immortals who have been forgotten: Leonard Goldberg, Creighton Hale and Leon Shamroy, whoever they once were. But Garbo, the indefatigable Zsa Zsa and – American showbiz is a broad church – the Reverend Billy Graham are not far away. Shops sell lurex bikinis, earthquake supplies and stills of Joan Collins being ravished by insects in *Empire of the Ants* or rounding up cowpokes in *The Wild Women of Chastity Gulch*. My sense of smell had recovered. I could distinguish the sweet reek of popcorn and coconut-flavoured tanning oil, plus the stench of a tramp who had fallen down in a stupor next to Joan Collins's star.

I remembered what she had said, up in the hills, about being 'surrounded by beauty'. We need our things of beauty (of which she is one), so long as we remember (as she does) that they are illusions, and that our tenure, like hers of the house off Coldwater Canyon, is temporary.

UNDRESSING TOM JONES

I N A WORLD WHERE THE IMAGE REIGNS, NO TRANSFORMATION IS impossible. In his early fifties, after two nose jobs, much cosmetic dentistry and a proliferation of paternity suits, after earlier lives as a builder's labourer and a door-to-door vacuum-cleaner salesman, as the sweaty balladeer of Welsh working-mens' clubs and the prancing phallus of Las Vegas floor shows, Tom Jones has become a yuppie.

This can't be him, I thought, as he strolled out to rehearse for an appearance on a television talk show. A dignified gent wearing a tie, a buttoned blazer and charcoal pants picked his way through dreadlocked technicians trussed in cables and some teenage musicians in mutilated jeans. I half expected him to produce a mobile phone and ask his office how he had been misdirected to this inner circle of hell: a flimsy room painted smoky pink and acid peppermint, with a red strobe searing the ceiling and dry ice fulminating on the floor.

Instead he produced a microphone and began to sing. Or rather to wail, yelp, grunt and gurgle in a coital frenzy which climaxed on a B-flat: 'Ba-BEE, here I am, the *MAN* that you see.' Yes, it was definitely him.

Having begun to sing, he unlocked his lower half. Tom Jones's centre of gravity is anchored a few inches below the belt. A hand swung to and fro in a suggestive arc across his groin, while the well-greased hips rotated in a circle, throwing in some suggestive thrusts. Given the grey advancing from behind his ears across that cropped, bristly head, given the wear and tear discernible beneath his orange tan, above all given the expensive respectability of his clothes, it was an incongruous and unsettling act: as if a stockbroker at a commuter station had discarded his umbrella, torn his *Financial Times* to shreds, and started to boogie.

That was not the only incongruity. What kind of voice was he squeezing up from his diaphragm? The lubricious lyrics oozed out with an American accent, as he volunteered to light the candles of the ageing, overweight women who were queueing to enter the studio. But the sound itself was African, a thumping tom-tom which evoked not the green,

green grass of home but a scorched desert or a raucous jungle. Was the music being piped through the solid citizen in the blazer? Then when he put down the microphone, fiddled in his pocket for a throat lozenge and, while sucking it, asked to have the monitors adjusted, there was another shock. Though he sings like a black American, Tom Jones speaks with the bucolic lilt of the Welsh valleys.

Jonathan Ross, the host of the show, appeared from behind one of the peppermint partitions to greet his guest. Wrinkle-free and sleekly gelled in green gabardine, Ross took stock of Tom's revised image: 'What's that you're wearing today?' he asked. 'Gaultier, is it?'

Tom tugged his blazer open and checked the label on the inside pocket. 'Yamamoto', he read or rather spelled, checking when he got to the end of the word that he had said it all.

'Where are you staying this time, Tom? Inn on the Park, is it?'

'No, no', said Tom with his cosy, all-confiding Welsh burr. 'Nice little place. 47 Park Street they call it.' Ross nodded knowingly. 47 Park Street is a hotel in Mayfair so snootily self-effacing that it has no sign outside and uses its address as a name. Like Tom's blazer, it represents affluence gone minimalist, capitalism turning dead cool. The merely rich are ostentatious; the very rich can afford to be discreet. A business magazine recently revealed that Tom's tonsils and hips are together worth 382 million dollars.

Irrepressible, Tom sang the incognito hostelry's praises: 'Great restaurant they've got there too. Now then, what do they call it? The Grosh, is that it?'

Ross smiled with thin lips and, after a pause, helped him out: 'Gavroche. Le Gavroche.' He audibly separated the syllables for Tom's benefit.

'Yeah, that's the one. French, isn't it? French is a bit hard for me. So's English, come to that. Anyway, we get the grub from the restaurant up in the room.' Tom is an amiable innocent. The sophistication goes no deeper than the designer clothes, under which he still sports – as I later ascertained – a crucifix large enough to qualify as a deadly weapon, tied to a gold rope which reposes among the shrubbery of his greying chest hair.

Ross, it transpired as they passed time between rehearsals, had an item in his collection of pop memorabilia which he wanted to present to Tom: a beer mat advertising Double Diamond lager, signed – no doubt before Ross was born – by Tom and all the members of his early band, The

Squires. Tom missed the point of his being a curio, a beer-stained museum piece, and reminisced enthusiastically, 'Ah, the old Double Diamond. That was a good drink. You don't find much of that around these days.'

He sauntered off to sing again, with the usual ululations and the usual miming of coitus. 'Can you see my erection on camera?' Ross asked the producer, and pretended to hammer it back into the folds of his elegantly baggy trousers. 'Sorry Tom,' he winced. 'It's not your singing that's to blame, really it's not.' Tom grinned, amiable and innocent as ever.

Ross begged him as a special favour to sing 'Dalilah', and when Tom obliged he muttered, 'I know he can't get that top note any more.' It was a malicious dig: a singer's high Cs are his virility symbols. Tom groaned and ground his way through the little melodrama of lust, betrayal and righteous anger: 'Forgive me Dalilah, I just couldn't take any more.'

As he keened 'Why *why* WHY, Dalilah?', another voice gutturally harmonized and demanded 'Dalilah, why did you fucking do it?' Ross was singing along. (He deleted the expletive after the rehearsal.) Leaping on to the bandstand, he gyrated through a parody of a prehistoric Tom Jones routine, swinging his microphone like a cowboy's lasso and rortily caterwauling. Tom's own moves, no longer insinuatingly languid, looked weary. Once billed on a record cover as A-TOM-ic Jones, he now seemed distinctly un-nuclear. To his credit, he continued gamely, bravely smiling.

The next afternoon in Mayfair, his overtaxed pelvis was sleeping in. At 2.30, with the uneaten breakfast sent up from The Grosh still under covers on the table, he stepped into the shower, where he stayed for twenty minutes. Never having had a shower which lasted longer than three minutes, I reflected that you need to be very fond of your own body to spend twenty minutes soaping it.

Barefoot, his lolling hips scarcely covered by a skimpy bathrobe, Tom sauntered in to choose clothes for a photographic session. His wardrobe in the hotel bedroom was classified like the shelves of a library: a rainbow of shirts; boots (augmented by one-inch build-ups) being worn on his behalf by a forest of shoe trees; a pile of freshly laundered underpants, puffed up by an extra dose of fabric conditioner or by the impress of Tom's privates. The floor was strewn with items donated by the designers he favours – donated with some reluctance in the case of Comme Des Garçons, whose press officer feared that Tom would accessorise the suit with the gold crucifix and a shirt leering open to the navel. His taste, it is true, needs policing. He sifted through the Armani blazers and Mugler shirts, lingering over the most gruesome garments: a two-toned leather jacket, black with white panels, which made him look like an upright piano, and a diaphanous shirt with sequinned sleeves, perhaps suitable as formal wear in Mexico.

Mixing and matching, he asked 'Is this *me*?' He put the question with evident anxiety, and – since he has survived by adapting to the expectations of each new decade – it was one which only someone else could answer for him. His aesthetic conscience is his son Mark, a burly and florid blow-up of his father. Mark is also his manager, and manage him Mark does. He briskly weaned him from the shirt with the spangles and told him who him who he was to be this afternoon, or this year.

Their relationship oddly reverses roles. Tom, padding about in underpants and crucifix, tried on what Mark told him to, and meekly looked to his son for approval. 'No, that's not you', snapped Mark, and the trousers were peeled off (a process as intimate as a flaying). 'Yes, that's you', he decided, and Tom, relieved, glanced down to see what identity Mark had wished on him. Mark resembles a pushful stage mother, forcing a timid tyke into the offices of producers. In between telling his father who to be, he lectured the stylist: 'Have a look at those straight pants on him – they look good, there's no pleats or anything. Ooh, that's a nice shirt, he likes that, can we have it? We have to *buy* it? Well, how much is it? £165? No problem. Do we get a discount? And make sure you get him into those leather strides. Leather, that's what they want.' They are the elegiacally randy grannies of the world, for whom Tom symbolizes the receding memory of desire.

Now Tom had to be ferried across London to the photographer's studio. Mark abandoned his musings about the leather strides and turned bossily maternal. 'What are you going to wear to go over there?' It was a major decision, because Tom had several yards of corridor, lobby and pavement to traverse before reaching his Range Rover with its black-tinted glass. When he arrived at the studio, he would immediately have to change into something else. 'Do you want to wear your jeans? The black ones, not the blue. Yes, the Gap jeans. And the cowboy boots. Make sure it's the right leather jacket – the one with the fur lining. Have you got your throat sweets?' I remembered my own mother's check-list of preliminaries, to be worked through before leaving the house: have you been to the toilet / blown your nose / got your bus fare / put on clean underclothes (in case you get run over and have to be taken to hospital)? Mark closed the bedroom door, and completed the fabrication of his father in privacy.

Waiting for Tom to be finessed into his jeans, I considered his sweet-natured compliance in allowing himself to be bullied by his son and to have his leg pulled by Jonathan Ross. The day before, Ross had said to him 'You are a bit of a hip geezer, Tom.' Tom chose to assume that Ross meant it. To keep the customers interested, you must update yourself regularly. Madonna invents a fresh outrage each season; Tom plaintively trusts that Armani's double-breasted jackets and Mugler's iridescent cottons will renew him. He has also had some help from the surgeons, inside and out – they straightened his nose, and sliced a nodule off his vocal cords – and from the engineers: in 1988 he collaborated with the pretentious techno-pop group The Art of Noise on a Prince song, 'Kiss', negotiating an extra instalment of credibility with the kids who buy records.

In most shops, however, Tom's albums are banished to the twilight zone known as 'Easy Listening'. Despite his current honorary yuppiedom, there is no hope of remaining young or of retaining the attention of those who still are young. Ultimately, a performer who trades on sexuality can continue only by consenting to become a joke, mocking his or her own graceless refusal to grow old. Mae West and George Burns made careers from a senile imitation of lechery. Allowing Jonathan Ross to laugh at him, Tom must have foreseen a future when the Armani camouflage would no longer work. What do you call a superannuated sex symbol? A camp character.

He arrived at the studio an hour late: it had taken that long to persuade his nether half into those cruel, circulation-arresting jeans, and another shower may well have been necessary during the operation. He was hustled into a corner, stripped, dressed, and consigned to the scrutiny of the lights and the lens.

'Move it', said the photographer. Tom obediently moved it. Even for a head and shoulders shot, he posed with his thumbs in his belt, hands spread like a picture frame around his crotch. 'Stomach in', yelled Mark, 'chest out'. The thudding, concussive disco music issued its own orders, and Tom danced as you might do in your sleep, like an aching automaton. Each attitude he struck seemed to quote from some defunct cult figure. He shadow-boxed like Bruce Lee, froze with one arm poking upwards like John Travolta in *Saturday Night Fever*, crouched to aim an imaginary gun like Sean Connery in the credits of the James Bond films. Every few minutes he was hauled back into the corner and made to change his clothes.

Late in the afternoon, there was an emegency. Tom was supposed to wear a brown suit, but no one had thought to bring a compatible belt. I was summoned to the corner and asked what colour my belt was. I had to look: it was black, so I missed my chance to make my own small contribution to the stitched, patched, eclectic persona of Tom Jones. The stylist ironed a temporary turn-up on to a pair of unfinished, borrowed trousers, and the make-up lady repaired a blotch beneath Tom's tired eyes. Reduced to his underpants once more, he gripped his crucifix and steeled himself for whatever the next incarnation might require.

A Consultation With Vidal Sassoon

In the history of hair, Vidal Sassoon counts as what the old-time historians used to call a Great Man. The 1960s were a hirsute decade, when hair – which is the body's unruly excrescence – symbolized the rebellion of nature against the crew-cut conventionality of the 1950s. Sassoon's achievement was to transform this jungly natural growth into art. His celebrated bobs treated hair as an extension of the head, not a rigid hat-like imposition on it. Faces became sculptures, softly carved from the planes and indentations of bone. Hair, too, acquired volume and angularity. Thanks to Sassoon, the hair-do became – along with the protest march and the rock concert – one of the era's new modes of expression, delighting in its own ephemerality. The crimper, formerly synonymous with limp-wristed fussing, was promoted to a culture hero.

'Actually', said Sassoon when we met in Los Angeles in 1992, 'it's very difficult to be in the sixties in my head – and I don't mean the 1960s.' He was referring, with the defensiveness compulsory in eternally youthful California, to his age. He had just turned 64. It was fifty years since he left school to work as a shampoo boy in the East End. He still looks spry and faun-like, with a carrot-coloured tan which owed more to ray lamps than to the smoggy winter sun. He no longer dyes his greying hair, since a girlfriend had told him this was uncool, but the creases have been smoothed away from the corners of his eyes. 'Sure, my eyes have been done. I'd have it all done if I thought I looked tired. I'm entitled to half price at the movies now, but I refuse to ask for it. I'm too proud.' The cinemas near Sassoon's apartment – in a gated, sentry-guarded settlement at Century City, built on the artificial scenery of what was once the Twentieth Century Fox backlot – advertise Twilite Discounts for senior citizens; this is what California awards its elders instead of a bus pass.

The next best thing to remaining forever young is remaining in fashion, which Sassoon has deftly managed to do: 'Hair is the only art form that constantly evolves, just because hair doesn't stop growing. It's a now job. I was always involved in trying to discern what was happening. Was it intuition or cogito? I never knew, yet I always pulled off something in time to stun them at the Paris collections. An architect could have the same style for twenty years. I had to change mine every six months'.

The changes have been ideological as much as stylistic. The 1960s were a decade of feckless indulgence: the most emblematic hair of the era belonged to Sassoon's collaborator Mary Quant, who shaved her pubes into the shape of a heart and thus relocated the body's centre of affectivity. But as the beautiful, brainless young things of swinging London got older, they began to worry about the abuse they had inflicted on themselves. Hair-cutting, which already overlapped with the pseudo-science of cosmetology, allied itself now with faddish research into health, and eventually made its peace with a religiosity which the 1960s had blithely derided. Sassoon, sniffing the wind, suspected all these futures before they came to pass. 'Way back in 1961 I opened a health bar in my salon at the Grosvenor Hotel, with a nurse who gave vitamin B and C injections – until the authorities closed her down because we didn't have the right licence.'

Sassoon's move to California during the 1970s solemnized this merger between the hedonism of the 1960s and the more conscience-stricken concerns – nutritional, ecological and spiritual – of the New Age. He no longer cuts hair, or even owns the salons which are operated in his name by two former employees; his gels, sprays, fixes, mousses and body glazes belong to and are marketed by a pharmaceutical company, for whom Sassoon himself travels as 'an exponent and example of corporate philosophies and policies.' These days he broods about the end of history rather than split ends; he philosophizes about globalism and greenness, dreams of a Middle Eastern Economic Community uniting Israel with the Arab states surrounding it, and – still scarred by his childhood memories of Fascist marches through Whitechapel – he has endowed the Vidal Sassoon Centre for the Study of Antisemitism and Related Bigotries at the Hebrew University in Jerusalem.

He seldom appears at his salon on Rodeo Drive in Beverly Hills, but he does not need to, because the hair-cutters who work there are graduates of his academy in Santa Monica. His ethos adapts itself neatly to California, with its reverence for the image, its worship of youth, and its fetishism about its intestines. Los Angeles has enriched the world through the invention of valet parking and a cornucopia of related fulfilments. It is the birthplace of wellness and bio-feedback; of tennis therapy and dream workshops; of wishcraft, mind gyms and emotion management.

Local publications advertise 'clothing-optional retreats' and a mind-boggling species of massage which is guaranteed to be an 'erogenous, alleviatory, utopistic experience'. Beauty here is a substitute for godliness, and puritanism has been updated as a theory of dietary salvation. At breakfast in my hotel, while the joggers around me made life-and-death decisions about rolled oats, skimmed milk and cholesterol-free eggs, I sent a seismic shock through the room by ordering a fry-up; stopping for my elevenses on Rodeo Drive, I caused a similar ripple by asking for what the city's limber angels scathingly term 'leaded' coffee instead of decaff.

These alimentary manias are a trusting investment in immortality. Rodeo Drive is prowled by nubile female cadavers wearing the immovable, mirthless grins which tell of plastic surgery. Beverly Hills, as pure as Plato's republic, outlaws hospitals, funeral parlours and cemeteries, serenely denying death. As if to illustrate how hair has proliferated since the 1960s into a many-stranded symbol of aesthetic grace and moral hygiene, the salons around Rodeo Drive combine the functions of art gallery, movie studio and psychiatric clinic. Umberto's passes itself off as a museum of sculpture, with bronze busts and posturing torsos in its lobby. At Dusty Fleming's, would-be starlets squirm in beach chairs, pretending that they are about to be summoned on to the set. Concepts, which specializes in 'complete image make-overs', is a laboratory where you can reconceive yourself. Tova's, owned by the wife of Ernest Borgnine, claims to be a Mind, Body and Spirit Salon, mystifing whatever that might mean behind the black glass favoured by stretch limos. Sassoon's establishment is starkly didactic. It has no street frontage: above the pavement a video monitor shows a cut in progress, as gruesomely incisive as an anatomy lesson; behind it a steep marble staircase leads upwards to beauty and the renovated you.

The experience – as much therapeutic as cosmetic in this Californian version of Sassooning – begins with what is solemnly entitled 'The Consultation'. A hairdresser like a head-shrinker has to be intimate with your unconsciousness. I eavesdropped while a tiny Korean girl dressed as a harlequin interrogated her client, the wife of an army officer in a training camp for desert warfare near Las Vegas.

'When was your last hair cut?' she asked. She might have been inquiring about the woman's last visit to the confessional.

The client, as if replying to a priest, shifted in her seat and guiltily murmured 'It's been a while....'

The Korean tugged a lock dismissively. 'Who cut it?'

'It wasn't you', said the army wife, by now desperately flustered. 'You weren't here that day.'

I left them to their recriminations. In an adjoining booth, a cutter called Jason – small, bearded and cheekily Mephistophelean – painted crimson sauce on to someone else's hair and wrapped it in armadillo scales of aluminium foil. He too, like a censorious priest, was prescribing penances. 'She got her hair over-coloured. There's routine punishment that goes with bad colour jobs. About a third of our work is corrective here in Beverly Hills. She gets a double penalty because the damage wasn't done at Sassoon. People in this town all want TV hair – you know, like the news anchors have, all flossed and varnished. Or they put gunk on their hair, then go to the beach and get it full of chlorine. English hair is healthier. You guys don't have the elements over there that we have. Just all that moisture, I guess.'

Ever since Figaro plied his trade in Seville, the barber has been a connoisseur of secrets. Women told him about their marital woes, men bought their condoms from him. In California the services rendered extend to spiritual counselling. Another client, burdensomely pregnant, was blurting out her disgust to a solicitous cutter: 'I mean, just look. Isn't it gross? I don't feel it's me any more. You've gotta do something.'

Sassoon, who had turned up to be privately titivated in the VIP room, joined me in my snooping. 'Hairdressers are so privileged', he whispered. 'We're touching human beings, getting feelings out of them. Even a psychiatrist doesn't run his fingers through your hair. You're lying there stiff on the couch. It's all so much more formal. Most hairdressers are gentle souls. It's in the nature of the work. Eyes speak to us. We send the clients out looking so much better, and the thank you is in their eyes.'

Also, I thought as I listened to this breathy homily, in the signatures on their credit-card vouchers.

Now, however, two plaintive eyes were speaking to another cutter, who began the consultation by asking, in that unctuous tone shared by priests and therapists, 'Have you been into the salon before?'

I thought that the speaking, imploring eyes would burst into tears. 'No, no', she said. 'I'm just a little Canadian girl.' The mention of Canada was a heart-rending bid for pity. 'I hate my hair. My face is so round, and I don't want puffy hair. Can't you thin out my face?' She closed her eyes, trusting that when she opened them she would be looking at a remade person.

The cutter was then derailed by a woman who hurtled in from Rodeo Drive, all her ornaments clattering and her frizzed hair electric with anguish. 'Jeffrey', she screeched, 'help! I can't do anything at all with this. I'm in trauma here! I need you.'

Jeffrey, hustling her off to sob as she was shampooed, yawned at me 'That lady's having what I call a hair tragedy. And when you're having a hair tragedy, believe me it can ruin your day'.

Summoning all my courage, I volunteered for a personal consultation. I chose a cutter whose own hair was moulting, on the assumption that he would be sympathetic. 'You've got a crown', he sighed. 'There's nothing you can do about it. You've just got to work with it....'

'That's exactly how the Queen feels', interjected Sassoon. 'Peter, I'd say something Grecian for you.' Seeing me frown uncomprehendingly, he added, 'You know, the Romans? Those old films with Olivier?' I suppose I should have been flattered: everyone in Los Angeles aspires to be made over into someone from the movies.

Sassoon did not pause to classicize me, since he was off spreading sweetness through the salon. He does not pick up the scissors these days, but he likes to hover, mopping and mowing balletically as he fluffs a client's hair and watches it bounce back. Hairdressing, like faith-healing, consists for him in a laying on of hands.

Back home in Century City, where the ground is ruled into a map of the night sky and streets are called Galaxy or Constellation or Empyrean, Sassoon himself became astral. 'A good book these days is better than a good party. I'm taking time out to study. It's the ideas, the thinkers I feed on. Look here, this is a heavy cat.' He was referring to Martin Buber, whose biography had been wrinkling his tanned brow. He also tugged out a book on comparative religion, which he had taken to the Caribbean on holiday. It was full of the autodidact's earnest underlinings. Beside his bed – shared at the time with his fiancée Rhonda, familiarly known as Ronnie, a graphic designer from Cincinnati – lay a paperback entitled *From Socrates to Sartre: The Philosophic Quest*, its spine bent out of shape by Sassoon's nocturnal wrestling with his angel. His sacred text is Camus' *L'Etranger*. 'It's so right about the intrinsic loneliness of the human being. You can be alone even in a crowd. Have you ever thought of that?' Sassoon's fondness for this existential fable is not entirely fatuous. Hair-dressers, as I discovered at the salon, see panic and emptiness staring back when clients look in the mirror; they are experts on the tenuousness of identity.

'We're building a new house, in one of the canyons above Beverly Hills. I tell Ronnie we'll need a librarian.' When I looked quizzical, he added 'You know, to sort out all the books.' I can indeed testify that Sassoon owns several dozen.

The most impressive rooms in his apartment, however, are the bathroom and the kitchen. The former is a positive palace of thalassotherapy, the latter an apothecary's shop of herbal remedies and death-delaying tonics. Sassoon used to gobble sixty pills a day, gorging on cohosh, prickly ash bark, boldo leaves and mistletoe. After chomping his way through the shrubbery, he then purged himself with a draught of Acidopholus, made from bacteria found in live yoghurt. His intake now is more moderate: a sachet of two dozen tablets prescribed by his Sikh kinesiologist ('I feel spiritually awakened when I leave him'), plus a health drink which has the colour and consistency of a Malibu mud slide.

Ronnie, lured out from the heartier mid-West, was at first bewildered by this Californian diet. Offering me dessert – frozen yoghurt, accompanied by some wizened, intestinally cleansing prunes – she feigned astonishment when I accepted. 'Oh wow, you like to *eat*! That's so rare in LA. When I moved out here, my friend called me from Cincinnati to see how I was doing, and I said to her "They're weird, they think cheese is the devil." On our first date, Vidal took me to the symphony. I asked him whether we were going to eat afterwards, and he said "Oh, I'll just blend us a health drink. Then we won't have to chew." I'm corrupting him. Now I have him moaning at dinner. About the food.'

As well as demonizing cheese, California has excommunicated white sugar. To counter my scepticism, Sassoon called for a cup of the controlled substance. Ronnnie indignantly denied that they had any on the premises, as if fearing a raid from the dietary police. But Sassoon's housekeeper – a rollicking black blancmange called Tommie, who sings as a soloist with a gospel choir – revealed a supply which she kept hidden for Dionne Warwick's visits: 'Miss Dionne swears by that stuff. She says it makes her sing sweeter'n a bird.' Sassoon used it to demonstrate his doctor's technique of muscle-testing. He had me hold out an arm at right angles, then pushed down on it like a lever; it didn't budge. Then I was given the cup of sugar to grip against my solar plexus while I extended the other arm; this time when he pressed, the arm gave in. 'You see, sugar drains all the energy from you, it saps your vitals.'

Two days in California make you credulous: only when I got home and tried the experiment using flour, muesli and even soy protein did I realize it was not the sugar's fault. What weakens the protruding arm is the fact that its fellow is clutching a cup, which engages the muscles across your chest. Refined sugar in this case got a raw deal; but California requires scapegoats, since something other than our own biological alarm clock must be held responsible for the fact that we inevitably sag, sicken, age and die.

Sassoon's apartment was cluttered with sculptural totems: the hand of a gigantic Buddha, flopping in benediction; a tube of glass twisted like a spastic colon; a chair of coiled wire to punish you for possessing buttocks. These objects please him because they recall the chunky geometry of his earliest cuts: 'I didn't just make people look pretty. I drew attention to bone structure, I cut according to the shape of the head.' Like Michelangelo hacking away with his chisel until he liberated the human form imprisoned in stone, Sassoon's scissors snipped in order to excavate a hidden self. He also rather grandiosely acknowledges the influence of architecture: 'Mies van der Rohe, the Bauhaus – I was heavily into that movement. Less is more was my motto too. I wanted my cuts to look like that building of Mies's on Park Avenue, the Seagram. It's so huge, yet you feel you could lift it up like a piece of cake. And I love the design Richard Rogers did for our Frankfurt salon, the exoskeleton look. I wish I could have been an architect.'

This made me curious about the house currently under construction in the canyon. Talking about it, Sassoon used a telling cosmetic metaphor: 'There was a house on the site before, but we're stripping it back to its bones. Luckily it's got very good bones.'

Ronnie at this point took command, and explained what she called the design concept: 'The guy who's doing it is very hot right now in LA. It's going to be part Mexican, a tiddly bit Italian, and a tad Japanese. It's very us.'

Since I had trouble visualizing this stylistic salad, I went off to investigate the much-touted designer's masterpiece, a clothes store on Melrose Avenue next to the cobalt-blue breaking wave of the Pacific Design Center. It is a concrete bunker, windowless with doors of rusted iron; trowels account for the only texture on the façade, and the paved floor has a crack as if the San Andreas fault travelled beneath the racks of dresses.

Simian monoliths rear in the parking lot. Domestic comfort is not this designer's priority: perhaps, in a city where beauty is obligatory and thus almost banal, ugliness is the ultimate chic. Reporting back to Ronnie, I said I would sooner live in an accident on the freeway.

Ronnie, undismayed, smiled at my philistinism and blinded me with her teeth. Still, she conceded that there were problems at the site. 'The house is on bedrock, but we want to extend the pool to the edge of the hill, and the soil is loose. We have to put a caisson in.'

'That's compressed concrete, Le Corbusier type', said Sassoon, deploying another item in his bibliography.

'Beverly Hills', said Ronnie, 'is full of fill. No, I said fill, not filth. Some of it's compacted, some of it's not. There were certain times when the soil was non-certified.'

Such is the tragic ecology of Los Angeles: the hillocks above Sunset Strip have been coated with an icing of concrete, to prevent them from decanting the houses they prop up on to the road beneath. It all comes down to the same decaying instability which Sassoon's salon and the plastic surgeons ratcheting skin back behind the ears aim vainly to combat, for facial slippages are here held to be as fatal as those of geological kind.

Sassoon saw me nodding sagely at the thought of his Mexican-Italian-Japanese mélange casting off its anchorage, and appealed to me as a human being who also possessed a heart and hair. 'Come on, no-one can begrudge me a house. I've worked fifty years for it.'

In truth, it is hard to begrudge him anything, since those years have traversed such an arduous allotment of experience. There is more to history than the rapid turnover of hairstyles, and Sassoon in one lifetime has careened through a century or more of social evolution. His father was a rug trader from Turkey or Salonica – Sassoon does not know which, and stoically affects not to care – who frequented Petticoat Lane until one day, unregretted, he disappeared. His mother worked in a sweatshop, and when she could not afford to feed Vidal and his brother she committed them for six years to a Sephardic orphanage in Maida Vale. Sassoon calls her 'a Golda Meir type, a socialist and a Zionist. She radicalized me'. He was gaoled for brawling with neo-Fascist thugs in a Kilburn pub in 1945; in 1947 he was recruited for the Israeli army. 'It was the only honourable thing to do. It gave me my dignity. I found myself as a human being.'

He looks back with a surprising lack of bitterness, though he is aware of how different his life might have been if he had belonged to the other

Sassoon clan, the assimilated grandees whose ranks included Sir Philip, the cabinet minister, Sir Victor, the Derby winner, and Siegfried the poet: 'Then I could have gone to university. I might have been an architect after all.' He notes that the integrated clan's biography banishes him to a footnote, where it takes care to point out that he is not a member of the family. What the book means, of course, is that he belongs to an inferior social class. 'Yet I didn't want to be a hairdresser. I never even enjoyed it much. I just wasn't allowed to think of anything better. In those days you had to leave school at fourteen, and get apprenticed to some sort of trade.' He is also able to grin, at this distance, about the three humiliating years of elocution lessons with a plummy gorgon from the Old Vic which were necessary before he was considered fit to cut West End hair. After all that, I think he deserves the absurdly eclectic house, and the Jaguar which he frets about being photographed in, knowing how prone to envy are the readers of the British press.

Perhaps because his own artistic creations were so short-lived, growing out within a month, he says that he venerates above all 'the thinkers who created the ideals that carry on today.' Hence his veneration of Buber, the 'heavy cat' whose theory of dialogue – permitting the believer to speak with but not about God – links Judaism with the inquisitions of psychotherapy. 'In Hegel, it's all thesis and antithesis. But in Buber, everything is hypothesis. There's no divine revelation, and everything is arguable. People argue with God, imagine that! I don't know if there is a God, that doesn't concern me. What matters is that you can extend and prolong thought in disputation. I don't go to synagogue every week, it's not me. But I am fascinated by these extraordinary minds who decided they would argue with God and man equally.'

A naturalized citizen in the country of the bland, Sassoon seems to have no quarrel with anyone. All the same, his gospel of spiritual awareness and environmental kindness is the extension of his hairdressing expertise. For him, every haircut is a parable of radiant self-transcendence. He tells the story of a client in the 1960s who came in fat and miserable, complaining about her marriage and begging Sassoon to make her happy. He refused to cut her hair until she promised to diet; meanwhile he asked Mary Quant to design a dress for her, basing it on the figure she could look forward to having after six months of abstinence. When she lost the prescribed amount of weight, she came back in the new dress and he gave her the longed-for haircut, because now she qualified for it. Next he had a visit from the grateful husband, who said, 'I lost my wife - but I found my old girlfriend.'

Can we allow a hairdresser to be a highbrow? Over dinner, Sassoon mentioned Ted Koppel, a political interviewer on American television. 'What do you think of his hair?' I opportunistically asked. Koppel boasts a florid mane of what Jason in the salon called 'TV hair': it looks like a burnished ersatz helmet.

His reply was unemphatic, but closer to being snappy than anything he had previously said to me. 'I don't care about his hair. I'm more interested in what's in his head.'

Sassoon has written a preface for a history of the Jewish resistance to fascism in the East End, in which he remarks that 'the monstrosity of the Holocaust was a Christian tragedy.' He is a good and honest man who recognizes that some problems defy the laving, redeeming agencies of shampoo, even if it's combined with conditioner by the synthetic action of silicone. He knows at least, unlike many of his clients, that there are worse things in the world than hair tragedies.

THE UNIVERSE AND OPRAH

WHAT'S IN A NAME? PERHAPS AN OMEN, EVEN IF IT IS MIS-SPELLED.

Oprah Winfrey's parents in poor, rural Mississippi thought they were naming her after a Biblical character called Orpah, but they reversed two letters when filling in the form. Despite the error, Oprah thinks of her ascent from starveling childhood through delinquent adolescence to global fame and undreamed-of wealth as a pre-destined affair, perhaps overseen by her allegorical patron Orpah. 'I was born for greatness', she has avowed.

She refers to *The Oprah Winfrey Show* as a ministry. Winnie Mandela, before her headlong lapse from grace, chummily assured her 'Your mission is sacramental.' In a programme shortly before Christmas 1993, Oprah turned reflective. 'Every day', she said, 'I ask God or the Universe or whatever what the purpose is – my purpose. 'Cos I don't think the purpose is just to do no talk show.' The show, for its hostess, is an earthly allegory of higher things, the manifesto of a destiny. Combining the roles of earth mother and sob sister, New Age evangelist and investigative muck-raker, Oprah 'talks through' the diurnal miseries of the twenty million Americans who watch her each weekday afternoon in that slack, beached time-slot between the end of the midday soap operas and the start of the early evening news; she exhorts them to 'turn their lives around.' 'I am highly attuned', she purrs when discussing her vocation, 'to my divine self.'

Money is decanted on to her directly from heaven. 'The Universe just goes and picks people', Oprah has remarked. In much the same way her Biblical colleague Mary, the wife of a humble carpenter, must have pondered the choice made by the inseminating angel. 'I've been blessed – but I create the blessings. The money is symbolic of what I am supposed to do in life.' In 1993 the industry gossips of *Entertainment Today* calculated that proceeds from syndication of her programme brought Oprah

27 million dollars a year. This made her 'the highest paid entertainer on the planet.' The astral phrasing is fair enough: someone with a divine self cannot be expected merely to exist in the world, like the rest of us. I quibble only at the category of 'entertainer'. Healer, surely? Redeemer? But in the land of Aimee Semple McPherson and Tammy Faye Bakker – where radio and television stations must be acquired to disseminate the good news and theme parks constructed as a preview of the New Jerusalem – religion is a sub-section of the leisure industry.

The *National Enquirer* (which has made Oprah a symbolic figure on the communal totem pole by chronicling her struggles to lose weight and keep boyfriends) did some extra sums for the benefit of readers in the supermarket check-out line who might be leafing through a copy while waiting to buy groceries with food stamps. The paper computed that Oprah earned – though it might be more accurate to say that her income was – 5,421.06 dollars per minute. These figures do not quite match those of *Entertainment Today:* at this rate, Oprah's annual takings would be just short of three billion dollars. The *Enquirer* naturally does not employ fact checkers, and they may not have a calculator in the office. Since such figures are science fiction, any unspendable, unimaginable sum will do. As they are apt to remark in America, go figure.

In quest of Oprah's divine self, I thought I would look up her prototype in *The Book of Ruth*. Orpah, it turns out, was a Moabitess, the sister of Ruth and the daughter-in-law of Naomi. When Naomi returned to the land of Judah, she puzzlingly advised her sisters to remain with their own people and their own gods. Ruth, foreseeing an opportunity to say 'Whither thou goest I will go', followed Naomi to Judah and its alien corn; Orpah stayed at home.

Not much of an augury, it would seem, for the upwardly mobile Oprah, who used to feed hogs and empty bedpans on the Mississippi farm but now occupies a vast Chicago condominium and tapes her show in a lavishly post-modernized studio – done out in green and violet, with marble staircases and distressed-timber ceilings – which she herself owns. Yet the source of Oprah's appeal, despite her wealth and the lofty detachment which goes with her celebrity, is her populism.

Like Orpah, she keeps faith with the folks at home, and attends to their griefs and gripes and domestic tribulations: sexual abuse, teenage abortion, drink, drugs and marital infidelity. What she calls her ministry is a psychotherapeutic seminar for ailing America. 'We are here', she will say, 'to try to understand. We are here to explore your feelings.' An earlier, small-time version of her show, which she hosted in Baltimore before moving to Chicago in 1984, was called *People Are Talking*. The people talk, while Oprah's main talent, like a shrink's, is for listening. Reaction shots reveal her versatility in doing so. She nods her head sadly or shakes it in disbelief, clutches her microphone for moral support, waves it like a fairy's wish-fulfilling wand, or raises it at malefactors like a truncheon. Sometimes her gaze goes out of focus as she listens. Perhaps she is surfeited with sorrows, though she may be listening to the tinkling of that sky-descended gold, which – if you believe the *Enquirer*'s accounting – arrives at the rate of just over 93 dollars per second. (I omit the cents from my long division, assuming that Oprah gives them to charity.)

This career might seem to be the happiest of accidents, except that Oprah's divinely superintended world-view does not allow for the fortuitous. 'Luck', she opines, 'is a matter of preparation.' The producer who has been with her since Baltimore, Debbie Di Maio, remembers that Oprah would arrive for work at the Baltimore studio humming 'Chi-ca-go, Chi-ca-go, that todd-e-ling town,' and believes that she was sending out 'a subliminal message.' Somebody up there was on her frequency. A Chicago station flew her in, auditioned her by setting her to pry into the anguish of a group of sexually impotent men, and encouraged her to reminisce on camera about the deprivations of her childhood, the sexual abuse she of course suffered, her spell as a teenage runaway. Her astute merger of prurience and uplift proved irresistible. By 1990 hers was the most popular programme on American television, overtaken only by the unbeatably moronic game shows *Wheel of Fortune* and *Jeopardy*.

Oprah can be forgiven for believing that the move was providential, because Chicago is in fact the capital city of a populism like hers. It keeps an equal distance from the egg-headed east coast and the air-headed west; with its mythical stockyards and gangsters, its gales and ice and grime, it is the headquarters of American realism – the home base of Theodore Dreiser and Upton Sinclair, of Nelson Algren, Saul Bellow and David Mamet. Studs Terkel, the Oprah Winfrey of the radio waves, broadcasts his own talk show from here, substituting a socialist desire to redress wrongs for her blithe mystical conviction that 'anyone can be what the Universe wants them to be.' *Ordinary People*, Robert Redford's film about suburban psychological qualms, was set in Chicago: where would he have found ordinary people in New York or Los Angeles?

Oprah's studio is located in an area of the inner city as downcast as the quietly despairing people who watch her show in the hope of salvation: a district of abandoned warehouses and repair shops for electrical appliances. These 'service outlets' are a sure sign of impoverishment: affluent America throws its gadgets away when they go on the fritz and buys replacements, rather than sending the old models to be mended. The elevated railway clatters by on its way into the Loop, littering the street with sparks and cinders. A bum dozes in a doorway. The wind from Lake Michigan whips up small cyclones of crumpled newspaper.

On the corner, the studio audience docilely waits to be admitted. The women are bravely smart in their synthetic fabrics, with make-up working overtime to soften their case-hardened faces. And why are those men here, at nine on a Monday morning? Are they all unemployed? The queue has the shuffling stoicism of the line at a labour exchange, or the procession of penitents awaiting turns at the confessional box. 'We don't have tickets to the show', Debbie Di Maio explained to me. 'We do it by reservations, kind of like a restaurant. That way people can come to a show they're interested in.' Menus are posted in advance. You can choose between wronged wives confronting 'the other woman' next Monday and rape victims confronting their attackers on Tuesday; later in the week there may be teenage prostitutes turning tricks after school or foreign tourists being gunned down in Miami. If the show is a restaurant, then its daily specials consist of miseries.

Oprah used to be matriarchally chubby, and waddled amiably through a role in Spielberg's *The Colour Purple*. Then, deciding that the Universe wished her to be glamorous, she shed sixty-seven pounds and unveiled her svelte new body on the show as if performing a miracle. She subsequently gained the weight back, then lost it again: the *Enquirer* must be fed with copy. Her studio has been through as many make-overs as its mistress. It began life as an armoury, then served as a roundhouse where streetcars could reverse; during World War II it was a roller-skating arena. Now reclaimed and redecorated, with streamlined glass bricks on the façade and a fanatical security staff who demand that you surrender a driving licence or a passport or a credit card into their custody while you are inside the building, it is both a temple to the cult of Oprah and the brain-box of her media empire. Here she incorporates herself: the Oprah who should have been Orpah has jumbled the letters once more and anagramatized the studio and her company as Harpo, Inc. That name might also be an omen. Oprah lucratively trades in talk, whereas Harpo was the mute member of the Marx family. Oprah's divine self, however, possibly has designs on Harpo's celestial harp. Perhaps there is also the punning hint of a hippo, in recognition of Oprah's heavy-set, pre-divine self.

The studio is churchily hushed as the audience awaits her appearance. She used to begin the show by saying 'Hello everybody, my name is Oprah Winfrey.' She has given up the introduction. Nowadays we all know who she is; we were all there, unnaturally early on a Monday morning, to see her. Having got money and spent weight, she is the precious proof of the self-improving gospel of 'personal growth' which she propounds.

Before she appears to us, we must be made ready, changed from a crowd into a congregation. 'Hi there,' says the warm-up man, 'I'm the audience co-ordinator.' He sets out to co-ordinate us by asking how we are doing this morning.

'Good', people dubiously grunt. The reply is not enthusiastic enough; he makes us repeat it until it is a roar of affirmation. *The Oprah Winfrey Show* is in the feel-good business. 'We want you to have a lot of energy. I want you to clap like you're really happy to be here. Do you all know how to clap for television?' I realized that this was a skill I did not possess: it has to be done with palms visibly raised in front of the chest, bashed together like cymbals. 'Look as if you're having a good time, otherwise you won't get on television today. You've gotta be animated for our cameras to catch you.' All the creased, care-worn faces mimic rapture.

When we have been heated to the right temperature, Oprah moseys on among a gaggle of technicians and beautifiers. There are shrieks and screams: 'Here she *is*!' Oprah is royally courteous, but cannot be said to share her public's ecstasy. 'We are recording', shouts the director. 'What a thrill', mutters Oprah, with the scornful inflection of Bette Davis declaring, 'What a dump' in *Beyond the Forest* or Elizabeth Taylor imitating her in *Who's Afraid of Virginia Woolf?*

As the applause crescendoes, she opens her mouth, only to close it again abruptly. Just what *is* the show supposed to be about today? 'There is not a single thing in that prompter, so I don't know what y'all expect me to do.' Her employees run in panicking circles to wake up the autocue. She snarls an aside to the audience: 'We got the *best* people here.' Tapping a tiny, peremptory foot while she waits, she muses aloud on her ubiquity in the Universe: 'We're in Japan this week. "Why?" I say to myself. I can't wait to see me translated.'

At length the autocue informs her that today she will be fearlessly investigating 'dating service scams': lonely-hearts agencies that fleece their clients. The subject doubly evinces the alienation Oprah supposedly succours but actually exploits. How sad in the first place to entrust your love life to a computer, which matches you (for a large fee) to a partner of its choice. How much sadder to describe your misalliance with a stranger to twenty million other strangers on television. Nevertheless, Oprah has the usual row of victims eager to 'share' – this is the talk show's buzzword, claiming that confession is contagious and mutually beneficial – their sorry tales.

She calls them her 'guests', although she meets them for the first and only time on air. They include a stockbroker whose dating service fixed him up with a hooker, and a female accountant who was dispatched by the computer to brunch with a barbarian. The accountant's bleary eyes spoke of sleepless nights, her sunken cheeks chronicled decades of disappointment. She described the grossness of her electronic date, who had omitted to shave, comb his hair or brush his teeth. He ate with his fingers and – this seemed to be his gravest breachest of etiquette, causing me to twist in my seat and flush with shame – he held his coffee cup with both hands. 'And Oprah, he wiped his mouth with the back of his hand. Of course he had a napkin, but he used that for blowing his nose. When he laughed he snorted, and sprayed me!' Harrowing testimony indeed; as she relived the traumatic brunch, she was close to tears.

The manageress of the service then defended the match-making know-how of her computer: 'The individual in question', she said, referring to the unwashed snorter, 'is a scientist and a MENSA person. We should not expect an intellectual to have the same dress code as a business person.' (I will plead my intellect in mitigation, I told myself, if ever I am ostracized for holding a cup with both hands.) Prodded by Oprah, the electronic madam admitted that the man was 'not a 10. Maybe a 7 on a physical attractiveness scale.' Her computer, I suppose, assigned numbers to quantify sex appeal. 'He's going through some stuff – there are some things in his life – we hope he can get it together.'

Another of this woman's dissatisfied customers was able to outdo the accountant: 'She charged me 700 dollars, Oprah, and all I got was a man who was bald, with dental braces. Oh, and his wife had killed herself the night before.' The manageress, it transpired, had immediately transferred to the moral high ground, and was suing the angry client for twenty thousand dollars. What damage had she sustained? 'She's harassing me Oprah, can't you see?'

Audience members, having made reservations for this particular psychic feast, went on to volunteer horror stories of their own. One woman worked for an agency which sent out decoy salesgirls in miniskirts or leather pants to scour laundrettes or McDonald's outlets for clients. The men doing their laundry or chomping cheeseburgers signed up of course, but soon discovered that the sexy procuresses were married to the owners of the agency. Only frumps were available for dating. Someone else denounced a service which signed up dozens of black women although it had no black men on its books to mate them with. This prompted Oprah to plant her hand on her hip and pout, 'Those black men must have said "Hey, we don't need no dating service, we c'n git our own women."'

Her vamping was welcome in a discussion conducted otherwise in that merger of psychobabble and technocratic jargon, mixing in metaphors from sports and shopkeeping, which Americans use when trying to re-engineer their emotional lives. The stockbroker defensively explained that he did not mean to sign up with the agency at all: 'I went to solicit the woman who runs the service as a possible client for my own firm. I work on Wall Street, I thought she was a highly networked individual.' The accountant desolatingly reflected that 'A date is like a job interview: you've gotta impress. When a service like this goes wrong, it's not a broken toaster.' (I remembered the repair shops in the streets nearby, with their pile-ups of broken toasters.) The woman who fielded the messy eater and the bald widower with the braced teeth philosophized, 'In the game of life, just like baseball, you don't make a hit every time. Sometimes you strike out.' A man who owns another agency snatched the image and ran with it: 'It's up to us to carry the ball by making good phone. I can do it intuitively because I'm a psychologist. We need to build a consumer-smart approach to dating.'

Oprah benignly absorbed this mess of tormented feeling and muddled thought. She does not interview people. She permits them into her presence, and that – combined with the lights and the cameras – unties their tongues. To gain her attention, they will say anything. She is capable of aggression and accusation. When making a programme in red-neck Forsyth County, Georgia, where 'niggers' are ordered to go home and Jews are considered an 'alien race', she did hector her all-white audience. Unfortunately her indignation lost some of its righteous force when she chose to attack her audience's viewing habits rather than its bigoted views: 'Don't y'all even watch *The Cosby Show*?'

But in a 1990 programme about shoplifting, a rare moment of self-awareness threatened to halt the proceedings. This, the Universe must have muttered into Oprah's ear, is not why you were chosen. A reformed kleptomaniac was whining 'Basically I'm an honest person in every other way, but I had this problem.' Oprah looked as if she had finally had enough of the self-extenuating drivel through which she daily wades. She shot back '*How* can you be an honest person in every other way if you *steal*? In this age of talk shows, we label everything a disease. Well, you can't stop yourself from getting cancer, but you can stop yourself from stealing.'

It is interesting that Oprah thinks of modern times not as the nuclear age or the age when history ended, but as 'the age of talk shows', epitomized by her own talent-free art form. She is right, of course. The talk show takes the soothing rationalizations of popular psychiatry and constructs an entertainment from their sunny moral escapism. All your wrong-doing derives from some problem or compulsion or non-medical disease of which you are the hapless victim. The devil – in the form of an abusive parent or an addictive snack food – made you do it. A contemporary murderer has after all excused his crime by blaming the sugary Twinkies he had been eating.

Oprah's testiness was short-lived. Recovering, she gave a demonstration on the same show of how the transference of blame is effected. 'I've only told one other person this,' she whispered with a confidentiality which is only possible when you are addressing twenty million people. 'When I was eight years old, I stole a bag of Fritos. It would be food, knowing me.' Then came her notion of making amends: 'A while ago I ran into the President of the company that makes Fritos, and I was *so* relieved that I could tell him what I'd done!'

This hardly counted as a penalty, since the anecdote allowed her to boast about her acquaintance with captains of industry, and the President – I assume – did not ask her to pay the price of those Fritos plus thirty years' interest. Nevertheless, the 'expert' invited on to that day's programme to anoint the sinners with the unction of his professional jargon congratulated her on her courage and proclaimed a victory: 'That negative feedback really helped you, Oprah. Now you can let that guilt feeling go.'

Oprah waved goodbye to her albatross. Absolution is easy and automatic, as in the commercials which she is always pausing for, where happy endings are ensured by purchase of the correct mouthwash or deodorant or dandruff shampoo, and guilt like grease can be magicked away by a new detergent. The talk show depends on a double paradox. This is talk to be watched, not to take part in: conversation as a spectator sport. Increasingly it is also talk which you do not listen to but rather empathize with. Its purpose is to make you feel better, and *The Les Brown Show* – a morning talkalong with a young black host on Oprah's network, ABC – advertises this in a catchphrase whose last word ingeniously replaces the expected verb, 'hear': Les purveys 'The Best Talk You'll Ever Feel.'

Freed from the Fritos, Oprah at once slipped back into her inimitably cosy style, which confuses psychiatric inquisition with seamy curiosity. A department-store official in charge of 'loss prevention' was asked 'What happens when you catch people stealing? Do they really lose body control? I mean is it true they break down and wet themselves?' The man disappointed her by refusing to be graphic about puddled linoleum.

During the investigation of dating services, Oprah roused herself to a brief spasm of scorn when quizzing 'two women who go out with loser guys. They prefer loser guys because the losers give them money.' On flounced the bimboes with that blissful absence of shame which is the moral mood of contemporary America, made possible by the ministrations of talk shows. They were called, as befits bimboes, Cindy and Chrissie: those names are omens too. They told Oprah how they shake down no-hopers sent to them by a dating service. With the profits, they buy hairspray. I could see that they needed a lot of it: teased, frizzed, highlighted chimneys teetered above their venal little faces. They might also have considered investing in stockings or pantyhose, since their agile-looking but bristly legs were bare.

'How old are you guys?' Oprah asked, reeling at their cheek.

'Eighteen', chirruped the bimboes.

'Only in America', Oprah sighed. It was the truest thing she had said all morning.

Next she crossly curtailed an experiment which required members of the studio audience to answer the kind of question a dating service asks when inducting clients. Two teenage girls were press-ganged to their feet and made to rate their sex drive on a scale of 1 to 10. They were next asked to estimate – oh, to the nearest hundred – the number of sex partners they had so far tallied up. The girls were young and squirmingly awkward enough to abash even Oprah. 'I'm the President', she snapped, 'drop the question. They shouldn't have to answer that. Oftentimes on television, producers think of ideas which don't work in execution. *This* is one of those ideas.' A couple of producers, I imagine, scurried from the room to execute themselves.

Oprah's presidential edict reminds us who we are dealing with. Presidents – I mean those who merely preside over the United States – often begin speeches by addressing 'My fellow Americans.' Oprah is alert to the locution, although she dispenses with its pretence that presidents are only citizens, indistinguishable from their fellows. Bypassing the plurality of voters, she speaks directly to the personified country. After a 1993 programme in which she and her team of therapists arbitrated a dispute among five feuding sisters, she turned to the camera and breathtakingly said, 'This was a difficult show for me, America.' Her quiet assumption that an entire continent was tuned in to her is beyond presidential: it is prophetic.

The fat and folksy confidante of the early shows has become both a beauty and a mogul, grandly condescending to the poor, tired, muddled masses. When, in a programme about race relations, a white woman admitted that she would be uncomfortable about inviting a black person to a meal in her home, Oprah hoity-toitily shrugged and, raking in a few syndicated dollars in the time it took her to say the words, replied 'I could care – I could bring my own cup, you know what I mean?' And I dare say she would daintily hold it in one hand only.

Such asides reveal how the scenario has altered. The programme is now less a forum for the investigation of issues than an arena for Oprah's self-display. Her guests have no quarrel with this upstaging of their problems. The show's true function, after all, is to usher them into Oprah's presence. She has become totemic, magical: like medieval kings whose touch supposedly cured scrofula, the celebrity she possesses might well be contagious.

On the programme about the five feuding sisters – a mess of bickering, slander and threatened fisticuffs, with legal injunctions hurled around the studio like swear words – a therapist asked each of the sisters in turn why they had chosen to air their personal vendettas on television. What had they expected to gain from coming here today? What problem did they hope the exercise would solve? The eldest, a brutal termagant called Jackie, – accused, among other petty villainies, of pocketing money donated by the church for their mother's burial expenses – stared balefully at the therapist when her turn came. Then she said, with the growl of a dog behind a gate, 'I wanned ta meet Oprah'.

With all of bellicose, embittered America lining up to meet Oprah, who does Oprah want to meet? Celebrities exist in the closed, self-referring world of their fellows. Madonna recently complained that life had lost its some of its savour because she had 'met everybody': everybody, she meant, famous enough to be meetable. Oprah presumably wanted to meet Michael Jackson who – at least until his life began to unravel in the summer of 1993 with charges of molesting juveniles, followed by a medical breakdown – represented celebrity at its most astral and unreachable. His image was omnipresent, while he remained invisible. Since the tabloids knew nothing about him, they had to make stories up, and their fantastications counted as miracle-mongering, a lowly form of devotional literature which told of strange habits and hinted at supernatural powers. Chimps and cheetahs roamed through his house, they said. He slept in an oxygen chamber to frustrate the effects of ageing. If and when he died, he intended to have his body cryogenically stored, in readiness for immortality. Meanwhile he was preparing himself to become an angel by bleaching his skin a spooky, lunar shade of white.

Early in 1993 Michael Jackson invited Oprah to Neverland Ranch, his private paradise outside Santa Barbara. Oprah was agog about the global significance of the encounter. 'We are on live television all around the world!' she said. 'Today Michael will let the world know the truth.' Her demeanour was awestruck, as if she were covering St Antony's return from the desert or shouting up to St Simeon Stylites on top of his pole. 'You went inside yourself, you became a recluse', she reverently reminded Jackson. 'You have not spoken to the world for fourteen years.' All she meant was that he had not given a television interview during that time, and now he was only talking to her rather than addressing the assembled nations from a mountain top. But her wonderment was understandable: for a celebrity, not giving interviews is like succumbing to a harsh monastic vow, or undergoing some saintly self-mutilation.

Oprah tried to remain calm, and brandished her credentials as an investigator. She was anxious to establish that she had made no deals. Questions had not been vetted in advance; she had not promised to use

Jackson's honorary title, 'The King of Pop', conferred after an impromptu coronation by Elizabeth Taylor at an awards ceremony. Unfortunately, Oprah's excitement prompted her to an even dizzier excess of flattery than the one she was disavowing: 'I didn't get this interview by contractually agreeing to call you The King of Pop. I haven't called you The King of Pop once here today, have I? Anyway I frankly think that the King of Pop is too limiting a title for you....'

Jackson clearly had nothing to fear from this inquisition. Oprah's technique for eliciting truth is not concerned with facts but with feelings. The responses she wants are entirely subjective. With sycophantic tact, she broached the subject of the Jackson family romance as described by Michael's sister La Toya: the usual saga of violence and sexual maltreatment. 'Do you feel that some of the things she's been saying in her book are true?' purred Oprah. This is very different from asking if they are true; instead it meekly enquires about how Michael feels about her saying them. What is truth anyway, in a culture where who you are and what you have done matters less than how you are subjectively 'perceived' by others? America's swindlers and bomb-droppers are all the time declaring on television that they 'feel comfortable with' their actions or themselves. Oprah derived comfort from Jackson's comfortable reply: he loved his sister and he hadn't read the book. She forbore to acquaint him with its contents and then ask the question again.

In one area – the area in which she specializes – she did subject him to a grilling. The area in question was the groin. Oprah protested that the whole issue was unpalatable to her, but she felt obliged to raise it because 'the mothers in my audience are always asking me to ask you this: Why do you grab your crotch?'

Jackson, who obviously watches *The Oprah Winfrey Show*, knows that if you have a problem or a bad habit – shoplifting for instance – then someone or something else must be responsible. The devil makes you do it. 'It's the music that compels me to do it. I'm a slave to the rhythm.'

As the deputy of America's mothers, Oprah was not so easily appeased. At the end of the session she asked him for an undertaking about the future: 'Are you gonna lay off the crotch then?'

The moral stance could hardly be maintained. Censorious about the crotch-clutching, Oprah returned to the assault with more prurient motives. 'I'm gonna to ask you this, and I'm embarrassed to be asking it, but I'm gonna ask – are you a virgin?'

'How could you ask me that?' piped Jackson with sweet, ephebic indignation.

'I just wanna know', said Oprah. So, she must have thought, did America, and the world.

'I'm embarrassed', murmured Jackson by way of a reply. End of exchange: television talk is not about what people say but about how they squirm and blush while saying it. Oprah had managed to embarrass both Michael and herself, so the investigation could be declared a double success.

At this point Oprah, as if able to conjure up celebrities at will, called for someone to 'bring out' Elizabeth Taylor, who by chance was lurking in Michael Jackson's kitchen. On tottered Liz, her little legs in tight jeans valiantly supporting a large chest and an even larger hair-do. There had been some feigning of reluctance backstage: 'I know that you didn't want to be on camera at first', said Oprah. Liz oriented herself with surprising speed, and began to recite the litany of accomplishments or ailments which linked her to Michael: 'I was a child star at nine, I had an abusive father....' Stardom like this is shamanism. Elizabeth Taylor no longer acts; her job is to agonize on behalf of us all.

The show then moved to the private theatre where Jackson was in the habit of entertaining terminally ill children, who watched from hospital beds connected to intravenous drips. Oprah's inquiries became more solemn. 'I believe that everything in life happens for a reason', she told Jackson. She long ago settled the question of her own destiny. Now she proposed that – as recompense for his lost childhood – his reason for being lay in doing good to minors. He suffered little children to come unto him and succoured them with free candy and rides on his private carousel and dodgem circuit.

Jackson accepted her interpretation of his purpose here on earth. 'I try', he said, 'to imitate Jesus.' He added, with a modest twinkle, 'I'm not saying I *am* Jesus. But I try to follow his teaching – to be like children, to be as pure as children.'

Oprah then asked what it felt like to receive, through the roar of stadium crowds, the love and gratitude of the entire world.

He whispered his reply. Was it after all some internal radiance which had blanched his skin? 'I feel very blessed and honoured to be an instrument of nature that was chosen to give them that happiness.'

Oprah mused on the difference between his metaphysic and her own.

'Hmm, an instrument of nature....' In her own case, of course, the instrumentality belongs to 'the Universe'.

Jackson explained it to her again. 'I have been chosen as an instrument to give music and love and harmony to the world, to children of all ages.' Like nature playing through the strings of an Aeolian harp, divinity strummed him like an electric guitar.

In practical terms, this meant that his Heal the World Foundation was setting out systematically to heal the world. 'We're doing Heal LA right now. We're gonna go all over the world – we've done Sarajevo.' It was good to know that the besieged folk of that tragic city had been morally re-armed, made ready to cope with the next celebrity evangelist who visited: Susan Sontag arrived later in 1993 to explain Sarajevo's predicament to itself by staging *Waiting for Godot* among the rubble. Sontag was perhaps unaware that the city's wounds had already been bandaged by Jackson.

'You have this child-like aura about you', said Oprah. 'I see you with children and they play with you as if you were one of them. You relate to them so much.'

Jackson, combining the identities of Jesus Christ and Peter Pan, simpered prettily and led her off to the fun fair which he installed on his grounds in order to 'bring out the child that lives inside of everybody'. In obedience to the Messiah, Oprah regressed. At the end of the programme she removed her executive high heels and scampered off down a yellow-brick road, intending to treat her own inner child to a ride on the ferris wheel.

Oprah still insists that her shows are 'hour-long life-lessons' and 'learning experiences', but these days this is liable to mean – as on a recent programme when she was partnered by her tuxedoed fiancé – a quick course in the life-saving skills of ballroom dancing and hip hop. The morals extracted by Oprah at the end of the hour tend to be as platitudinous as the prairies. All she could salvage from the tawdry scandals and hurt feelings of the dating services episode was the warning 'Buyer beware'. The issues have dwindled to a pretext. The shows are about Oprah – her success, her diets, the good she does in the world and the divine superintendence which made it all possible. Debbie Di Maio believes that 'we help people take that first step towards changing their lives.' The paramount transformation in Oprah's own life – more mythologically potent than her rise from the Mississippi pigsty to the Lake Michigan condo – is her weight loss. Thinness for Americans is next to godliness, perhaps interchangeable with it. It functions as a physical remedy for psychological maladies: if you shed fat, your worries will evaporate like perspiration. When Oprah removed the wraps from her new physique, she became an icon of the metamorphosis she preaches.

But because all these mysteries are domiciled on television, which is an electronic supermarket, the life-lessons of *The Oprah Winfrey Show* are often parables of contented consumerism. 'We're a heart-oriented show', said Debbie Di Maio. 'Our interests are in the quality of life. Like recently we did one on gadgets everybody has at home and no-one knows how to use. We showed people how to programme their VCRs, what to do with their Cuisinarts.' The new and diviner you, once released from its coffin of flab, will also need to invest in a new wardrobe. Accordingly, the second show Oprah taped on my day in Chicago was a display of spring fashions. Lace jeans and suede shorts were paraded, together with ensembles in rubberized nylon.

Distantly mindful of people on budgets, Oprah complimented one of the designers: 'Your clothes are affordable, and that's a word we all like to hear. Isn't it outrageous what clothes cost?' (She was probably thinking of her own Ungaro- and Valentino-stocked closets.) 'How much does that one retail for?' She frowned sternly when told the price, although she once assured an interviewer 'I can afford *anything*', and at Christmas is liable to take loyal staff members to New York where she unleashes them in Bloomingdale's, goads them to grab all they can in an hour, and signs the credit-card slips with a generous flourish when the rampage is over.

The same designer was quizzed about fashion taboos. Is it still true that you can't wear white before Easter, and is patent leather strictly forbidden in winter? Oprah the liberator – the Martin Luther King of the kitchen sink, who set out to free us from our hang-ups, our hatreds and our chemical dependencies – was on this occasion merely liberating us from our fear of being unfashionable. But her divine self also had an interest in the subject. 'How about wearing high heels if you're short?' asked Oprah, who is very short.

The designer gave an answer which was the distillation of the talk show's therapeutic gospel: 'It's all in your confidence, the way you carry yourself. It's a matter of self-presentation.'

I remembered the fashion show when I happened to see a programme in December 1993, on which Oprah's guest was an Alabama quack who, having consulted the spiritual lore of the ancient Greeks, had rigged up a 'psychomantium' in his house. This, cheaper to furnish than one of Wilhelm Reich's orgone boxes, is simply a room with thick curtains containing an easy chair and a mirror. The bereaved, having paid a fee, are left alone in the darkened room, where the loved ones they have lost promptly reappear to them in the mirror. *The Oprah Winfrey Show* teaches you to be surprised by nothing: psychomantia apparently are big business, as plentiful in the Bible belt as hot tubs in California. A lady from Georgia had a decorating tip: why not convert that spare bedroom you seldom use into a salon for entertaining your dead relatives?

Nor, in god-starved contemporary America, is there any shortage of spirits eager to pay calls. Members of the audience vied with each other to report on sightings. One woman described a door blowing open of its own accord at a family reunion. Through it, she said, walked her grandfather, recently dead but determined not to miss the party. She knew it was him because he was wearing his favourite pair of old overalls.

'Wait a minute', said Oprah. 'If he's dead, what's he doing with overalls on?'

He always wore them, the woman insisted.

Oprah, who daily presides over a torrential Mississippi of gush, decided that she could not permit this particular nonsense to swirl past. Remonstrating with the woman, she explained the problem: 'I was with you until the overalls. But when you go on ahead, you're a spirit. You don't need no body any more, or no overalls.'

Then, addressing the audience, she made a cosmic detour: 'I see bodies just as outfits. So there's black outfits and Asian outfits and white outfits....' Applause signalled that there was no need for her to complete the thought, since everyone in the studio had followed her into outer space. She meant that the body itself is a pair of overalls. When you die, the spirit undresses. Back in the changing room, it tries on another outfit. In Oprah's world, all is one. Interior decoration overlaps with parapsychology, metaphysics and *haute couture* conjoin. Reincarnation happens inside your walk-in wardrobe. Surveying the models who paraded those slinky lace and rubber numbers on my day in Chicago, she perhaps was shopping for future lives.

At the end of each session, Oprah ritually farewells the flock to which she ministers. 'I'll say goodbye now', she tells the studio audience. 'I do it every day, just like after church. I don't sign autographs, because I can't do

160 – and y'all will all want extras for your friends! But I will shake your hands.' Audience co-ordinators co-ordinate the sheepish audience into a single line; people file past Oprah and shyly tell her that they love her. She has meanwhile clipped on a body mike, to amplify and record their whispered thanks: 'Don't forget you're still being filmed for our programme. We're going to use this in some promo spots.' Is this glad-handing the action of a concerned, gregarious minister or of a canny self-publicist?

The ambiguity is the point. It is from such snarled-up, opposing motives that Oprah and her show are created – the contradiction, for instance, between a television studio and a church; between passively watching television and changing your life; between handing out the telephone number of Shoplifters Anonymous and administering the sacraments; between feeling good and doing good. The show's guests contradict themselves by professing penitence while revelling, like Cindy, Chrissie and the ferocious Jackie, in their wickedness. Oprah's manner contradictorily merges sneaky, lewd inquisitiveness and altruism. She herself sums up her country's contradictory splicing of thinness and moral merit, of enrichment and spiritual evolution, of puritanism, capitalism and showbiz. Only – to quote Oprah – in America.

AMERICAN DREAMERS

EVERY HOUR THE PLANES AND TRAINS AND BUSES DISGORGE THEM INTO unimpressed, overstocked New York: the pilgrims and the seekers, kids from the dreary hinterland who long for the city to realize their dreams, or at least to recognize their existence. Some are driven by a creative itch. For others, their sole creation is themselves, and they announce their arrival by 'giving attitude', as they say, to the blasé metropolis, imagining their names on the neon signs along Broadway or writing themselves into the tabloid headlines.

One of these seekers came to New York in the mid-1960s with the usual exorbitant desire for fame or else infamy, and the usual meagre advantages: the son of a Jewish grocer from Worcester, Massachusetts, who had nothing to recommend him but a law degree, a slick tongue and a large endowment of the above-mentioned 'attitude'. His name was Aaron Richard Golub. Now, having swallowed the ethnic Aaron and coughed it up as a discreet initial, he is rich, successful and, on the global island of Manhattan, famous, belonging to the city's clan of celebrities who – like Donald Trump or the chiselling hotelier Leona Helmsley or the junk-bond merchant Michael Milken – are celebrated not for their achievements but for their swank, their swagger, their bad behaviour and their unrepentant self-esteem.

Golub is a loud-mouthed, slangily eloquent trial lawyer whose cases cluster at the tackier end of show business. He defended the photographer who sold unauthorized nude snaps of a pubescent Brooke Shields, and represented Ken Russell when the proprietor of *Penthouse,* Bob Guccione, sued Russell for defaulting on a contract to make a soft-porn film-version of *Moll Flanders;* he prosecuted William Hurt on behalf of the actor's common-law wife, and after losing the case he famously or infamously claimed that the female judge was hostile to the plaintiff because she had a crush on Hurt.

For Golub, law is one of the performing arts. In the courtroom, he dresses and accessorizes to kill, plots his lolling, shimmying moves across the floor like a choreographer, and is occasionally rebuked for flirting with jurors. To preserve what he calls his 'charismatic flashiness', he has recently had a facial tuck. In his spare time, he makes amateurish music videos, in which he plays a louche private eye, or a messianic preacher who liberates Sing Sing, or a cavorting shrink who lobotomizes a Hollywood star to administer shock therapy for greed.

Installed in a house on the Upper East Side, Golub has got what he came to New York for: he is a legend in his own mind. 'I've been doing my act for so long, I'm not sure it's an act any more', he says. 'Sometimes I wonder, when I'm walking round the house alone at night, What is this I've become?'

Another seeker – who has not yet managed to become what he dreams of being – arrived in New York in 1981, with the statutory desire for a life which would somehow be better than other lives. His name was David Hampton. The day after this young black man from Buffalo hit town, a gormless deb married the Prince of Wales and became the most visible and therefore the most celebrated person in the world. The moral of her ascent was not lost on Hampton. He had vaguely planned to 'pursue an acting and dancing career', even though, like Golub in his music videos, he possessed no discernible talent; but desperate measures would be necessary if the city were to take him at his own grandiose valuation.

He therefore transformed his creativity into confidence trickery, and with the aid of a purloined address book bluffed his way into various exclusive New York households, where he introduced himself as the son of Sidney Poitier. Found out, he spent nearly two years in prison for the imposture. Still, the act conferred stardom on him, because one of his victims told the story to the dramatist John Guare, who used the anecdote in a much-praised play, *Six Degrees of Separation*. Here the young hustler who passes himself off as Poitier's son is revered as a symbol of art, of the imagination's dazing advent in ordinary life; he ends as a martyr to the snobbishly proprietorial bourgeoisie. Unappeased by such homage, Hampton decided that Guare had stolen from him the commercial rights to his own life-story, and in 1992 he sued the dramatist for an alleged three hundred million dollars. Litigation represents the American dream switched to the fast-forward mode: riches arrive without having to be worked for, so long as you can invent a sufficiently expensive grievance. Hampton's lawyer, inevitably, was Golub.

Golub, who lost this case too, paid his client the heart-felt tribute of one huckster to another: 'Hampton's more imaginative than me. I may have developed this superstructure with my suits and my cuff links and my cowboy boots and the whole manner, but what he did is something else. He's like some errant weirdo writer who invented the character of Sidney Poitier's son, and Guare stole that from him.'

Weren't they both, I wondered, stealing from Poitier, who surely retains the right to invent his own sons?

Golub overruled the objection. 'Guare's just like a cheat in a school exam. He threw a sheet of tracing paper over David Hampton's life. The New York courts have never recognized that an individual should be able to exploit his own story, so I have to change the law in this matter. I've gotta be creative too.'

The alliance of client and lawyer was predestined, because both Golub and Hampton are pretenders, spoiled artists who – unable to make art – conceive of life itself as a performance. Golub apologetically concedes that 'civil litigation is basically about the exchange of money. You've got a bunch of cheap defendants on the stand who don't want to make out a bank draft. A lawyer is an economic catalyst. We move the money around.' Hampton relied on Golub to make him rich, and in return would – if he had won – have made Golub richer. Nevertheless, more was involved here than profiteering: the affinity went deeper. Golub's notion of the courtroom as a theatre of verbal virtuosity where your version of the truth will prevail if you present it with enough histrionic energy was matched by Hampton's vision of society as an arena of deceit and sub-terfuge where you will prevail if the persona you fabricate for yourself is ostentatious and audacious enough.

Both men are illusionists. 'The courtroom is a stage for the truth', said Golub, 'but there's truth and then there's legal truth, and here the truth is what comes out in the presentation of a case. You've got to prepare, rehearse, put on a show. We even audition jurors; it's not like England, where the barristers have to keep their distance. There's no difference between my presenting David Hampton's case in court and Barnum and Bailey's circus presenting some act in the ring. It's all about getting a jury to suspend disbelief. Belief is mechanical. You can manipulate it if the details are plausible. That's why I like using props – I mean exhibits, things the jury can handle. That way they know they're taking part in a play.'

This does not sound much like the patriotic creed of Superman, who touched down on the grubby soil of Gotham City to fight for truth, justice and the American way, but Golub was unconcerned. 'Is it justice or not? So what if it isn't? David Hampton could be Hermann Goering or Attila the Nun for all I care. You just have to leave it to my artistic devices.'

For Hampton, truth was equally relative. He could lie with impunity because he knew that in New York social credentials are never checked. Every guest at a cocktail party is protectively clad in some act or other, reinvented with the aid of hairdressers and clothes designers and plastic surgeons and elocution teachers; the tacit accord is that you will not challenge my claims about myself for fear that I might challenge yours. Hampton convinced himself that there was justice of a kind in his masquerade, claiming that his victims were being punished for their credulity and vanity – in this case, their lust for a vestigial association with Hollywood, and for bit parts in a film supposedly directed by Poitier which Hampton distributed among the WASPs who fed and lodged him. The con man is a twisted moralist, just as the shyster is a warped philosopher whose aim is to demonstrate the slipperiness of truth.

Of course there is the gap of a generation between Golub and Hampton, with an intervening deterioration of the American values they simultaneously appeal to and parody. Golub is a traditionally industrious meritocrat, who hauled himself out of the grocery shop by studying. 'Mostly the law is just about pushing papers around', he says. 'It's all research. In order to gain your power of persuasion, you have to suffer pain.'

In the new world to which Hampton belongs, the painful work can be dispensed with, because graduation to stardom should be instantaneous, automatic. The requisite is neither intelligence nor talent but skill at touting a product which is yourself. Hampton admires the self-merchandising of Andy Warhol and Madonna; he was viciously gleeful because, after attempting to crash a party, he rated an entry in the fatuous, ephemeral Warhol diaries, whereas Guare, who merely happens to be a writer of distinction, did not get a mention. He is also symptomatic of a new American morality in the way he turns disgrace to his own advantage. Criminality is a fast lane to fame, with book contracts and movie deals almost guaranteed after the sentencing; notoriety is the nocturnal side of the celebrity everyone covets. Hampton may have gone to prison, but he qualified as what he calls a 'celebrity inmate', sequestered from the common herd of malefactors with other criminal stars like the mass-murderer Son of Sam and Mark Chapman, who shot John Lennon.

Despite Golub's brashness and Hampton's larcenous cheek, there is something wistful and touching about both of them. They are authentic American dreamers, excluded creatures who first imagined a life for themselves and then set about attaining it. 'My family was poor', says Golub with a shudder. 'If you don't have a rich father who leaves you a company to run, what do you do? I wasn't a great athlete either. I managed to grow to five feet ten inches, though I always say I'm five eleven; actually I'm pissed off I didn't make six feet. What assets did I have? Only a good speaking voice, which I cultivated. So I began to concentrate on learning words, especially big words which no one used in my family – words like conflagration. That was the quiz-show era on TV. Polysyllables were a proof of smartness. I was attracted to law because I thought I could dazzle people with language.' The adolescent Golub's work on his word-power is pathetically reminiscent of Jay Gatz's timetable for promoting himself to greatness and living up to his own invented character, Gatsby: Fitzgerald's hero allocated one hour a day to practising elocution, and also resolved to 'read one improving book or magazine'.

The motive which goaded Golub was emulation. 'I have a theory that everyone in America chooses their job because they've seen someone doing it on TV. I used to go down to the basement and watch Robert Taylor playing a lawyer in a movie called *Party Girl* – very sleek and elegant, telling the jury some sob story about the pocket-watch his dying father gave him. I even got myself a pocket-watch, and it used to be one of my great moves in court. I can't use it any more because everyone knows about it. And as a matter of fact the story about Robert Taylor isn't true, though I've told it so often I almost believe it. I wasn't watching *Party Girl* in the basement, I was fucking the babysitter. She only got four and a half bucks an hour, she deserved a bonus.'

Hampton's motive, more disturbingly, was envy. He saw, on display through the high, barred windows of Fifth Avenue, a life he could never earn, and could only penetrate for a while by fast-talking dishonesty. He has said that 'the most dangerous person on the face of the earth is someone who is poor, smart and hungry. When you're poor, you want for more. And when you're smart, you devise ways to get it.' He too did his homework: like Gatsby and Golub he changed his diction, learning the dandified languor of the privileged, and was offended when he saw

Guare's play because the black actor who played him was too demotic; he made a field trip to Harvard and memorized the lay-out of the campus where he claimed to be studying, like Gatsby fantastically enrolling himself at Oxford. The force of his alienated envy was positively nuclear, as the analogies he used when explaining himself made clear. He likened his hoodwinking of the rich to Saddam Hussein's annexation of bloated Kuwait, and said about the aftermath of his prison term, 'when a catastrophe like this happens in life, you have to deal with it diplomatically, the way the United Nations does.'

In this society of simulations, where the tenure of reality is terrifyingly lax, everyone has a fanciful alter ego, a fictional model on which the self can base its performance. David Hampton's was Sidney Poitier (chosen because Harry Belafonte already had a son, and Sammy Davis junior was too gaudy for his name to ensure access to East Side salons), just as John Guare's, in a work of fiction which is parasite on this fictional incident in real life, was David Hampton. To begin with, Richard Golub's may or may not have been Robert Taylor, depending on whether you believe it when he says he was lying. Nowadays his object of emulation, curiously enough, is his adversary Bob Guccione, who lives on the same block of East 64th Street in a Beaux-Arts mansion complete with swimming pools, prowling mastiffs and photo studios for the exposure of nubile flesh.

Golub has tangled with Guccione and his corporate lawyers on so many cases that the man has become an obsession with him: 'Sometimes I feel when I'm free on weekends that I should go over and cross-examine Guccione. I'm suing him again at the moment. We claim that The Gooch stiffed one of his Playmate Pets – he never gave her a car she was promised. Do I ever see him outside of court? Well, The Gooch has not invited me over for linguini in quite a while. It could be the water's not boiled yet. No, I know why it is. He's having his hair rewoven, or maybe it's his forehead that's being lowered. Don't you love that hair of his? It's a low-pile carpet of low quality. The thing about The Gooch is that he's from New Jersey, poor guy. So's Sinatra, and Springsteen too. These rough-round-the-edges characters who've made it big are always going on about how they're self-made men blah blah blah.... Who needs it?' Golub, however, appears to need it, and behind his animosity I suspect there is a covert admiration for Guccione's lounge-lizard sleekness and his shrewd translation of economic power into erotic success.

Celebrity counts as an aphrodisiac, and Golub – who believes that 'you've gotta be sexy in court, very angular, so you appeal to all the senses; you've gotta *attract* those jurors' – shivers with narcissistic delight at his own allure. While we were talking, he was telephoned by a woman who had plagued his answering service at three in the morning. 'I get a lotta these broads bothering me', he yawned. 'One of them planted a tree in Israel for me. I just got the document to say so yesterday. Another one sends me gifts every afternoon – candy, gum, brownies. I need a food taster in this house.'

He took the call from the importunate unknown, luxuriating in his own lewd, husky change of vocal register and paraphrasing the woman's contributions for my benefit as he went along. 'Do I remember you? Yeah, I did live on 83rd Street, but that was twenty years ago, when I was married. Did I fuck you when I was married? You wish? So listen, what's your name? Alison, how come you're calling me after seven years? Because I'm so handsome? Actually I've gotten very old and ugly, I wear a lotta makeup'. At this point, Golub bared teeth which shone like a row of footlights, and ran a casual hand through an underbush of wavy hair which endows him with the extra inch of height he always thought he deserved. 'What are you doing now, Alison? Tearing your hair out and having sex? Oh I get it, having *fits*. What are you – brunette, tall, short, fat, skinny? How old are you? You sound to me about fifty-eight. I'm forty-nine, you might be too old for me. Why not come on over? I'll check you out, see if I remember you. OK?'

He hung up, and gradually worked his voice back from the nether regions to which it had plunged. Upstairs, awaiting Alison on the floors above a lobby where leopard skin climbs around the walls and ferally invades a sofa, is Golub's private pornotopia, as lurid as the decor in Guccione's *Penthouse* centrefolds: a bedroom with a frieze of copulating satyrs, a bathroom with a painting of a steamy seraglio. Afterwards there might be breakfast in a kitchen where the cabinet sprouts mammaries and you hang an apron on the prong of an erect penis. America always promised the poor that it would make their dreams come true. To the rich, it additionally promises that they can live out their fantasies. Hampton likewise understood that sex is a negotiable currency, and obtained the address book which was his passport to the East Side from a preppy with whom he slept; in Guare's play he strips in exchange for information about the families whose names are listed, removing one of his garments for each biography which the boy who owns the book surrenders.

Because Golub has demonstrated that the truth consists merely of big, bogus words and Hampton that society consists of the falsity and fraud which go by the name of good manners, unreality adheres to both of them, even haunting them. Hence Golub's existential discomfort in the small hours: 'I used to think, Wait a minute, I'm just this little kid, the grocer's son. What·is this glitzy world I'm in? But now I've grown into the person I used to play at being.' Hampton, morally blither, escaped from blame in a paper-chase of forged and discarded identities. In 1991 he was found out while conning the business manager of a theatre, claiming to be the actor who played David Hampton playing Sidney Poitier junior in John Guare's play. Warned, the victim summoned the police. Hampton's supremely nonchalant response was to deny that he knew the man who filed the complaint and to suggest that he had been ripped off by someone impersonating Hampton the celebrated impersonator: 'You know, I had this trouble before.'

On his staff, Golub retains a figure as fictitious and outlandish as Hampton or as Golub himself, whose function is apparently to keep him vestigially attached to a truth which cannot be reduced to verbal games and a reality which cannot be reduced to cheating images. This is his butler, a blissfully smiling, vertiginously turbaned Sikh called Mr K.

Without seeming to displace any air, Mr K glides into the room, offers to be shaken a hand moist with sandalwood oil, presses his palms together in a solemn bow, and in his melodic Indian accent begins a litany of praise to his demi-divine employer: 'Oh sir, I exist only because of my master's qualities of heart and mind. He is a good master who has eighty suits and forty-five pairs of shoes made from leather. The taps in my master's bathroom are of gold.'

Mr K makes it sound as if he is a butler in some vulgarly lush Muhammadan paradise. He is Golub's straight-man and kicking-post, his reliably obsequious in-house flatterer; but he is also, as a holy fool, the embodiment of his master's residual conscience. In Golub's latest music video, Mr K plays Freud. He serves Golub a squashy human brain on a silver salver, bedded on lettuce leaves. Golub then steals Mr K's mind and identity, and the befuddled Sikh ends up as the internee of a grim Gothic asylum in Golub's home town of Worcester. 'First he shrinks my brain,' explains Golub, 'then I shrink his. I like that kind of role-reversal.

When I defended Ken Russell against The Gooch, I was the director, I gave him orders. Now in the video I let Mr K do that to me.'

Golub affects not to know how long Mr K has been on his team. 'It was a misty day, and along came Mr K – you get the rhyme? A blue turban kind of floated round the corner. He's just exponentially around. He seems to live here, but he has no assigned room. Do you want the truth? OK, I killed the real Mr K years ago, this one's an imposter.'

'It is as you say, sir', said Mr K, beaming transcendently.

'Actually K,' said Golub, 'it was a mistake to cast you as Freud. You don't look Viennese. You look more like Malcolm X today.'

'Oh sir, that is your gracious outlook.'

'K, who was Malcolm X?'

'A very great millionaire sir. I have heard you speak of him.'

He meant Malcolm Forbes, the elderly motorcycle-riding tycoon who briefly, before he died of AIDS, had Elizabeth Taylor as a pillion passenger. Celebrities constitute a repertory company, and are always turning up in one another's lives: Forbes, curiously, had an incidental walk-on in the fictional life of Hampton. Caught in bed with another young man by one of his hosts, Poitier junior forestalled criticism by coolly introducing his pick-up as Malcolm Forbes's son.

'He's somewhere in the ether', marvelled Golub. 'He's not in the same material universe as the rest of us. Listen to this. K, who is Mick Jagger?'

'Sir, Miss Jagger is an honourable lady, devoted to you, very, very blindly behind you.'

'That's Bianca he's talking about. She's my client, he goes round there on errands. He's never heard of Mick. K, who are the Rolling Stones?'

'That, sir, is a very old true English maxim. A rolling stone will not gather moss, oh my goodness no.'

'You know about Shakespeare though, don't you K?'

'Indeed sir, a great bard, bloom of the word and priest of us all....'

'K, don't you have to go to the post office, or somewhere?'

Exiting, K clasped my hand and begged me, 'Do a good justice to my master, sir. He will bring the reality before the judges, his intelligence will reveal the truth. It is, oh sir, his uprightness.'

'Sikhs', shrugged Golub, and threw me a tissue to dry the unctuous sandalwood oil. Though massaged by the flattery, he seemed astonished at the innocence of one in whose eyes he could stand for truth and justice, not the meretricious arts of packaging and presentation. 'They're completely unselfish. My father was like that, a Jewish Sikh. He didn't care about making money. If his customers were hungry, he gave them the groceries. Hey, maybe I'm a secret Sikh myself. Some of my clients never pay me.' The wisecrack covered Golub's discomfiture at the thought of generosity and goodness, and of a mental world so far from New York that the name of a gilded nonentity like Bianca Jagger could mean exactly what it was worth: that is, nothing.

Then, the turban having dematerialized, Golub caught sight of another domestic drudge in an adjoining room: 'Dora, what are you carrying? Why are you always buying toilet rolls? How come there's so much bullshit going down in this house?'

On the corner of Madison Avenue, among the throng of poseurs and predators, of would-be artists and self-sanctified monsters, a homeless man who no longer hopes that the city will notice him has bedded down in a coffin-shaped canvas hutch with walls made of milk crates, outside a jeweller's window full of Cartier sparklers and iridescent Lalique vases. Along the block, the pleasure palace of Guccione faces Golub's house with its library of law books, its gallery of fetishes and its plethora of toilet rolls. The Roman empire is in its last, lunatic, decadent days.

AMERICA THE MUSCULAR

PRIMITIVE MAN MUST HAVE IMAGINED SOMETHING LIKE IT, WHEN peering out of the cave in which he cowered: giants rearing against the sky, ogres swaggering through the swamps; the crunch of bones; the howls of the vanquished, and the unholy war-cries of the victors. The perpetual clashes and combats of monsters make up our earliest myths.

Now, once more, the myths have taken on flesh – an armour-plating of it, beefed up by steroids and toasted by tanning machines – and the primordial monsters waddle out again to snap one another's spines and sit on one another's heads. The race of mastodons is not extinct. Among the current crop are Animal and Hawk, thugs with faces scarified by red paint and collars of spikes, who team up as the Legion of Doom; Hacksaw Jim Duggan, a bulging-bellied oaf who totes as his weapon a plank ripped from a tree he probably uprooted with his bare hands; and Jake 'The Snake' Roberts, whose neckwear is a python. These are some of the bogys invented and exhibited by the World Wrestling Federation. They criss-cross the United States, with monthly stops at Madison Square Garden in New York, and appear twice each weekend on television. In London, during their European tours, they often bludgeon each other at the Royal Albert Hall. It must look as if the dinosaurs had lumbered up the hill from the Natural History Museum, to stage a last atavistic bout before evolution dispensed with them.

Each match in a World Wrestling Federation event is the re-enactment of a myth, dramatizing the fears of the audience and choreographing terminal battles between good and evil or – since it amounts to the same thing – between America and whoever its current enemy happens to be.

A Hercules in a classical breastplate of plastic worsts a heathen rowdy called Warlord. The Nasty Boys, two punk bullies in the leather coats of storm troopers, slobber into the ring like bikers invading a peaceable suburb, and are beaten back by twin archetypes of Americana: the ursine logger Duggan with the length of wood, and a Marine with a pugnacious, protuberant jaw who goes by the name of Sergeant Slaughter. Slaughter has in recent years trounced the Iron Sheik from Iran and an Iraqi school-friend of Saddam Hussein who wrestled as Colonel Mustafa. The national stereotype he pulverizes these days is a Japanese man-mountain called Kato (who prudently wears a stocking over his head, because in this theatre of fakery he is more than likely a Pole or a Puerto Rican). Slaughter's bouts are accompanied by a rhythmical massed chant from the audience: 'U-S-A! U-S-A! U-S-A!'

Inimical values are righteously thrashed. A character known as The Model minces out, clad in pink briefs and a matching bow tie. His pecs play peekaboo inside a cutaway tuxedo jacket. He preens, prances, squirts the air with a spray can of cologne, and is summarily humbled by the Texas Tornado, a cross-eyed simpleton who personifies American virility and has a map of the Lone Star State embroidered on the seat of his shorts.

This is a factory where, between hyperbolic grunts and groans, you can watch old myths being revised and new ones created. Among the WWF's so-called 'superstars' is a necrophile from a horror movie whose stage name is Undertaker. His home, the company's publicists insist, is Death Valley, California. He stalks out with a creaking Karloffian gait, his face ashen and his eyes staring. His theme tune is an organ threnody, and he is attended by a manager who brandishes an urn reputedly containing the cinders of previous opponents. He does not need to wrestle. He frightens victims to the floor and then, having paralysed them, lays them out as lovingly as a mortician.

On the night early in 1992 when I saw Undertaker at work in Madison Square Garden, he was crossing a loser's hands on his chest and tenderly closing his eyes when someone in the audience yelled 'Hey, it's Jeffrey Dahmer!' Dahmer, the cannibal who had oral sex with severed heads and stored frozen strips of meat cut from the lovers he murdered, was in court that week in Milwaukee. His trial was being televised, so he too had become a superstar. When the man in the audience suddenly identified him with Undertaker, I felt I was present at one of those inspired, unexpected moments of synthesis by which popular culture operates, fusing different narratives to renew a myth and plucking characters from the surreal reality of America to fit the fantasy. I expect the WWF to have a wrestler named after Dahmer one day soon, who will make a meal of the partners he knocks out.

Popular culture is a collaborative venture, allowing everyone – the heckler who invoked the name of Dahmer, for instance – to be an artist: these tournaments are a species of Pop art, comic strips which have come noisily to life. The WWF's most celebrated performer, Hulk Hogan, is the trademarked property of Marvel Comics Inc, and the man with the jutting jaw who plays Sergeant Slaughter in his earlier career impersonated GI Joe for a toy company. Cartoons unfurl as endlessly as medieval sagas or as reels of film, with their eternal antagonists fighting it out indefinitely inside their boxes and always arriving at a cliff-hanger when they get to the edge of the page. These are modern myths churned out for mass consumption, and so are the orgies staged by the WWF.

Because the kicks and punches never connect, the violence is all pretence, supplied by sound effects, as in the paintings of Roy Lichtenstein where bursts of harmless gunfire and fatuous explosions which do no damage are signalled by silently stentorian capital letters: POW! WHAM! BOOM! The Pop sculptor Red Grooms designs similar soft tragedies. In the installation called *Ruckus Manhattan*, subway riders are sliced in half when the train doors shut on them, but they can bounce back to wholeness moments later because their bodies are made of foam rubber. The same comical logic is built into the souvenirs hawked to young fans by the WWF. You can buy a replica of Hacksaw Jim Duggan's menacing length of timber: to ensure that the kiddies don't use it to brain their playmates, it too is made of weightless, frivolous foam.

The wrestlers, whose personae are as excessive as their musculature, carry their symbolic burden with the knowing archness characteristic of Pop art. They are not to be confused with that rival and equally mythical figure, the boxer, who fights in deadly earnest. American popular culture venerates the boxer as an existential underdog, using his fists to wound an indifferent world into noticing him. The sport has its own theatricality: the character of a boxer has been a virtuoso turn for a series of Method-trained actors, from John Garfield in *Body and Soul* to Marlon Brando in *On the Waterfront* and Robert de Niro in *Raging Bull,* because a desperate masochism is common to the sport and the acting technique. These boxers wear out their brutalized bodies in pursuit of some precious ideal, some tenuous notion that their lives matter. 'I could,' as Brando brokenly sobs, 'have been a contender.' Even Sylvester Stallone in the first of his *Rocky* films – long before he megalomaniacally proposed that the Cold War should be settled in the boxing ring between himself and a blond nominee of the evil empire – paid tribute to this self-improving idealism by having Rocky Balboa train on the steps outside the Philadelphia Museum of Art.

The wrestlers have no such sweaty aspirations. They lack the integrity and authenticity which comes from actually being hurt. They may not be so insulated by blubber as Japanese sumo wrestlers, whose bulk prevents physical contact and turns a match into a polite, formulaic encounter like the tea ceremony, but their bodies, by contrast with the boxer's battling athleticism, are laughably inflated, even effeminate. 'Bitch tits!' jeered someone in my row at Madison Square Garden when The Model jiggled his pectorals. 'Steroid queen!' added someone else.

They are invested with grand ideals, but they wear these as costumes, like the map emblazoned across the buttocks of the Texas Tornado, and the values they supposedly embody can be switched to and fro with whimsical, cynical ease. In 1990, for instance, Sergeant Slaughter deserted the flag, misled – according to the 'storyliners' in the WWF, who move the adipose puppets around – by Mustafa and bribed by gifts from Saddam Hussein. The timing was inconvenient. No sooner had he changed sides than the Gulf War broke out, which made his treason seem dangerously plausible. The offence was all the more heinous because Slaughter, before his present life as a cartoon and his previous existence as a toy, had been in the Marine Corps. The WWF surrounded his home with security guards in case his fans sought revenge. No one torched his house, but – rather more alarmingly – sales of Slaughter memorabilia (camouflage pyjamas, uniform hats for tiny heads) faltered. The WWF's myth-making had only too successfully erased the difference between art and life. Slaughter was abruptly ordered to see his error, and to vouch for his patriotism he made an expiatory tour of army camps and veterans' hospitals; he was photographed saluting the graves of the fallen – with his jaw set in stoical concrete – at the Arlington National Cemetery in Washington.

Capriciously shuttled between good and evil, the wrestlers suffer from the same moral mutability as characters in television soap operas. Blake Carrington's son Stephen in *Dynasty* began as a homosexual drunkard, then was gratuitously cured of both kinks because viewers could not 'identify' with them. (He later reverted, when the imperative was to keep those listless viewers interested.) Despite their vast bulk, Slaughter and his colleagues are meekly mortgaged to those who write the scripts, who in turn obey the market researchers. In themselves they mean nothing: their vacant faces make them obliging screens on to which we project emotions which they then counterfeit.

At Madison Square Garden, therefore, the only violence is verbal, and it comes from the audience. A harried mother, haranguing a brat who demanded hot dogs, had taken lessons in child care from the Nasties. 'Shuddup already,' she snarled, 'or I'll beat the shidouttaya.' Beside me sat a small girl dressed in WWF regalia: a lime-green head band honouring Macho Man Randy Savage and an acid orange Hulk Hogan T-shirt, with one of Hacksaw Jim's featherweight cudgels gripped in her little fist. All night, her young lungs maintained a barrage of invective.

She warmed up with the nerdy announcer: 'Quit, you blabbermouth. Get off, you bald-headed bozo.' Then she disqualified a referee: 'Boo, you make me puke, bug head.' When The Model wiggled on, she let fly a paragraph of homophobic hatred: 'You crapola, you fag, you sissy boy! You stink, you weenie!' She egged on Texas Tornado for the kill: 'C'mon Texas, kick his butt. Destroy this creep. Sit on his face. Eat him for breakfast.' When Texas got the dandy's arm in a lock, she yelped like an infantile psychopath: 'Break it. Just break it. Jeez Tex, I think he wet his pants.' Her father feebly added 'Kick him in the balls', and the girl roared in triumph, 'He don't have none!'

Kato excited her to an all-purpose xenophobic frenzy. 'You Japanese freak! You Ching Chow Chinee monkey!' So did the arrival of the Canadian Mountie, who marched out in regimental gear, brandishing a cattle prod: 'Take your stick and suck it. Ram it up your butt.' The Mountie's opponent was a Neanderthal meatloaf with golden ringlets and cobalt blue briefs, whose soubriquet is Sid Justice – or Shit Justice as the Mountie put it. Sid pumped up with frightening ferocity. His skin seemed transparent, a fraying membrane stretched too tight over his distended muscles. The pint-sized virago for once became reverently hushed, and as Sid laid waste to the representative of Canada she repeated a mantra: 'Justice,' she said over and over, 'will be served.' For Jake the Snake she turned up the volume again: 'Jake, you're a faggot, you and your corny snake. Your mother wears pink underwear. On your knees, eat my crap.'

At the end of the evening, still not hoarse, she tweaked her father's cuff and demanded, 'Dad, is this live? Are we on TV? What channel will we be on?' Her animosity had also been an act; her barracking was as mythically specious as the rest of the spectacle.

The myths are manufactured thirty miles north of Madison Square Garden, far from its raucous revelry and its stench of rancid frankfurters. WWF has its corporate headquarters – a glistening glass box with a marble foyer and corridors carpeted in plush purple – at Stamford, Connecticut. Stamford is in New York's affluent commuter belt, and WWF has banks and insurance companies as its neighbours.

This incongruity is deliberate, as one of the nattily suited Executive Vice-presidents pointed out: 'Our owner, Vince McMahon, had this vision. And what he saw in his vision, Peter, was this – he saw that wrestling could be an entertainment product.'

Here a pause was inserted, allowing me to react to the Edisonian brilliance of the idea igniting in Vince's head. I spent the interval, however, brooding on that hateful word 'product', a corporate euphemism for whatever you happen to be selling.

When he judged that my pulse rate was back to normal, the Vice-president went on. 'Mr McMahon wanted to get wrestling out of the smoky small-town arenas, get the guys into costume, give them theme tunes, and put them on TV. And he knew that if we were gonna convince people that we weren't gangsters chomping cigars, we had to position ourselves in the media centre. So here we are, right in the middle of corporate America, just as dedicated to our product as IBM or Toyota or General Motors. Of course we also needed to get ourselves an image. What this building tells you is that we're a well-oiled, functioning corporate structure, marketing a product with a family demographic. We're a business that plans to be around. Hey, we're not Ninja Turtles! Many weekends we hold inspirational seminars in the building: if you sign on you get nutritional advice from our Dr Squat and a video of yourself training with your favourite World Wrestling Federation superstar. We've got Macintosh 2FX in our art department. The gym here is high tech, state of the art. No, the wrestlers don't use it, they don't live around here. It's for us, so we can tone up after a day behind the desk.'

Vince the Visionary contemplates the results of his brainwave from a corner suite overlooking Long Island Sound, silvery in the winter sun. Outside is Titans' Terrace, available for barbecues. The passages are decorated with posters of the Federation's grimacing geeks, but the only people you meet are yuppies with degrees in merchandising and oral communications. From inside the glass box, even the wrestlers are seen as corporate clones: 'They live just like regular professionals. They travel round the country, arrive at an airport, check into a hotel, then go to the gym and work out. The gym is their office.'

Here, in the laboratory of myth which the WWF calls 'our talent-booking department', images are invented which the wrestlers slavishly abide by until altered political circumstances or commercial trends prompt a revision. 'These guys', said the three-pieced Veep, 'are our product. They're our property, our copyrighted characters. We own them, and we have design approval over them. They can't change their hair-style without asking us. We reserve creative control.'

In America reality has been subsumed by the image, and imagery is negotiable for cash. In the week I was at Madison Square Garden, an ethical controversy was stirred up by the decision of Michael Jordan to prevent the National Basketball Association from exploiting his image. Contending that he was the sole owner of that image, Jordan planned to license it exclusively to Nike. He then earned some twenty million dollars a year from the sale of sneakers and sportswear bearing his face or name; the deal with Nike was intended to deprive the NBA of its share in the profits. David Hampton's case against John Guare – who in Richard Golub's view had 'thrown a sheet of tracing paper over my client's life' – raised the same issues: to whom does your image legally belong, and (more importantly) how much is it worth? The wrestlers enjoy no such recourse. Their images are monopolized by the corporation which created them. For all their belligerent posturing, they are robots controlled by Visionary Vince and his slick team of marketers.

I discovered the extent of this creative control when I spoke to some of them backstage at Madison Square Garden. 'Our guys give their interviews in character,' a publicist advised me. Nevertheless, confronted first with a surly black called Virgil, I made the mistake of asking what he had done before he became a superstar.

'I bodyguarded,' glowered Virgil. 'I guarded some very famous bodies. I was one of the greatest bodyguards in the en-tire world. You better believe it.'

I was going to ask for references, but thought better of it. In any case, the publicist, who insisted on sitting in as chaperone, interrupted: 'That's real life Virgil's talking about. Peter, I told you the guys don't like to get into that stuff. Let me update you on Virgil's character.' He did so while the disaffected subject simmered in silence. 'Virgil here used to be valet to our Million Dollar Man. He cleaned house for him, he made his reservations, he carried his bags...'

'Yeah, and checked his chicks out', interjected Virgil. 'Like Mike Tyson, ya know what I mean?' Like the mention of Dahmer, this was another opportunistic insertion of reality into the myth: that same week Tyson the boxer was on trial in Indianapolis, accused of raping an entrant in the Miss Black America beauty contest. Popular culture has a genius for synthesis, discerning patterns in randomness. It's also worth noticing how many American celebrities end their careers – or, like Hampton, begin them – in court.

The publicist over-rode Virgil's impromptu aside. 'Like I was saying, Peter, Virgil had his uprising. He rebelled against the Million Dollar Man. He saw he was being maltreated, and he went against tyranny. The fans love to see a victim get even. Are you familiar over there in England with the idea of the morality play?'

By now Virgil had tired of hearing the story of his supposed life told for him, and was ready for another insurrection. He trumpeted the phrases he had been taught, taunting his anxious monitor: 'I was blinded by the mean green. Oh yeah. I let money buy me. How 'bout that? But my dignity got hurt. Ouch! Ain't no-one gonna take my dignity away. No, sir, no way! And now I'm gonna show the people – get this – that there's more than money in the world. That Million Dollar Man was the eighties. I'm the man of the nineties. You hear what I say? Hey, you betta write that down.' He flexed his fists, causing his biceps to haemmorrhage. I took dictation.

Virgil was hustled from the room and replaced by the ingenuous Sergeant Slaughter, who has fewer qualms about exemplifying his assigned image.

'There's a lot of me in the role. I was a drill instructor in the Marines. Being Sergeant Slaughter is a twenty-four-hour job, because of what I represent. Yes, it's an even bigger responsibility than being GI Joe. I got death threats when I was in league with the Iraqis, but I'm back with the USA now. They also love me in Europe, especially in the England area. I was invited to the White House three different times during the Reagan years. The first time I went to do a Salute to him. There were two hundred celebrity sports stars there, and after we took the group picture he called me over and said "Sergeant Slaughter, I've always wanted to meet you. I'm a big fan of yours." '

It must have been a piquant encounter, between two figures who had given up trying to separate invidious reality from the fictions which were second nature to them both. The Sergeant – whose friends have learned to call him Sarge rather than Bob (the name he was born with) – believes his spurious biography; Reagan likewise used to expatiate on his non-existent combat experience during World War II by reciting the plots of the movies he stayed in Hollywood to make during those years.

Advising me to keep my chin up and my chest out, Sergeant Slaughter dismissed himself, and Macho Man Randy Savage was ushered in.

The Macho Man conceals a profoundly pockmarked face and a concussed nose beneath the brim of a neon stetson. With fringes flapping from his leatherette tunic and green leggings, he looks like an anachronistic, shell-shocked hippy. Perhaps he is still bemused by the reversals his creative controllers have forced on him. He used to be a bad guy, an abusive loudmouth, but has recently been bundled on to the side of the angels. To solemnize his conversion, he has married his manager, a sequinned brunette known as Miss Elizabeth. In titleless America, to be referred to as Miss is the equivalent of a peerage. Miss Elizabeth, I was awe-inspiringly informed, is 'the First Lady of the WWF.'

I began by asking Macho Man what I thought was an innocent question: where was he born?

Instead of answering, he gulped. His frightened eyes, retracting into that cratered face, sought assistance from the publicist. What dark secret had I chanced upon? Finally he mumbled, as if in shame, 'Columbus, Ohio', and looked to his creative keeper for the expected rebuke.

'Randy,' sighed the publicist, 'you know the industry bio says Sarasota, Florida. Can we stick with that for the story, Peter? We don't want to confuse the folks, do we?'

Having taken in this warning, Macho Man began to assert his incredible credentials by psychobabbling. 'See, that's just how I am, I can't help it, I guess that's what the fans like about me: I'm honest. I'm not a giant or a monster or nothing, I'm just an ordinary guy. I was pink-slipped out of baseball, I failed at that, so I had to rethink my goals, and I worked hard at becoming what I am.'

Then he uttered the anthem which is the grand delusion of America, where the founding myth – or lie – is that you can attain success or fame by simply wishing for it. 'You know, everyone can be the best they can be. You've gotta go for it.' This was how the Universe brought forth Oprah, and why Hampton and Golub measured themselves against the Empire State Building.

Now Macho Man had talked himself into character, I asked about the period when he ran amok in the ring. Adhering to the script, he pieced the truisms and trite slogans together into his own philosophy of personal growth, like one of those hollowed-out recovering addicts who purge themselves every afternoon on the talk shows.

'I've made my mistakes, they're in the history books. To get myself psyched up for a match, I had to be focused, and I guess I focused on the wrong things. It was just me going crazy – you know, paranoic. Sure, my halo's not on perfectly straight. But where I'm at now is this: I'm trying to be a better person. Maybe that's the way of the world in America today. People are getting themselves straightened out. Now I'm married to Miss Elizabeth I've got my feet on the ground. I'm not bouncing off the walls no more. I still reach for the stars, but if I fall I don't have far to fall, 'cos I'm planted. That's what I'm about. Hell, the way I see it, we've gotta care for each other.'

At this point, perhaps recalling the similar bogus promise about a kinder America made by George Bush before the 1988 election, Macho Man became mistily sentimental. 'Wisdom comes with age. I've gone through each and every one of the stages to get where I am today. I have a tremendous following – tremendous. And I accept that responsibility. I will not lead the people who believe in me astray. I know I'm a role model for them. And I *will* help them.'

Overcome by this covenant, or choked by his own rhetoric, Macho Man asked to be excused.

'That's one sweet guy', said the humid-eyed publicist, prepared to forgive the infraction of corporate rules concerning Columbus.

On the morning of their performance at Madison Square Garden, the wrestlers gave a demonstration of their social conscience and humane compunction by appearing in a free show for handicapped children. There was the inevitable photo-call, since a good deed is valueless if it goes unpublicized.

The most severely handicapped of the children were selected for presentation to the superstars: a black girl with a beatific face and meticulously braided hair, who inexplicably ended at the waist; a paraplegic boy whose limbs were twisted at unusable angles, and whose head poked quizzically behind him. Hacksaw Jim swung his length of wood and hollered, while Texas Tornado – his eyes almost meeting in his conical head – said to the wracked, twitching boy, 'C'mon now, show me your moves.' As Texas feigned punches, the boy's unsynchronized legs managed a spasm. This was as much as he could make his body do

The scene became suddenly painful, like the mutual puzzlement of two species contemplating each other on either side of the bars at the zoo. This was a meeting between two kinds of bodily deformity, the macabre truncation or contortion of the children in their wheelchairs and the absurd, artificial over-development of the wrestlers – both, perhaps, equally tragic, since the wrestlers as much as the children are the prisoners of physique. They truly are sweet, pitiable creatures, not so much emblems of strength as of our shared weakness and our necessary gallantry in accepting defeat when our bodies decide that they can no longer be bothered to hold us up.

What made it additionally painful was the thought that, at a convenient distance from the brawny arena, the air-conditioned and deodorized brains in the glass box were tallying receipts from their sale of these humanoid images, and busily transforming ancient myths into modern money.

IMAGINARY CITIES

HOLLYWOOD, FLORIDA

A N AMERICAN HIGHWAY IS A ROAD GOING ANYWHERE AND EVERY-
where, an emporium of universal possibility.

This particular one, carved out the day before yesterday through
the fetid swamps and orange groves of central Florida, passes an Italian
restaurant in the shape of a Palladian villa called Caruso's Palace. Next
door is a half-timbered Tudor hangar advertised as King Henry's Feast –
also a restaurant, with wenches to wait on you and jousting between
courses. Further along is a green-tiled Ming temple (another restaurant)
and the campanile of a Spanish missionary church (a shopping mall).
Signs point to streets which do not exist yet: Samoan Row, Austrian
Court. Soon the bulldozers will arrive, and there will be grass huts
and baroque castles where the oranges once grew. Against the sky –
flamingo-coloured at sunset, then shredded by sheet lightning – rears a
colossal coiled intestine: the looping water-slide of an aquapark called
Wet 'n Wild. In the distance, rockets stand to attention on the launch-
ing pads of Cape Canaveral, ready to Americanize what remains of the
universe.

If you turn off this infinite, all-inclusive highway at an oasis of transplanted palms, you arrive in another small world, an imploded America
inside a fence, which sends up a blitz of searchlight to scratch the bellies
of the thunder clouds. This is Universal Studios, Florida's outpost of the
back lot in the Hollywood hills where tourists can wander through the
false fronts of actual movie locations. Here – beyond the silvery globe
with the Art Deco equator which is Universal's logo – you glimpse a
silhouetted New York consisting of cut-outs mounted on flag-poles:
Citicorp with its shelving roof, the snail-shaped Guggenheim Museum.
Nudging this toytown Manhattan are the heretical monuments of Los
Angeles: the Aztec pinnacles of the Pantages Theatre, the minarets of
the Garden of Allah Hotel, and that absurd article of geodesic headgear,
the Brown Derby Restaurant. On a clump of sunburned grass stands the
skeletal *Psycho* house, with the derelict cabins of the Bates Motel beneath

it, as a warning of what might await you on any innocuous side road branching off the highway of normality.

It sounds like a war zone over the fence. Buildings drop to their knees during shoot-outs in the Wild West town, cops detonate a drug-runner's trawler on the lagoon, and the Ghostbusters celebrate their fumigation of the New York Public Library by giving a percussive rock concert on its steps. Inside a congested, encyclopaedic enclave of four hundred acres you have America in little, with all its dreams on parade and all its terrors pyrotechnically exploding.

Rearranging the map, Universal Studios compresses the scattered cities which are the continent's mythical destinations. After passing through the turnstiles, you stroll into New York, where so many ambitious fantasists have preceded you, their egos looming like high-rises. Here is Tiffany's, where Audrey Hepburn imagined herself breakfasting, as well as the Embryo Bookshop in which she primly worked in another film, *Funny Face*, before Fred Astaire whisked her off to Paris to become a fashion model. The Palace Theatre, where Barbra Streisand caterwauled her way to fame in *Funny Girl*, is across the street from the rusty fire-escape on which Natalie Wood pined in *West Side Story*.

An alley which abridges three thousand miles curves beneath an arch and lets you out in Los Angeles. Here the mottled pavement is inlaid with stars, and the street is bordered with different dreams: Schwab's, the drugstore where Lana Turner's cleavage was discovered on a stool at the soda fountain; the baronial Beverly-Wilshire Hotel, whose bathrobes Eddie Murphy pilfered in *Beverly Hills Cop*; Mel's Drive-In, the streamlined resort of the cruising teens in *American Graffiti*. Along from the cool grey marble façade of Max Factor, Hollywood's cosmetic sanctuary, are billboards announcing Ciro's and Mocambo. The night clubs, like everything else, are only fronts with names displayed across them – but what names! Magic names, for use in evoking other dreams of perished glamour, complete with big bands and Brazilian dancers wearing salad on their heads, glimpsed through the filtering incense of cigarette smoke.

In these cities of simulation, you can search out addresses which mean something special to you. I went on a sentimental pilgrimage to a sheet of painted board purporting to be the newspaper office where Orson Welles conspired with his cronies in *Citizen Kane*. The space inside turned out to contain the serpentine queue for the *Ghostbusters* show, in which the posse of exorcists atomize a giant marshmallow on the demon-guarded roof terrace of a Central Park West apartment block. In a different, adjacent New York, a bleary sign touts the home-cooked fare of LOUIE'S RESTAURANT (L. CORLEONE, PROP.). This is the dive where Al Pacino graduated to manhood in *The Godfather*, retrieving a gun from behind the lavatory cistern and shooting the dinner out of Sterling Hayden. Through the door, they serve fast food – Italian, of course.

On the other side of the street or the continent is the place which for me was the most sacred of all: the Empire Hotel, supposedly perched on one of the vertiginous hills of San Francisco. Upstairs, in a room you have to imagine, inside a mist of green, sickly retrospection quickened by the pink throbbing pulse of the neon sign outside the window, James Stewart transformed Kim Novak into the facsimile of her own dead, fetishised self, while Hitchock's camera swooned around them in a light-headed circle and Bernard Herrmann's soundtrack quoted from the necrophiliac yearning of Wagner's *Tristan und Isolde*. The lobby door of the Empire Hotel was locked. Like the gates of Manderley at the beginning of Hitchcock's *Rebecca*, perhaps it opens only if you are asleep.

These buildings are no more than imitations of junked, discarded imitations, but anyone who loves the movies will be happily deceived by them. The Universal lot also contains a graveyard of props, presided over by the fibro shark from *Jaws 3*, its teeth worn down to stumps. Jumbled in a scrap heap of rusty metal and worm-eaten wood, you can find the dented shell of a chariot from the 1929 *Ben-Hur* and the tattered buggy, mounted on springs not wheels, in which Vivien Leigh fought off the rapist in *Gone With the Wind*. They even have the funereal bell from the Mission tower which tolled for both of Kim Novak's deaths in *Vertigo*.

All these treasures decay together on the gravel, soaked by the monsoonal downpours of the Florida summer. Who knows whether they are what they pretend to be, and who cares? The true believer lends them credibility by the force of his faith. They amount to a picturesque and venerable ruin, as ghoulishly wistful as the open graves and ivy-glutted catacombs of Highgate Cemetery. These are the pathetic remnants of our dreams, abused by the daylight, and they remind us that America too – like the movies, with which it is more or less interchangeable – is a dream.

Glancing around at the hordes of well-fed tourists from middle America in their rainbow-coloured fabrics, I had to admit that not everyone's reasons for visiting Universal were as nostalgic as mine. Middle America's motives are, if anything, more complicated and curious. These people had driven thousands of miles and paid thirty dollars each at the gate in order to be jolted, jerked and battered on the cinematic rides for which Universal is famous: they had come in the hope of being frightened.

America, which started out as a messianic dream, is always threatening to degenerate into a trauma, and the movies, from *King Kong* to *Halloween* or *Ghostbusters*, have made a speciality of articulating the country's fears. The cinema's creepiest and yet most endearing bogy is Hitchcock, who has his own pavilion at Universal. The interactive area makes you the victim of his special effects: you can be hurled off the demented carousel in *Strangers on a Train*, tumble from the Statue of Liberty's torch like the Nazi spy in *Saboteur*, or share James Stewart's seizure at the top of the tower in *Vertigo*. With the help of a pair of 3-D glasses, you can withstand bombardment by a squad of beaked, squawking gulls, like Tippi Hedren in *The Birds*.

Inside a theatre there is one more version of the *Psycho* house, together with a cross-sectioned motel cabin where during the summer of 1991 Anthony Perkins (looking like his own cadaver after he had filmed *Psycho 4*) talked audiences through Janet Leigh's last shower. America abounds in men who fancy themselves as murderous transvestites with Oedipus complexes: on my tour, a Texan called Elmer shimmied eagerly into Mrs Bates's nightie and hair-net, then aimed his rubber knife at a blonde employee who showered in a body stocking. This gory little playlet is repeated three times an hour. Meanwhile, posing in front of the outdoor *Psycho* house, the cosy nuclear families of Montana and Tennessee smile as they practise stabbing one another. These are bad dreams, apparently, which everyone is adept at acting out.

Each of the illusory environments at Universal has its own resident nemesis. The quaint clapboard New England village of Amity, smelling of saltwater taffy and crab cakes, has not forgotten the Fourth of July weekend when it was reduced to hysteria by the fin of Spielberg's shark. Behind the New York and San Francisco façades are rides which exploit the particular paranoia of those cities. In New York, King Kong still prowls through the siren-lacerated night. A ride called *Kongfrontation* bumps you above the trench-like streets in the elevated train which crosses the East River to Roosevelt Island; your carriage is punched by the rabid ape who swings from the chassis of the 59th Street Bridge.

Universal's Kong is as prone to nervous breakdowns as the stressed-out, overloaded city he personifies, and on the second day of my visit he was closed for emergency repairs. 'Oh, I guess they're just feeding him some more bananas', smarmed an attendant, fending off angry customers. 'Why don't you go for the earthquake? It's an 8.3 on the Richter scale.'

The earthquake is San Francisco's home-grown, only-too-prophetically true bad dream. One of the restaurants at Universal copies a wrought-iron warehouse which survived the quake and fire in 1906; its tablecloths are newspapers reprinting the doomy headlines of that day. 'I remember this', said a child eating fries at a nearby table, 'I was watching the ball game on TV when it happened. The whole ballpark shook, it was great....'

'No, honey', said his mother, 'it wasn't that quake you saw. This is another one.' Her own information about that earlier occasion probably derived from the movies: those crevasses which split the laminated studio floor beneath Clark Gable's feet, and Jeanette MacDonald trilling a hymn as reconstruction gets under way.

The adjoining ride is subtitled The Big One, and you watch San Francisco rehearsing its downfall from a BART train stalled at Embarcadero Station. First the street above caves in, exposing a frieze of flaming skyscrapers. A truck loaded with tanks of propane gas skids into the gulf towards you, followed by an annihilating tidal wave (which gurgles away down a convenient drain). Everyone in the train screams with a vengeance: video cameras claim to be auditioning for extras in a disaster movie.

This motorized mayhem, which excites such ecstatic alarm, hints at a secret truth about the movies and the culture they so accurately inter- pret. All of Universal's factitious sets are anxiously waiting for their moment of consummation, which will come when they are destroyed. My personal guide, a college drop-out who identified himself on his walkie-talkie as VIP Paul, explained that the marble of Max Factor's chapel on Hollywood Boulevard was actually fibreglass: 'That way, they don't have to be fancy when they tear it down. These sets take three weeks to build, but we can knock 'em down in two days! Isn't that neat?' The thought of the wrecker's ball made his eyes glow. I remembered the bangs, crashes and luminous cataclysms with which the lot resounds at night. America dotes on destruction because it makes possible a new beginning, and that's what the country is all about. If the gorilla levels Manhattan and the San Andreas fault gobbles up San Francisco, then we are freed from the past and can start the world all over again. On holiday, America flirts enjoyably with the idea of apocalypse.

The freakiest and most breakneck of the rides is based on *Back to the Future*. Stern health warnings from the Institute of Future Technology debar anyone with neck or back disorders, epilepsy or heart problems; ushers patrol the queue with first-aid kits. Waiting in a concrete cell to be shovelled into your own flying De Lorean car for the simulated roller-coaster jaunt through time and space, you listen to the screams of those who have gone before. Doc Brown, the crackpot inventor in the film, warns that 'This could be the end of the universe as we know it.' The oafish Biff has entered the institute disguised as one of us – scrutinize your loved ones, Doc advises – and stolen an experimental car for a joy-ride through the cosmos. Doc has been imprisoned; he needs us to give chase to retrieve the car. The voice of Buthead Biff cackles through a loudspeaker: 'Doc Brown's guinea pigs never make it back.' Then the steel shutter opens, and you are catapulted into the worst three minutes of your life.

I had to ride on *Back to the Future* twice because the first time, when I tried to make notes afterwards, I found I remembered nothing: I had my eyes screwed tightly shut throughout. The second time I managed to keep them open intermittently, so long as I muttered to myself every few seconds that none of this was really happening. The trip treats you in advance to sights and sensations like those reserved for the freshly dead:

> Ay, but to die, and go we know not where;...
> To bathe in fiery floods, or to reside
> In thrilling regions of thick-ribbed ice;
> To be imprisoned in the viewless winds,
> And blown with restless violence round about
> The pendent world....

As the car shudders, bucks and heaves, a video screen seven storeys high involves you in an acrobatic dogfight above the drowsing town of Hill Valley. Then, forcibly ejected from gravity, you plummet through chasms of ice, lunge into a dinosaur's gullet and are nauseously coughed up to bounce across a volcano. Finally, after ramming Biff's vehicle, you are hurled back to your starting point.

VIP Paul laughed about a little old lady unused to such adventures who gasped at the end of her ride, 'Oh, so we came back to the same room!' Of course she had never left it. I sympathized with her disorientation: your aerodynamic stomach makes a fool of you, and convinces you that you have been somewhere. The movies are celebrations of motion, and they have the power – like Hitchcock infecting us with James Stewart's vertigo by setting the camera to dolly forwards while its lens was tracking back – to make us feel motion sickness.

With their safety-netted perils, the rides offer a controlled and licensed joy in watching the world blown apart. But middle America expects to go home to its leafy, somnolent suburbs when the holiday is over, so Universal supplies reassurances that all is well in the land, despite the rampages of Kong or Biff and the unseaming of California. On the *ET* ride you pedal a bike through spangly galaxies and visit the extra-terrestrial's planet, which is a jungle of singing rhododendrons. On the way out you are personally farewelled by ET, who has been programmed by a computer to remember your name. What a consolation it is to hear the lovable monster with the staring eyes and the scaly, waving arm – America's elected guardian angel – croak 'Goodbye, Peter, friend'! Disembarking on earth again at the Wild West show, you find yourself in a country whose ancient verities are still enforced by the gun. Between shoot-outs, a maudlin hymn sings the praises of those silver-screen cowboys who stood tall for what they believed to be right, and sighs in conclusion, 'God knows, this is what America still needs.'

Inside the front gate of the studio, on the landing of a lofty staircase which leads nowhere, hangs a portrait of Orson Welles, the cinema's self-confessed faker. Everything at Universal is phony, or (to be modishly polite) fictional. The cobblestones of old New York were carved with pastry cutters in wet cement, and the concussed rubbish tins in the *West Side Story* alley were distressed to order by the art department. The most studied pretence is that the lot functions as a working studio. You are warned that your entry implies your consent to appear in any films being made that day, and alerted to look out for off-duty stars, but it is impossible to discover just what is happening in those sheds which are alleged to be sound stages. 'I guess you could say we're in hiatus', said an attendant who had exhausted all other excuses.

True, some doddering cowboys were winched on to horseback and put through their elderly paces for the premiere of the Wild West show: Chuck Connors with his craggy Mount Rushmore profile, and Harry Carey junior, once a member of John Ford's repertory company. They too, I suppose, are romantic ruins. Actors without better offers wander around dressed up as Blues Brothers or Ghostbusters, and a solitary stunt man can be found perpetually dying – shot down by the mob in Little Italy, or diving from the top of a building in Hollywood on the blithe assumption that the street is a swimming pool – for the benefit of a camera which has no film in it. There are doors everywhere forbiddingly marked PRODUCTION CREW ONLY. Investigating, I found that they led to the broom cupboards of the Cuban janitors.

What the crew busily produces is illusions, and the grandest of these is that of the studio itself. The mystique of the movies was inseparable from that of the old studios, with their imposing heraldic insignias: the Metro lion and the Paramount mountain, Columbia's slim and elegant version of the Statue of Liberty as a debutante, the futurist skyline of Twentieth Century Fox, and Universal's serenely rotating globe. But after decades of corporate take-overs, the studios now are only false fronts, renting premises to the producers of television game shows. In the absence of authentic movie-making, Universal cozens its customers by telling them they are in a movie of their own. Whenever you make a purchase – of a shower curtain from the Bates Motel or a cuddly ET or a plate of Corleone meatballs – the cash register prints its congratulations on your receipt: 'IT'S A TAKE! YOU'RE A STAR!' At Universal, there are at least two ways of being taken, or of being taken for a ride.

No-one complains or feels defrauded, because this is a lie which everyone is strenuously willing into a truth. After a day in Florida, it occurred to me that all the people I met were behaving as if they were in the movies. Well, perhaps not in the movies – they didn't quite have the transcendent allure demanded by the big screen. Rather they were behaving as if they belonged on television, with its sassy patter and its grimacing mannerisms.

My first encounter was with a rollickingly obese female immigration officer at the airport in Orlando, who inquired about my business and admitted me to the United States after I promised her on pain of deportation that I would have fun at Universal. She groaned about the sweltering humidity outside: 'Ain't it the pits out there? Mind you don't sweat to death!' She guffawed as she stamped my passport. Her name-tag said JEWELEE, but her act was modelled on Roseanne Arnold.

Next morning a waitress called Skeeter, her hair tightly curled by sheer force of personality, took my order for breakfast by demanding, 'Are you ready now? You better be ready boy, 'cos I'm dangerous! You want an OJ?

I'm gonna squeeze you that sucker with my own hands!' She then bustled off to fetch me a fluffy, cholesterol-friendly omelette made from egg substitute. Skeeter's chosen prototype was Carla from *Cheers*.

And VIP Paul, with his acne and his crinkly perm and his habit of telling his walkie-talkie 'I'm in New England now, just coming up to San Fran', endlessly enthusing that everything was 'neat', he was a latter-day version of Richie from *Happy Days*.

Humankind cannot bear very much reality, which is perhaps why God gave us the movies. As I returned to the highway, the whole experience seemed quite continuous: what difference was there between the makeshift cities on the Universal lot and the Ming temples, Palladian villas and Tudor manors out there? The highway led, I noticed, to Kissimmee, the town which is the proud birthplace of Tupperware. Reality in America has a plastic malleability, ready to be moulded into anything or everything you wish, and life – as you speed down the road, looking out at the pageant of transitory follies from inside your micro-climatized capsule – is a motion picture.

THE FORBIDDEN CITY: EVERY MAN AN EMPEROR

THE FORBIDDEN CITY MIGHT HAVE BEEN CONSTRUCTED FOR USE AS A film set. Insulated from lowly, teeming Beijing by its moat and its sunset-coloured battlements, it is a montage of supercilious façades and intricate tableaux whose purpose was to forbid the real world from entering: an empire of illusion.

For Bertolucci in *The Last Emperor* it is the ultimate back lot, a stage for deploying armies of colour-coordinated extras, with ready-made decorative recesses around every corner – streams tormented into serpentine courses and indoor gardens of polyp-like, porous rock; crazily convoluted pavilions with gilded dragons writhing on their ceilings; throne rooms where incense burners worked overtime to manufacture the same air breathed in heaven, and bridges suddenly raised their humps above non-existent rivers in the middle of the floor so as to delay your approach to the enthroned deity.

Pu Yi, the Emperor in the film – who was crowned as a child, deprived of power by the revolution, reinstated as a puppet by the invading Japanese, then captured and brainwashed into penitence by the Maoists – wants to escape from his prison of exorbitant artifice into the modern China beyond the walls. The Emperor's desire to dismantle the set acts out the director's misgivings about an art form in which he, omnipotent behind the camera, is an absent, ubiquitous god. In Bertolucci's *La Luna*, the retracting roof of a cinema suddenly slides back to reveal the night sky, and in *The Spider's Stratagem* the proprietor of an outdoor cinema, afraid of the rain, rolls up his screen as if it were a window blind. But these alienating criticisms of illusion never damage the screen on which Bertolucci is arranging his images; instead they open into a further, even-more-illusory depth behind that screen. In *La Luna*, the galaxies are suspended above, like chandeliers. In *The Spider's Stratagem*, the furling of the screen – useless, anyway, in daylight – causes the imaginary room to collapse and exposes an overgrown garden which the sheet had cordoned off: a hiding-place for the political and psychological mysteries which the hero investigates.

Like Hitchcock, Bertolucci prefers his curtains to be torn, violently gashed by truth. But film, despite his efforts to make it engage with society, is an art form expressly designed for the cave-dwellers in Plato's fable. In 1987 *The Last Emperor* may have looked like the documentation of a China which was no longer forbidden to Western eyes. Seen again a few years later and checked against the actuality of Beijing, it is impossible not to notice how much it leaves out or overlooks, and how vainly it strives to rid the Emperor of his dreams. Like the self-enclosure and labyrinthine endlessness of the Forbidden City, Bertolucci's film is a tribute to the power and the inescapability of cinematic fantasy.

The geomancers who ordained the lay-out of Beijing designed the Forbidden City as a many-mansioned house of fiction. Their symbolic magic ruled the world into orderliness with a fanatical but spurious logic. The palaces inside the walls were arrayed along a north-south axis, reciting a spell which supposedly brought earth and sky into equilibrium and the warring elements into harmony. The Emperor, directly descended from the sun, sat on his throne facing south. A man-made hill behind the Forbidden City shielded him from noxious spirits of the north; extra defences were supplied by the mountains on the northern edge of the city and then – since paranoia never entirely trusts its own soothing therapies – by that last, most stolid and insanely literal-minded barrier, the Great Wall.

Installed at the sacred mid-point of creation, the Emperor could preside over a universe whose immortality he allegedly shared. His domain contained 9,999 rooms, falling just short of the ten thousand which would be at his disposal in heaven: there had to be something for him to look forward to. From Coal Hill, the Forbidden City's maze of dragon-guarded peaks resembles the cross-section of a preposterously ingenious, multi-cameral brain. Each roof caps a different idea, or houses a separate function. The Emperor did his schoolwork in the Hall of Mental Cultivation, he marched forth to battle through the Gate of Martial Valour, he spent his retirement in the Hall of Permanent Longevity. Even immortals must possess a digestive tract, but this architecture took responsibility for the Emperor's regularity: his excrement was evacuated through the Gate of Certain Peace. The Forbidden City was an ideogram, a model both of the world and of the mind.

The grand delusion of the symbolist is to construct a system, obliging all phenomena to fit its equations. Confucianism did so, and by encoding everything sought to abolish chance. The Forbidden City mapped the Emperor's formal progress through life, from the green-tiled palaces in the east where he grew up to the yellow-tiled, central headquarters of wealth, honour and physical plenitude; Dowager Empresses were housed in the west, confined to a region whose presiding atmosphere was dryness and whose identifying colour was a ghostly white.

On this dogmatic scheme, Bertolucci imposes a symbolism of his own, replacing Confucius with a combination of Marx and Freud. Symbols are arbitrary, even though they pretend that the connections they make are self-evident; they can be reversed at will. Maoist China switched the traffic code back to front: because red was the colour of revolution and thus of progress, it would hardly be proper for a red light at a street corner to mean stop. Cyclists were therefore ordered to interpret green as the stop signal, and to pedal forward when they saw red.

Bertolucci made similar alterations when deciding what the Forbidden City would mean for him. The fluttering banners of imperial yellow in *The Last Emperor* are screens obscuring truth, curtains which must be torn. Pu Yi and his bride, undressed by others after their wedding, twine together in a filmy gauze which prophylactically isolates them from each other. The red-lacquered, impassable gates block the way towards enlightenment. Pu Yi hurls his pet mouse against one of these in frustration when he is not allowed out. 'Open that door!' he cries ineffectually, like the Italian peasants in Bertolucci's *1900* who remember being herded by their master into a feudal compound which he padlocked at night. They are freed by the radical rallying-cry of Gérard Depardieu, 'Now the doors are open.' Bertolucci's political purpose was to besiege the Emperor's impregnable city, to overthrow it by rereading its symbols.

Pu-Yi in the film craves psychological as well as social liberation. His predicament is not so singular after all: pampered by eunuchs who appreciatively sniff his stools, guzzle green ink at his command, and permit him to do anything he pleases, he is the infantile monster we all once were. Freud called this midget despot 'His Majesty the Child'. All babies see the world beyond the crib as a court, with their parents as sycophantic attendants. To grow up is to be weaned off flattery, and to recognize our marginality in the world. When he is dethroned, Pu Yi has to renounce the megalomania of childhood, which his position had prolonged: he ends his life as a diffident, anonymous, well-adjusted citizen of Mao's new state.

The agent of his re-education is Bertolucci's own art, that of film. He breaks down in tears and admits his complicity when he sees newsreel evidence of the military atrocities committed by the Japanese. In addition, the camera deconsecrates him, taking away his aura. As Emperor, he was officially invisible. His profane subjects had to turn their backs when he passed. Bertolucci's camera confers visibility on him, and calls his supernatural bluff. Yet the film-maker, as if berating himself for ideological crimes in one of those auto-critical purges beloved by revolutionaries, simultaneously points out that his own art cannot be trusted, because cameras always lie. Crowned a second time by the Japanese occupiers of Manchuria, the powerless Emperor stands on a makeshift dais beside some smoking factories; the occasion is solemnized by a recording of a Viennese waltz and fictionalized by the newsreel cameras. Amakasu, the ugliest and most callous of the Japanese agents, carries a camera as his alibi. Labouring the point that technology supplies us with artificial bodily aids, Bertolucci allows him only one arm.

The two systems of symbolism – medieval geomancy and modern, leftist psychiatry – did not quite match in the film, and both are discounted by the present state of things inside the Forbidden City. The place is no longer the cosmic centre the ancient Emperors assumed it to be. Neither is it the schoolroom where Bertolucci's last Emperor, eavesdropping on the rumours of historic change which convulse the city outside his walls, learns about moral and civic accountability from the Scottish tutor played by Peter O'Toole. The Forbidden City today is in part a romantic ruin, and in part a tourist trap.

Bertolucci's designers spruced it up: the film does not prepare you for its dilapidation. Among the ceramic ogres which rear and romp on the orange eaves grow hanging gardens of weed. Electric wires are plaited like unruly noodles around the walls. The courtyards are muddy, and the stream which wriggles beneath five bridges, symbolizing the virtues, is thick with algae, studded with bottles, and cruised by helicopter-like formations of dragonflies. The apartments where Pu Yi lived are tatty, the wallpaper cracked and peeling, the furniture threadbare.

This dereliction could well be a mordant Chinese joke on the imperial cult of perpetuity. All the Emperors sought an elixir of eternal life which was supposedly available on three islands of the coast; at the

Summer Palace in the hills above Beijing, three such islands were built, with wishful symbolism, in a lake. For want of eternity, Emperors were hailed as the lords of ten thousand years, but their abode in the Forbidden City has begun to moulder only decades after their eviction. An exhibition about Pu Yi is ironically installed in the Palace of Permanent Longevity. A nearby pavilion contains the dynastic collection of clocks and watches, with timepieces sprouting from flowerpots, riding on elephants or unicorns, floating suspended from helium balloons or charging through space in the shape of locomotives. In the 1930s visitors would assemble to hear their synchronized chiming, and to see clockwork dolls write Chinese characters with a brush while toy birds sang and crystal water trickled. By now all the clocks have wearily ticked themselves to a stop – another ironic judgment on this kingdom of timelessness, which kept history out and was therefore condemned to obsolescence?

Bertolucci's disciplined, kowtowing courtiers have been replaced by an equally numerous but rowdier cast of characters: teenage soldiers wearing slippers with their uniforms, a bewildered crush of Tibetan peasants, and a tout whose wares include ginseng and a sterilizing unguent called Love Solution: the packet shows a couple in starched white medical jackets enjoying an infection-free embrace in a hospital room. On a bench in another courtyard, a boy sprawls with his head in his girlfriend's lap; she spends the afternoon patiently delousing him, searching for parasites in his hair and squeezing them to death between her finger nails. Two off-duty caretakers play ping-pong in a shed. Plugged into head sets, foreign tourists amble along while film stars whisper in their ears and tell them what to look at. English and German commentaries on the taped tours are fruitily intoned by Peter Ustinov. If you speak French, your guide is Fernando Rey, the drug-runner from *The French Connection*. Inside the Forbidden City, film retains its delusive power, with Ustinov and Rey encouraging you to treat life as if it were an interactive movie.

What of the city beyond the blotchy, bleeding walls? *The Last Emperor* permitted stray glimpses, after Pu Yi's rebirth as an ordinary citizen, of Beijing in the 1960s: orderly cavalcades of bicycles, a contingent of propagandizing Red Guards. The contrast reverses that between the closed apartment and the turbulent, dangerous streets in Bertolucci's *Last Tango in Paris*: the empty room where Brando and Maria Schneider copulate serves as the stark and clinical place of truth, while Paris itself is a noisy, congested vacancy. The Emperor, however, has advanced from the lonely exclusiveness of the Forbidden City into a companionably collective life, and can be seen shopping happily for a cabbage. Today in Beijing the relationship between what the courtiers called 'the Great Within' and the city outside seems more complex and sinister. Pu Yi locates humanity and the bliss of anonymity outside. But in fact the front gate of the Forbidden City opens on to a paved wilderness which no-one had ever heard of when *The Last Emperor* was made: Tiananmen Square. And in it is the mausoleum of the sage and ogre who was truly China's last – or perhaps only its latest – Emperor, Mao Zedong.

Mao decreed the area's clearance to make a place for mass congregation. He announced the creation of the People's Republic from a rostrum above it (where the choice of muzak when I visited was 'Some Enchanted Evening'); when he died, a million of his subjects forgathered mournfully below. Three images of him posthumously keep watch on Tiananmen. A portrait is strung from the rostrum, with the dawn sky allegorically brightening behind his pink, jolly face. Inside the mausoleum, an effigy in stone implacably sits in one of those leatherette armchairs, complete with doilies and antimacassars, which communist despots used to favour for photo-opportunities. Behind it, in a transparent coffin, the waxy embalmed head of the man himself peeps out from beneath a red security blanket.

Infinite and featureless in the moist, pearly summer air, the totalitarian emptiness of Tiananmen suits a theory of society which abolished the past and the private life. That society can be overseen by one man from the rostrum; it can also conveniently be surrounded by tanks. Such a vast vacancy is useful for regimentation, and for extermination. The square is a calculated affront to the riddling subtlety of the subdivided Forbidden City. Beside it is Mao's populist rebuke to the Emperor's palaces, the obtuse, pharaonic bulk of the Great Hall of the People. Its wastes of marble and acres of grubby, scruffed parquet are a desert with a roof on top. Like the square, it is full of nothing. It exists only to symbolize the exhausting, incomprehensible massiveness of a mass society. On the front steps of the Great Hall, I saw a family from the provinces stretching out their arms to encircle one of its elephantine Egypto-Soviet columns. There were six of them, and they strained every muscle to reach around it, but even so they could not manage to touch each others' fingers. The brutal thing, like a jackboot in concrete, kept them apart.

After his therapeutic remoulding through manual labour, Pu Yi wrote an autobiography (or rather had it ghosted for him) in which he piously gloried in his conversion. In the book he zealously joins in Chairman Mao's campaign to eliminate flies by swatting his alloted quota each day; he assiduously makes briquettes in prison, and for a treat is allowed to go on educative inspections of public utilities. He claims that his first desire on returning to Beijing was not to revisit the Forbidden City as a paying tourist (which is how Bertolucci's film ends), but to see Tiananmen Square, and take part in a political demonstration there. Having done so, and having exercised his franchise in the 1960 elections, he declares his life's ambitions to be fulfilled.

At the end of the film, Pu Yi is implausibly Lear-like: humble, tender, sweetly reconciled. I longed to know whether Pu Yi's fellow citizens today share his contentment. Crowds of them wander through Beihai Park – a Maoist Disneyland, where the different agendas of fun fair and doctrinal seminar are combined – gazing at automated allegories. Puppets perform in a festival of flags on behalf of a coal mine, and a dance of female marionettes dramatizes the 'unbroken thoughts of love' connecting China and Taiwan. A display by the Xuangang Mining Administration, beneath an archway of coloured lanterns on which two plastic giraffes are grazing, comes complete with a placard prescribing a politically correct emotional response: 'The spectators are faintly aware that they are intoxicated with the spirit of joyousness.' There are, all the same, mechanical malfunctions in this promised land. I noticed a worker rowing out into a lake through choking lotus leaves to repair the cardboard cut-out of another coal town on a floating stage, above which two silvery Soviet figures shook their fists in a proclamation of economic virtue and marched into the future. A second operator had his hand up the skirt of one of the Taiwanese marionettes, fiddling with her prosthetic metal leg to make sure she still moved through her stilted routine of reconciliation.

Beneath the walls of the Forbidden City and behind Tiananmen Square, Beijing reverts to a dusty, fetid, endlessly unravelling shanty town. Its people squat in the gutters swigging from jam jars of green tea or spitting with the force of flush toilets. Their huts have lids made of tar paper held in place by chipped rock, and their amateurish television antennae are twisted together from coat-hangers. An open door discloses a Marlboro packet on a display as a mantelpiece ornament. As I wandered down alleys carpeted with chicken feathers, avoiding rickety bicycles and the tiny turds spontaneously vented by babies through slits in the back of their pants, a local would occasionally lower his germicidal face mask and try out the one English word he knew: 'Hallo.' Beyond that, there was no chance of communication. If I had been able to ask, I dare say the slum-dwellers would have expressed the same enthusiasm the Emperor professes in his autobiography – and for the same prudent reasons.

But if you watch them carefully, you can see them repudiating Bertolucci's loyal view of their recent history. They have learned the lesson of his art too well. All of them have cameras: it is one of the few human rights China recognizes to be inalienable. And having themselves photographed in the courtyards of the Forbidden City, they appropriate the place by posing in front of it. Though the bridges and ramparts are glutted with people, a discreet protocol sorts out the crush. The moment a camera is produced, everyone stands back – with the deference of Pu Yi's eunuchs – to avoid obtruding in someone else's holiday snap. Raised aloft in his sedan chairs, travelling through streets where no buildings were permitted a second storey because his subjects could not look down on him, the Emperor fancied that he owned the sky. Nowadays anyone with a camera possesses exclusive rights to the view, and for an instant shares the Emperor's visual dominion and Bertolucci's directorial authority.

Tourism is mass society's revenge on the forbidding aristocratic past. At the Summer Palace, one of the becalmed, absurd relics of the old regime is a paddle steamer made of stone, its rudder paralytic, its wheels sunk in the silted lake. Symbolism is dangerously fickle: the marble barge was supposed to exemplify the stability of imperial rule, though it might also symbolize the titanic sinkability of that power. Around it families on holiday pedal other, more buoyant boats, with the heads of plastic dragons laughing on the prow. In the last scene of Bertolucci's film, the Emperor's throne room is stormed by a mob of day-trippers: democracy asserts common ownership, just as Pu Yi in his memoir claims to have felt proud that he and his countless proletarian colleagues shared the land and all its goods. But did Bertolucci notice how these madding tourists long for a past they officially despise? Above one of the gates to the Forbidden City, there is an open-air studio where children can be dressed up in the robes of Qing princes and princesses and perched on a make-believe throne to be photographed. Their parents giggle at the ideological naughtiness of the imposture. Every child is a temporary Emperor; to become an adult entails a painful abdication. Pu Yi may have recanted, but every Chinese family – perhaps because reproduction is so sternly rationed – wishes royal status on its offspring.

In *The Last Emperor*, the dialectic serenely works itself out so that history can arrive at a happy ending. Events have supplied a sequel which repudiates Bertolucci's fade-out. The Forbidden City may have thrown open its gates, but power in China continues to immure itself behind barricades and protect itself with armed sentries. The evil dotards who sent the People's Liberation Army into Tiananmen Square inhabit villas around a willow-fringed lake in an estate adjoining the Forbidden City. When they quit their fortified sanctum, the old imperial rule of invisibility reapplies. You no longer have to turn your back when they pass, as the courtiers did, but all the same you cannot see them: they are obscured and guarded by the tinted glass of their elderly limousines. No wonder Mao complacently referred to Pu Yi as 'my predecessor'.

Meanwhile, other forbidden cities are rising everywhere in Beijing, glistening above the squalid alleys. These are the luxury hotels built to accommodate foreign tourists. Inside them, fawned upon by platoons of flunkeys, bowed to, smiled at, wished a nice day on all sides, every man is an Emperor – so long as he is a Westerner with credit cards in his wallet.

As power drains from him, Bertolucci's Pu Yi calls the Forbidden City 'a theatre without an audience'; the actors only remain on stage so they can steal the scenery. The new hotels, ridiculously lavish and mostly quite empty, are also palaces of pretence. Like the thick crimson walls behind which Pu Yi masqueraded, or the pavilion in which the Dowager Empress Ci Xi celebrated her sixtieth birthday in 1894 by watching operas for ten days, they are designed to deny the truth of China. The most dizzily fatuous is the Sheraton Great Wall. External elevators waft you above the meagre factories and poky shops of the suburbs and let you look down at a garden where the hotel's playfully dwarfish version of the Great Wall girdles a miniature golf course, a satellite dish for the relaying of American cable television, and a pool which spurts computer-timed water jets. The Chinese raised the original Great Wall to keep the barbarians out. This replica serves to keep the barbarians snugly in, and to debar the Chinese themselves, unless they are employed as scullions.

Inside the hotels, no expense is spared to uphold the promise of modern international tourism, which is to persuade you that you have never left home. Their restaurants pamper Americans with burger nights;

a British bobby announces fish and chips (wrapped, improperly, in the *International Herald-Tribune*). Their lobbies are loud with Mozart quartets or with a serenade of a mariachi band whose members are Filipinos pretending to be Mexicans. Once I heard 'Edelweiss' played on a Chinese harp. In a would-be Bavarian beer cellar, I was served by a wait-ress in a facsimile of a dirndl whose name-tag said HSI PING (THEL-MA). She cheerfully explained that 'Hsi Ping is my Chinese name, but I choose English name of Thelma for myself too. I like English name best. Is nicer.' Thelma, she must have thought, is what all the voguiest girls in the West were called this year. It could have been worse: she might have opted for Demi, or k.d. The last Emperor was accused of cultural treason when, during his exile in Manchuria, he rebaptised himself Henry. Now such borrowed names are not shameful; they confer a pathetic prestige.

Bertolucci found in the Chinese a 'pre-consumerist innocence. They were still at the pre-McDonald and Coca-Cola phase of Western colo-nization.' No longer: in 1990 Kentucky Fried Chicken opened a three-tiered pagoda of greasy batter at the southern end of Tiananmen Square, with queues round the block at lunch time and marshals on duty to cram the eaters in and speed them out again. Its only concession to China is the pointedly Confucian cast given to the features of Colonel Sanders on the sign in the window. In the scramble for profit, ancestral symbolism has been casually discarded. At the Avenue of the Animals – an honour guard of monolithic elephants and camels near the Ming tombs – the positioning of the ticket office outrages the edicts of the geo-mancers, who insisted that paths should always curve to the left. The booth is located at the wrong end, so as you walk up the avenue it bends to the right: disastrous magic. The paradoxes of the country are so much acuter now than when Bertolucci was there. Gunning down demonstra-tors in 1989, the regime expressed China's abiding contempt for the rest of the world, while simultaneously – desperate for foreign capital and for the foreign currency tourists spend – it was permitting the construction of hotels which advertised the forbidden delights of capitalism.

Perhaps the mistake of Bertolucci's film was to assume that Chinese history has a Western tempo, progressively accelerating throughout the twentieth century, like Italy in his *1900*. One day I walked for miles and hours beside the swampy languor of the moat around the Forbidden City, awash with dead fish. This, the outer edge of what Bertolucci called his 'universe of yellow tiles', was off-limits to his camera; here history had already ceased to exist. A girl gnaws at a melon rind. A boy chases dragonflies with a net. A man pedals a cart-load of vegetables to market. An old woman does her martial-arts exercises in soporific slow motion. They have all been performing these actions for millennia, no matter who their Emperor happens to be and whether he calls himself the Son of Heaven or the Chairman of the Communist Party. The ancient inertia of China resumes, interrupted for only a moment by a revolution, or a massacre.

THE FIERY ANGEL ON ICE

PETRIFIED BY ICE, THE OPTIMISTICALLY RENAMED CITY OF ST Petersburg waited in the last week of 1991 to see if it would crack apart, like its own stiff river, when the thaw began. The day before I arrived, Gorbachev resigned; the day after I left, the Soviet Union wished itself out of existence.

The city's alternate tyrants, as unmoved as the frozen river, remained at their posts: Peter the Great rearing in bronze on his stallion in the square where the Decembrist rebels were slaughtered in 1825, Lenin atop a tank outside the Finland Station where he left his train in 1917 to take charge of the insurrection. When I went to see him, Lenin was haranguing a non-existent crowd in a park of muddied slush. Beneath the image of the Tsar, a bride shivered in filmy polyester, her high heels bedded in snow while her dented taxi steamed at the kerb. She was being photographed with her posy, perhaps in the hope of a benediction from the autocrat who – with the help of slave labour – caused this phantasmal city with its lemon, green and scarlet neoclassical terraces to rise from the marshes.

Dostoevsky, remembering Peter's megalomaniac will and the deranging endlessness of the perspectives he laid out, called St Petersburg 'the most *intentional* city in the world'. Even the lions and gryphons which gobble the cables of suspension bridges across the canals seem to support the platforms by the painful rigidity of their diaphragms: if they ever relax, the bridges will fall. Peter imprinted one absolutist intention on the city, and Lenin – during the city's career as Leningrad, stoically outlasting a Nazi siege – endowed it with another. At the end of 1991 it was between intentions, in one of history's nerve-wracking intermissions. Only the rigor mortis of cold held it together.

I went to St Petersburg to see an opera, slightly sceptical that anyone would bother putting on a show when a society was re-creating itself, or perhaps disintegrating. When I arrived, I found that the theatre, like the city, had changed its name: the Kirov Opera, so called to commemorate a party boss killed by Stalin (who blamed the deed on terrorists, and thus justified his vicious purges), had reverted to its imperial title, the Maryinsky. But the show – Prokofiev's *The Fiery Angel*, a parable of religious fanaticism and sexual hysteria, co-produced with the Royal Opera at Covent Garden where it was due to open a few months later – went ahead as planned, because it too was a post-Soviet act of restitution.

In 1917 Prokofiev's first opera, *The Gambler*, based on a Dostoevsky story, was performed at the Maryinsky between the February and October revolutions. Valery Gergiev, the theatre's current artistic director, describes the score as 'machine music, like roulette', as frenetic as the runaway engine of history. The following year Prokofiev was grudgingly granted permission to leave for the United States, although the People's Commissar for Education warned that the revolution from which he was excusing himself would not forgive him. He began work on *The Fiery Angel* in Bavaria in 1922. After a production arranged for Berlin was cancelled, he disassembled the drama and rearranged the score as his Third Symphony. A production in New York seemed possible in 1930; nothing came of it.

Returning to Russia for a brief concert tour in 1927, Prokofiev warily noted the size of the Comintern building in Moscow, which he described as 'a kind of huge jar full of microbes destined for world-wide distribution'. In 1936, despite these misgivings, he was lured home to live in what he sneeringly called 'Bolshevizia'. Other exiled artists, like the painter Repin and the bass Chaliapin, remained abroad; Prokofiev was enticed back with promises that the operas and ballets he had composed in the West would be performed. But the ethics and aesthetics of socialism could not condone the mysticism and erotomania of Renata, the obsessed heroine who is inflamed by visits from a demon lover; he never saw *The Fiery Angel* on stage. Instead he became an immediate victim of Stalinism, harried by censorship, required to prepare craven birthday odes for the bogy and to glorify the war effort against Hitler in his operatic adaptation of *War and Peace*. The theatre director Meyerhold, who had vowed to stage *The Fiery Angel* in Russia, was arrested while working on Prokofiev's *Semyon Kotko*, an innocuous socialist parable about a Ukrainian partisan in 1918; he was tortured by the secret police and shot. Prokofiev's first wife was plucked off a street corner and sentenced to a labour camp. Her only crime was being Spanish, and having friends in foreign embassies. The Maryinsky, at the end of 1993, the composer's centenary year, was determined to make amends.

If St Petersburg is an intentional city, the Maryinsky is a monument to the driven intentions of one man, its resident autocrat, whose pedestal is not an armoured car like Lenin's or a spar of rock like Peter the Great's, but a podium: the conductor Valery Gergiev. Vowing to change the Russian attitude to Prokofiev, Gergiev said, 'He is simply not known here. It is not neglect, just ignorance. For me, it was the usual fight with stupidity and obstruction – the same fight Prokofiev had against the bureaucrats and Bolsheviks when he came back. But the theatre owed him this tribute.'

Gergiev's talent and energy have restored the Kirov company to international prominence since he took charge in 1988. He instigated the association with Covent Garden, blithely telephoning in 1989 with a request to borrow the company's production of *Boris Godunov*, which he coveted because its director was one of the last Soviet artistic exiles, the film-maker Andrei Tarkovsky, and because the opera itself – about a ruler's loss of legitimacy, and his inability to comprehend a country in chaos – could serve as a remonstrance to Gorbachev. This *Boris Godunov* was the first Western production to be seen in the theatre since 1917. Next came a co-production of *War and Peace*, telecast from St Petersburg by the BBC in the summer of Prokofiev's centenary year, followed by *The Fiery Angel*. Inviting Plácido Domingo to appear in Covent Garden's *Otello* at the Maryinsky, Gergiev made a symbolic attempt to place St Petersburg on the circuit of capitals between which the world's great singers fly; he has also earned the company a subsidy from foreign tours, with extended visits to Edinburgh, London, New York and Japan.

A tour of Gergiev's domain makes clear the difficulty of his task. The theatre is a microcosm of the city, mixing Tsarist swank with the squalor of the Third World. Around the peppermint-green building, bedraggled queuers wait for trams which blitz the street with sparks as they lurch along; above the canal, the plaster of the theatre's back wall looks leprous. Under a crumbling roof the auditorium is opulently golden, though a hammer and sickle are suspended like a curse above the Tsar's box. Ancient women swathed in shawls with violently tinted hair sit on guard beside every door, knitting like Norns. In the canteen, stocked only with stewed cabbage and sweet tea, the cash register is an abacus. One backstage tunnel, as in a house of horrors, contains a rusty railway track: a train had to be used as counterbalance to shift the cumbrous scenery for Graham Vick's production of *War and Peace*, and could be heard huffing

and puffing through the opera's orchestral interludes. Cats prowl the corridors, along with the scent of deodorant which is supposed to repel them
and the curling fumes of toxic local cigarettes. Wandering around
between acts of *The Fiery Angel*, I was puzzled by the acid tang of oranges:
it couldn't come, surely, from the massive orange halves made of painted
wood which were parked on a landing? No, these were props left over
from Prokofiev's spooky farce *The Love for Three Oranges*, in which the
heroine travels inside the fruit. The smell belonged, I discovered, to the
oranges meagrely shared out as a special treat on first nights. The
linoleum catacomb of the Maryinsky is not exactly awash in champagne.

Gergiev's command centre is a cubicle hung with ragged tapestry and
wanly lit by naked bulbs, where fussing matronly helpers keep him alive
with infusions of raspberry tea and slices of a creamy wafer cake which
seems to be the exclusive perk of the conductor and his star singers. He
fills a power vacuum, and nothing in the theatre can be done without
him; when he closes the door of his cubby-hole, a crowd of jabbering,
excluded petitioners accumulates outside, helpless without him.

The man himself is a Dostoevskyan figure, wolfishly stubbly, wild-eyed
and wilder-haired, with a pustular skin which seldom sees the daylight.
He wryly acknowledges his historical necessity, and hopes that it is merely transitional: 'For the West, it looks strange – one man trying to control
everything, as I am. But we can live no other way for the time being, and
I don't mean only in the theatre. I have sacked two chief administrators
since I came here, and not because I am a dictator; we need someone to
think into the future. Meanwhile I must do everything myself. If we have
to contact Covent Garden or La Scala, I'm the one who speaks the languages, and a phone call from me can get more done than months of letters from state agencies.'

Exhausted by the need to be ubiquitous, Gergiev fuels himself with
music. One morning, after a run-through of *The Fiery Angel* (which concludes in a literal pandemonium, with Renata rampant in her nunnery as
an Inquisitor booms anathema), he paused neither for breath nor a lunch
break but called out the tenor Gegam Grigorian and the chorus, who
lined up on the front of the stage and hurled themselves into Prokofiev's
apocalyptic cantata *Seven, They are Seven*. This work, which uses as its text
'a Chaldean invocation engraved in cuneiform characters on the walls of
an ancient Akkadian temple', was composed between February and
October 1917; its muttering imprecations and its final cataclysm of sonic

violence convey Prokofiev's sense that the entire country was seismically shuddering beneath him. Under the circumstances, performing it was group therapy for Gergiev and his cohorts, as well as a distracting substitute for lunch.

On the night before *The Fiery Angel* opened, I watched from a side box as Gergiev – not content with rehearsing the crazily propulsive, freakily haunted opera all day long – conducted the Third Symphony which Prokofiev derived from it in 1928. The symphony muddles up the order of the opera's scenes. It begins with the duel fought by Renata's infatuated lover Ruprecht, goes on to the episode of her ordination, jumps back to an earlier seance in which she experiments with the black arts, then leaps ahead to the final torturing exorcism. In the absence of a plot, to whom do these paroxysms belong? When Gergiev conducts, they belong to him: he is the sorcerer whose coercive arms and febrile hands summon up the demons.

I recall being startled, during the BBC's telecast of the Tarkovsky *Boris Godunov* from Leningrad in 1989, to hear Gergiev in an interview refer to the city as St Petersburg. He dismissed this minor act of defiance with a grin: 'I wouldn't want to be remembered just as someone who said something!' He did more than simply use the erased, prohibited name: he carried out his own counter-revolution inside the theatre. 'When I took over, we had regional party committee meetings every Wednesday, then the unions met on Tuesday, and on Friday a city hack came to lecture us on Marxism and Leninism today. Everyone was obliged to go, even the violinists. I cancelled the lot. So in this theatre you have a small example of how in Russia things are possible, if you work. The reason for it all is to keep a tradition alive, or to make it up again from our memories, since the communists took it away from us by the way they dictated to artists. And not only the communists: Mussorgsky was broken when *Khovanshchina* was rejected by this theatre, and that led to his early death. You're right, I am a bit like Renata. She has the vision of her angel or devil in flames. I am that way with Mussorgsky and Prokofiev. I feel I am called to do this for them: it is my mission.'

This sense of an inherited responsibility is pervasive in St Petersburg. The statues represent a past which supervises the present, still creeping into its dreams. In the streets you look for characters from Russian literature, which was invented here: Pushkin's maddened clerk, fleeing from the vengeful bronze horseman; Gogol's downtrodden civil servants;

Dostoevsky's scuttling dissidents. Music, too, is inescapable, since it has made its own maps of the place. The Eleventh Symphony of Shostakovich measures the baleful, glacial immensity of the square outside the Winter Palace on Bloody Sunday in 1905, and his Twelfth records the electrified urgency of revolutionary Petrograd (as the city was called, in a fit of anti-Germanic revisionism, between 1917 and Lenin's death in 1924, when it adopted his name). His Seventh Symphony, subtitled 'Leningrad', commemorates the city's stoic resistance to the Nazi siege in 1941: a trampling march for the invaders, a requiem to inter the defenders. For forty seconds in Prokofiev's *Visions fugitives*, an agitated piano describes the crowds on Nevsky Prospect during the February revolution, in a tripping stampede of notes.

As Gergiev says, this tradition has to be reconstructed, because Stalinism interrupted or perverted it. Stalin personally denounced the lewd cacophony of Shostakovich's opera *Lady Macbeth of the Mtsensk District,* and the cultural commissars endlessly deferred performances of *War and Peace*, ordering extra military choruses in praise of Marshal Kutuzov, Stalin's official predecessor as the saviour of Russia. Shostakovich turned to subterfuge, wordlessly trumpeting his own name in the form of an abbreviated musical motto; Prokofiev, in his deceptively naive Seventh Symphony, took refuge in the sad recollection of a lost, childish innocence.

Shostakovich, still a child in 1917, never had the chance to leave. Why did Prokofiev make his apparently fatal decision to return? 'You may as well ask', Gergiev replied, 'why I have decided to stay. Prokofiev was a son of this earth, he had a longing for the landscape. I feel the same way, I am depressed if I don't see the birch trees or the river or the fortress every day.' That possessive, castrating female, Mother Russia, hovered lumpily in the air. Gergiev, who has guest engagements all over the world, understands Prokofiev's fear of deracination. When Stravinsky's *Oedipus Rex* was first performed, Prokofiev sourly commented, 'The libretto is French, the text is Latin, the subject is Greek, the music is Anglo-German (Handel), and the money is American – true cosmopolitanism.' Gergiev could make a fortune conducting Tchaikovsky lollipops with American orchestras, but he dislikes the industrialized music-making of the West: 'The problem is to find a live performance. You go to a concert and you hear a recording. No soul.' (The cavernous Slavic soul is a holy ghost often found in the company of Mother Russia.) 'It's all technology, geared to whatever new appliance the Japanese want us to buy. Besides, despite all his suffering, there were gains in Prokofiev's music after he came back. Sometimes it sounds as if they had broken his spirit. He lost that phenomenal energy you hear in the Third Symphony. The Seventh Symphony worries me with its nursery rhymes. I'm trying to understand if that is great music or not. But though there's less fantasy in the later music, there's more emotion.' He cites the solemnly resigned death of Andrei in *War and Peace*, and also the slow movement of the Sixth Symphony, where a sequence of wrenching modulations leads to a quote from Wagner's *Parsifal*: excerpting the motto which stands for the Grail knight's healing spear, Prokofiev makes a worldess plea for redemption.

For reasons which are equally personal, Prokofiev's decision perplexes Sergei Leiferkus, the baritone who sang Ruprecht in *The Fiery Angel*, although he explains it more briskly. 'Prokofiev was tricked. Stalin needed some famous people so he could get the West to trust him. At least Prokofiev wasn't sent to Siberia straight away, he succeeded better than some.'

Though born in Leningrad, Leiferkus himself now travels on three different passports and makes his home in Oxford. Why not London? 'I need a garage for the cars', he said, his perfect diction making sure that the sibillant plural buzzed. He returned to St Petersburg for *The Fiery Angel* as a guest star, amused by the fact that he qualified for a pension after two decades of service in the state theatres. His son has been forced into exile, punished by the bureaucracy because Leiferkus could afford to pay for him to study abroad. Commuting between Boston and Montreal, Barcelona and Bregenz, Leiferkus enjoys the lucrative cosmopolitan life Prokofiev renounced, and he does not share Gergiev's doubts about the Western transformation of music into a business. He hallows the memory of Margaret Thatcher, gratuitously frets about the red peril in the neutered Labour Party, and wonders how the students who sell *Marxism Today* on the streets of London would enjoy living in communal flats. To him, his chosen art symbolizes the freedom of markets and the rough justice of laissez-faire: 'I think competition is basic for a good life. After all, I'm an opera singer, and we're in competition – with others, with ourselves – all the time.'

Leiferkus sports the trophies of success – including a jewelled signet ring and some expensively reafforested hair – with understandable pride, and grumbles about the Russian customs officials who have impeded his migration: 'Here we are slaves. We are allowed to own nothing. No one asks Plácido Domingo at the border why he takes out a diamond ring or a gold statuette to put in one of his houses. But me they ask. They tell me these things are not mine, I'm just using them! They say I must promise to return the possessions I took out for my house in Oxford.'

'Will you?'

The lips of Leiferkus tightened in an acid smile: Verdi's Iago is one of his best roles.

Leiferkus's most valuable possession is a voice which may well be the most beautiful of its kind in the world, and it gives him an endearing sense of privilege. One afternoon, as I was about to faint from hunger, he produced from a polished leather briefcase another of those sugary wafers which had materialized the day before on Gergiev's desk. Remembering the famished, scavenging lines in the streets outside, I asked how long he had queued for the cake. His eyes, a polar blue behind contact lenses, sparkled naughtily. 'Oh', he said, 'ten – maybe fifteen seconds'.

For Leiferkus, Russia's abiding social and economic problem is its need for a law to protect private property: 'What is mine', he says definitively, 'must belong to me.' For Prokofiev's Renata, the more urgent need is a law protecting the artist's right to a private and socially irresponsible vision: her infatuation with the angel is an imaginative rapture which can only be interpreted – in sixteenth-century Germany, where the opera is set – as madness and heresy. Visionaries of whom Stalin disapproved ended in concentration camps; Renata sentences herself to a nunnery, and is eventually executed by the Papal Inquisition. Galina Gorchakova, the Siberian soprano who sang the merciless role with a youthfully invincible disregard for its difficulties, understood the relevance of Renata: 'I think she could find a proper place in our lives today. Probably she would be seen as a soothsayer, or a healer.' She might also have been reincarnated as the babbling female seer from Kiev who set the date for the end of the world in November 1993, only to announce a temporary postponement when the police locked up all her acolytes. Collapsing societies are apt to produce prophets.

Leiferkus the eternal competitor, perhaps irritated by the secondariness of his own part, scoffed at Renata: 'That stupid mad woman. She is a medical case, of course.' Instead he emphasized the contemporaneity of Ruprecht, a bold humanist who consults a cabbalist and attends a witches' sabbath in his quest to comprehend eternity: 'The opera shows

how it was dangerous to be a scientist at that time.' The time he meant
might be either the sixteenth century, or the twentieth. Ruprecht is
befriended by the infidel philosopher Faust, but he could equally well be
a colleague of Sakharov.

David Freeman, who directed the production, also underlined the
work's admonition to a country which was hearing it for the first time: 'I
hope that never again will a politician tell an artist or a scientist what to
do or think or create. You can kill off what makes life possible that way.'
Freeman accordingly ensured that the production made no moral judgment on Renata's spiritual transports. He surrounded her with a troupe of
acrobatic familiars, white devils whose nakedness provoked shifty titters
from the puritanical Russian audience. These demons slid through the
walls, metamorphosed into dogs, ravished nuns, then retired to writhe
high up on the walls. They served to make visible a reality which only
visionaries can see. Freeman told his spirits, 'Don't assume that you're evil.
You're just unknown. It's like Russia and the West in the past: each
demonised the other because of ignorance.' In the final scene the
Inquisitor, his rite of exorcism ruined by the hallucinating nuns, calls in
halberdiers as representatives of state power to batter the rebels. The two
acts of Freeman's production conclude with radically un-Soviet images of
individuals confronting mystery, casting off an old ideological certainty.
Ruprecht interrogating the black magician stares up into the dark while
skeletons jig and rattle behind him; Renata is raised aloft in a profane crucifixion as the sky opens and a scorching, blinding eye stares down into
the shadowy cave which is our world.

Freeman spoke of 'a wilderness in the middle of culture'. During
Renata's seance in Cologne, there are rumblings and bangings behind the
walls, as the spirits she has roused demand entry to the room. 'Society is
just a fence', said Freeman. 'It's like the wall you build around a city. We
think that we can push the wall back and recover the wilderness, civilize
it. The witch, like Renata, knows you can't do that. She doesn't live inside
the fence like the rest of us, she walks on the wild side of it.'

The suspended flats and flimsy partitions of David Roger's set underlined the frailty of our defences, the improbability of civilization. That
view could be confirmed by looking out of the window of the malachite
room in the Hermitage. Across from this tropical conservatory of precious
stone is the log cabin where Peter the Great lived when the place was still
a humid, uninhabitable bog. Now on the white crust of the river men sat

on chairs, fishing through holes they had drilled: I suppose this chilly vigil beats queuing. The same view coincides with the landscape of Prokofiev's music. His early scores were made from fire: the industrial heat of the foundry in his ballet *Le pas d'acier*, or the searing radiance of Renata's angel. The music composed after his return to Russia – the skidding battle on the frozen lake in *Alexander Nevsky*, or the blizzards at Smolensk which punish Napoleon's army in *War and Peace* – inclines to the condition of ice, jagged and lethal. One reason for Prokofiev's return was his desire 'to see real winter again', though in his diary he sardonically reported watching ice on the Dnieper blown up with dynamite. It might have been a prescription for inducing change in a sclerotic society.

When the ice breaks, of course there is floundering chaos. David Roger studied the workings of Russia from a hospital ward, where he was being treated for a kidney stone. A cat occupied the bed before his arrival; the sheets were not changed. A nurse resembling a secret policeman took a blood sample by slitting his thumb with a razor blade, sucking out blood into her own mouth through a pipette, then spitting it into a saucer. When he protested, he was proudly shown the complaints book, a prime exhibit of Gorbachevian openness. He was also told that although the bureaucrats had passed a law insisting that every state institution should have such a book, they had omitted to pass a supplementary law nominating someone to read the complaints. He bargained pairs of tickets for *The Fiery Angel* in return for the promise of clean syringes.

While he was lying in his eiderdown of cat fur, the doors of his set were built back to front and the costumes sewn inside out. The acrobats began to suffer from an allergy to their second skin of white make-up. (When the production reached Covent Garden in April 1992, they developed another problem, and began inexplicably to fall off their perches. It was discovered that they were starving, since they consider buying food to be a waste of their expense allowance.) And at the dress rehearsal, the bear-like bass who sang the Inquisitor – a totem of rectitude – staggered on stage drunk and had to be propped up by two prompters, one at each elbow.

'The director says it's a disaster', shrugged Leiferkus. 'What can you expect when the whole country is a disaster?'

'I don't care about the whole country', wailed Freeman. 'I just want this show to work! These people talk about being Russian as if it were a disease. Why can't they be responsible for themselves?' He suspected that inefficiency was their canny means of self-defence: 'It's the way they learned to deal with being oppressed from above and mismanaged for so many decades, or centuries. When you ask them to do something, they say yes straight away. Then they don't do it. I've screamed more here than ever before. Usually I'm not a screamer.'

After the opening, Freeman planned to travel east to Uzbekistan: 'I've always wanted to go there – the silk road, not the hippy trail. I'm supposed to arrive two days after the place becomes a country. They still don't know if they can give me a visa because they don't know who should issue it, and they can't sell me an air ticket because they can't work out what it will cost. Plus there's a civil war there.' Freeman savvily cancelled his trip.

Gergiev meanwhile had discovered that theatrical politics recapitulated traumatic national events. 'Next week all the republics become different countries, so my company is suddenly international. Our tenor is Armenian, we have twelve Ukrainians. Everyone was horrified when I invited a Georgian here to direct Prokofiev's *Gambler* – I am Ossetian, you see, and our two peoples are officially at war. You can't expect paradise when you put a hundred and twenty nationalities together in the same country. Gorbachev's mistake was when he did nothing to stop the nationalist killings in Azerbaijan. It was the miscalculation of an enormously messianic man. It worries me because I come from the Caucasus, from a city with a whole mess of different ethnic groups. In the Baltic states they dramatized their protests, and that got the Western press interested. But many more people are dying in the Caucasus. How can I hold on to this ensemble? I suppose, like Gorbachev, I'm struggling to save the Union! Somehow or other, this poor country has to go through a catastrophe every fifty or seventy years.' It was a cue for Mother Russia – a booming, bosomy contralto – to groan.

Gergiev, however, trusts opera to tell Russia the truth about its tormented past. He is fascinated by the parallel between Mussorgsky's initially progressive Godunov and Gorbachev: hailed as saviours by the crowd, then promptly rejected in favour of someone else. On a recent visit to Moscow, the Kirov company had presented *Khovanshchina* during the Congress of Deputies. Yeltsin, Gorbachev and the hard-liner Ligachev attended, and were astounded by the scene in the opera when the Europeanizing reformer Golitsin, the conservative keeper of the faith Dosifei and the aristocrat Khovansky with his private army quarrel inconclusively over the fate of Russia: 'They saw themselves on stage. And they saw that the problems are still the same as they were in the seventeenth century, when the opera happens, or the nineteenth, when Mussorgsky composed it.' This perception gives *War and Peace* a convulsive power in Gergiev's performances of it. Kutuzov's lament for a Moscow he is tactically abandoning becomes the anthem of a tragic history, levying sacrifice as the price of survival.

In a society where language was for so long tainted by lies, music can retain a clear conscience. One day, in the Peter and Paul Fortress where the Tsars knouted opponents to death, a tout sidled up to me and muttered a magic, seditious password in my ear: 'Vishnevskaya?' From inside his overcoat he produced not caviare or cocaine but a compact disc of Shostakovich's Fourteenth Symphony, with Galina Vishnevskaya singing and her husband Rostropovich conducting. This was artistic contraband: in disgrace because they had harboured Solzhenitsyn, Vishnevskaya and Rostropovich were hustled abroad in the 1970s, then summarily deprived of their citizenship. Anna Akhmatova, another casualty of Stalinism, wrote a poem about listening to Vishnevskaya's voice on the radio. She interpreted the ululation of anguish in it as a protest, safe because it communicated through tone not words. But when I asked Galina Gorchakova which singers she had admired and learned from when she was a student in Novosibirsk, she surprised me by naming Callas and Sutherland. Why not Vishnevskaya, I wondered. 'She was a non-person then', said Gorchakova. 'Officially she did not exist. After she left Russia, all her records were banned. They took her name out of the history books.'

As usual with Shostakovich, the dissidence of the Fourteenth Symphony is oblique, ironic. It protests against butchery and political violence, but the poems it sets are cautiously distant from Soviet reality: Apollinaire's Bishop is perturbed by the Loreley, a witch like Renata, and instead of burning her at the stake sends her to repent in a convent; Rilke's poet lies dead, decomposing, safely apathetic at last; the Zaporozhean Cossacks, in another Apollinaire poem, denounce the Sultan of Constantinople as an evil angel, horned like Beelzebub, and add some even more furiously scatological abuse whose target, for Shostakovich, was closer to home. Vishnevskaya sings her contributions with a venom which chills the blood and a distraught compassion which breaks the heart.

I bought the disc, of course, and my five dollars earned the tout the equivalent in roubles of a doctor's monthly salary. As a souvenir, it summed up my experience more justly than those nesting dolls which place Yeltsin inside Zhirinovsky, Gorbachev inside Yeltsin, Brezhnev inside Gorbachev, and so on backwards until you reach a smugly glowering Tsar. In a society where language for so long propagated governmental lies, music retains a clear conscience. The Maryinsky *Fiery Angel* was a gesture of repentance for the Soviet corruption of culture, and an offering of hope that, when the static thraldom of ice relents, scathing truth-tellers like Renata will be tolerated, perhaps even cherished. In Russia it is the composers – rebuffed and left to destroy themselves like Mussorgsky, brutally intimidated like Shostakovich, frustrated and coerced into compromise like Prokofiev – who are the unacknowledged legislators of mankind.

SEEING AND BELIEVING

GIELGUD: ABJURING MAGIC

WHEN SIR RALPH RICHARDSON DIED IN 1983, A PACK OF journalists was dispatched from London to Sir John Gielgud's house in the country to report his reaction to the news. As Gielgud came downstairs, he overheard one of the hacks speculating about 'which of the old farts will go next'. Next, as it happened, went Olivier, followed by Dame Peggy Ashcroft. In 1990, at the age of 87, Gielgud remained the sole survivor of his fabled acting generation, and he was undergoing something perilously like an apotheosis.

In Peter Greenaway's film *Prospero's Books*, intended by the director as a homage to Gielgud and to his 'mastery of illusion', he returned to the terminal Shakespearean role of the magus who renounces his supernatural powers in disillusion and despair. Greenaway not only equated the actor with the part he played but fused both with the dramatist. Gielgud's Prospero is Shakespeare, and having rehearsed the action inside his head, speaking the lines which he later ventriloquistically distributes among all the other characters, he concludes the film by sitting down to write *The Tempest*. The performance is also a revelation of Gielgud himself: simultaneously naughty and noble, a high priest and a joker, contemplating at the end of a long life the value of the art he practises.

After completing the film, Gielgud proceeded to another role for which only he had the requisite venerability: God. The BBC engaged him to narrate *Genesis* in a radio serialization of the Bible. The casting was inevitable. What other voice – a sinfonia of effects, as mellifluous as a violin, as plaintive as a clarinet, occasionally as ominous as a kettle drum – could be entrusted with the task of creating the world over the air waves? Nevertheless, Gielgud turned up at the studio eager to learn, not to sing an over-familiar aria: 'They gave me five pages of pronunciations to watch out for – and they were all new to me!'

Castaway in exile on his island, Prospero dreamed bitterly of regaining power. In his early seventies Gielgud quit London and retired to his own magic kingdom, a pavilion built in the late seventeenth century and secreted – down thickly hedged, twisting lanes which might be leading to the heart of England – in the dense Buckinghamshire greenery. Here, instead of Prospero's fairy familiars, he keeps company with three Tibetan terriers, as fawning as fans at the stage door, and a peacock as given to strutting as its master was in his theatrical heyday. Having already made his last appearance on stage in Hugh Whitemore's *The Best of Friends* during 1988, Gielgud accepted that *Prospero's Books* would be viewed as a summary of his career and a formal farewell; but when I called on him late in 1990 he had no Prospero-like regrets, and despite his recent assignment intoning the Old Testament, he was as undivine as could be. Slightly unsteady after a trip that morning into Oxford for a session of acupuncture ('to perk me up'), he resembled a cross between a rural colonel, with his velvet smoking jacket and thin white moustache, and an impish, ruddy, worldly abbot.

He tried hard to dissociate himself from the grandeur of his surroundings and pointed out that he lived in an adjunct of the main house, which is owned 'by a lady who is' – he said with a nervously confidential titter – 'rather a terror'. In the hall he opened a wall cabinet and displayed a favourite toy: an elaborate model of an Elizabethan theatre, with Shakespeare rehearsing his actors in *The Winter's Tale*. Among the motley audience was a boy with a tethered bear, presumably the beast which Antigonus exits pursued by. 'Yes', said Gielgud, 'and if you look closely you can see that the bear's got an erection. I was so pleased when I discovered that!' The house was the man: apparently haughty, actually a box of tricks and wicked surprises. 'I suppose it looks rather palatial, but it's quite snug all the same.' He led the way to a tiny den beneath the stairs, rather like Prospero's occult cell, where the sofas bore the imprint of his dogs and beside the fire lay a basket of toy kittens for them to maul in play.

Like Prospero, Gielgud the anecdotalist looked mostly backwards. 'I'm so old', he said of Greenaway's film, 'that I was terrified I'd die before seeing it.' But Prospero's retrospection is morbid and miserable, whereas Gielgud shed years as he recalled the past. *Prospero's Books* was the consummation of a life-long affection for the play. 'I don't know whether Greenaway ever saw me in it on stage, I didn't dare to ask him.' At the Old Vic in 1930 (with Richardson as Caliban) his Prospero was 'Dante without a beard'; in 1957 for Peter Brook he played 'an El Greco hermit', dishevelled and decrepit; in 1974 for Peter Hall he was a crabby, bespectacled academic, modelled on the alchemist Dr Dee. The film required him to rethink the part yet again, since Greenaway was less interested in Prospero's psychology than in his bibliography. Facing up to a blizzard of cultural icons, bombarded by books, Gielgud here presented Prospero as Renaissance man in person, exercising a universal power through the volumes in his library, but confounded by his own sorry mortality.

'I was glad I knew the text so well, because there was so much going on in the studio to distract me! I had to try to stride around wearing that cloak with the symbols sewn into it, which was so heavy it took four people to lift it on to my back. Everywhere I looked there were supers with their private parts on show, and I had papers flying in my face all the time. And it was terribly cold in the bath.' Gielgud began the filming naked: for the sequence in which Prospero ordains the shipwreck he spent four frigid days immersed in a tank during the grim Dutch winter. 'It wasn't the first time. When I made *Orchestra Conductor* in Poland with Andrzej Wajda, we started in a nasty hotel room, and the first thing he said to me was "Now take all your clothes off." I blinked. "Yes," he said, "it's the middle of the night, you're telephoning your wife, you wouldn't have any clothes on." I said to him, "You might have warned me", but of course I did as I was told. I'm very obedient. Except when I'm the director. Then I'm a tyrant!'

Before meeting Greenaway, the deferential, insecure Gielgud spent years pleading with other directors to film *The Tempest*. Ingmar Bergman, who would only work with a clique of intimates, turned him down, as did Alain Resnais. Giorgio Strehler replied to Gielgud's request with a video tape of his stage production. Gielgud could find no go-between through whom to approach Kurosawa, but eventually worked with him by proxy: the onerous cloak in *Prospero's Books* was made by the costume designer from *Ran*, Kurosawa's feudal adaptation of *King Lear*. An actor's life consists of rejections, and Gielgud remained philosophical about such setbacks. 'We're so easily hurt and so easily downed, yet we're very resilient. One has to plod on. It's the only thing I'm any good at, so I thought I should keep going. Somehow, I must have had a feeling that Greenaway was just around the corner.'

Early in his career, Gielgud sniffed at cinematic Shakespeare. 'I'd seen the Hollywood *Midsummer Night's Dream* with Mickey Rooney and Mendelssohn's music, and I hated it. So I turned down the chance to film

Hamlet for Alexander Korda, and then I said no to MGM's *Romeo and Juliet*, which they made with Leslie Howard. Hitchcock seduced me into doing *The Secret Agent* by telling me it was *Hamlet* by other means, but of course it was nothing of the kind, and when I got the script I found that all I had to do was be skittish with Madeleine Carroll.' Recollection burblingly proliferated: 'I don't think Hitchcock liked me much, he was very contemptuous of West End actors. I was swapping with Larry in *Romeo and Juliet* at the time. We alternated between Romeo and Mercutio on different nights with Peggy as Juliet, so for the six weeks it took to shoot *The Secret Agent* I'd get up at five to go to the studio, leave twelve hours later exhausted, snooze on a sofa for ten minutes, then be off to the theatre. And during the day Peter Lorre was so wicked, he used to hide so he could give himself a fix, and everything had to be held up while they searched for him.'

Gielgud's suspicion of the medium covered a deeper unease. 'I was frightened of film. I was terrified I'd somehow be found out!' About acting for the camera, he once remarked – with a characteristic mixture of stuffiness and mockery – that 'seeing one's own back and profile is an experience usually limited to one's visits to the tailor.' He worried that film would expose his physical flaws. 'I was thought very effeminate and affected. I walked like a camel. And my hair was so thin, even then. Everyone told me I must wear a toupee, but I hid under hats instead.' This mortifying self-consciousness was shared by Olivier. 'Larry always thought he wasn't handsome enough for the camera. He disliked his nose and was always altering it, he even padded his legs. Actually I had rather good legs, better than his. People said I should have been a dancer. Strong calves! But they never did me any good, because I didn't have Larry's athletic zest. I couldn't leap about and jump off things like him. I'm such a coward. Larry also ragged me about my voice. He used to say, "You're singing, not acting!"'

Eventually Gielgud overcame his doubts about himself, film and its adequacy for Shakespeare. He longed to play the chorus in Olivier's *Henry V*, but was too proud to ask. Olivier, slyly competitive, cast him as one of the crookback's first victims in his film of *Richard III*: 'Larry was an autocrat, rather frightening at times. He had a very dark side.' His experience as Cassius in the *Julius Caesar* directed by Joseph Mankiewicz in Hollywood, with Marlon Brando as a bare-chested, mumbling Antony, was not entirely satisfactory. 'It was all done on the cheap. They shipped in the set for the Forum from Italy, where they'd used it in some epic or other, and they had to film the battle in the Hollywood Bowl. I spent hours on top of horses and underneath them, and had to have three baths when I got home at night. I must say Louis Calhern was more like a bank manager than my idea of a Roman Emperor. And I was very unhappy with the American actors when I directed Richard Burton's *Hamlet* on Broadway: they were always wanting to know what their motives for everything were!'

Gielgud also played the moribund Henry IV in Orson Welles's digest of the history plays, *Chimes at Midnight*, with Welles himself as a Falstaff too sweetly ingenuous for this crafty world. At least it is sometimes Gielgud you see in Henry IV's intermittent scenes. Filming in Spain, Welles could not afford to pay anyone for more than ten days' work, so his cast dispersed whenever he declared temporary bankruptcy. Funds were not available for air fares to recall Gielgud from other engagements, so whoever was hanging around on the set took his place. Henry IV is mostly seen in the indistinct distance, or else from behind. 'Orson was so maddening. He had everything you need for Shakespeare – the voice, the appearance, the imagination, the education – but never any money, and there were always bailiffs and mistresses and unfinished films in the background. As an actor, he could give a wonderful *picture* of a Shakespearean character – except that, come to think of it, we none of us ever saw him in make-up as Falstaff. But it never developed, perhaps because he had no experience of the stage, or of doing things in sequence. It was the same with Brando. He did his Antony in bits, back to front, so he never knew where the climaxes should be. Orson's life was such a tragic waste. And then I did him out of his wine commercials on television, poor man!' Gielgud took over from Welles in fruitily commending Paul Masson's Californian vintages; he remembered the usurpation with a guilty giggle.

After so many aborted or only half-successful projects, *Prospero's Books* was a source of gratification, even though Gielgud added, with his usual artless frankness, that the cap Prospero wears in his cell 'makes me look like an old lady, and I wish they'd given me a plain white robe to play the last scene in.'

He went on to intimate that some of his younger colleagues — chosen for their looks not their talent – were woefully over-parted. Ensconced in the country, he maintains a more or less diplomatic detachment from the contemporary theatre, but has never been able to counterfeit discretion:

'Vanessa Redgrave is our greatest actress, but she's such a bore. No humour at all, except on stage. Ian McKellen I don't warm to. His personality doesn't appeal to me.' Remembering his long association with Noël Coward, I asked – rather deviously – if he had been to see Joan Collins sashaying through *Private Lives*. 'I sent flowers', he said rapidly, as if referring to a funeral. 'I do like her, but oh, I couldn't have sat through it.'

There are anthological stories of Gielgud's inadvertent truth-telling. At a clubbable lunch, he gave a loud, relieved sigh when a table-hopping playwright passed him by: 'Thank God, he didn't stop, he's even more boring than Eddie Knoblock.' His host, to whom he addressed the remark, was of course Eddie Knoblock. From anyone else in the profession, such scurrility would be an exercise of the star's power to hurt and humiliate others with impunity, while continuing to eat lunch at their expense. But no one ever blamed Gielgud for his incapacity to edit his thoughts; his gaffes appeared to be evidence of an unspoiled, unsocialized naïvety. The lives of his closest colleagues were theatres of cruelty: Olivier with his 'dark side', ventilated in his Richard III or the Nazi dentist in *Marathon Man;* Richardson with his dangerous, anarchic caprices, which so suited the menace of Pinter's *No Man's Land.* Gielgud, by contrast with their controlled madness, seemed sweetly reasonable. His gaffes, however, gave the lie to his swanning, silver-tongued poise, and revealed the flustered insecurity of the man, sure that others were thinking the same uncomplimentary things about him that he was blurting out about them.

His comments on his bandy-legged walk – Ivor Brown in 1924 remarked that Gielgud's Romeo had 'the most meaningless legs imaginable' – and his baldness hinted at a self-disgust which might have been a motive for his creativity. He reminisced about reinventing himself to play the seedy litterateur (based physically on the unkempt Auden) in *No Man's Land* in 1975: greasy hair, crumpled suit, sandals with socks. And, I remembered, an improbable sagging belly. 'Oh, that was my own, I'm afraid', said Gielgud with a flush. 'I must have grown it out of sympathy.' The actor's trade is an odd blend of exhibitionism and self-denial, maybe self-hatred. Why else make a living out of being other people? Gielgud owned up to the contradiction. 'I must say I do rather like being famous! I've got five fan clubs in Germany. I did a small part in a film with Michael Douglas there a while ago – very dreary, four days work took three months – and all the time there was a crowd outside my hotel, and

I had people following me everywhere.' Yet what use is the adoration of all these strangers, and to what personal inadequacy in the celebrity does it appeal? Often in his career, Gielgud castigated himself for being too keen to make an audience love him.

Perhaps he remained a great artist by keeping his wounds open, by not recovering from slights and put-downs administered to him seventy years before. 'Nobody thought I was much good when I was young,' he told me. 'I think I only succeeded because I had so many family contacts in the theatre, which is rather shaming.' His mother belonged to the acting dynasty, the Terrys; but the English gentility in Gielgud was countered and complicated by a Slavic melancholy inherited from his father's family – Polish aristocrats, ousted by the revolution in 1830. This ancestry made up Gielgud's mind for him when Tony Richardson tried to entice him out of retirement in 1990 to play the grumbling, doddery retainer Firs in a stage production of *The Cherry Orchard* with Vanessa Redgrave, Alan Bates and Paul Scofield: 'It's not the right part for me – it has to be a little old man, a peasant – I'm not the type at all!'

The brooding East European mood adapted itself to England in Gielgud's temperament by mutating into a sense of humour. To laugh at yourself was a socially acceptable way of dramatising irony, uncertainty, even anguish. 'The old actresses like Marie Tempest took themselves *so* seriously. My first Lady Bracknell in *The Importance of Being Earnest* was my aunt, Mabel Terry. She was superb in farce, though she hadn't a grain of humour herself. She used to look out front and mutter "Whatever are they laughing at?" Maybe our generation had too much sense of humour. Noël and Ivor Novello sent themselves up before anyone else could. I suppose we were frightened, so we made a joke at our own expense.'

This shy, awkward self-mockery perhaps made the sublime fury of Shakespearean tragedy inaccessible to Gielgud. He gleefully acknowledged that his Othello, crushed by the ornamentation of Zeffirelli's production, was dire: 'I should have played Iago when I was younger. Larry was the only *English* actor who ever made a success of Othello.' About Lear he said 'I had four goes at it – the first when I was only twenty-five – with enough success to please me and enough failure to convince me I should never have done it at all. Peter Hall begged me to do it again at the National Theatre, but they kept on changing the director, and then they wanted to take it on a world tour. Eventually I refused, but one day before I decided I ran into Larry. He looked at me rather cunningly and said "Johnny, *surely* you don't want to do Lear again – do you?"'

The fraternal rivalry between the pair persisted, in Gielgud's imagination, even after Olivier's death, and in scoffing about London's citadels of subsidised drama – the concrete ziggurat of the National Theatre and the Royal Shakespeare Company's subterranean bunker in the Barbican – he was especially cheeky about the gaping auditorium at the National which commemorates its founder: 'The National's an airport, and the Barbican's a hospital. You simply can't hold the house in the Olivier, as you could in the old Edwardian theatres. They should keep it for things like *The White Horse Inn.* Or *The Miracle*, if they ever revive it!' As Gielgud well knew, neither work – the cutely folksy operetta, or Max Reinhardt's religiose pantomime – is ever likely to be admitted into the canon.

He rhapsodised blimpishly about the days when theares were built of golden wood not steel and were upholstered in red velvet, and when actors rehearsed in suits rather than being put through Tai Chi warm-ups. 'There was a kind of mystical grandeur to the stars of my youth, one didn't dare approach them! The Edwardian actresses were such prima donnas. Actresses today are very housewifely and ordinary, like Judi Dench. The change started in the Twenties, with Noël coming on in his dressing gown. From the dressing gown period we advanced very quickly to the kitchen sink perod. I've always tried to be as matey as possible, but nowadays you have to go to all extremes, take your clothes off, use filthy language....'

I quietly reminded him about his own nude scenes for Greenaway and Wajda, and about the Oscar he won as his reward for saying, while a sozzled Dudley Moore romped in the bath in *Arthur*, 'I suppose I am now expected to wash your dick, you little shit.' He blushed, and grinned at being caught out. Gielgud, like any aged gentleman, might anathematise modernity – 'London is so awful now!' he wailed to me. 'The plastic bags in the streets and the beggars and the motor bikes and the tourists, the vulgarity of it all!' – but as an actor he long ago made his peace with modernism. In the 1950s he dismissed *Waiting for Godot* as gibberish; in 1970 he recanted by joining Ralph Richardson at the Royal Court to play two inmates in a lunatic asylum in David Storey's *Home*. 'Ralph and I', he remembered, 'got on so well with all the hippy young men.' The butler in *Arthur* with the foul mouth and the impeccable diction should not have been a surprise.

There is a supremely touching moment at the end of *Prospero's Books* when Gielgud, having waved away his shaky mythological masque, says with tears in his voice:

> We are such stuff as dreams are made on,
> And our little life is rounded with a sleep.

He speaks these lines against a black backdrop, and having done so he slowly closes his eyes. He might have been acting his own death. Yet it would be wrong to identify Gielgud with the exhausted, disillusioned actor in this scene. His own eyes remain wonderingly open. His memories are not an obsequy but a means of rejuvenation: he glowed and glistened with joy as he talked. He never pondered a Shakespearean role intellectually, he said: 'I throw myself in, like a boy tackling charades.' There is bravado and abandon and exhilaration in that. In his late eighties, his genius still had its roots in a lovable, candid, mischievous childishness.

OTHELLO: THE AUTOBIOGRAPHY OF ORSON WELLES

'HE WAS', MARLENE DIETRICH FAMOUSLY GRUNTS AS THE BLOATED, punctured body of Orson Welles bobs down a scummy canal in *Touch of Evil*, 'some kind of a man'. Quite so, but no one bothers to ask Dietrich (who plays a taciturn Mexican whore) the essential follow-up question: what kind of man exactly?

Should we remember Welles as the prodigy whose first film, *Citizen Kane*, instantly revolutionized the art of cinema, or as the self-indulgent wastrel later described by Walter Kerr as 'the youngest living has-been'? We have a choice between the Luciferean sewer-rat he played in *The Third Man* and the innocent, abused goodness represented by his Falstaff in *Chimes at Midnight*; between the elegist for genteel, pre-industrial America in *The Magnificent Ambersons* and the self-merchandising Welles who appeared in commercials for sherry, lager, fish fingers or anything else that could be drunk or eaten, who hired himself out to play a succession of Biblical potentates, over-ripe Roman Emperors and grease-ball dictators in bad films made by others, and suffered definitive disgrace when he impersonated the obese mogul Lew Grade in *The Muppet Movie*. Did he end his career as a spurned genius or a corpulent self-parody?

Pathological explanations seem to be called for. Mark Robson, who worked on the editing of *Citizen Kane*, surmised that Welles had a 'need for failure': the boy wonder, having outgrown his juvenile promise, sabotaged his work – afflicting his films with inaudible or unsynchronized soundtracks, leaving them unfinished or else (like the *King Lear* which was his last, most cherished project) unmade – in order to preserve his mystique.

Mostly, however, it was others who willed Welles to fail. He refused to work within the Hollywood system; he therefore had to be destroyed. *Citizen Kane* was almost suppressed because of threatened reprisals from the press magnate Hearst, whose megalomania it lampooned. RKO discarded a third of *The Magnificent Ambersons*, and – with Welles safely absent in Brazil at work on a documentary, *It's All True*, which was also cancelled – traduced it with a happy ending. *The Lady from Shanghai*, a nightmarish exercise in paranoia, had soft-focus close-ups of Rita Hayworth inserted into it for the sake of glamour. *Touch of Evil* was casually chopped about to clarify the plot.

Driven out of Hollywood, Welles spent the last three decades of his life soliciting funds from dodgy European backers, who of course all let him down. He managed to complete a self-justifying autobiographical film called *The Other Side of the Wind*, with John Huston playing Welles; but the money was advanced by an Iranian entrepreneur, and after the revolution the Ayatollahs impounded the footage, which remains inaccessible in a Paris bank vault while lawyers squabble lucratively over it.

When he died in 1985, Welles owned just one of his twelve completed films, his version of *Othello*. He willed the rights to his daughter Beatrice; she was the offspring of his marriage to the Italian aristocrat Paola Mori, who plays the daughter of Welles's homicidal crook in *Mr Arkadin*. In 1992 Beatrice Welles organized the restoration of the film which was her patrimony, touched up its hiccuping soundtrack, and secured its rerelease. For her, this began a campaign to salvage her father's disputed or misappropriated work, and to recuperate his reputation. '*Othello* was the place to start', she told me in Las Vegas (where she manages a cosmetics franchise in a shopping mall), 'because it was his most personal film. It was his crusade. He financed it himself, so the studios couldn't ruin it, but the whole operation took four years. He had a nervous breakdown in the process, and then when they trashed it in America, it really broke him. Who should have to go through all that just for a movie?'

The play may be a tragedy, but the filming of *Othello* was a protracted, delirious farce. Welles regularly closed down the production so he could act in other films (including *The Third Man*) and thus raise money for the next instalment. Once he made a nocturnal mercy dash from Italy to the south of France to plead for a loan from Darryl F. Zanuck; he slept in the hotel lobby while waiting for Zanuck to wake up, and disarmingly handed over the bill for his 420-dollar taxi fare. One can hear Welles's Falstaff exiting with an impenitent reminder of unpaid debts: 'Master Shallow, I owe you a thousand pound.'

Casting was a saga of endless substitutions. Everett Sloane, who played the crippled cuckold in *The Lady from Shanghai*, was to be Iago, but quit because he thought himself unphotogenic. Welles appealed in vain to

James Mason, then settled on the effete and snakey Micheál Mac Liammóir, best remembered for his impersonation of Oscar Wilde in a travelling stage show called *The Importance of Being Oscar*. This Iago came with a ready-made motive for resentment. In 1932 Welles wanted to play Othello in Dublin, where he had been given his first acting job in Mac Liammóir's company; Hilton Edwards, Mac Liammóir's lover, insisted that Mac Liammóir should be Othello, with himself as Iago. Planning the film in 1949, Welles enjoyed a belated revenge: he demoted Mac Liammóir to Iago, and relegated Edwards to Brabantio, Desdemona's father. Mac Liammóir kept a journal during the filming, published as *Put Money in Thy Purse*: the title employs a cynical aside of Iago's to jeer at Welles's financial distress. Welles wrote a jovial preface to the book, but was stung by its anecdotes about his absenteeism and his sexual peccadilloes ('Orson disappeared to unknown destination: may be the Moon but suspect Casablanca', or 'O. again disappeared, this time with Belle of Stockholm'), and in later years he retaliated with stories of Mac Liammór's extracurricular adventures. On location in Morocco, Iago spent his nights pursuing swarthy policemen; while filming in Venice, he targeted gondoliers, and almost drowned one of his conquests when the boat in which they were boisterously copulating capsized.

Welles got through four, perhaps five, maybe even six Desdemonas. He began with his fiancée Lea Padovani, who turned out – as if intent on confirming Othello's suspicions – to be simultaneously sleeping with a member of the crew. 'She had a face like a spoon', Welles later snorted. She also spoke no English, which had not seemed a handicap at the time. Next came Cécile Aubry, who left for a better job in a swashbuckling epic called *The Black Rose*. Welles was briefly indignant, then followed her to play a Mongol chieftain in the same film. Aubry's replacement was Betsy Blair. This time the misogynistic Mac Liammóir was ready with a metaphor: he likened her face to a golf ball. Finally Welles cast a French-Canadian actress, Suzanne Cloutier, who soon afterwards married Peter Ustinov. Cloutier's predecessors can still be seen in the film's long shots, and since Welles reassembled the dispersed company in a hurry whenever he had a windfall, he sometimes replaced Cloutier with whoever he was currently dating. 'I'm sure that's my mother in one or two scenes', said Beatrice Welles. Crucial scenes – the reunion with Desdemona in Cyprus, for instance – are played out by shadows flickering on a wall, presumably because no actress at all was available.

A sixth, invisible Desdemona, Gudrun Ure, apparently spoke Cloutier's lines for her. Welles, a fiendishly skilful ventriloquist ever since his radio days, lent his own versatile voice to as many parts as he could in his films. Still, even he did not dare to essay Desdemona, although he once played mewling quintuplets in a broadcast. The dubbing was his practical joke on Cloutier: he remarked during the filming that he was saving the scene in which Othello strangled Desdemona for the last day, for fear that Cloutier, described by Mac Liammóir as an adamantine butterfly, might not survive to do a retake. Cloutier herself, now retired in Montreal, remains faintly miffed by all these usurpations. 'I know I did all those long shots', she insisted when I asked about the multiplicity of Desdemonas. 'And I think I recognize my voice!'

Beatrice Welles refused to arbitrate, but mentioned her own experience as an actress in an Orson Welles film. Aged nine, and growing up as a gipsy in Welles's Spanish entourage (he did not believe in sending her to school, except for flamenco lessons), she played Falstaff's page in *Chimes at Midnight*, which he was filming in tandem with a version of *Don Quixote*. Welles, as if making home movies, cast a different child in each of his Shakespeare films: his daughter Christopher, born to his first wife, Virginia Nicholson, appeared in *Macbeth* as Macduff's precocious young egg, and was murdered by her own father; Rebecca, born to Rita Hayworth, carried someone's train in *Othello*. For Beatrice, Welles augmented a role which in *Henry IV* scarcely exists. 'I'm the one who announces "Falstaff is dead", and I push his enormous coffin. Only it's not my voice, and not my body either most of the time'. When she fell ill with rheumatic fever, Welles found a minuscule double who was smuggled into the page's armour; Beatrice's voice was provided by a middle-aged cockney sparrow. The Welles who delighted in magical sleight of hand and in *F for Fake* announced 'I am a charlatan', thought that film was the art of bemusing the ear and deceiving the eye.

The making of *Othello* depended on inspired improvisation. The armour was cheapskate bricolage, pieced together from sardine cans; Othello's ship was a shadow, since the budget forbade anything more substantial. The opening sequences undertake a relaxed tour of Othello's adopted city, where the sets were free, provoking Kenneth Tynan to joke that this was 'the movie version of Ruskin's *The Stones of Venice*'. Fuzzily visible and seldom audible, characters perambulate in long shot across the Piazza San Marco, while Roderigo's dog – a Wellesian addition to the cast – scatters the pigeons, or scampers up and down the picturesquely coiled staircase of the Palazzo Contarini.

The action of the play then transfers to Cyprus. Welles at first proposed to construct the entire embattled island in a studio near Carcassone. He adored what Truffaut called 'the closed-universe principle'. His model perhaps was the glass ball with the snowy landscape inside it which is Citizen Kane's most treasured possession: a brittle microcosm, like Hamlet's nutshell which contains an infinity. Welles enjoyed packing worlds into a small room. His film of *Macbeth* took over a set which had already served as the interior of a mine in several Westerns and turned it into a cerebral cortex of porous papier-mâché rock, with cataracts seeping down its walls. For *The Trial* he squeezed Kafka's labyrinthine Prague into the disused Gare d'Orsay, and for *Touch of Evil* he transformed the other Venice – a few blocks of plaster arcades and sluggish rivulets on the beach below Santa Monica – into a scabrous Mexican border town. Eventually he relocated Cyprus to a fortress at Mogodor, on the North African coast, where a cranial architecture of riddling tunnels and recessive crannies maps Othello's obsessions. His editing spliced continents together, in a triumph of imploded geography: Iago strolls out of a church on the Venetian lagoon and into a cistern in Morocco.

When the cast and crew arrived in Mogodor, the costumes Welles had commissioned from a fancy Florentine couturier were not available: the dress-maker refused to deliver them until he was paid. Local Jewish tailors ran up cut-rate substitutes. Meanwhile, financial necessity forced Welles to be inventive. In order to justify a scene in which the characters would be wearing only loin cloths, he shot the murder of Roderigo in a fish shop converted by vaporizers into a steam bath. This desperate contrivance resulted all the same in an episode which distils the miasmal humidity and sexual sweat of the play's atmosphere.

There is still controversy about Welles's acting of Shakespeare. Eric Bentley disqualified him altogether: 'He never acts; he is photographed.' Olivier thought he lacked the breath control for Othello, and John Gielgud, when Welles told him he intended to play the role on stage in London, simply repeated the information in a crescendo of incredulity: 'You're going to play Othello? On stage? In London?' It is true, as Gielgud went on to admit, that Welles knew how the character should look: his Othello is a beautiful buccaneer, with that baby-faced ingenuousness which never entirely disappeared beneath his fat.

He also possessed the voice – the richly lubricated, insinuating instrument of the salesman he became. Those television commercials must have attracted Welles because they often required him to impose a personality in his own physical absence, as if he were still playing his radio role of The Shadow, who whispered his knowledge of 'what evil lurks in the hearts of men'. He never outgrew his delight in the aural enchantment of radio. If Christopher Isherwood could say that he was a camera, Welles identified himself by pointing a camera at a microphone: at the end of *The Magnificent Ambersons*, reciting the credit titles aloud in order to exercise that leonine authorial voice, he announces – over a shot of a microphone – 'I wrote the script and directed it. My name is Orson Welles'. Vocal self-indulgence sabotages Welles's Macbeth, spoken in a slurring, drunken brogue which is more Boston Irish than Scottish. The same mannerism ought to suit Othello, already almost an operatic tenor, in love (like Welles) with the sound he makes. Challenged in the street, he does not merely tell his adversaries to lower their swords but elaborates the command into a conceit: 'Keep up your bright words, for the dew will rust 'em.' Yet in this regard, astonishingly, Welles's Othello disappoints. He speaks the verse lethargically. Sometimes he rewrites it, and whole paragraphs are blown away by the Atlantic gales in which he filmed.

He may have had reasons for this maddening negligence. A film cannot contain the sound and fury of a theatrical performance, which is why the cinematic record of Olivier's Othello at the Old Vic looks so grotesque. On Shakespeare's stage, dense verbal imagery made up for the lack of scenery; on film, scenery necessarily replaces language. In *Macbeth*, Welles cuts away from his own delivery of the hero's 'Tomorrow, and tomorrow, and tomorrow' to a scene in which clouds coagulate in the sky. Instead of listening, we watch as the metaphors are visualized. Welles understood that, in a film of Shakespeare, the camera should do the talking and the emoting. 'Did you know', a character cheekily asks in *The Other Side of the Wind*, 'that there are dissolves in Shakespeare?'

This is perhaps why Welles was so lackadaisical about synchronizing sight and sound in his films. In *Chimes at Midnight*, the words on the soundtrack hardly ever correspond to the motions being made by the actors' mouths. As well, the wrong voices frequently emerge from those mouths – Welles dubbed the role of the conspirator Worcester on Fernando Rey's behalf. Perhaps the bad lip-synching, together with the camera's perpetual motion, is meant to separate images from words.

Whenever during editing Welles found that visual and verbal rhythms did not agree, the words yielded right of way. He added an extra exclamation to one of Othello's crucial, quotable lines – turning 'It is the cause, it is the cause, my soul' into 'It is the cause, it is the cause, oh my soul' – in order to underline the lurching of the camera. Later the sequence was re-edited and the 'oh' removed, but not because Welles acknowledged the sanctity of the text: now the line is whispered over a blacked-out screen as the camera, following Othello through Desdemona's dark, draughtily cavernous bedroom, momentarily loses him in the shadows.

In *Othello*, the camera is the hero's eye, and it registers all the convulsions in his consciousness. We do not see Othello's epileptic fit; instead the camera swoons, and we stare up at a frame of craning bystanders and the unblinking, inquisitorial sun. At the end, in Othello's dementia, the camera goes on a vertiginous dance of death through the bedroom, bumping its head on the ceiling before slumping back to ground. Welles knew all about the hallucinatory subjectivity of the cinema. To film Shakespeare is not to photograph people speaking verse; it is to create – as he does here, or in the gruesome, gruelling battle in *Chimes at Midnight*, or even in the primeval sludge and viscous fog of his *Macbeth* – a poetic phantasmagoria. In a play, primal scenes may occur off-stage, like the murder of Duncan. The event is unseeable, rather than unspeakable. Macbeth and his wife speak of nothing else, but they use language and metaphor to alter what they have seen and to deny what they feel: thus Duncan's skin is improbably silver, his blood golden, or else the welter of gore is Latinized and sanitized by the oddly pictorial word 'incarnadine'. A film can have no interest in such verbal equivocations. Neither can it elide what has happened in the wings, or between the scenes: it is a visual form, making images to match our dreams. Therefore Welles shows the murder, adds the episode in which Macbeth slaughters the grooms, and invents a protracted ceremonial beheading for the Thane of Cawdor, which the play merely mentions in passing. In a staged performance of *Othello*, the most rending shocks come when we watch as a conquering hero falls on to the floor, gibbering and incapable, or share the consternation of the other witnesses as we see him strike his wife. Film cannot take the measure of these social lapses; rather it represents from within what the hero's world looks like to him as it collapses. A theoretical method always underlies Welles's technical madness.

Welles has to be accounted a great Shakespearean, if only because the roles which preoccupied him told the story of his own tragicomic life. Beatrice Welles and Suzanne Cloutier both find a personal pathos in *Othello*. 'He was always being betrayed by the people he trusted', said Beatrice, and added, firmly setting the jaw which formerly belonged to her father, 'I don't want to talk about it.' Cloutier was more expansive. The film, for her, is about Welles's quixotic idealism, and its inevitable disappointment. 'He always put women on a pedestal. He thought of them as goddesses, and then when they proved unworthy.... Look at the way he attacked Rita Hayworth in *The Lady from Shanghai*. I was lucky. He and I were only ever friends, so I stayed on my pedestal.' She also believes that Welles shared the neurotic insecurity which destroys Othello. 'Orson was always baffled by his talent, surprised by what he did. That's what being a genius means – you don't know where you get it from. It was the same with Marilyn Monroe. She was also a friend of mine, and she didn't think she was beautiful. Orson had no faith in himself; he thought he was a fraud. Othello used to be a slave, and he's always asking himself, "Why should this woman love *me*?"' Beatrice Welles agreed: 'He was apologetic about everything he did, and so insecure and ashamed that he hid behind make-up. The only film in which he really shows his face is *The Third Man* – and Harry Lime is the most hateful character he ever played.'

All the other Shakespearean characters were present inside Welles, adding up into the repertory company of his myriad selves. In *Chimes at Midnight*, his tottering, sorrowful Falstaff nods his head over 'the days we have seen'. It was Welles's obituary for Merrie England, and for his own radiant youth, just as the uncompleted film of *Don Quixote* was his elegy for chivalry: 'Je suis', he told a team of interviewers from *Cahiers du cinéma* in 1958, 'un homme du Moyen Age.' As Falstaff, he needed a Prince Hal, a substitute son to whom he could transmit his tricks and by whom he felt he would inevitably be rejected: that role, in Welles's life, was played by Peter Bogdanovich. Gielgud rather tactlessly tried to interest him, when he was at his most bulbous, in playing Caliban, but Welles had already made an ersatz *Tempest*: in *F for Fake* he is a disenchanted Prospero, exposing his own virtuoso charlatanism.

The film he planned to make of *King Lear* was to be his final, angry resumption of an authority which the moguls had stolen from him. Brooding about de Gaulle and Mao, he told Bogdanovich that 'Lear became senile by giving power away. The only thing that keeps people alive in old age is power.' The end, he thought, might bring him back to the confident beginning: 'The enemy of life is middle age. Youth and old age are the great times.' In order to play Lear, he was prepared to busk again as Falstaff the old toper: in 1985 the Californian winery which had replaced him with Gielgud in its commercials rehired him. 'He told me he had a new contract', said Beatrice, 'and now there would be enough money to make *King Lear*. But a week later he was dead.'

So Welles was as mined by self-doubt as Othello, as happily improvident as Falstaff, as sceptical of his own sorcery as Prospero, as furious at declining capacities as Lear; a combination, like all his Shakespearean prototypes, of nobility and folly. He was that kind of a man, as Marlene Dietrich would surely have gone on to say.

BOXING *OTHELLO*

WHEN I ARRIVED AT THE STUDIO ON THE NORTHERN OUTSKIRTS OF London early in December 1989, I found Trevor Nunn struggling to fit Shakespeare into a box. With the hooded eyelids and impassively cogitating face of Fu Manchu, headphones clamped over his ears, he was crouched in front of a television monitor, which shared a rostrum with a litter of styrofoam cups, some screwed-up tissues, a flask of throat spray and a tiny prayer-book. Was the last item, like everything else in the jumble, an actor's little helper? Over his shoulder, I saw that the monitor's screen showed a claustrophobic muddle of human limbs among a gimcrack scattering of furniture. 'Now *how*', wailed Nunn, studying the cramped composition, 'do I get around that chair?'

Earlier in the year, Nunn's Royal Shakespeare Company production of *Othello* had packed The Other Place in Stratford and the Young Vic in London. Nunn chose these venues – a shed in a field, and a concrete bunker which used to be a butcher's shop – because he believes that in *Othello* Shakespeare was writing an intimate drama about emotional corrosion, possibly intended for a smaller theatre than the world-enclosing Globe. Now his experiment in reducing the play's rhetorical volume and adjusting it to a domestic setting faced its hardest test, as he battled to fit his actors, their grand passions and some some shaky chairs and tables into the even more exiguous theatre of a television screen.

He was working on the scene in Desdemona's closet, when Othello abuses her by pretending she is a whore, with Emilia as the brothel-keeper. Once the problem of manoeuvring around the chair while staying within the camera's range was solved, another tactical impasse replaced it: how to get the weeping Desdemona from her stool to the prie-dieu where she would consult that prayer-book. 'That's a non-move!' groaned Nunn at the tenth try like a befuddled chess player, and jeered at himself: 'Another naturalistic triumph for this show.'

When the bluff, bustling Iago of Ian McKellen arrived to investigate the fracas, Nunn had to shoehorn him into the already-congested frame.

'You're going to bend over a little bit, aren't you?' asked Nunn.

'Well', leered McKellen, 'not permanently....' Comic camping helps actors get through the day even more effectively than coffee, throat spray and prayers.

Nunn then called for the Desdemona of Imogen Stubbs to be swivelled into profile as Iago leaned over her, pretending to commiserate. 'You're not getting this profile, are you?' asked McKellen. 'My panty line?' He pointed with a grimace to his bottom, which Nunn promptly angled out of the shot.

Facial expressions were put through the same minute adjustments as the bodies of the actors and the sticks of furniture. McKellen over the years has grown himself a doleful, puffy, rather puddingy face. When not working, it looks like a tired mask; switched on, it can express anything. Hurrying in, he pulled off his regimental cap and – since he had never been in Desdemona's bedroom before – quickly, furtively looked around. Not quite furtively enough the first time: 'Perhaps the pause was the *teensiest* bit too long?' suggested Nunn. 'Fair enough to register that you're in the bedroom, but you don't need to appraise the interior decor.' At the next take, the pause was even more infinitesimal, and thus even more telling.

As he left the room, McKellen peered back at the two women whose lives Iago was ruining. 'I think I caught a little twinge of guilt there at the end', Nunn remarked. McKellen took joking offence at the notion that his psychopathic character could feel guilt. He stroked his chin, lifted his finger as if to say 'I'll fix that', and next time chillingly purified the glance of emotion. In a later scene, after a quarrel with the put-upon Roderigo, Iago is startled by a knocking at the door and scuttles away. 'It's the only moment of cowardice we see in him', Nunn reminded McKellen, who at once supplied a nauseous gulp of fear at the sound. His face has became transparent: looking at McKellen, you see a physiognomic stream of consciousness.

The camera spies on those thoughts, the microphone overhears them. Sitting ten feet away from the performing area, I was unable to hear the actors. Intensity did not entail declamation. Willard White's Othello, accusing Desdemona, could scarcely utter the word 'whore'. Most Othellos sing the lines, sometimes adding a calypso beat like Olivier. White – who played Porgy in Nunn's production of Gershwin's opera – is actually a singer, yet as Othello he gave a stringently anti-operatic performance, lowering his ebony voice at the climaxes.

Staggering off-stage after repeated takes, however, White could not help reverting to music in order to relieve his anxiety. He gasped and sweated while wardrobe assistants mopped him down; then he began to sing. On-stage he had to hiss a line about Emilia's 'mystery', meaning the sexual trade she plies; out of range, he boomed through a free-associating reprise of 'Ah sweet mystery of life, at last I've found you'. When he fluffed a line he strode around the perimeter of the studio and – while girls with Polaroids checked that the hair of Desdemona was correctly dishevelled and Zoë Wanamaker, playing Emilia, returned to roll a cigarette and read a novel in the corner – he chanted 'I wanna do it again' to the tune of the Beatles song 'I wanna hold your ha-a-a-and'.

A week later, in Lisbon, I saw another *Othello*. To be exact, it was *Otello* I saw – Verdi's opera, in which Plácido Domingo was making his Portuguese debut.

The performance was sponsored by a local newspaper which, in return for underwriting Domingo's fee, received permission for its photographer to record the occasion inside the opera house. Domingo entered, made love, raged and died in a blitz of bulbs. Everyone knows Hazlitt's remark about Edmund Kean, whose acting was like reading Shakespeare by flashes of lighting. This, however, was Shakespeare by the popping of flash bulbs.

Otello's first word, as he rushes on after surviving a storm at sea on his way to Cyprus, is 'Esultate!' Exultancy and uproar are the signatures of opera: Verdi's *Otello* is everything that Nunn's view of the play refuses to be. Here the action did not stay tidily inside its boxy frame. Domingo, throwing Desdemona to the ground in front of the Venetian amabassador, accidentally ripped off her necklace in the process. The pearls clattered to the floor and rolled slowly one by one down the slope to pelt like hail into the orchestra pit; the soprano might have been weeping for the loss of her jewels. During the grand ensemble which followed, there was an unorchestrated crash. A female chorus member had fainted, overcome by the lights or by the proximity of Plácido. Some musketeers abandoned their posts to haul her off. Having stabbed himself, Domingo crawled towards the nuptial bed in a night-gown split up the side, inadvertently exposing a white leg which he had not burnished to the same negroid tone as his face.

Moments after expiring, he was back in front of the curtain, arms upraised in a victory salute as the audience bawled its approval. He began his career, after all, as a bullfighter. Though Nunn's *Othello* is a psychological drama, tensely internalized, the play can also be – as it was for Verdi – a duel in the sun, loud, Latin and extroverted, leaving blood on the sand and pearls in the orchestra pit.

Back in London in January, I asked Trevor Nunn about the opera. Not surprisingly, he disapproved. 'It's an alternative work and a fascinating one, but Verdi got *Othello* wrong. It's all so refined and spiritual. There's so much lewdness and vulgarity and ugliness in Shakespeare, which Verdi excludes.'

Verdi has often been praised for eliminating Shakespeare's first act in Venice and preserving the unity of place by starting with Othello's arrival in Cyprus, having vanquished the Turkish fleet and vocally surmounted an orchestral storm. This, from Nunn's point of view, is a loss: 'Shakespeare shows these people transposed from a mercantile civilization and a life of luxury to a barren place at the rim of the world, where there is no law to appeal to and no way out.' Nunn's set for Cyprus is a cage of slats with a dirt floor. Roughing it in a combat zone, the pampered Venetians must make do with shoddy, temporary rooms. Like castaways, they have to confront the frailty of culture, the barbarity of human nature.

Nunn mistrusts Verdi's melodies – so eloquent and so fluent, a form of special pleading for the imperfect and even inarticulate people of the play. The 'Willow Song' of Verdi's Desdemona and the 'Ave Maria' which follows it are the character's means of sublimation. By the time she finishes singing, she has gained herself admission to heaven. Imogen Stubbs, on the contrary, chants the 'Willow Song' with deliberate, impatient tunelessness. 'There are so many interrupted thoughts in the play', said Nunn. 'Broken thoughts, thoughts without verbs, thoughts that lose their way – no cadences. In filming it, I wanted to shoot language, which means shooting thought-processes.'

'I believe in Shakespeare the novelist', said Nunn. In quest of novelistic veracity, he insisted on an Othello who was 'born black and raised black. How can you do a play which is so much about sexual chemistry if the actor is disguised head to foot in make-up? Whenever there's any contact, he'd come off on her! I would look forward to the time when it would be universally unacceptable for someone to be bewigged and blacked up as Othello.' Willard White took care to cause the Venetian senators a moment of shifty unease when Othello remembers being sold into slavery. Nunn's former wife, the actress Janet Suzman, had recently made the same point by staging the play with a black Othello in South Africa , where she was born. To me, the argument has the literalism and the ignorance of history which are honour badges for the politically correct; more importantly and more oddly, it implies a theoretical objection to acting itself, and to the simulations of the theatre. But I am forgetting: Shakespeare wrote novels.

For Nunn, the characters in the play possess an obdurate, annoying truth to life; those in the opera are seraphic or infernal fictions. 'I don't think Desdemona is an angel, which is what Verdi takes her for. She's a risk-taker. She wants adventures, she likes the idea of going native. She's capable of deceit too, as her father says, because she has unconventional ambitions. Look at the way she chooses to *fight* for Cassio, whereas most women would think that was mens' business.' In the film, Imogen Stubbs wears a military greatcoat when testifying to the senate, and harangues the reluctant Brabantio into submission. As a feminist demonstration that she must not be patronized, she carries her own bags aboard the ship to Cyprus, and she warms herself up with a dram on arrival. Visiting the barracks, she insists on trying out the hard beds of the soldiers. Emilia, her consciousness raised by association, defies taboos by smoking a pipe, and dies with her hand clasping Desdemona's in earnest of sisterhood. To believe in Shakespeare the novelist entails devising acres of such extraneous business, perhaps in order to distract attention from the fact that these characters, while coping with the luggage and attending to household chores, are uttering blank verse.

Having grounded Desdemona, Nunn was equally keen to rationalize the metaphysically malevolent Iago of Verdi. 'In the opera, Iago is the devil. That dehumanizes him. Verdi misses the point about all the people in the world who are like Iago. It has to be uncomfortably recognizable. You have to admit to yourself that you would trust Iago.'

Although the play is about the romance of heroism, no man is a hero to his valet, to a resentful subaltern like Iago, or to a novelist. Nunn therefore unseated the domineering protagonist: 'I want to get away from this fetish about the title role. It's actually about a quartet, even a sextet of people.' The two marriages – Othello's to Desdemona, Iago's to Emilia –

are equally important, with the demoralized Emilia arriving at the nauseous knowledge that the man to whom she has devoted herself is a fiend. Emilia emerges as a tragic heroine whose magnanimous flaw is her liberated bravery: she insists on telling the truth, on making her voice heard, and is killed for her liberality by Iago – 'I will speak as liberal as the air', Wanamaker positively roars (having rewritten Shakespeare's more enigmatic 'liberal as the north' in order to justify herself), 'yet I'll speak.... So speaking as I think, alas, I die.'

The third couple are Cassio and Bianca, who matter to Nunn because they reveal the society's double standard in sexual matters: Cassio idealizes the divine Desdemona, but simultaneously relieves himself with a harlot. A novelistic biography, neglected by Shakespeare, must be invented for these minor characters. 'When you think about Cassio,' said Nunn, 'he becomes a very interesting case. Just what *is* his problem?' The film answers that question by having Bianca unbutton his shirt and start kissing his belly. Nunn's Cassio is spotted with commonness: he throws up in self-disgust into a slop bucket after the drunken brawl incited by Iago.

I began to understand why Nunn had set his *Othello* in the nineteenth century, with military costumes which vaguely suggest the American Civil War. Shakespeare the novelist is a colleague of Jane Austen and George Eliot, and like them he concentrates on marriage so as to inspect the abrasive relationships between men and women, and between individuals and society. Tragedy is no longer an affair of spectacular fates and magniloquent gestures; its agonies are ordinary. Desdemona scavenges in a rubbish tin to look for her lost handkerchief, and Othello rifles her dressing table to find evidence of her infidelity. There has been a murder in the house over the back fence.

In the theatre, the only test of an idea is whether it works, whether you can 'play' it. I was persuaded by this *sotto voce* suburban approach to Shakespeare until, a few days later at Covent Garden, I saw *Otello* again. Domingo was the hero once more, vaulting on to the stage to sing 'Esultate!' across a bridge from his anchoring ship which the sailors hurriedly constructed over the pit. Strobe lights lanced the air from the dome of the theatre, the floor rumbled with thunder, and Carlos Kleiber, conducting, lashed the orchestra into an audible, upheaving, foaming ocean, which he calmed in a moment with a motion of his hands.

Nothing could have been further from Nunn's confidential domestic intrigues. Kleiber called into being a universe of sound which extended around, above and below the drama. A trill of jeering malice seethed beneath Iago's satanic credo. A serpentine wriggling of strings accompanied Otello as he advanced to denounce Desdemona; when he called her a courtesan, a cymbal clash struck like a concussion. The castle was split apart by fanfares when the ambassador arrived from Venice, as if the Last Judgment were being announced. Drum rolls and a cleaving blast from the brass seemed to slice the earth open as Desdemona was hurled to the floor.

In her 'Willow Song', Desdemona says that the lament she is repeating is so sad that it frightens the birds from the trees. As Kleiber conducted the passage, you could hear the birds instrumentally fleeing in dismay: distracted strings, shrill alarmed woodwinds. I remembered Nunn's desire to 'shoot language, shoot thought-processes'. Translating language into music, Verdi (with some help from Kleiber's genius) had made the audible – as in that metaphor about the birds – seem visible. The orchestra spoke Shakespeare's poetry wordlessly, with a hundred different voices. Surely Nunn's quartet or sextet of muttering, monologuizing actors could not compete with this symphony of grief? Nunn had said that the television camera 'needs to scrutinize what is real, and it exposes what is unreal.' But the television camera also has its own definition of reality, and the emotional energies unleashed by *Otello* or by *Othello* can't easily be contained in a box, or even in a theatre the size of the Royal Opera House.

Backstage in an office at the National Theatre, on a day in January when the staid reality of London outside was being overturned by a hurricane, McKellen returned to the attack on the supernatural Shakespeare of Verdi. 'It would be impossible to play the devil. Iago is not the incarnation of evil. For the actor, the problem is to make him real, and frankly I didn't find that difficult, once I looked at what he says when he's alone on stage. Shakespeare's characters never deceive the audience in soliloquy, so I trust what he says: he's jealous, too, like Othello, and afraid of being cuckolded.'

McKellen himself had exchanged realities since December. Shedding Iago's military moustache, he was now crew-cut for the concentration camp of Martin Sherman's *Bent*. Iago's deceptions were behind him; he was now playing someone like himself – a homosexual pressed into militancy by political circumstances. Or was he?

Nunn had described to me a rehearsal in which McKellen, to convince the sceptical Othello that he is telling the truth about Desdemona's adultery, suddenly burst into convulsive sobs. 'Iago believes in his own lies, he backs them up with extraordinary emotional conviction. Ian is astonishingly adept at this sort of thing. As a person he's incapable of disguising anything, but as an artist he's fascinated by deceit and falsity.' One of his greatest performances was as Face in Nunn's production of Ben Jonson's *The Alchemist*: a character who is no more than a collection of dishonest, constantly alternating façades. As a man, McKellen feels the need to be confessional; yet the art he practises depends on lying. How could he confer reality on a character who reinvents himself on the run, and who is called 'honest' by the other people in the play simply because he obligingly fits their notion of what he ought to be? Perhaps Iago engaged McKellen so deeply because the part – aesthetically though not morally – was a self-portrait: a master feigner, a consummate confidence trickster; when deprived of his technical skills, perhaps a hollow man.

He described the scene – another novelistic addition to the character's biography – in which honest Iago, impersonating a good bloke, debags a soldier at a party in the barracks. The scene was intended by Nunn to show 'how soldiering unfits these men for marriage, for all human relations other than military ones'; the coarseness of their profession has vulgarized other feelings. Despite his crew cut and an incongruously tweedy suit, and despite being late for an appointment to discuss his next Shakespearean con man, Richard III, McKellen began to act out the nasty little macho jape in a corner of the office. As he did so, his face turned wan and waxy, his eyes emptied and began to stare at me with a dull mesmerism; the joke lost all its humour as he stood aside from it to watch himself exercising power over his victim. He was changing back into Iago.

Time, I thought, to get out of here. It is possible to play the devil, and you don't need a red cape. All you need is a mortifying indifference to other people like that which was written temporarily across McKellen's features.

At the stage door Joan Plowright, in her capacity as Olivier's widow, was being ushered from the building with all due deference. She had dressed for the hurricane in her best fur coat, and wore (on a day when the sun was hiding its own face) those wrap-around dark glasses with which celebrities affect anonymity while signalling that you ought to recognize them. Out in the street, the weather was as described in the first scene of *Otello*, though without the music.

'The problem with filming Shakespeare', Nunn told me, 'is scale. You've got a heightened poetic language trying to cohere with naturalistic settings. But *Othello* is wonderfully appropriate for television, because it's so intimate.'

Shakespeare the novelist determines the scale of Nunn's film. While Plácido Domingo has said that he thinks of his voice as a cello, gravely melancholy, Willard White grunts 'Rude am I in my speech' and does his best to mean it. At Covent Garden, Katia Ricciarelli's Desdemona had been a Raphael Madonna; Imogen Stubbs is feisty, frisky and disconcertingly worldly as she larks about in the military outpost, climbing all over Othello like a kitten while he tries to concentrate on his paperwork. McKellen's Iago is embarrassed by Othello's occasional proneness to operatic bombast, and punctiliously dusts off the papers scattered when White bangs the table in a tantrum.

Yet no matter how conscientiously McKellen attempts to explain away Iago as a disgruntled officer motivated by petty jealousies, his performance goes well beyond the sober, diurnal limits of Nunn's production. The novel has not yet been written which could analyse this character. He is an invention of the theatre, dangerous because he creates, destroys and recreates himself as we watch, while remaining a mystery to us and to himself. Why does McKellen first say 'I hate the Moor' matter-of-factly, then repeat it in vomiting violence, almost gobbling his own hand as he runs his hand along his lips? Is that open mouth in soliloquy after the brawl a bored yawn or a silent scream of despair? Why does he rock and cradle the broken-hearted Desdemona, in the scene I watched him filming, with such obscene tenderness? Why the great, gratuitous sob on 'This is the fruit of whoring!' after he stabs Roderigo, and why the scampering run as he leaves, like a naughty child propelled half by terror and half by elation? What does that numbed look at the dead bodies of Othello and Desdemona mean? It speaks volumes, but they remain unspoken. Watching this moment, I had to admit that there are things opera cannot do, states of mind too complex and self-contradictory for it to register.

'I am not what I am', says Iago. Is he, or McKellen, anything at all? He retreats into silence at the end because he has no idea any more of what he should say. 'I am not what I am' is the actor's creed – a boast of power, an admission of impotence. No man can ever know himself, or be certain about where his desires and aggressions have their source. What you see on the television screen, when McKellen occupies it, is a black hole into which the illusion of human identity vanishes. That is not a sight which fits comfortably into a corner of your living-room: it dissolves the sedate, cushioned domestic box, and everything else as well.

THE REDGRAVES, THE RICHARDSONS AND REBIRTH

THIS, LIKE *HAMLET*, IS A FAMILY ROMANCE AND ALSO A GHOST STORY. In January 1993 Vanessa Redgrave paid a visit to Adelphi University on Long Island in order to see a rare newsreel clip of her father, Sir Michael Redgrave, playing Hamlet. The snippet had been discovered in a Moscow archive and brought to Adelphi by a Russian scholar. Travelling out to see it, Vanessa Redgrave was like a detective in quest of a clue to the meaning of the past: *Hamlet* recurred in her father's life, and it continues to make spectral reappearances in that of his acting family.

Vanessa herself was born during a performance of the play in 1937. Her father was on stage at the Old Vic playing Laertes, the vengeful brother of Ophelia; Olivier, the production's Hamlet, announced the birth from the footlights and predicted that the baby would be a great actress. In 1950 Redgrave graduated to the role of Hamlet after Olivier renounced it. In 1963, for the National Theatre's first production at the Old Vic, he stepped aside to play Claudius, Hamlet's adulterous uncle and the murderer of his father. Olivier directed, Peter O'Toole was Hamlet, and Redgrave's second daughter, Lynn, was a lady-in-waiting. In 1985, enfeebled by Parkinson's disease, he was taken in a wheelchair to another production of the play, now down the road at the Young Vic. In this *Hamlet* Vanessa's daughter Natasha, born during her brief marriage to the film director Tony Richardson, was Ophelia. By then Redgrave could hardly speak, although he managed to tell Vanessa, after a painful pause which lasted the whole way back to the nursing home, 'She's a true actress.' Having legitimized another successor, the next week he died.

At the time of Vanessa's sentimental pilgrimage to Adelphi, her sister Lynn was preparing a different, more tormented tribute to Michael Redgrave: a one-woman play called *Shakespeare for my Father*, which she took on a zigzagging tour of the United States, before settling into a long Broadway season. The play struggles to resolve Lynn's relationship with an adored but indifferent parent, who discouraged her while nurturing

Vanessa and their brother Corin (also an actor, and also the father of an acting daughter). Vanessa's birth had all the proper auspices, with a professional blessing from Olivier. Reading through her father's diaries, Lynn found that her own birth merited no auguries; in fact the entry for the day in question did not mention the event at all. The shock of the omission was like Lear's disinheriting of Cordelia. It made her feel that she had no lawful right to exist; it also persuaded her that, although her father had ignored her birth, she should take responsibility for her life by engineering her own rebirth.

The therapy she prescribed was a re-enactment of scenes from Shakespeare. The episodes selected for her play all have a personal subtext. Sometimes Lynn plays the faithful Cordelia, clinging to and comforting a father who rejected her. One incident of personal reminiscence resembles a supplement to *King Lear*. Dying in a noisy hospital ward, the bewildered Michael Redgrave is surrounded by his family. Curtains have been drawn around his bed to supply a pretence of privacy. When someone peeps out to summon a nurse, Redgrave – terminally imagining that he is on stage waiting for a performance to begin – grumbles that it is against the rules to twitch the curtain and peer at the audience. Lynn pats his hand and agrees with him. Vanessa, however, sternly insists on telling the truth, and tells her father that they are in hospital: there is no audience, only a disconsolate line-up of his fellow sufferers, also waiting to die. 'My sister the Marxist realist', Lynn tartly comments in her play. At the beginning of *King Lear* it is Cordelia who, like Vanessa, brushes aside the tender flatteries of love; Lynn clearly feels that such callous honesty is better suited to Goneril or Regan. Elsewhere she casts herself as a female Hamlet, addressing one of the prince's soliloquies to a dead father who seemed to her, she says, like a ghost communing with his own reflection in a make-up mirror.

The emotional climax of *Shakespeare for my Father* comes with Lynn's location of her grandfather's grave in Australia. Roy Redgrave was a profligate barnstormer who decamped to the southern hemisphere soon after his son's birth in 1908. The baby was carried on stage as a novel prop during performances of a melodrama in Sydney, but Roy had no interest in the roles of husband and parent. Michael's mother took him back to England, and he never saw his father again. For Lynn, the quest ends when she discovers the unhonoured burial plot beside Sydney harbour. She picnics there, stretches in the sun, even joyfully kicks her legs in the air. Frozen out of her father's life, she has found a way of bypassing him: she retreats a generation to celebrate her kinship with this unknown ancestor. At the play's conclusion, she drags her trunk of costumes into the wings like a coffin which can now be buried. The female Hamlet has disentangled her Oedipus complex, and laid to rest that troubling ghost.

Migration to America in the early 1970s – after Olivier curtly told her that she was a 'darling flopsy bunny' but that she could never expect a leading role while he was running the National Theatre – enabled Lynn to establish an identity apart from her invidious, encroaching family. She became a sitcom actress on television and, after some drastic slimming, made commercials for WeightWatchers. To shed fat is, for the New Age, to be born again. Lynn has written a book extolling this latest mutation of American puritanism: combining psychic self-help with low-cal recipes and explaining that she over-ate because she was under-loved, it is called *This is Living*.

America has supplied the same service to Natasha Richardson, who has transferred her base to New York because, as she puts it, 'here no one cares about the Redgrave baggage'. At home Vanessa and Corin are execrated for their support of the flakily leftist Socialist Workers' Party, which considered Thatcher's Britain to be a police state and claimed that IRA bombings were a Tory provocation, staged to damage the republican cause. The odium extends to America, where Vanessa's advocacy of Palestinian liberation has made her unpopular: acepting an Oscar for *Julia* in 1978, she took the opportunity to harangue the 'Zionist hoodlums' who were burning her in effigy as 'Arafat's whore' in the streets outside. When the Boston Symphony, after engaging her to narrate Stravinsky's *Oedipus Rex*, cancelled the contract to appease its Jewish subscribers, she sued the orchestra, accepting a donation of 150 thousand dollars from a Saudi Arabian prince to pay her legal expenses. Dropped from a national tour of a Peter Shaffer play, she again suspected political persecution and sued the producer, who happened to be married to Natasha.

America, however, exists to relieve newcomers from a burdensome, inherited past. Natasha has stepped aside from her difficult heritage by using her father's name and pursuing his love-affair with the country to which, cursing drab and class-bound England, he moved after the end of his marriage to her mother. Her major successes have been in American roles: she played Patty Hearst, the kidnapped heiress converted or brainwashed by her radical captors, in Paul Schrader's film; she was the traumatized Catharine, threatened with a lobotomy to cut a forbidden knowledge out of her brain, in a television version of Tennessee Williams's *Suddenly Last Summer*; she made her Broadway debut in 1993 as Eugene O'Neill's reformed harlot in *Anna Christie*. (She received a Tony nomination for best acress as Anna Christie; so did Lynn Redgrave for her Shakespearean memoir. Luckily, preserving the peace in their fractious family, neither of them won.)

Despite her adoption of another country, Natasha has ghosts to ward off, demons to exorcise. She has inherited her mother's smoky voice and her talent for emotional revelation, yet is determined to make her way independently. 'She's afraid of having her mother's career', Paul Schrader told me. When I remarked that her mother's career was not a bad thing to have, he countered with an assessment of Vanessa Redgrave's bankability: 'Her mother was never a commercial star, she was never hot – not on the A list.' He went on to liken the Redgrave family romance to that of the Renoirs, Auguste the painter and his son Jean, the film director: 'When I was at graduate school in Los Angeles, I used to spend Saturdays at Renoir's house, and he was always talking about the curse of being his father's son. He used to say, "My father hated movies, but it was fortunate for me they came along when they did – they saved me from having to be a painter." Then of course Jean Renoir went on to dump all over his own son.'

As well as competing with her mother, Natasha must cope with the distressing legacy of her father, who died of AIDS in 1991. Anna Christie travels from Minnesota to New York to reclaim the drunken father who abandoned her. Soon after Tony Richardson's death, Natasha found the manuscript of an autobiography locked in a cupboard in his house above Sunset Boulevard, and set about organizing its publication. The book concludes more happily than Lynn's relationship with the spectre of her father: it has an epilogue addressed by Richardson to his daughters, Natasha and her sister Joely (also, of course, an actress). Natasha says, 'It was his goodbye to us – which he never spoke in life.'

Actors emote on our behalf. They offer to share our miseries, or to be agitated by our madness. All families are complex and strife-ridden, incubators of guilt and conflict. At least the members of the Redgrave and Richardson clan can turn to Shakespeare or O'Neill for help in living down the past.

In 1967, at the age of four, Natasha Richardson officiated as a bridesmaid at one of her mother's cinematic weddings. Embarrassingly, she was herself, as she now admits, 'madly in love with the groom'. He was an actor called Mark Burns; her father masterminded the ceremony for a scene in his film *The Charge of the Light Brigade*, and it took place at the country home of Michael Redgrave and his wife Rachel Kempson (who is, it goes without saying, herself an actress). 'On the day we filmed the scene', Natasha remembers, 'a bee stung me. I screamed and cried so much they called a doctor, and my father said, "It can't hurt that badly!" But it wasn't the pain that upset me, it was the thought that I mightn't be in the film. Already the little professional!'

By this time, Tony Richardson had already left Vanessa. He attempted to protect his daughters from political indoctrination by making her sign a legal agreement not to take them with her to meetings of the Socialist Workers' Party. 'He wasn't really successful', says Natasha. 'I still remember a girl in a physics class pointing at me and saying, "Your mother's a commie." He tried to persuade me to come to Los Angeles and live with him.' But she remained in England, inevitably attended drama school, and got her first London job in a production of *A Midsummer Night's Dream* outdoors in Regent's Park. She played Helena, aware that there was almost a genetic inevitability to the choice of role. 'All the Redgraves play Helena', Lynn remarks during *Shakespeare for my Father*: she herself did so at the Royal Court in the mid-1960s, with Tony Richardson directing; her own daughter has recently inherited the part. The casting is predestined because Helena's height is an issue in the play. She laughs at the dwarfishness of her rival Hermia, who in turn mocks Helena's beanpole stature. Redgrave women, being uniformly tall, fit the description. Tony Richardson, briefly in England, attended Natasha's first night, then asked her to drive him to the airport at seven the next morning for his return flight to California. On the way, he shredded her performance. 'And I thought I was so wonderful! I cried, made excuses – and tried to keep the car on the road. He said I must find something more interesting than myself in the character. The next day he FedExed a copy of the play to me from Los Angeles, marked up with suggestions!'

For her West End debut in 1985, Natasha took over one of her mother's earlier roles, Nina in Chekhov's *The Seagull*. Vanessa played Nina in Sidney Lumet's 1968 film of the play. The character is Chekhov's Ophelia, and has a plaintive mad scene after a moody dramatist jilts her. It was a touring production. When it reached London, Vanessa Redgrave unexpectedly joined the cast as the exhibitionistic actress Arkadina. Impelled into a professional collaboration with her mother, Natasha was dumbfounded: 'She rehearsed like a tornado. It was completely crazy. She rolled on the floor in some scenes. I was terrified of being on stage with her. Then once when I was taking a short cut out of the theatre through the lobby I overheard someone who'd seen the play say, "Did you notice how she copies her mother's mannerisms?" Ever since, I've been scared of working with my family.' Joely Richardson was awarded her first film role by their father, in *The Hotel New Hampshire* (1984), and went on to play Vanessa Redgrave's younger self in David Hare's film, *Wetherby* (1985): Vanessa is a school teacher in desiccated, dwindling middle age, while Joely in flashbacks is the same character as an adolescent tearaway, not yet broken by life. Natasha, for her own competitive reasons, dreads the accusation of nepotism.

All the same, her family is inside her and, like Hamlet with his father's ghost, she cannot evade the dictation of the past. She found herself falling into line when her mother recommended Stanislavsky's books on acting to her: 'Michael discovered them in the 1930s, and told her about them. She passed them on to me. And they almost got me expelled from drama school! The principal disapproved of the theory that you should try to *become* someone else.' English actors, experts at vocal mimicry and social notation, typically approach roles from the outside: hence Gielgud created Spooner in Pinter's *No Man's Land* by studying the insalubrious clothes and finicky habits of Auden. A Stanislavskian actor tries instead to inhabit the character's skin (and if necessary bloats and distends his own skin in order to make room for the resident alien, like Robert de Niro conscientiously over-eating in order to look like Jake LaMotta in *Raging Bull*). Theories considered seditious in England gained easier acceptance in America. English actors play games of charades; American actors conduct experiments in life. Olivier, working on *Marathon Man*, whispered some advice to Dustin Hoffman, who staggered on to the set after keeping himself up all night in order to experience his character's insomniac torments: 'Dear boy, wouldn't it be easier to *act*?'

Michael Redgrave was among the first English actors to research his roles, which Stanislavsky recommended as an aid to emotional identification. Preparing to play Shylock in 1953, he visited ghettoes and consulted rabbis in Holland. At its finest, his acting was rawly neurotic, like the work of an American Method actor. He played Chekhov's Uncle Vanya, for instance, as a self-loathing Russian Hamlet, laughing nihilistically and babbling in dipsomaniac despair. His last stage appearance, in Simon Gray's *Close of Play* at the National Theatre in 1979, was his bravest and most pathetic venture in self-exposure: wasted by his illness and unable to remember lines, he sat mutely throughout the action, his face registering reactions to the brawls and confessions of his family, and at last spoke a single phrase – 'The door is open' – which signalled his readiness for death. Following his example, Vanessa Redgrave has developed an almost shocking candour. She is capable – when she plays a character like the thwarted, yearning Lady Torrance in Tennessee Williams's *Orpheus Descending* – of rendering her face translucent, baring every flicker of feeling behind it.

Natasha shares the family aptitude for emotional extremity. She described to me how she fancied playing Viola's first scene in *Twelfth Night*. The character usually strolls on and coolly asks what country she is in, nodding when she is told that the place is Illyria. Natasha impatiently sent herself off to start again: 'No, no, she's been shipwrecked, she's throwing up, she can't walk, she's coughing and spluttering because she's full of bilge, there would be tears in her eyes...' With a paroxysm like this at the beginning, *Twelfth Night* might never get underway. Natasha forced herself to live through Patty Hearst's ordeal, blindfolded and shut in a closet, so that when the bandage is removed from her eyes in Schrader's film we watch the blinking disorientation of a new-born child. The character's sufferings were matched by the deprivations imposed on the actress: she spent the first part of the film with her face masked, crouched inertly in a dark corner.

During that internment, a death and resurrection occur. When a Black Muslim later in the film asks 'Where's Patty Hearst?', Patty replies 'She's dead. I'm Tanya.' For Schrader, this experience dramatized the mystery of religious conversion; for his actress, it was simply a variant of her normal working method, destroying her own identity in order to assume someone else's. The same is true of Catharine's medical trial in *Suddenly Last Summer*. When she is injected with truth serum, 'everything comes out, decent and indecent, but always, always the truth.' This might have been a definition of Natasha's performance: with twitching hands, blurting mouth and staring eyes, she embodied the nausea of a woman destroyed by having witnessed obscenity. Her Anna Christie on Broadway was, she says, 'another extraordinary journey', tracing the character's progress from the battle-weary slut who slouches into a dockside bar demanding whisky, through the barefoot, liberated mermaid breathing fog like sustenance on her father's barge to the domestic angel, demurely reborn in a white dress, redeemed by her love for the Irish navvy played by Liam Neeson.

Vanessa Redgrave reports in her autobiography on the exalted, unintelligible moment when an actor feels that 'someone else has taken possession of him', uniting 'the conscious with the unconscious.' A strange transcendence enables Vanessa to exchange minds with another person, to alter her body and even – as the androgynous Rosalind in *As You Like It*, or the transsexual tennis player in *Second Serve* – her gender. It also licenses her to desert her political principles, allowing her to joke nostalgically about Nixon in *Wetherby* or to deliver Kate's speech of submission in *The Taming of the Shrew* with a quite beatific radiance. Making up for the matinée which marked her graduation from drama school, she was astonished to find 'a woman satisfyingly different from myself' looking back at her from the mirror. Like her mother, Natasha is attracted to roles which require the violent obliteration and recreation of herself. Backstage one night before a performance of *Anna Christie*, I spied on the strange ritual of the make-up mirror and watched her transform herself with a vengeful glee. While a transistor dispensed disco music, as if to pump energy into her, she smeared on a layer of white grease, giving her face a ghostly pallor which aged and estranged it. Then she added bruising purple shadows, fever spots of rouge, a tarty crimson mouth and some specks of soot as souvenirs of the train ride from Minnesota. She checked the result against a print of Munch's 'Scream', which hung on the dressing-room wall: her purpose, like that of Munch's painting, was to turn her face inside out. Pleased with the result, she wandered off to paint a graphic scar on Liam Neeson's back. 'A kind of bonding thing', she explained: actors have a special affinity with one another's wounds.

Acting like this can seem indistinguishable from a nervous breakdown. After *Anna Christie*, Natasha was preparing to follow Zelda Fitzgerald from early hedonism into madness, for a television biography. 'Right up my street', she reflected with humorous grimness. 'Self-destruction, I mean. But at least, on the way, I get to dance, throw myself into fountains, all that stuff. It could be my Isadora.' Having said this, she bit her lip, because she had trespassed on her mother's terrain: Isadora Duncan is one of Vanessa Redgrave's defining roles, played as a recklessly free spirit in Karel Reisz's film *Isadora* in 1968 and as a disillusioned revolutionary in Martin Sherman's play *When She Danced* in 1991.

Such coincidences, like Natasha's inheritance of Nina in *The Seagull*, are inescapable. Both mother and daughter underwent a frenetic initiation with Ken Russell: Vanessa played a hunchbacked nymphomaniac nun in his film *The Devils* in 1971, while in 1988 Natasha was Mary Shelley in Russell's *Gothic*, reeling through an orgy of truth games in a haunted house with her demented husband and the depraved Byron. As a result of these occult revels during a summer in Switzerland, Mary Shelley wrote *Frankenstein*, delivering into the world a monster she discovered inside herself while she slept – a metaphor, perhaps, for acting, which in the Redgrave family often resembles a state of demonic possession. Before the rampages of the bewitched Vanessa in *The Devils*, her father appeared in the 1948 thriller *Dead of Night* as a ventriloquist whose mind is overtaken by his dummy. The life he creates by projecting his voice is somehow more real than he is: the man lapses into degeneracy and madness while the wooden automaton gloats in triumph. The story might be a parable about the psychological risks of acting. Michael Redgrave's own behaviour confirmed the warning. During her childhood, Lynn learned to stay away from him if he was appearing in tragedy. When he had a comic role, he was more approachable at home. In either case, his mood was determined by the alter ego he assumed when he went to the theatre at night.

Natasha, with almost savage relish, remembers the filming of *Gothic* as 'an emotional roller-coaster. By the end I was black and blue, and in tears all day long.' Actors are masochistic creatures, taking the agonies of others upon themselves. Vanessa Redgrave starved herself and scarified her shaved head with needles when cast as a concentration-camp inmate in Arthur Miller's *Playing for Time*: She put herself through an unwatchably brutal fist fight with Keith Carradine in the film of Carson McCullers's *Ballad of the Sad Café*. Natasha too tends to judge the veracity of a performance according to the emotional strain and physical damage it inflicts on her. The ropes which trussed Patty Hearst left her arms numb for weeks: during the scene of Patty's humiliating gynaecological inspection in prison, she briefly lost control and fled from the set in tears.

Her medical tribulations during the run of *Anna Christie* were worn like merit badges. First she developed conjunctivitis after an off-stage collision with a tennis ball. This was exacerbated by all the crying Anna has to do, and by the production's atmospheric fog. Rubbing her face with her fists, she transmitted the infection from one eye to the other and then passed it on to Liam Neeson (who repaid her in kind by muddying her hair at every performance with the slick coat of baby oil he wore on his torso to give him the lock of a castaway). Then, during the iciest weeks of the winter, she treated her sinuses with a brand of extra-strength nasal spray to which the membranes – as she discovered when she belatedly read the small print on the bottle – became addicted. As a result, the high notes in her voice were burned away, although she always recovered them when she went on stage: 'Performance is therapy, I suppose.' Fidgeting nervily when we met for lunch, biting her nails and chain-smoking, she pleaded with me not to look at her too closely: 'I put Anna's make-up on and take it off so often that I'm suffering from nappy rash. I'll have hardly any skin left after this show.' That, however, is what being an actor is all about, at least in her family: flaying the face to make thought visible; possessing one fewer skin than the insulated, evasive rest of us.

Because acting involves turning the self into a stranger, like the dummy in *Dead of Night*, Natasha is quietly proud of her own anonymity. 'Didn't Flaubert say that in order to be a great artist you have to be a boring person? I love tennis, and it always surprises me that if you watch a great Wimbledon final and then see Agassi or Connors being interviewed afterwards – well, they're so *dull*. But that's how it should be. They're not interesting when they're just being themselves. On stage I try to expose myself totally, which I would never do in life.' She tells a story about her discomfort at having to be herself, without a role to inhabit. 'I was once in a steam bath being massaged, and the woman who was pummelling me looked down and said "Don't I recognize you? Aren't you an actress?" I lied, I said I wasn't anyone. It was horrifying to me, to have to be me when I was just a naked slab of meat like everyone else. If I must be recognized, at least I want to have my face on!' Her husky laugh acknowledges that it will most probably be someone else's face.

Her quest to annihilate herself in another, invented person has an occasionally comical literalness. Paul Schrader remembers that in their second film together, *The Comfort of Strangers* – a melodrama of sophisticated evil in Venice, tricked out in Armani clothes – Natasha vexed the elliptical Harold Pinter by quizzing him about her character's life outside his script: 'The woman is supposed to be a single parent, and although it's not relevant to the story – you don't ever see the children – Natasha insisted that she had to know what happened to their father. Did he die? Were they divorced? Harold said, a bit indignantly, "I've never answered a question like that. Read the script."' I don't doubt that Natasha invented a biography for the spurious figure.

She told me about a similar exchange with her mother, when Vanessa came to see *Anna Christie*, which disclosed some secrets of their make-believe trade. 'She's so reluctant to say anything about a performance; she's afraid of being hurtful. When I begged her to tell me what she thought, she said that maybe the suitcase Anna stuffs all her belongings into for the trip to New York should be more beaten up. She was quiet for a while, and then she said, "I hope you know what's *in* the suitcase."' The suitcase is never opened on stage, but Natasha could indeed recite an inventory of its contents, the sum of Anna's tawdry past. As Shylock in 1953, Michael Redgrave wore a silver bracelet and a belt acquired from antique dealers in the Amsterdam ghetto. In her dressing room, his grand-daughter unlocked the case and produced an ancient photograph from among Anna's crumpled garments. 'You see', she said, 'she carries a picture of her mother.'

'Whose mother is it though?' I asked, peering at the faded, sepia-tinted scrap. It certainly was not the gauntly, austerely radiant Vanessa Redgrave.

'It's Anna's mother', insisted Natasha.

'Oh, come on...'

'All right, I don't know *whose* mother it is. It's just a photo someone gave me to put in the suitcase. But I'm sure that's what Anna's mother looks like.' The use of the present tense was telling. Anna had not been relegated to the past, at the beginning of the century: she was alive – for as long as the run lasted, until her eviction by Zelda Fitzgerald – inside Natasha's body. Filling up the case like a time capsule, Natasha invented Anna's memories for her, and even recreated the mother who had created her.

These transformations can occur without the application of make-up: they begin from a minute, invisible change of gear inside the throat. Natasha, in quest of other identities, has become a virtuoso of the American accent, or rather of various regional accents, all precisely differentiated. She began with the patrician Palo Alto drawl of Patty Hearst, speaking as if through a wired jaw. Paul Schrader remembers a surreal incident at a Cannes film festival press conference in 1988: 'There, sitting on one side of me, was Patty Hearst, talking in *exactly* the voice Natasha used in the film. And on the other side was Natasha, who had no choice but to use her own voice and her English accent – except that she sounds just like her mother! It was very hard to tell who was who.' Since then, Natasha has extended her repertory of voices with a dreamy New Orleans lilt for *Suddenly Last Summer*, followed by the harsher blare of Minnesota for *Anna Christie*. Next on the agenda was Zelda Fitzgerald's sector of the South, not to be confused with Tennessee Williams's domain. In the restaurant, I coaxed her into giving me an aural preview. She uttered one word, 'Alabama', elongating it like a lazy river of molasses and sounding the four 'a's directly from her diaphragm.

Politely ignoring my astonishment, she at once reassumed the flat London voice which is her own. Or is it, actually, her mother's? 'We both smoke like chimneys; maybe that's why we sound alike. If I answer the phone in her house, people think I'm her.' I sympathized with Schrader's bemusement: how could you be sure, if you were making the call, that you were talking to Vanessa or to Natasha, or to one of them impersonating the other? I also sympathized with Natasha's sense that to live in America, and to speak with her rota of new-found accents, means freedom – the freedom to be someone, anyone, other than her mother's daughter. This vocal expertise is a particularly cunning way of declaring her difference, because Vanessa Redgrave has never managed a plausible American accent, and even – half way through rehearsals for *Orpheus Descending* – decided that Lady Torrance, whose father is Italian, should sound like Anna Magnani.

But what of the classic Shakespearean roles left behind, like discarded family heirlooms, on the other side of the ocean? Natasha is relieved to have escaped that obligation. She is unafraid of comparison with the sacred monsters of the movies: she has played the Garbo role in *Anna Christie*, the Elizabeth Taylor role in *Suddenly Last Summer*, and the Grace Kelly role in *High Society* (in a revival at the Old Vic). But there is one part she avoids, one comparison she dodges. The role is Rosalind, Vanessa Redgrave's most rapturous Shakespearean performance, still spoken of breathlessly by those who saw it in 1961: a sapling in bud, agitated by the breezes of desire. 'I know that she listened to tapes of Edith Evans in the part, because she knew she had to do it differently if she was to make it her own. So perhaps if I watched the bits of my mother's performance you can see on video, I might be able to banish the ghosts.... But no, no, it's better not to.'

'Doesn't it worry you, though – that you're in danger of becoming an American actress?'

Natasha roared with laughter and said, when the fit subsided, 'I don't think it's a danger any more. It's just a fact.'

America has also made it easier for her aunt to be a Redgrave. Initially distancing Lynn from her family, it eventually provided her with the means of reconciliation, as she testifies in *Shakespeare for my Father*.

Natasha remembers Michael Redgrave as a vague, remote eminence. She saw him more often on television, affecting a stiff upper lip in patriotic epics like *The Dam Busters*, than in person. For Lynn, too, he was merely an animated shadow – capable of expressing all emotions when they belonged to someone else, yet null and void when required to be her father. Once during her childhood he returned from a year in America with some slippers as a gift for her. She was so diffident, and so bewildered by this interloper, that – like Cordelia stubbornly unable to tell Lear she loves him – she could not find words to thank him, and was ordered from the room in disgrace. She still shakes her head over an unhealed wound. 'The pity of it is', she told me after a performance on her tour of New England, 'that I really adored those slippers.' Later her father paid a courtly visit to her school, to see her act in her first school play. Shamingly, he walked out after her opening scene. 'He came to my bedroom next day to apologize, but I wouldn't let him in. I realized recently that this was the only time in my childhood that he ever came to my room.' He was more encouraging to Vanessa, assuring her that she possessed a 'divine gift'. Since the gift derived from him, in paying her the compliment he was deifying himself.

Lynn, who says that she looked and felt like a mushroom, was intimidated by her elder siblings. 'Vanessa wanted to be a ballerina. Dad had such hopes for her. When she grew too tall for ballet, he suggested she should take up tap dancing. Can you imagine Vanessa hoofing it in a musical comedy? Corin was the academically brilliant one with his scholarship to Cambridge, and a fencer of Olympic standard. Everything was expected of them, and they fulfilled all expectations. But I was the one of whom nothing was expected – shy, anaemic, always sick. I remember a game the three of us played. Vanessa was the President of the

United States, Corin was the British Prime Minister – and I was the royal dog. I quite enjoyed being the royal dog. I thought so little of myself that I wouldn't have wanted a speaking role. I only spoke to my nanny. I didn't know I was lonely until I discovered that there were other people in the world, not just the members of my family.'

Yet actors trade in pain, and can turn it to their own advantage by soliciting our sympathy. It was Lynn's lack of self-esteem and her dependence on food for comfort that made her a star, in the 1966 film *Georgy Girl*. She plays, poignantly and endearingly, a pudgy ugly duckling in swinging London, unable to make anyone love her. As compensation she adopts the unwanted child of a promiscuous flatmate; she is rewarded by marriage to James Mason, her friend's rich protector who is – significantly – a father-figure. 'I suppose Georgy was me. I was always plastering on Mary Quant make-up and painting my eyelids silver like Twiggy, but I never got the look right. When Olivier told me I was through at the National Theatre, I remember my eyelashes fell off into my tomato juice as I started to cry. I thought I'd always be at the National, that I'd grow up to be Sibyl Thorndike and die backstage after playing the nurse in a matinée of *Uncle Vanya*. I was so clumsy and inept then. I was sure I'd been given the wrong body. Yet I felt I had all those other characters inside me.' She releases this company of secret selves in *Shakespeare for my Father*: an ecstatic Juliet, an imperious Cleopatra; also a morbid Richard II and an anguished Hamlet, stalked by his dead parent.

America grants all immigrants the right to reinvent themselves. Settling in California with her actor husband, John Clark, Lynn acquired by force of will the body she thought she should have had all along. WeightWatchers signed her up as an icon of self-help and discipline: she remains reedily, elegantly slim. She has the eager vivacity of the sitcom performer, yet her elastic features often pause in puzzlement or self-disbelief. Her need to be loved has suited her to the cosy domestic theatre of television. But when the canned laughter ceases, her large face can lengthen, as it does throughout her Shakespeare show, into a tragic mask.

In her autobiography, Vanessa remarks that she and Lynn virtually lost touch for two decades. During that time, they devised their separate, incompatible strategies for redeeming the self and reforming the world. Vanessa the unrepentant socialist believes in revolution, Lynn the adoptive Californian puts her faith in dieting.

For Vanessa acting is, like the dialectical procedures of Engels, a scientific investigation of 'what we do not know': in her book she interprets *Macbeth* as an attack on totalitarianism and *Ghosts* as a prophetic diagnosis of AIDS. Communism may have failed historically, but in her view it has triumphed theatrically. Thus she argues that the revitalization of American drama by the Method was a belated bequest of the Russian revolution. Despite these efforts to equate acting with activism, she is doomed to ineffectuality. Actors specialize in altering themselves, not the world: they can only tell the truth by their proficiency at physiognomic lying. These contradictions torment Vanessa's conscience, making her refer with bitter irony to Kierkegaard's dismissive phrase about 'a crisis in the life of an actress'. She seems unable to forgive herself for the art she practises, and in her book she is scathing about the fact that in 1966 she turned down the chance to visit Vietnam and instead filmed *Camelot* among unseasonal orchards in simulated bloom on the Warners back lot in Hollywood. As an actress, she sees herself as forever the prisoner of a false consciousness.

For Lynn, acting serves not to liberate the masses but to release what New Age gurus call the 'inner child'. The chains she wishes to cast off are not social but psychological. Reflecting on her abandonment of England, she says 'I told myself I had to grow. So I became the butterfly. I got out of the cocoon, and I *flew*.' In *Shakespeare for my Father* she does exactly that, skipping flightily across the stage as Juliet or hauled aloft by imaginary pulleys as a fairy in *A Midsummer Night's Dream*. Performance allows her to escape from gravity, and from her personal anchorage in the past.

In 1990 Vanessa and Lynn worked together for the first time, in two projects which were implicitly autobiographical, continuations of sibling rivalry by other means. To begin with, they made a television film of *Whatever Happened to Baby Jane?*, reviving Robert Aldrich's grotesque thriller in which Bette Davis as a derelict nymphette sadistically tortured her crippled sister, played by Joan Crawford. Lynn was the witchy Jane, Vanessa her victim. Both characters are raddled former film stars: Lynn noted that the adaptation was updated 'to the 1960s, the time when Vanessa became a star', but declined to discuss a personal sub-plot. She did, however, admit that 'I understood Jane. It took me quite a while to stop being her.'

Immediately afterwards they moved on to their second collaboration, a London revival of Chekhov's *Three Sisters*. Again the roles were extensions of themselves: Vanessa was the strictly principled teacher Olga, Lynn the impassioned Masha. The third sister, Irina, was to be played by Vanessa's daughter Joely. When she withdrew to make a film, she was replaced from within the clan by Corin's daughter, Jemma. All went well until, having completed her film, Joely came to a performance and went backstage to give her mother some notes: she apparently thought that Olga's job would have made her tougher and more tyrannical. As a result, Lynn reported, Vanessa changed her performance, waving away the objections of the director, Robert Sturua. I wondered what sort of changes she had made. 'For a week', said Lynn very quietly, 'she played Olga as Hitler.'

Meanwhile, soon after the opening, the Gulf War began. Vanessa – who shook with unfeigned emotion when speaking Olga's final lines, which pray for the advent of peace and happiness, and sometimes sobbed during curtain calls – flew to Barcelona to address a rally on her day off. She called for 'the withdrawal of US, British and all imperialist troops from the Gulf', and added 'We must unconditionally defend Iraq' against Western aggression. An international scandal ensued. At later performances she was sometimes booed, for reasons unconnected with her acting (which was as usual, after she stopped being Hitler, searingly truthful). Lynn Redgrave, appalled, was heard wondering if it might not be too late in life to change her name.

Deriding the amateurism of Method actors, Natasha Richardson in one of our conversations laughed at 'people who go to classes and burst into tears and think it's great acting because they've remembered the day their mother died.' I recalled this remark during one of the chillier episodes in *Shakespeare for my Father*. In 1958 Michael Redgrave's mother died. Lynn was with him. They ate their meals together in anaesthetized silence. Then he went off to play *Hamlet* in the evening. He did his grieving, she assumes, on stage.

Natasha in a way resurrected her own father by unearthing his memoirs and making them public. For Lynn, using her private memories as the subject of a play, Hamlet's ghost continues to prowl the battlements at night. 'My father's remains are not yet interred', she told me. 'I've agreed that it's the responsibility of my sister and brother to decide about that. But, strangely, I find the fact that he's not properly laid to rest helps me when I'm doing this play.' Vanessa – who has no such misgivings about the family – has simply turned into her father. As Miss Amelia in

The Ballad of the Sad Café she is angularly mannish in dungarees; she wanted, she has said, to make the character look as Miss Amelia's father 'might have done when he was a young boy.' In fact she is the image – the frighteningly exact reincarnation – of Michael Redgrave thirty years ago. While Lynn plays young Hamlet, Vanessa is the ghost.

Acting, like parenthood, brings to birth new lives, which of course are variants of their source. Two of the most lyrical passages in Vanessa's otherwise strident and embattled autobiography describe the birth of her daughters. As if contemplating the creative miracles she achieves in her acting, she is frankly amazed by these alternative beings who have germinated inside her. Plugged to the breast, Joely's 'crumpled, wrinkled face began to fill out', and her minute fist opened tendrils like a sea-anemone. Natasha is a landscape awakening to life, as 'whorls and spirals of hair' on the crown of her head 'moved like water over sand stirred by the wind.'

Robert Sturua, observing the process during rehearsals for *Three Sisters*, likened Vanessa's engendering of a character to labour pains. The analogy holds good in the next generation. One of Mary Shelley's nightmares in *Gothic* shows Natasha watching herself give birth. In her research for the role, she encountered an incident which transfixed her: 'Mary had a miscarriage, and apparently they took the foetus out of the room and threw it into the fire.'

Saying goodbye to her after one of our meetings, I flippantly suggested that she should have some babies of her own quickly: 'Don't let those genes go to waste.'

'Enough already!' she shrieked, in another of her American voices – the gravelly dialect of a Jewish New Yorker. But then, in her own (or her mother's) English voice, she immediately added a smiling, sceptical request to be contradicted: 'Don't you think?'

John Boorman: The Chemical Magician

A NOTICE STUCK IN THE SCRUFFY HEATHER ANNOUNCED, 'THIS LAND is poisoned', to deter dogs which might decide to revert to savagery and attack the sheep. We walked across what seemed to be a bare moor, crossed a ridge, and found ourselves on the edge of an abrupt, unannounced cliff. An emerald ravine, the incision left by an ancient glacier, sliced the landscape in half. To the west, the mountains of County Wicklow like a dormitory of enchanted giants slumped on the horizon in a mystified haze. Below us there was a grey lake, its trapped waves whipped into fins. Up from it boiled a gust of wind, a blast of energy evacuated by the valley to buffet us.

'Can you feel that?' shouted John Boorman, before the wind ripped his words away. 'Where does it come from? It's just sheer force. If you lean into it, it supports you.' He did lean into it, dangling briefly over the abyss like one of the spirit-birds called up by the incantations of the Amazonian tribe in *The Emerald Forest*. Stretching his arms to embrace the furious air, he summoned the image of other, more lumbering birds with jets beneath their wings: 'We're just steering, like the pilot of a 747. Come on, come closer, don't be frightened. Our minds are an insult to our intelligence.'

Behind us, a gentler gale creaked through the trees. 'The early Christians thought that was the voice of the Holy Ghost', said Boorman. He folded those aeronautical arms of his and wandered among the trees, tenderly checking on their health. A summer storm had felled an ash: its torn roots clutched at boulders for anchorage. 'The land is poor here, but these great trees can exist in it because they take very little from their roots. They live off the air. In the days of the Celtic chieftains it was an offence to cut down certain trees – oak, holly, ash. They called those the noble trees.' I could see from the gleam in his eyes that he approved of this anthropomorphic feudal hierarchy in the vege-table world. Beside the lake at the bottom of the valley, he pointed out a tree he had planted at the summer solstice, during a night-long vigil:

'It was a ceremony. I recited all the proper spells.'

'How do you know which spells are proper?'

'I suppose I don't really, so I used the charms of making from *Excalibur.*'

The man who on the edge of the cliff resembled a bird looked now, camouflaged in turfy brown trousers and a mossy green shirt, like one of those ruminating elders of the forest, his arms spread into a suggestion of branches. But before he could metamorphose into a tree, he changed back from a Druid into a canny ecologist: 'You known that when the wind passes through the leaves like this, it stimulates photosynthesis and that produces oxygen. Wind creates a vacuum, which drags up the water. The whole cycle is happening all around us.'

The coupling of religion and science, magic and chemistry is typical of Boorman. He practises an art made possible by the technologies of the twentieth century, but he makes that art serve an ancient and primitive purpose. Like myths, films to him are forums for collective dreaming; beaming visions on to a blank wall, they are the continuation of a mystical trance. He sees the director as a species of witch doctor with power over our fantasies, like the freaky, cackling necromancer Merlin played by Nicol Williamson in *Excalibur*, or the healer Kokumo played by James Earl Jones in *The Heretic* (Boorman's sequel to *The Exorcist*). Behind the camera, he presides over a ritual like Wanadi in *The Emerald Forest*, who administers a hallucinatory drug to initiates while reciting, of course, the proper spells. In *The Heretic*, the Vatican dispatches a dubious priest (Richard Burton) to expel evil spirits from the adolescent Regan (Linda Blair, who is also plagued by puppy fat). The process of exorcism relies on a synchronizer, an apparatus for hypnotizing two people simultaneously and fusing their imaginations: the hokey device is a symbol of what film can do to us in our hundreds, as we sit in the darkness and envisage light. One of Boorman's coveted but, so far, unfinanced projects is an adaptation of Lindsay Clarke's novel *The Chymical Wedding* about eroticism and alchemy, the pseudo-science of transmutation which suggests another analogy for the mind-alterning agency of film.

Boorman has worked his own technocratic magic on the Irish valley where he lives. It is his personal lost world. 'Amazing how vigorous those ferns are', he said on one of our walks, pointing to a humid, overgrown hollow. 'They're a remnant of evolutionary history – they grow from spores, not seed.' He has transformed this landscape into the likeness of a speculative future and a subliminal past, bringing both epochs to life within his own present.

The valley's slumbering conical volcano and its glaciated crevasse were the despoiled waste of the Outlands in Zardoz, set in 2293 after an industrial apocalypse. Here Sean Connery as a jockstrapped exterminator called Zed rapes and pillages among the Brutals, before being captured by the Eternals. In their sacred city he learns that this distant future is an archaeological scrap left over from an infantile cinematic past: the deity Zardoz is a shattered contraction of *The Wizard of Oz.*

The same valley's swelling mammary hills, secret clefts and allegorical thickets also supplied Boorman with the Celtic wonderland of *Excalibur.* The lake we looked down on, which sent up that sudden vertical explosion of wind, had also in its time disgorged the sword won by Arthur. Boorman indicated a hump of rock across the gulf, where a single standing stone jutted portentously into the veiled, evasive western sky: 'That's where I built Stonehenge.'

Arthur in the film keeps watch by night there, like Boorman observing the solstice, and Merlin appears to him against the same dimly revelatory sky inside a stone circle completed with blocks of polystyrene. 'Of course, we had it easier than the Druids. You know those stories about how they had to haul the stones all that way across Salisbury Plain? Well, the land here is too boggy for that. We had to fly our stones in by helicopter, and position them from the air! Some American tourists passed by while we were filming. You should have seen them searching through their guide books for this megalith which didn't exist.' He laughed at the cheating facility of the movies, so dangerously potent a medium for making us believe in unrealities. 'In the cinema you can mythologize *anything*. You can change the world just by the way you look at it and photograph it.'

Further down the valley, near his house in the grounds of a sixth-century monastery, Boorman is landscaping his personal Camelot, planting stands of native trees and arranging walkways which will be as teasingly circuitous as chivalric quests. A brisk little river runs through the property, and converges with a colleague around the corner. 'The place where two streams meet', Boorman explains, 'is always crucial in Celtic mythology.' His lawn bumps and billows like an emerald ocean, interrupted by a granite boulder. 'This is a glacial valley, and that's a glacial pebble! A friend of mine who's a Benedictine monk carved it for me.' It is inscribed with a frieze of coiled, curling lines which store energy like springs; with the lawn seeming to gyrate around it, the rock is a Celtic omphalos. 'To me it shows all the power that's inert in nature – held there in equilibrium, just waiting.'

Excalibur does not, disappointingly, use the boulder as a scabbard. Instead of thrusting into a stone, the sword stands propped inside Boorman's front door, ready to ward off gipsy tinkers, French structuralists writing these about its owner, Hollywood moguls, and other itinerant riff-raff. It was made for Boorman – another disappointment – not by any lady in the nearby lake but by the Wilkinson's Sword factory, where they mass-produce the nation's razor blades. All the same, Boorman would not be parted from it when the film was finished. 'There were only two things I wanted as keepsakes, Excalibur and the Grail. I got them both, and then – would you believe it? – I lost the Grail!' He laughed at the accident, which cast him as one of Arthur's more befuddled, unreliable knights.

Boorman commutes between past and future, between Celtic glades or Amazonian swamps and the dubbing studios or editing suites of the film industry, between Ireland and America, and his house strains to accommodate his two lives. It used to be a presbytery, though it has been deconsecrated and subtly Hollywoodized. Palm trees like those which line the manicured thoroughfares of Beverly Hills have been painted on the drawing-room walls, to frame the nobler indigenous specimens outside. Through the window of a video den you can see a swimming pool, drained and adrift with fallen leaves like Gloria Swanson's in *Sunset Boulevard*.

Scorning the pool, Boorman takes his dips in the river: 'I suppose I have some great compulsion to test myself against nature.' Immersion is a providing ordeal for Boorman's heroes. His son Charley undergoes a baptismal dunking in *The Emerald Forest*. In *Deliverance*, the weekend hikers negotiate some angry rapids in their canoes, while Jon Voigt later plunges from a cliff into the river where, submerged, he tangles with a corpse. Lee Marvin defiantly swims from Alcatraz to the mainland in *Point Blank*. The director shares this need for risk and physical peril, like the hardships which the Arthurian knights must suffer. Boorman's films have regularly involved his own flirtation with death. He splashed among a shoal of piranhas in the Amazon during *The Emerald Forest*, and was poisoned by a scratch from a coral reef while making *Hell in the Pacific*. Filming *The Heretic* on top of a Manhattan skyscraper, he cavorted above Sixth Avenue wearing a safety harness which – he later discovered – was not tethered to anything. His films concern trials of physical resistance and spiritual valour: the suburbanites battling the river and some homicidal hillbillies in *Deliverance*, Richard Burton battling a plague of locusts sent by the demon Pazuzu in *The Heretic*, Lee Marvin battling the faceless Organization in *Point Blank*. Making those films has entailed similar trials for Boorman, who says, 'I'm tempted to make a film in the Antarctic – although as I get older, the temptation is easier to resist!'

More is at stake than personal bravado. Filming in Appalachia or the Amazon or on an isolated Pacific atoll, Boorman maximizes difficulties, not to advertise his dexterity in overcoming them, but in the hope of restoring truth to an art which – aware of its genius for fakery – has for too long been content with falsity and phoniness, like Boorman's own temporary and synthetic Stonehenge.

Behind Boorman's films lies his private history (or perhaps theology) of film. Its genesis he attributes to D.W. Griffith: 'Griffith invented the film as an epic form of story-telling, handed down from the sagas and the Arthurian legends. It combined all the arts. He was the first to show his films in proper theatres, with an orchestra behind the scenes and live sound effects. He even added painting to the mixture when he hand-tinted the blush on Lillian Gish's face. For him, film was the universal language prophesied in the Bible, where it's meant to announce the Millennium. It's a complex language, difficult to speak but easy to understand – a truly popular form. Within five years it made Chaplin the most famous person in the world.' Genesis was also happening at the same time in Russia: 'Eisenstein invented a different version of the form. He worked it out according to a political theory, not by instinct, eclectically, like Griffith. He didn't think that it announced the Millennium; instead montage copied the rhythm of revolution. And when he joined forces with Prokofiev in *Alexander Nevsky* and *Ivan the Terrible*, he linked film with another universal language, that of music.' The marriage of images and music persists in Boorman's work: the duet or duel of banjos in *Deliverance*, the Wagnerian score of *Excalibur*.

In this theological account of origins, the fall from grace and from universality occurred with the arrival of sound. Once Al Jolson had spoken in *The Jazz Singer*, films were restricted to one language only – at least until Boorman reversed this lapse by making *Hell in the Pacific* as a virtually silent movie: its two characters, an American and a Japanese soldier shipwrecked together, cannot understand each other's language, and since they communicate by playing mimed war games while grunting inarticulate curses, we don't need to understand what they say in order to follow the action.

More dismayingly, sound grounded films. It restrained the liberty of fantasy, shackled the cinema to realism, and kept directors under the supervision of studios which were run like factories. The disaster, for Boorman, was that the earliest sound cameras could not be taken on location. '*Gone with the Wind* is an example of the decline. It's supposed to be about the soil and the land, but they never went off the back lot. When Vivien Leigh is eating the raw carrot and throwing up, the trees behind her are all silhouetted cut-outs.' For Boorman, what greater impiety could there be than to carve a fake oak from cardboard? And what more appropriate place for the headquarters of this industry than Los Angeles, a city which to Boorman symbolizes the intolerable lightness and rootlessness of being: 'The problem about LA is that when you're there, it disappears. It's all made of neon and cardboard, it's just scenic flats. It has no structure.'

Boorman sees the studios as prisons. 'With everything being made on the premises, film fell into the hands of the moguls, men like Harry Cohn. It's the fashion to romanticize them now, as if they were Al Capone, but those studio bosses were bad men. As Scott Fitzgerald said, they took our dreams away – and that's the worst of all possible betrayals. After *Citizen Kane* it seemed that Orson Welles was going to change things and make films that were truly imaginative. Then the same system crushed him.' Boorman's inaccessible locations were his attempt to guarantee himself freedom from interference by the front office.

In his demonology, the tycoons and their mean-minded troops of accountants correspond to the Organization which eliminates Lee Marvin in *Point Blank*. His paranoia is entirely justified. A deputation was sent in to remove him from the set of *Point Blank* because the executives thought his clashing colour-schemes were evidence of certifiable lunacy. Without consulting him, the studio attached some stock footage of bombed buildings to the end of *Hell in the Pacific* so that the film would end with a vulgar bang not an expiring existential whimper. 'When I found out, I went on television to denounce the producers, and asked people not to go and see the film. I must say they obeyed me, in their millions! Later an Italian critic sympathized with me about what had happened. He said, "Isn't it terrible how they mutilated your film – they must have cut out all the action sequences!"' Producers vetoed his casting of Marlon Brando and Jack Nicholson in *Deliverance*, on grounds of expense; they demanded that he use Burton in *The Heretic*, lumbering Boorman with an actor who was never more than half awake: 'He refused to move, and film after all is motion. For me, the ideal was Lee Marvin – he was like a dancer.' Audiences nostalgic for the gore and green bile of *The Exorcist* reacted angrily to the metaphysics of *The Heretic*. 'They actually tore up seats and threw things at the screen', reports Boorman, delighted by his provocation of middle America. The studio recalled the film for surgery.

Now Boorman is his own producer, but he remains subject to the humiliating whims of the financiers. He was made arbitrarily to transfer the setting of *Where the Heart Is* from London to New York in order to qualify for funds from Disney. He complied, even though the film was about the solace of home. Then the backers changed their minds: 'They said it was still a Boorman film and not a Disney film. I really didn't have any answer for that.' He was equally depressed by the agenda of Mrs Thatcher's day-long seminar for film-makers at Downing Street in 1990: 'To her, we were just entrepreneurs, earners of foreign currency. All the discussions were about scrabbling for grants from the European Community. Nothing was said about film as a cultural value, a force' – a voltage of imagery which, like the wind detonating from that sunken Irish lake, can compel you to dream.

Independence has allowed Boorman's films to venture into explicit autobiography. *Hope and Glory*, about his boyhood in London during the blitz, confided the infantile sources of his myth-making. In a backyard in the suburb of Eden Park, the young hero pretends that his toy soldiers are knights exploring a misty forest; when he is evacuated to a villa on the willow-fringed Thames, he turns the river into a Jungian stream of recollection and submerged recollection which 'has flowed in my mind ever since'.

The blitz was Boorman's schooling in the surreal, alarming magic of film. The incendiary bombs melted reality down into the more obligingly sensuous lineaments of fantasy. 'I remember once being in the centre of London with my mother. Everything was burning. And I just couldn't take my eyes off some metal railings which the heat had bent out of shape. They were so straight and restrictive before. Now they were released from that, and they were *beautiful*.' The scorching metal wriggled like the serpentine patterning of Celtic ornament: Boorman – who was brought up as a Protestant although he attended a Catholic school, and has always yearned for the pantheistic religions suppressed by Christianity – still blames St Patrick for driving the snakes out of Ireland, which he interprets as a pious expulsion of snake-worshipping Bacchic women.

The fiercest, guiltiest excitement of Boorman's childhood, also recalled in *Hope and Glory*, was 'the night when our home was hit by a bomb!' He has restaged that joyful calamity many times. A Notting Hill terrace is besieged by revolutionary fireworks in *Leo the Last*, and a Georgetown mansion is dismembered by devils in *The Heretic*. In the opening frames of *Where the Heart Is*, a Brooklyn warehouse is torn down, collapsing to its knees in an incense of dust as gracefully as Pavlova's dying swan. Boorman often cabbalistically mutters Merlin's spell of making from *Excalibur*; film also indulges his fondness for unmaking, for a happy anarchy like the air raids in *Hope and Glory*. 'I'm very interested in the aesthetics of destruction', he admits a little shiftily, changing into a black magician. He thinks of a film's creation as a series of destructive spasms: first comes writing, then directing, finally editing, and each stage is a violent assault on the previous one. 'Casting is dreadful for me, because I have to give the characters away, allow actors to alter the way I've written them. But once I start to direct, I'm just as ruthless with my own script. And when I'm editing I always have to be restrained from hacking the film to bits.' His opposed impulses act out their antagonism in *Where the Heart Is*. Its two heroes, smilingly indulged and slyly derided, are Boorman's twin selves – destroyer and preserver, technician and magus.

Dabney Coleman plays a property developer whose speciality is blowing up buildings, a comic ogre related to the gun-toting campers in *Deliverance* and the engineer who scalps the land and throttles the river with a dam in *The Emerald Forest*. Coleman's firm is called American Demolition: he is one more gloss on Boorman's claim that 'America is a neurosis of the human race'. But he is also Boorman the director, a reluctant and somewhat ashamed dictator, shouting 'Action!' and ordering towers to crumble, houses to blaze, actors to jump into rivers. Chastened by the loss of his fortune, Coleman ends babbling ecstatically about the sun as it plays on water. 'I have seen the light', he murmurs. This is also Boorman's creed: film is a love-affair with luminosity.

Balancing Coleman is Christopher Plummer as a down-and-out magician whose tricks are almost exhausted. Padlocked like Houdini and dropped into a tank, he treads water in sputtering desperation and swallows the key with which he should undo his chains. This is Boorman the connoisseur of charms and pagan rites, the worshipper of oaks and pilgrim to remote Celtic shrines, guying his own superstitious susceptibility. He began by wanting to make a film about a modern dispossessed Lear: Coleman evicts his obnoxious son from his Manhattan brownstone, then is himself unhoused by a stock-market crash. He ended by making a film about a derelict Prospero: Plummer's insubstantial pageants fade, like a film when you turn the light on in the room. Except that – as a character remarks when one more house is blown up, destroying some surreally painted walls inside – this doesn't matter. The reality was only background, and the murals have already been photographed: 'It's all still there, on film.'

Despite the genial truce of *Where the Heart Is*, the contradictions in Boorman remain invigoratingly unresolved. He looked out of the drawing-room with its grove of imaginary palms at the cleared land on which he is reconstructing a primeval forest and said, 'I'm fencing it in – my God, the trees that have been cut down to make fence posts outnumber the new ones I'm planting. And the irony of all this concern for nature is that makers of film stock are among the worst chemical polluters of the atmosphere!'

How, I wondered, can Boorman manage to alternate between the primordial and the futuristic? How can he connect the visionary origins of cinema and its manufactured, mechanical end-product? Film, he has said, alchemically transmutes money into light. How does he both raise the money and praise the light?

'I do it', he said, taking a deep breath, 'with great difficulty.'

WIM WENDERS AND THE ART OF SEEING

THE HEROES OF WIM WENDERS ARE MEDIA MEN, INCAPABLE OF coping with life unless they can mediate it. Rüdiger Vogler in *Alice in the Cities* keeps a chaotic America at bay by freezing scraps of it as Polaroids, while Dennis Hopper in *The American Friend* mutters his psychic disquiet into a tape recorder. Hanns Zischler in *Kings of the Road* denounces his father, who is sitting silently across the room, by composing a headline on a linotype machine; Harry Dean Stanton and Nastassia Kinski in *Paris, Texas* numbly discuss their marital anguish by telephone from either side of a glass partition. Most dolefully or absurdly of all, in *Until the End of the World*, Sam Neill, pursuing Solveig Dommartin through the Australian outback after a nuclear catastrophe, reports that 'By the time I came to rescue Claire, the only thing she cared about was having fresh batteries for her video monitor.'

Wenders himself is an image of the indirect, insulated people he has imagined. He appears uneasy when not invisible behind the camera. Clutching a bottle of mineral water in his Berlin kitchen, muddlingly mystified when trying to pour from it with the cap still on, his only means of mediation was his glasses, whose thick frames surround his eyes with oblong cinema screens. While talking, he looked resolutely out of the window at a patch of concrete-coloured sky, perhaps squinting to see angels descending through the wintry haze. Occasionally he risked a glance at my notebook, trying to decipher – upside down across the kitchen tabe – what I was writing about him.

In his late forties, still awkward inside his own body and baffled by obtuse foreign bodies like the flask of mineral water, Wenders resembles a schoolboy who has elongated overnight, and in the process has acquired worry lines around those eyes which remain stubbornly fixed on the middle distance. He speaks so softly that you seem to be overhearing him. Whenever a thought reached its terminus, he was relieved by a pause which made me fidgety. Silence, like the obstinate catatonia of Harry Dean Stanton in *Paris, Texas*, is peace, or maybe power.

Such uncomfortable intervals constitute meditative havens in Wenders's films. Not speaking, you simply look, until at length sight becomes vision. *The Goalkeeper's Fear of the Penalty* is a double experiment in this patient, mind-emptying discipline. At the village match which concludes the film, someone proposes a mental test. Don't bother about the players running around the field; keep your eyes on the goalie while he's waiting for the ball, even though nothing is happening. Do it until your head aches. The goalie, a killer who feels nothing at all about the crime he has committed, practises the same sedative visual drill. On and off throughout the film he stares at an inexplicable apple, suspended somewhere in space. Wenders, who first wanted to be a painter, is fond of Cézanne's admonition that 'Things are looking bad. You have to hurry if you want to see anything. Everything is disappearing.' During our talk, he raptly gazed out of the kitchen window at empty air, as if taking a photograph without a camera.

The criticism Wenders published during his time as a film student in Munich between 1968 and 1971 deploys the same mute, hypnotic attentiveness. Nicholas Ray's *Johnny Guitar* is recommended because in it you can see 'an incredibly brilliant red'. A review of John Sturges's *Bad Day at Black Rock* simply lists, with an exclamatory ecstasy which the objects hardly warrant, the things in the film that can be looked at, if you let your eyes slide away from Spencer Tracy and Lee Marvin and disengage your mind from the violent plot:

The ventilator! The broken-down car!

The gas pump! The ketchup bottle!

At first this seems like the blissed-out blandness and idyllic banality of the 1960s: Pop Art with its endless duplication of soup cans, or Warhol turning the camera on and allowing it to make endless and unwatchable films about boring sights. But the intentions of Wenders were subtler. In looking at these films, he abstracts them: the point of *Johnny Guitar* is not its otiose romanticism or the perverse shoot-out between Joan Crawford (changing from a ball gown to cowboy gear) and Mercedes McCambridge; what preoccupies Wenders is that tone of red, as unrealistically vivid as the shine on the goalie's conceptual apple. It was particularly cunning of him to look at American Westerns in this way, because in doing so he weans the genre of its obsession with action and, stopping his ears to the noise of gunfire, celebrates its peaceful passivity. He praises the sequence of Westerns Anthony Mann made with James

Stewart because they are 'quiet', and likes Raoul Walsh's *The Tall Men* because it is 'slow'; he remarks on the gentleness of Delmer Daves's *3.10 to Yuma*, in which from the vantage-point of a saloon, 'you watch eternity go by.'

His own early films are essays in seeing as a vigil, the keeping of a watch, as if the eyes were indeed sentinels, on guard against the evanescence of visible reality. *Kings of the Road* contains an irrelevant but indispensable interlude in which Vogler suddenly halts the truck he is driving. He tells Zischler that he needs to pee. This, however, is not exactly what happens. He crosses the road with unhurried deliberation, and walks through some hillocks of industrial waste. Then he unbuckles his dungarees, pulls them down, squats, and – taking his time about it – lengthily, satisfyingly shits. The camera remains at a discreet remove, but is close enough for us to verify that Vogler is not acting. He fishes for paper in his pocket and wipes himself clean. We are required to watch all of this because a motion picture is about duration, and the film's German title, *Im Lauf der Zeit*, means 'in the course of time'. Of course, as in the underground movies of Warhol, the point of the scene is its defiance of a visual taboo: had a bowel movement ever been filmed before? Yet the mood is the reverse of sensational. We concentrate on the tropism of a living creature; once more, as pensive as Vogler himself during this daily moment of meditation, we watch eternity go by. A film, in this case, is what happens before the director thinks to shout 'Action!'

His company – which has its office on a building site in Berlin's Turkish ghetto – is called Road Movies, but the open road for Wenders is not the adventure-crammed film strip which unreels towards the horizon in the American movies he admires. The American road leads always to a promised land beyond the horizon, from Oklahoma to California in John Ford's *The Grapes of Wrath*, from California back to Louisiana in Peter Fonda's *Easy Rider*. American heroes travel in the confident, conquistadorial hope of arriving. But for Wenders and his vagrant characters – the goalie wandering from Vienna towards what used to be the border with Yugoslavia, Vogler and Zischler shuttling up and down along what used to be the border between the two Germanies – travel dispenses with the idea of a destination.

When travelling, Wenders prefers to drift. 'I don't necessarily want to get anywhere. I keep going because of the need to see. When you're on the road, you're a stranger where you are, so sight is a little more curious, even feverish. The eyes are more awake. My ideal is aimless travelling. Normally with movies an aim emerges, and you have to look for locations. I always feel that's a pity.'

Until the End of the World emerged by accident on one of these entropic journeys, when Wenders was on his way round the world in 1977. 'I was in Indonesia, travelling alone, living like a monk, just taking pictures. In a second-hand bookshop I found this novel by Nevil Shute, *A Town like Alice*. Then I saw it was just a hop across to Darwin, so I stumbled through the back door into Australia, this strange country – the oldest piece of the planet I'd ever seen, the planet in its natural state, with people living the same way they had for the last forty thousand years. Instead of going home to Germany, I settled in a motel in Alice Springs and began writing a film about the aborigines, a nuclear disaster, and a scientist who had collected ideas from all over the world of things that would never be seen again, and was trying to invent a way of transmitting them into the mind of a blind person.'

When, almost fifteen years later, Wenders got around to making the film, the scientist was played by Max von Sydow. In his laboratory – a version of Plato's cave, equipped with all the latest gadgetry yet entombed beneath the ancient, wrinkled Australian earth – he translates sight into brain waves, records these biochemical reactions as abstract paintings, and beams them behind the unseeing eyes of his wife, Jeanne Moreau. While von Sydow attempts to purify sight, the world outside his cave has fallen victim in 1999 to an inflation of images, a morbid visual saturation. William Hurt, von Sydow's son, suffers from tired, sick eyes, which have been bombarded for too long by the lurid ephemera of modernity. His complaint is the disease of images, of imagery in viral, virulent excess. Its symbolic incubator is American television, described by Wenders as 'optical toxin' or 'poison ivy for the eyes': Vogler on his behalf junks a set in a motel room at the beginning of *Alice in the Cities*.

In the visual culture of *Until the End of the World*, the eyes have been pre-empted by video cameras. Tokyo consists of wall-to-wall imagery, and every gyrating, pulsing neon logo has some extrasensory appliance to sell. Only the aborigines resist the predatoriness of those who would rather film the world than look at it: 'You think we want you walking through our dreamings with your fancy cameras?' Wenders admits to sharing this disquiet. 'I live by sight; I get first-degree nourishment from it. Yet we have this world where everyone feeds on reproductions, on second-hand images.' In *Faraway, So Close!*, his sequel to *Wings of Desire*, one of the angels who has fallen into contemporary Berlin descends further, exploring a hell which has its headquarters in a flooded bunker beneath the runway of Tempelhof airport. Here, where the Nazis stored the artillery which they intended to use in staging their private *Götterdämmerung*, the black marketeers of the new Germany have installed a more up-to-date inferno, a cinémathèque of sin: the catacombs house a library of pornographic videos, and batteries of machines for duplicating them. Pornography is one of Wenders' recurrent symbols for imagery as a sad, sterile simulation of life. In *Kings of the Road*, Vogler plays a mechanic who repairs projection equipment in cinemas. One of the theatres he visits now specializes in pornography. Entering the booth, he finds the projectionist listlessly masturbating. The ticket seller tells him about a couple in the audience who decided to join in the orgy on screen. The woman developed vaginal cramps, and her partner was unable to extricate himself; they had to be carried out together by the ambulance men, locked in a vice-like mockery of coition. As the girl describes the incident, she and Vogler vacantly stare at some looped frames of the current film, watching an act of mechanized, piston-pounding love which will never reach a climax. The avenging angel in *Faraway, So Close!*, who intervenes to destroy the subterranean image bank, fits the punishment to the crime: he uses a ribbon of celluloid as the fuse for his explosion.

Wenders acknowledges that, 'As a film-maker, I am contributing to that inflation of images. But I'm also showing a way out. Film guides sight, it studies images reverently. Films are a very moral institution regarding sight, especially by contrast with other electronic media. The quietest and most peaceful film – something by Ozu, for instance – can show up on TV and be interrupted by publicity, which makes the film itself publicity. The cancer is advertising, which has spread into every area of imagery.' Wenders is a visual puritan, like the crotchety old woman in *Kings of the Road* who closes the cinema she owns rather than screening trash. With a photograph of Fritz Lang on the wall behind her, his blind right eye covered by a patch, she repeats the first article of the faith which also sustains Wenders: 'Film is the art of seeing'. *Faraway, So Close!* even has a Biblical epigraph warning against the evil eye and the ocular lusts of materialism.

The goalkeeper's fixation on that gratuitous apple is a lesson in the art of seeing: a long moment when a motion picture stops moving and becomes a parable of static contemplation. Wenders remembers fighting with his editor about this insert. 'I was determined to keep it in, even though there was no reason for it, and he was determined to cut it. Then when I saw the film, I decided that it didn't fit, it had to go. And this time it was the editor who argued for keeping it. He said he couldn't imagine the film without it! Funny you should remember that apple. It's important, in some weird way.'

Mystics favour deserts because there, with nothing to distract the eyes, sight can be purged and converted to insight. Wenders shares this predilection, whether he is dealing with the aridity of the American south-west and the mirage-like glassy towers of Houston in *Paris, Texas*, with the man-made desert bifurcating Germany in *Kings of the Road*, or with the blitzed, strafed, churned and immemorially disputed no-man's land of Potsdamerplatz in *Wings of Desire*. He was grateful to the scorched red desert of Australia because he had the sensation that he was the first man ever to look at it, and because it cleansingly erased the images he retained of an American desert colonized by cinematic myth. 'I was so preoccupied with America, and in Australia I had no preconceptions to get in my way.'

For Wenders the cinéphile it was impossible to see Monument Valley without imagining John Wayne loping through it on some military crusade, or without mentally carving one of the pinnacles of rock into the craggy, eroded face of John Ford. 'The American desert is a catalogue of images, it's second-hand. It's not empty, it's full of ideology.' Wenders elaborates this thesis in a volume of photographs taken while location-hunting for *Paris, Texas* in the south-west. He called the collection *Written on the West*, hinting in a secret subtitle that the disregarded signs and rusted slogans he photographs may as well have been written on the wind.

His pun – illustrating the palimpsest of received ideas and parasitical allusions which makes up a European's America – picks at a tangled cinematic history. *Written on the Wind* is a family tragedy about oil wells and alcoholism directed by Douglas Sirk, a refugee from Germany whose Hollywood films were seen by Wenders's radical colleague Rainer Werner Fassbinder as insolent denunciations of the capitalism they seemed to glossily extol. Sirk's America is as oppressed by affluence as post-war Germany with its economic miracle: baubles rain down on it, during the credit titles in *Imitation of Life*, like brittle, icy hail. For Fassbinder, in this world of 'manipulated dreams' the madness of Dorothy Malone in *Written on the Wind* was as prophetic as Ophelia's: 'Insanity represents a form of hope... Douglas Sirk's films liberate the mind.' The photographs of Wenders omit the irate cyclonic wind which makes America shudder in Sirk's film and Fassbinder's interpretation of it. His view of the landscape has a flippant nihilism. America does not need to be shaken by a revolutionary storm: left to itself, it is placidly decaying.

In California, near a nowhere vaingloriously called Four Corners, Wenders photographs the symbolic act of writing on the west. Here a sign pokes up into a smiling sky and announces

Western World
DEVELOPMENT
TRACT 8271.

But there is nothing here, on this lowly horizon of sage brush, which can be developed: the sign has faded long before keeping its promise about an affluent future. In *Paris, Texas* the aphasiac Travis (Harry Dean Stanton), lost in a wilderness 'without language or streets', also attempts to write his name on this indifferent land. He asks his brother to drive him to Paris, and shows a photograph of a vacant lot there: sandy dirt, an anorexic sapling, the obligatory insignificant signboard. 'It looks just like Texas to me', says his bewildered brother. 'It is', says Travis, who like Wenders and his mythical America is the victim of a preconception: he believes he was conceived in the town with the incongruous, disorienting name, and wants to build a house for his family there. This is his consolidating fiction of home, his delusion of belonging to a terrain in which he is as impermanent and unrooted as tumbleweed.

Throughout the West Wenders found similar attempts to consecrate hostile open space by distributing names and invoking the gods to whom they once, elsewhere, belonged – a writing prophetically imprinted on the wall, or on any surface at all, instead of being ephemerally consigned to the wind. In the Texan town of Odessa, whose name counts as another nostalgic transplantation, he comes upon a cavalcade of school buses christened in homage to apostles and Old Testament sages (Paul, Luke, Noah and so on), while on Shaw Street in Houston he photographs a Gothic church wearing a 'Jesus Saves' placard on its tower, like a head-band. But the church is humbled by a sleek new heaven of mercantile filing cabinets. The shrines remain empty. In Lowell, Arizona, a derelict movie house has a billboard still labelled 'Now Showing', although nothing has shown there for years. *Paris, Texas* was Wenders's disbelieving effort to reveal these arid spaces without the benefit of ideological benediction.

His need to rid himself of ersatz imagery recognizes the predicament of his German generation, brought up on the imported sights and sounds of America, imposed by an occupying army. The culture of his formative years was the product of a cheating mediation. As an adolescent, his emotional life found an outlet in the rock and roll records he collected. Like the goalie treasuring a pocketful of unspendable American coins, Wenders did not understand the words being sung, but the inarticulate feelings seemed to fit. The characters in his German films converse obliquely by quoting American song titles at each other. Sometimes the dislocation of foreign words from native sensations becomes painful. During the getaway from Hamburg at the end of *The American Friend*, Bruno Ganz, too stricken and dispirited to save himself, sits behind the wheel with the face of a tragic clown humming 'Baby you can drive my car'. The car, after Ganz's fatal heart attack, contradicts the song by driving itself.

Wenders also saw Germany through the medium of a cinematic America. *Kings of the Road* was his indigenous version of *Easy Rider*, transferring the road movie to a continent where roads were not open, because of the narrow, impassable gulf between West and East. *Alice in the Cities* was his sardonic reversal of John Ford's *The Searchers*: instead of John Wayne's quest to rescue the child abducted by Indians and return her from the desert to what he thinks of as civilization, Rüdiger Vogler trails randomly through industrial Germany trying to get rid of the obnoxious little girl who has been deposited with him like left luggage. Wenders explains that 'There was so much mistrust of imagery and stories in Germany during those years. After all, from 1933 to 1945 film was used here exclusively for propaganda. So we felt that only Americans had the right to show and tell things, not us. My parents were worried when I started to make movies, because a film director is not something anyone could conceive of being in Germany. Even after my third film, my mother still worried about what I was going to do when I grew up.'

America became an adoptive parent to the young Germany whose dreams it invaded, so that for Wenders the anxious business of growing up entailed an Oedipal struggle both with his father's generation – implicated in the war, and additionally shamed by defeat – and with the artistic foster-fathers of his imaginary America. He has been quoted as saying, 'My father was a fascist, but I loved him.' He now denies, with a characteristic, quiet vehemence, ever having said this. 'My father was in the army, but only as a doctor. I started to study medicine, because like so many kids when they finish high school, the only job I knew was my father's. But I realized I wasn't made to be a student. I'm not aural. I can't learn by listening. I spent most of my two years in medicine as a nurse. Whenever I had any spare time I was writing and drawing. My father wasn't disappointed, he was delighted!' Even so, he concedes that the estrangement between von Sydow and Hurt in *Until the End of the World* is the latest instalment in a quarrel which has been going on since Zischler in *Kings of the Road* set up in type that headline which mutely accuses his slumped, demoralized father. 'In a way, they are battling it out for me, I hope for the last time. Still, I think my Oedipal situation is more with the American cinema than with my dad.'

From the American films he adored and imitated, Wenders inherited a succession of optional fathers: the directors his early films salute and then remorselessly execute. *Alice in the Cities* concludes with Vogler reading an obituary notice for John Ford. Fritz Lang in *The State of Things* reposes, as if in a grave, beneath his star on the besmirched pavement of Hollywood Boulevard. In *The American Friend*, Sam Fuller, playing the sleazy director of a porn film who doubles as a gangster, is gunned down beside the Hamburg harbour. In the same film Nicholas Ray is a painter who shams death in order to increase the market value of the canvases he posthumously produces.

Invited to Hollywood by Francis Coppola in 1977, Wenders pursued his argument with America by turning its most venerable cinematic genres inside out. He began with the detective story: his *Hammett* is a thriller from which all thrills have been scrupulously removed. The energetic, punchy Sam Spade is supplanted by his sick, broody creator Dashiel Hammett (played by Frederick Forrest). Spade's self-extension was his gun; Hammett's technological arm is his typewriter, and when his apartment is wrecked this is the first thing he pulls from the rubble. Checking that it still works, he smiles contentedly. The detective has been superseded by the artist. The Op who peeped through keyholes (the motto of the Pinkerton Agency, for which Hammett once worked) now has a god-like omniscience. Looking down through domes or up through glass floors at a tiered society poised on the steep hills of San Francisco, the

Hammett of Wenders anticipates the angels in *Wings of Desire*, who swoop from ledges to perform their redemptive errands in Berlin. The American tough guy mutates into a European seraph. Equally paradoxical, *Paris, Texas* was a Western about the new West with its air-conditioned corporate skyscrapers, where rowdy saloons have been replaced by antiseptic brothels in which intercourse occurs on the telephone; instead of saluting the conquest of territory and its settlement like the Westerns of Ford, it proposed a salutary disconnection from a land we can never own.

Even after Wenders returned to Europe, the Hollywood genres proved inescapable. *Wings of Desire* appended a sombre epilogue to Frank Capra's sentimental comedy *It's a Wonderful Life*, since Wenders allows his guardian angels only to commiserate with suffering humans, not to save their lives. *Until the End of the World*, haphazardly encircling the earth to conclude in outer space, was the ultimate road movie, a synopsis of human experience between the stone age of the Australian aborigines and apocalypse in 1999. 'We shot it', says Wenders, 'in fifteen cities in ten countries on four continents, and all for twenty-three million dollars. In America, that's what they spend to make a film in a house with only two people! I arranged the financing on condition that I could shoot the story in chronological order, even though that was more expensive. You take the spirit of adventure out if you can't react to what happens on the road as you're filming, so we rewrote scenes and worked on relationships as we went along.' Digressions and detours allowed him to revisit favourite places and editorialize about pet causes. When the budget would not allow for an expedition to Moscow, he found a disused Art Deco cinema (elegiacally called the Eden) in the centre of Lisbon and dressed up its labyrinthine lobby with a Piranesian cobweb of intersecting staircases, as a post-Soviet hotel. Thus, like a postscript to *Kings of the Road*, the film appeals for the preservation of one more site sacred to the faculty of seeing.

Wings of Desire had a doddering bard called Homer, who recites the history of Berlin before it was bombed by the Allies, and grumbles that epics always sing the praises of war, never of peace. In *Until the End of the World*, the garrulous epic story-teller was Wenders: 'I told the story to Peter Carey when I was trying to persuade him to write the screenplay, and it took me six hours! He said: "How can I write a three-hour movie if it takes you six hours to summarize the plot?" Really it's my *Odyssey* in reverse. Instead of Ulysses wandering round the world on his way home to Penelope, it's about Penelope following him. And – because there's never really any end to the story – she's being followed in her turn by another man.' That other man, Sam Neill, is a novelist who weans Solveig Dommartin from her addiction to the video monitor. Then, discovering a battered typewriter which the aboriginal children are using as a toy, he sits down in the outback and begins to write the epochal tale of their travels: 'I didn't know the cure for the disease of images, but I believed in the healing power of words.'

By now, Wenders has freed himself from his invidious fascination with America and the moribund cinematic ancestors he acquired there. When you reach your forties, you no longer want to kill your father, because you have now arrived at the same age he was when you first remember him. Having become him, you must forgive him. 'I'm gaining a little ground', Wenders said to me, shyly congratulating himself on his evolution. 'It's the ageing process, I suppose.'

He now thinks of his American career as a detour: 'I was in Alice Springs when I got Coppola's telegram. I abandoned my Australian project, and went to America to make one film, though I ended up making four.' During acrimonious production delays on *Hammett*, he dramatized his discontent with the industry in *The State of Things* and cathartically rid himself of his filial anger in *Lightning over Water*, a home movie about Nicholas Ray's terminal illness. 'When *Paris, Texas* was finished in 1984, I gave up my apartment in New York, returned my green card, and came back to live in Berlin.' From this disenchanted distance, he recognized the emotional inadequacies institutionalized by American film. The genres which obsessed him – the road movie, the buddy movie, the Western – were all, he says, 'so male, so much about men, about fathers and sons. But when I ended *Paris, Texas* with the shot of the little boy hugging Nastassia, his mother, I knew that was the beginning of whatever I was to do next. I had to start a film with a female character at the centre.'

The film was *Wings of Desire*, and the character turned out to be the lissome aerialist on the trapeze played by Solveig Dommartin, for whom the angel Bruno Ganz renounces immortality. The upper atmosphere is photographed in ethereal black and white, while human beings live in a world of garish, carnal colour. The moment when Solveig's silvery naked body warms into flesh tones proclaims the arrival of Wenders at emotional maturity. He once thought his vocation might be the priesthood, and he seems to favour women he can worship. He was married for a time to Ronee Blakley, who played the saintly, martyred gospel singer in Robert Altman's *Nashville* (and whom Wenders, before Coppola used his veto, tried to cast in *Hammett*); Solveig is his current embodiment of the eternal, elusive woman. She announces herself in *Until the End of the World* by whispering to William Hurt, 'I am the angel again', and she ends the film restored to the firmament, this time as an astronaut surveying the oceans for evidence of pollution crimes.

In *Wings of Desire* the camera, following an angel as he glides through the air, weightlessly vaults over the fortified Berlin Wall and goes for a ramble in the mined strip which separated East and West. In 1987, this seemed like the fond wishful thinking of Frank Capra: a happy ending made possible by technical sleight-of-hand. When the Wall was breached in November 1989, Wenders was off the map in Turkey Creek, in the inaccessible north-western corner of Australia, filming von Sydow's experiments in the geological bunker: 'I was euphoric when the news came through. If we hadn't already spent so much energy and money, I'd probably have said "Hold it!" and come straight back. It was something *Wings of Desire* hardly dared to dream about. But that was a fairy tale, and no fairy tale can cope with all the reality which came pouring through the Wall. When I got back here, I realized that I felt more divided than ever.'

Until the End of the World jokily glimpses a reified Berlin, with a matte-painted backdrop of skyscrapers rearing above the Brandenburg Gate. Wenders, however, found it difficult to rejoice about a victory which the West had won not because of its spiritual superiority but because of its acquisitive allure. Mercedes-Benz, Benetton and American Express promptly secured lavish frontages on Friedrichstrasse, which used to be a desolate, frowning alley, its façades pitted by the bullets of snipers around Checkpoint Charlie. Does our much-envied civilization amount only to cars, stripy sweaters and credit facilities? 'Before 1989 the division was artificial, and you could be angry or appalled about it. The emotions were easy. Now the country isn't separated, but it's still split: the division is inside people's heads. Those who lived on the eastern side for so long come from out of the past. They're so naïve, so innocent, with all their moral scruples which are now no use to them in a society that's all about consumerism. They've undergone all these changes too suddenly. It's like a gigantic jet lag. And that's what I thought my second angel should find out about.'

The first angel unregretfully shed his wings for love of the nubile Solveig; the second, Otto Sandler, has a bumpier landing in *Faraway, So Close!*, tumbling into an officially united Berlin where two irreconcilable world-views are still at war. Sandler laments the tyranny of the visible – earthlings, he says, believe only in what they can see – and reports that capitalism has corrupted the art of seeing: now the eyes of humans do nothing but take, they can no longer give. In a city forsaken by gods, where all creeds are questionable, the angels have been replaced by celebrities flown in from America. In a back street Rüdiger Vogler as a bumbling private eye bumps into Peter Falk, and wonders if Columbo could really have dropped from the sky; when Sandler is reduced to sleeping rough, the apparition of the rock singer Lou Reed – 'one of the greats', says Wenders, who took advantage of his presence in Berlin for a concert during the filming – hovers over him and donates a handful of dollars.

Wenders' angels fall from black and white into a world of polychrome illusion. Bruno Ganz first learns about the existence of colour from the blood on his forehead, then from the searing graffiti on the Wall. Otto Sandler, when his turn comes, winces at the neon lighting in the Alexanderplatz station – the glare of a cold sun, unhealthily vivid. Wenders himself remains a soberly monochrome man, dressed on the day we met in black jeans and braces and a grey shirt, with two Mont Blanc pens showing their molten ice-caps in his breast pocket. Perhaps it was one of these pens which Gorbachev used during his walk-on in *Faraway, So Close!*, where he signs an official document with an angel looking over his shoulder; possibly Gorbachev, aware that the Mont Blanc is as much a trophy of capitalism as a Rolex watch, supplied his own.

In Wenders's case, the pair of pens might have been his homage to the alpine exhilarations of the nineteenth-century German poets. His youthful rebelliousness has run its course: student riots in 1968, lots of drugs, then the compulsory stint of psychoanalysis. He is now growing back into a moody German romantic solitary, like the frock-coated wanderer above the mountain mists in the painting by Caspar David Friedrich, whose work he venerates. (He is himself 'a Sunday painter'.) Even his itineracy has a romantic source, since his early film *Wrong Movement* adapted Goethe's account of Wilhelm Meister's leisurely spiritual pilgrimage; and Goethe's theory that colour is an optical deceit perhaps lies behind his notion that angels see in black and white. Certainly he sounded like

Caspar David Friedrich's self-communing wanderer when he described his visit to Ayer's Rock in 1977: 'There was no Sheraton there then, just a motel where I was the only guest. A mongrel dog followed me everywhere. When I climbed the Rock, he stayed at the base of it. I was up there all day on my own, and the dog was waiting for me when I came down the mountain in the evening.' His oblique gaze, still focused to finicky precision on some neutral spot in the sky, might have been watching the scarlet and purple monolith materialize, like the goalie's Platonic idea of an apple, above the pebble-dash tenements of Kreuzberg.

Faraway, So Close! fades out with a warning from the angels about the media and the walls of mediation they construct around us. A medium inevitably gobbles up the messages it is supposed to be sending us: hence the indiscriminateness of American television, mixing up a film by Ozu with a plug for McDonald's. The angels therefore insist, 'We are the messengers, we are not the message. We are nothing. The message is love.' This shatters the glass of the isolation booths between which Harry Dean Stanton and Nastassia Kinski converse in *Paris, Texas*. In *Wings of Desire*, the angels often appear outside windows, solicitously longing to be inside with us. *Faraway, So Close!* grants that wish, and extends the Pietà with which *Paris, Texas* concludes. Ganz, the first angel to demote himself, has fathered a daughter; Sandler impulsively lapses from heaven in order to rescue a child who topples over a balcony, and then dies in order to save her a second time when she is kidnapped by gun-runners.

After another ruminative pause had ticked past, Wenders detached his eyes from the other side of his kitchen window and said, 'The mood is a bit lighter these days. Maybe, slowly, I'm getting there. You know, I always fancied myself as eventually shooting a comedy.' Then, as the grim, guarded, taciturn face relaxed, he looked directly at me, and laughed out loud at the sheer implausibility of it.

JIM JARMUSCH: ON NOT BEING BILLY IDOL

UNDER THE GROANING, WHINING MANHATTAN BRIDGE, ON A VERGE of mud and cinders between the F. D. Roosevelt Drive and the bituminous East River, a man who had fallen out of society emerged from a cabin of plywood to stoke his brazier. Prodding the fire, he stared in bemusement at a passerby: a lanky figure with a sulking face, dressed in the black uniform of the urban dandy but wearing cowboy boots – a cross between a moody Hamlet and a displaced ranch hand. It was the figure's hair which puzzled the tramp. Prematurely white, it bristled like a cockatoo's crest above his forehead, then declined into a curly duck's tail.

At last the tramp remembered the name which eluded him. 'Hey man', he shouted, 'are you Billy Idol?'

'No', said the cowboy-booted Hamlet. 'Sorry.' He appeared faintly irritated at the error. Billy Idol the pop singer is younger, and more mindlessly cherubic. Besides, his quiff comes from the peroxide bottle, not from whatever unguessable nightmare bequeathed this man his anachronistic hair.

When the tramp had withdrawn into his cabin, I asked, 'Wouldn't you like to be Billy Idol?'

'Not really', shrugged the figure with the inky cloak and the ashen locks, 'I prefer to be myself'.

That entails being Jim Jarmusch, and remaining suspicious of showbiz and its custom-made, ephemeral idols. Jarmusch, though Manhattan down-and-outs might not know his name, is the idiosyncratic, stubbornly independent writer, director and producer of several films which apply the technical experimentation of Warhol's underground to the sacrosanct Hollywood genres of the road movie and the buddy movie, infusing the amalgam with a larky, absurdist humour and a knowing literary sensibility.

Down by Law, hilarious and moving, deals with the improvised adventures of three ill-assorted prison escapees. John Lurie (who resembles Frankenstein's monster, with an automaton's scissoring limbs) plays a grumpy pimp, Tom Waits is an autistic disc jockey, and the balding pixie Roberto Benigni is cast as a deconstellated Italian tourist in New Orleans. Stumbling through the bayous, the escapees resolve their quarrels thanks to the mediation of American literature. The film traces the origins of the road movie to Whitman's 'Song of the Open Road', and derives the buddy movie from the doctrine of comradeship promoted by Mark Twain. Benigni sings the muddled praises of a poem by Whitman which he calls *Leaves of Glass,* and when the others leave him shipwrecked on a mud-flat they promise that Mark Twain will come by on a paddle-steamer to rescue him.

The hidden plots of Jarmusch's next two films allude to European literature. *Mystery Train,* in his own description, is 'a modern minimalist's version of *The Canterbury Tales*: three errant groups of rock and roll pilgrims visit the shrine of Elvis at Graceland in Memphis, and are consoled by different visions of the spectral, sequinned fatty. *Night on Earth* follows five consecutive taxi journeys through five different cities in the course of a single winter night. The short stories in this portmanteau add up into a single myth: the various taxi drivers – who range from the gum-chewing tomboy Winona Ryder in Los Angeles to the antic, sacrilegious Roberto Benigni in Rome – play Charon in reverse, ferrying their fares back across rivers of oblivion and through tunnels of obscurity from death into life, while the world optimistically revolves towards daybreak.

The cosmopolitanism of this compilation is typical of Jarmusch, whose original title for *Night on Earth,* jumbling the globe into a Joycean mouthful, was *Lanewyorkparisromehelsinki.* 'Helsinki didn't really fit, it was a joke, an anticlimax, like a punctuation mark at the end of this one big word. But I like the Finns. They're different from other Scandinavian cultures. The men are big rough bears, yet they don't mind crying in public, especially if alcohol has loosened up their feelings. They like to tell you, "We are shy forest peoples."' Jarmusch – although his father's family is Czech and his mother's Irish – has the same recessiveness, hiding behind his funereal costume, and also, once his guard is down, the same unabashed emotionalism.

Born in Ohio, he studied in Paris, where he watched American movies at the Cinémathèque and rediscovered his own country through the defamiliarizing eyes of the *Cahiers du cinéma* critics, who turned cornily innocent Hollywood melodramas into existential fables and religious parables. He returned to live in New York, which he considers 'the cultural capital of Europe'. His first film, *Permanent Vacation,* was about a young American preparing for his grand tour to the ancestral continent. His next, *Stranger than Paradise,* concerned the befuddled American dreams of two immigrants from Hungary who travel aimlessly between New York, Cleveland and Miami. The Memphis pilgrims in *Mystery Train* include two teenage Japanese style-victims, an Italian widow, and a yob from the north of England. In *Night on Earth*, the New York taxi driver is a recent arrival from recently defunct East Germany who speaks pidgin English and has not heard of Brooklyn (or, as he calls it, Brookland).

Such quizzical cultural relativism is rare in America, a world power compounding a world's worth of nationalities which yet remains obtusely provincial in its outlook. Jarmusch dislikes 'the white apartheid corporate party line' about the country. 'America is a mélange of people from all different cultures. Unfortunately it was founded on genocide, but the beauty of it is in this cross-cultural energy. Where I live on the Bowery there are Sicilians, Dominicans, Puerto Ricans, Hassidic Jews and Chinese. I go for a walk and I hear every language. It's natural for me to have three subtitled episodes in *Night on Earth*. It's a circular thing, a continuing dialogue between America and everyone else. French *nouvelle-vague* directors and their criticism made me focus on American film, but then I realized that Hollywood in the 1930s and 1940s consisted of European refugees – Sirk, Sternberg, Stroheim, Tourneur, Lang, Billy Wilder. Anyway, if we communicate it's not through languages. In *Down by Law* it's the Italian guy who gets the two Americans to talk to each other.'

Jarmusch enjoys America's garbled digest of the rest of the world, which it blithely rewrites or else breezily mispronounces. He assumes that his own family name ended in a z until a harassed immigration officer at Ellis Island decided to alter it, and he points across the Bowery to a furniture store whose owner's name is advertised as William Koniak: 'Can't you just see it? Some disoriented French guy gets to Ellis Island and they ask him what he's called and all he wants is a cognac, so they rebaptize him on the spot.' The name of Jarmusch's business manager, Demetra McBride, is a similarly eclectic *trouvaille*. 'She's half Greek and half Scottish. That sums up our social history. We're all mutts.'

Jarmusch's oblique, ironic view of his native land corresponds to the personal geography of Wim Wenders, who oxymoronically transplanted Paris to Texas, and Jarmusch in fact photographed the first part of *Stranger than Paradise* on surplus film stock donated by Wenders. His career overlaps with that of Wenders, but national temperament divides them. The characters of Wenders remain paralysed and incapable, immured in their separate silences. The two drivers in *Kings of the Road* travel on parallel tracks, one in a truck, the other in a train, and helplessly stare at each other across the distance in between. Their journey takes them up and down the border which bifurcated Germany, connecting their emotional difficulties with the country's internal mutilation. Jarmusch's companions also drift apart at the end of *Down by Law*.

Benigni remains in the south, while Lurie goes east and Waits wanders off in the direction of California. However their dispersal allows them to evangelize in all corners of the waiting country, spreading their matey gospel. In the films of Wenders, communication is obstructed by the technological media which are supposed to ease it. Film itself can be a substitute for seeing. The remorse of Wenders about his own medium is laughed away in *Down by Law*, when Lurie gives Benigni a lesson in English prepositions. He draws a window on the blank, impassible wall of their cell. The window, he explains, is on rather than in the wall; nothing can be seen through it. Lurie's grammar is correct, but he misses the film's point. The cell is a window on America, a vantage point for observation of democracy at its convivial, equalizing work. Still in the cell, Lurie coaxes Waits into giving a demonstration of his skills as a disc jockey. Waits, after a tantalizing pause, goes into his routine, and with his voice lowered to a nocturnal drone he whispers into an imaginary microphone every detail of the weather and traffic conditions in a non-existent city. Wenders might have interpreted this episode as a parable about America and its virtual, vicarious realities. For Jarmusch, Waits's act is not a fraud: he is chanting a lullaby to slumbrous, vulnerable America.

Jarmusch worked on *Lightning over Water*, the film in which Wenders documented the terminal illness of their mutual mentor, Nicholas Ray – 'I was a gofer, I made sure Nick had his coffee, I house-sat when they took him to the hospital' – and he began to make *Permanent Vacation* on the morning after Ray's death. This ghoulish alacrity suggests the Oedipal feelings of Wenders towards the founding fathers of American cinema, but again there is a difference. Jarmusch's relations with his adoptive parent were less fraught than those of Wenders, who guiltily worried that the strain of making *Lightning over Water* might have killed Ray. Despite these misgivings, Wenders did not relent: the artist, as Picasso brutally counselled, must slay his father. Ray co-operated in the deadly charade, even performing in his sickbed a scene he had adapted from the moribund Lear's reunion with Cordelia (played by Ronee Blakley); he knew that old age, as Lear bleakly says, is unnecessary. Jarmusch, one of Ray's students at New York University, was spared this lethal struggle between the generations: 'I was a big fan of Nick's before I met him, but he taught me not to idolize people. He didn't hide unpleasant things in his past, like his compromises with the studio system.' Ray was a wisely forbearing father-figure who encouraged filial rejection.

He also enabled Jarmusch to arrive at his own style by contradiction. 'I showed Nick several versions of the script for *Permanent Vacation*, and he always said, "There's nothing going on here, there's no action." And I'd always go home and take more action out of it. I think he was testing me. He knew I'd do the opposite of what he said; he used to smile mischievously when I came back with the next rewrite.' Ray's films are studies in the elegant virtuosity of action, valued not for itself but as a distraction from anxieties within. The teenagers of *Rebel Without a Cause* relieve their frustrations in knife fights and car races. The rodeo in *The Lusty Men* serves the same purpose for Robert Mitchum and Arthur Kennedy. Bogart is spasmodically violent throughout *In a Lonely Place*. But not much happens in Jarmusch's films, and as little as possible is said. In *Down by Law* Tom Waits sits in the cell for three days without uttering a word. Lurie frantically appeals to him to speak. At last he consents: 'Fuck you', he succinctly remarks.

Disregarding the precedent of Ray, Jarmusch is fascinated by mesmeric pauses. In the films of Wenders, such pauses enable the camera to consider the awkwardness or agony of sheer duration. Jarmusch characteristically allows his characters to fill up the vacuum, as bored people do, with zany stratagems for passing the the time: *Mystery Train* contains several interludes in which Screamin' Jay Hawkins and Cinque Lee, as the night clerk and bellboy in the slum hotel, keep themselves awake by playing tricks on each other or exchanging friendly abuse. 'I like the spaces in between things', Jarmusch says. 'Narrative is always secondary.' The stories he tells lead always to an anticlimax. In Wenders the same habit reflects a disbelief in happiness and a contempt for endings which legislatively impose it: father and son are not reunited in *Paris, Texas*. The omissions of Jarmusch are more often a joke, coolly deadpan but still good-humoured. *Down by Law* overleaps the episode of the prison break. The tourists in *Stranger than Paradise* go to see Lake Erie which – invisible in freezing fog – is not there. Those in *Mystery Train* do get to Graceland, but we are not allowed to accompany them.

Ray also made his apprentice promise never to go to Hollywood – 'not even to visit!' Jarmusch has, of course, disobeyed the command, and *Night on Earth* begins with a journey from the Los Angeles airport to Beverly Hills, but he remains true to the spirit of his vow to Ray. In the film's opening episode, Gena Rowlands is a casting director who tries to tempt her taxi driver into accepting a movie role. Winona Ryder, however, has ambitions to be a motor mechanic. Rowlands desperately pleads that everyone wants to be a movie star; Ryder responds, 'That's not a real life for me.' Her truculence expresses Jarmusch's indifference to the industry. 'Agents bug me a lot. I get offered teenage sex comedies, or episodes of *Miami Vice* – you know what I mean? But I'm not what they think of as a film director, I'm a film-maker. I couldn't just step in and do what the producers expected. I don't want to package my films, and I've always raised the finance for them myself.'

The accidents and interruptions of this fund-raising have even even worked to Jarmusch's creative advantage. Money for *Stranger than Paradise* ran out after Jarmusch had completed the first half hour, in which the Hungarian cousins edgily coexist in a New York tenement. It took eighteen months to find more funds, but the characters continued to exist in the interim, although they wandered off to Ohio: the film's fresh start coincided with their new lives. Jarmusch compares his methods with those of a nineteenth-century serial novelist: 'Even if my characters split up before the end, I think of them as staying alive after the film is over, like Dickens in those epilogues telling you where Mr Micawber is now.' His favourite actors similarly commute from film to film, like coincidentally recurring characters in the novels of Balzac: John Lurie meanders out of *Stranger than Paradise* into *Down by Law*, where he plays (as he previously did for Wenders in *Paris, Texas*) a pimp; Tom Waits, an imprisoned DJ in *Down by Law*, is also heard on the radio as an insomniac DJ in *Mystery Train*; and Roberto Benigni, who naturalizes himself in Louisiana in *Down by Law*, is repatriated to Rome in *Night on Earth*. The world is held together by a network of friendships: Jarmusch himself has a walk-on in *Leningrad Cowboys Go America*, a surreal Finnish road movie directed by Aki Kaurismäki; Kaurismäki was originally cast as one of the purgatively tearful Helsinki drunks in *Night on Earth*.

Jarmusch's role in *Leningrad Cowboys* is that of a slippery used-car salesman, who unloads a hearse-like limo on the members of the egregious Russian rock band. 'Why did Aki think of me for that part? We have cars in common, I guess – and bikes. He drives a Cadillac, and I have a white 66 Caddy with fins. You can see it parked outside the bar in *Mystery Train*. I don't leave it on the street in New York: some creep would be sure to paint SATAN all over it. Aki and another guy also have the only Harley-Davidson dealership in Finland, and I used to have two Harleys. Whenever we met we were always exchanging gripes – you know, "My transmission's fucked up" or "I need a new ignition switch". So I just walked into the role. When I grew up in Akron, it was a car culture, like *American Graffiti* except with a post-industrial backdrop. Cars meant freedom. I like to be on the road, owning nothing, hiring cars and then leaving them behind like disposable razors. I have a '79 Buick for the city. It looks a piece of junk, so no one fucks with it, but it has a great engine. I want to do a biker movie one day.'

He values the performers in *Night on Earth* as much for their driving as for their acting. 'Benigni is an amazing driver. We had a stunt driver to stand in for him, but he couldn't make a turn in one of those narrow Roman streets at the speed we wanted. Roberto did it himself. And the guy who drives the cab in Paris could race professionally.' This itchy addiction to mobility explains the fondness of Jarmusch for those shots which French cinéastes call 'le travelling'. *Down by Law* begins with a sequence of travelling shots as indefinitely extensible as a cross-country highway, speeding up and down drab streets in a New Orleans slum. This overture is exhilarating but quite superfluous: it allows Jarmusch the biker loudly to rev up his engine. The same desire for perpetual motion prompted him to make a film set entirely inside taxis.

He thinks of the cab as a squeezed, confidential theatre on wheels, an arena of pretence and also of self-revelation. 'You're in an intimate space with someone you'll never see again, so none of the rules apply. You can talk freely about politics or sex, or you can lie. Gena Rowlands told me she uses cab rides to try out fake accents – like, can she convince the driver she's a German or something? But you have moments of truth in a cab too. Sometimes it's easier for a relationship to develop between strangers.' The role reversal in the New York episode – where a street-wise black passenger assumes control and takes the bewildered German driver to Brooklyn – was based on the experience of one of Jarmusch's friends. 'He hailed a cab driven by a Pakistani who was new to the country and to the job and couldn't handle an automatic shift. So my friend drove, and he took the Pakistani on a tour of Manhattan, showed him Central Park, told him about Macy's Thanksgiving Day parade. He said the guy was like a kid on vacation, his eyes were alight. You know, there are warm, lovable people in New York.'

We took a battered cab across town from the East River to the Bowery; the driver, who spent fourteen hours a day on the mean, pot-holed, perilous streets of the city, told us that his upwardly mobile son was a merchant banker in London. 'Since making this film, I always tip cab drivers more', said Jarmusch when we got out. 'I give them thirty per cent now. It's a rough job. The poor guys are always getting murdered.'

Jarmusch's cabbies could not be more different from the noctambulant vigilante played by Robert de Niro in Martin Scorsese's *Taxi Driver*. De Niro listens in disgust to the bilious maunderings of his fares and wipes semen off the lacerated upholstery at the end of every shift, while the good-humoured drivers in Jarmusch's film dispense homiletic wisdom as they take their passengers home. Winona Ryder in Los Angeles serenely castigates the false values of Gena Rowlands, Isaach de Bankolé in Paris ditches some obstreperous revellers who show him no respect, and Matti Pelonpää in Helsinki talks his car load of drunks through a cathartic cry.

Closest to yet most distant from de Niro – who on one journey through the inferno listens to the self-loathing confession of Scorsese himself – is the maniacally funny Roberto Benigni in Rome. Benigni, having picked up a priest, takes the opportunity to ease his conscience. The sins he confesses, which include carnal relations with pumpkins and a pet lamb as well as his brother's wife, so convulse the priest that he dies of shock, and is unsanctimoniously dumped at the roadside. De Niro, deranged, quits his cab in order to slaughter the social vermin of the city; Benigni, disburdened, speeds off with a comedian's impunity, hurtling in the wrong direction down a one-way street.

Shuttling through various countries, the film allows Jarmusch to test his theories of communication. The characters suffer from problems of vision: Gena Rowlands complains of night blindness; Béatrice Dalle in the Parisian cab is literally blind, though clairvoyant; and Benigni drives at night wearing dark glasses, which he eventually transfers to the dead priest, whose eyes won't close. 'It's funny,' commented Jarmusch, 'but I didn't see all that myself. It was a friend who said to me, "This film is about blindness." A work of art is like an electrical circuit, it doesn't exist until there is some receptor for the current.' When I added that blindness is an odd subject for a film-maker, whose medium depends on sight, Jarmusch retrieved another psychic source: 'Maybe it was something my landlords on the Bowery did eight years ago, when I was three months behind on the rent. They came up to threaten me – they're these massive Italian-American bruisers, with polyester suits, gold chains, the lot – and one of them said, "Hey Jim, did you ever hear of any blind film directors?" They don't mess with me now, ever since I found out I could sue them for rent gouging and got the city to send them a warning letter. That convinced them I was a player, as they say in Hollywood.'

Even when they learn to recognize each other, Jarmusch's transients arrive at communion in spite of the muddling intercession of language. Although his first ambition was to be a writer, Jarmusch has a playfully dismissive attitude to words. He treasures the mistakes which occur across linguistic borders. The irrepressible Japanese girl in *Mystery Train*, convinced that she understands English, brightly proffers matches when someone asks her if the train is headed for Natchez. At Columbia, Jarmusch's creative-writing teacher encouraged him to translate poems from foreign languages which he had never learned: 'I just found a few Latin roots that looked familiar and invented the rest. It was a roundabout way of creating a new poem. I like not understanding stuff. I love riding the subway in Tokyo without being able to read the signs. Roberto Benigni has a tape he made one night in Rome, with Tom Waits declaiming Dante – and Tom doesn't know a word of Italian! It's great, someone should pirate it. You can get by without the vocabulary. When I first met Roberto we couldn't speak English to each other: we became friends in broken French.'

A philosophical hooker in *Down by Law*, castigating John Lurie because he doesn't beat her up often enough, remarks that 'America is a melting pot, and when it comes to the boil all the scum bubbles to the surface.' Jarmusch enjoys stirring languages into the cauldron, and serving up a stew which is as polyglot as rainbow-coloured America. His puns skip across frontiers and confound nationality. When the blind girl in the Paris taxi says that she often goes to the cinema, her fellow passengers – self-important drunks from the Ivory Coast, off to keep an appointment with the Cameroon ambassador – jeer that she sees nothing ('y voit rien'), then realize that they have inadvertently named their own slice of Africa ('Ivoirien'). Jarmusch hears the same Babel of voices in the singing of Tom Waits: 'People talk about Tom's voice being raw and whiskey-soaked. But he hasn't just got one voice, there's a different voice for each track on an album. He can croon or snarl or bark or squeal, he's got all the instruments in his throat.' Another of Jarmusch's eclectic fantasies – boozily dreamed up in league with Benigni – is of a heaven where all the artists he admires live together as buddies, sharing cabs and standing each other drinks. In *Night on Earth*, Benigni locates this clubbable Parnassus at a nondescript hostelry he drives past called Hotel Genio. He imagines Shakespeare and the jazz man Charley Parker as residents of the Genius Hotel, happily confabulating in the bar, no doubt employing the Esperanto of the after-life.

Although his manner has a cool, studied taciturnity, beneath the forbidding black get-up Jarmusch is as soft-hearted as one of his blubbering Finns. To be mistaken for Billy Idol irked him, I suspect, because he thinks of himself as a tough guy, not a pretty boy. He and Lurie, whose head was apparently sculpted by some hasty, inexact hatchet, have formed a secret society called Sons of Lee Marvin, jokily enrolling the late actor's scattered progeny: 'We're keen to have some female members, so long as they resemble Lee.' But the armoured grimness relented when Jarmusch began to talk about Waits: 'Sure, he sees things in a way that's very funny. You can go into a coffee shop with him and he'll say, "Hey, look, all the donuts have got names like prostitutes – Twinky Princess, Miss Jelly Hole . . ." Still, what I like most in his music is the emotional investment, the pathos in the details. There's a beautiful anti-war song, "Soldier's Things", where all he does is list the possessions left behind in the dead guy's room – boxing gloves, a broken radio, medals for bravery, all waiting for the garage sale. It breaks your heart.'

Nor can the minimalist laconicism of Jarmusch's films conceal their geniality. *Down by Law* concludes with a fortuitous love-feast, and Benigni in a typically mispronounced effusion embraces Lurie and Waits and tells them 'We are a good hegg.' Although Chaucer's disputatious pilgrims never reach Canterbury, the Japanese tourists in *Mystery Train* – who traipse down a grubby thoroughfare called, in their version of it, 'Chowcer Street' – are allowed to visit two holy places in a single day: Graceland in the morning, and Fats Domino's house in New Orleans by nightfall. Jarmusch boldly trusts in the atoning, reconciling powers of comedy: the Japanese girl, thinking that her boyfriend looks glum, paints a clown's smirking mouth on his face with her lipstick; the German taxi driver in the New York sequence of *Night on Earth* is a former circus clown, who cheers and charms his feuding passengers by playing on Pan pipes.

A comedian, for Jarmusch, is a healer. 'I was driving down the Via Veneto with Roberto one night. In Italy he's recognized everywhere; everyone wants something from him. Anyway, some guy raced out into the traffic and starting banging on the car window. He was crying, distraught, he said he'd attempted suicide, that Roberto had to help him. And Roberto talked to him for a long while. Afterwards I asked, "What did you tell him?" He said, "Oh, I told him many stupid things – that this is our life, we must cope with it, I told him to go have a coffee, I said coffee is one of the things worth living for..." Roberto won't turn anyone away. He probably saved that guy.'

I remembered the incident in *Down by Law* when Benigni, wandering through a seedy precinct of New Orleans, solemnly remarks to an old black man on a street corner, 'It is a sad and beautiful world.' The old man takes up the phrase, adds a beat and quickens it into a melodic riff, like the optimistic accompaniment to one of the city's jazz funerals. There is a postscript to this near the end of *Night on Earth*, where – while the globe swivels in space, transporting all its fugitive passengers through the night – the voice of Waits, as cracked and desolate as that of a ghost exiled to the interplanetary void, sings of his yearning to be 'back in the good old world'. Jarmusch's films convince us that, even though the meter is remorselessly ticking, our ride around the world is worth the price. As he improbably assured me, 'There are warm, lovable people in New York.' Well, I can think of at least one.

CULT FIGURES

LEONORA CARRINGTON: THE WITCH'S OILS

I RANG LEONORA CARRINGTON'S DOORBELL WITH SOME TREPIDATION. I was paying a call, after all, on a woman who in her youth served as an inflammatory muse to the surrealists – a wild embodiment of erotic impulse and maenadic madness – and who now in her old age, as a devotee of the White Goddess and the cult of female creativity, an adept of alchemical lore and a student of assorted Eastern arcana, had the reputation of being a witch. What spells and sorceries awaited me upstairs?

Her occult, outrageous career began innocuously enough. She was born in 1917, the daughter of a Lancashire cotton tycoon. After her expulsion from two convent schools and a 'finishing' academy, she moved to London to turn herself into an artist. In 1936 she ran off to France with Max Ernst, who was 46 and still concurrently fulfilling what Leonora called his 'genital responsibilities' to his wife. Ernst was interned when war began; Leonora, bereft, suffered a breakdown and – babbling wildly about a personal cosmology – was locked up in a Madrid asylum. Released by the intervention of the family nanny, she fled to Lisbon, shipped out to New York, and in 1941 settled in Mexico.

The collector Edward James first applied the witchy metaphor to her art. Her paintings, he said, were 'brewed ... in a cauldron at the stroke of midnight'. Surrealism always hurls form, identity and the sane, solid structure of things into a seething crucible, where objects undergo disintegration: think of Dali's molten watch, modelled on a runny Camembert, or his sofa which is the ripe, moist mouth of Mae West. In Leonora Carrington's paintings, pigs hatch from eggs, trees grow out of human heads like twitching thoughts, and people migrate between the species, merging with animals or birds.

To complement the paintings, she has written stories which are parables of the surrealist project, repellently decomposing and radiantly reconstructing persons and things. A debutante is escorted to her first ball by a hyena; the famished animal eats its own face at the table. A pagan priestess in Mexico ritually boils the Archbishop of Canterbury in a casserole dish. A bearded crone incites a revolution: Armageddon ensues, followed by the earth's regeneration, overseen by covens of weird sisters on Hampstead Heath. Her paintings hybridize the serene allegorical processions of Botticelli with the infernal revels of Bosch. Her stories mix together Celtic fairy tales, the cabbalistic recipes of Renaissance magicians like Giordano Bruno, Jung's collective unconscious with its sea-bed of symbols, and the instant theologies of the New Age. In this eclectic mental and physical mayhem, surrealism achieves what Antonin Artaud called the crucifixion or the excruciation of our so-called real world.

Back in that real world, a few days before Halloween in 1991, the doorbell I rang was in the suburbs of Chicago. Dismayed by the Mexican government's brutish repression of student protests in 1968 and its corrupt mismanagement of earthquake relief in 1985, Leonora Carrington now lives mostly here, close to one of her sons from a marriage to a Hungarian photographer. Waiting for her to let me in, I consulted my images of the young Leonora: a raven-haired and armoured warrior in a painting by Léonor Fini, legs aggressively spread as she confronts and defies a man-made society; a muse materializing from the depths in Max Ernst's portrait of her, picking her way through a brambly garden of skeletons and horned demons in a green dawn, her hair a forest and her flesh pearly.

Already, before she appeared, I had begun to doubt the trustworthiness of the reality I was standing in. The imagination of artists seems to infect and alter their surroundings. Leonora could have dreamed the building where she lives: a down-at-heels, incongruously Gothic apartment block, decorated with spurious crests and second-hand heraldic props, bristling in a cheery, average suburban street. On the tiled floor of the lobby, among a surf of discarded junk mail, a dozen earthworms wriggled, dilating, throbbing and twisting themselves into wet brown coils. Refugees, I wondered, from the cauldron upstairs?

The woman who opened the door required a quick adjustment of my ideas. Neither Fini's embattled virago nor Ernst's sensual savage, Leonora Carrington turned out to be a genteel and elegant old lady; no cackling sorceress either, although there was a sly glint of mischief in her eyes.

She at once disclaimed responsibility for the serpentine tangle of worms. 'They've just crawled in under the door to get out of the rain.' (There was a late-October monsoon in Chicago, for which – bouncing through the air between lightning bolts – I had also privately blamed Leonora.) 'It doesn't surprise me. This place is a mess. Look here, in the hall we've got a fountain which has been dry for years. That's the laundry room, none of the driers works. The light bulb on the stairs is always broken.' The surrealist in her resurfaced as she pointed to a brown, squelching blob trodden into the stair carpet outside her apartment door: 'I don't know what that once was, but whatever it was you wouldn't have wanted to touch it. At least it's quiet here, and cheap. Most of my neighbours are black. No, of course they don't know who I am. And even if they did, they wouldn't be interested. To be really famous in America, you have to read the news on television.'

Her apartment is small and bare, furnished mainly with a distracted jumble of air conditioners which malfunctioned long ago and disembowelled humidifiers, plus a smattering of sacred texts on Taoist physics. A Mexican cactus miserably hibernates in a corner. On a window ledge in front of a tattered blind sits a single sculptural familiar, a papier-mâché mermaid with ratty braids of string. She has none of her own paintings. The only signs of creative brewing and stewing were a French cooking apron slung over an empty easel, and a pile of clear plastic boxes, meant for storing left-over food, which contained her tubes of paint – the witch's oils, as Coleridge said when describing the phosphorescence of the water snakes. She excused herself, and made a trip to the bathroom. 'If you want to look around while I'm gone,' she said, 'you'll find my hard-core porn under the bed.'

Back in her kitchenette, she lowered herself into a padded rocking chair – a more sedate and sedentary allusion, perhaps, to the rocking horse which stands for her spirit animal in an early self-portrait, and looks towards a live version of itself galloping to freedom through the window. Next she apologetically lit a cigarette, after opening a door on to the fire escape. Then she produced a small, dog-eared, ring-bound notebook, scribbled full of prophetic utterances.

'You see I've done my homework for you. The campuses here like to have artists in residence, and they expect me to make pronouncements. So I've prepared a few, and I'll get double value from them. If it's too much for you to write down, we can go along the street and get this photo-copied. Then you'll have your article. No? All right. But you've got to let me read them out. Stop me if I go too fast. I'll start with some quantum jokes. I had a competition with some young women I know here, to see who could make the most pretentious statement of the year. "I sit where the quantum fears to leap." How about that?

Somewhere here, there's a little verse. Yes, this is it:
> Disintegration is bliss,
> 'Tis folly to be solid.

Do you like that?'

She chuckled, and I thought I could smell the broth from the caul-dron. The lines sum up her surrealist creed, with its desire to force bod-ies and minds (her own included) through a deforming metamorphosis. She looks back on her nervous collapse – despite her paranoid hysteria, her bouts of catalepsy, and the seizures provoked by the drugs she was given – with a certain gratitude: 'Well, at least being mad gets rid of all your fixed ideas about yourself.'

As the little notebook touchingly testified, Leonora feels obliged to be oracular. But in the process she mocks her own pretension: 'Here there's something about paradigms. That's a word I use a lot, I've just learned it, it sounds so impressive; they lap it up on the campuses.' She also has a way of suddenly grounding the higher nonsense in a very earthy good sense. Thus, as the recitation from the notebook continued, a reverie about morphology diverged into a cheeky practical joke on reality, and my particular tenure of it. 'Painting is the creation of form. You're creat-ing a body or an image. A symbol is the body of a real psychic identity. A sign is a name, a symbol is a body. Yet we're also disintegrating and reforming the body as we create it. We have to escape from the existential habit of existing in a certain shape, as I did when I was mad. We should think about *what* we are, not *who* we are. I'm seeing you, but are you real-ly here? Do I dare to come over and pinch you?'

I tensed, remembering the Witch in *Hansel and Gretel* who tweaked the flesh of her captives to test their readiness for the pot.

'No, don't worry, I won't. You might go "Phut!" if I did. And yet even though you're an illusion, you're also a celestial body. Everything is cos-mic. The worms down in the lobby are cosmic bodies too. So there. Those are all the notes I have. What else do you want to talk about?'

What I wanted to talk about was how a privileged, respectable girl had changed herself first into the passionate rebel who eloped with Ernst and then, after marriages to a Mexican diplomat and the Hungarian photog-rapher, into the elderly sibyl in the rocking chair. Leonora's motive has always been provocation. She has spent her life disowning her family nickname, Prim. Introduced to a Catholic priest at the age of fourteen, she pulled up her pinafore and demanded, 'What do you think of that?'

She had, of course, no knickers on. 'Oh, I hated those convent schools – having to wear a uniform, to walk in a line, to conform. Of course I hate all patriarchal religions. They expelled me for general insubordination. No, I wasn't caught *in flagrante* with the officiating Jesuit. General insubordination to them was even worse than immorality. And then there was the finishing school. Two maiden ladies ran it, one thin and one fat, like Laurel and Hardy. They found a hot book under my mattress: Michael Arlen's *The Green Hat*, such a tame thing. I hadn't even read it. It was being passed round the dorm, and I was last on the list.'

Hers is a particularly English variant of surrealism, because it originated in a compulsion to twit and tease a stuffy, pious bourgeoisie. The young Leonora railed against 'the spiritual maladies of the English', and declared that their souls had the consistency of pork brawn. In one of her stories, it is snootily decreed that 'one's got to suffer to go to heaven. Those who do not wear corsets will never get there.' Hypocrisy is the cement of this society. A precocious child whispers that 'Mummy says it's vulgar to say "Mucky", but we use it in secret.'

Leonora's long campaign of desecration began as an assault on the prohibitions enforced by Mummy, who permitted no muckiness. 'I didn't have any problems with my father, though he was appalled when I wanted to become an artist. My grandfather was a mill-hand; my father was proud of his brass and had no snobbery. He was a bit like a mafioso: he had a shoot, he enjoyed killing things. My mother came from a long line of Irish gipsies, but she went posh. We were awfully conscious of being nouveau-riche. My mother shamed me so. She never liked to say we were from Lancashire, she thought that was common. You should have heard her when we were abroad, convinced she could speak French or Italian. I cringed. She had me presented at court, in a rented tiara. The discomfort of it! The tiara was like a thumb screw around my skull. And all the oom-pahpah music the royals like! Then we had to go to Ascot. We weren't allowed to bet, and we knew no one in the Royal Enclosure, but my mother sat there in bliss, spotting people she'd seen in *Tatler* or *The Bystander*. I spent the time reading Aldous Huxley – *Eyeless in Gaza*, where the fox terrier falls out of the aeroplane.'

Snobs suffer from an over-excitable imagination, conjuring up for themselves a grandiose vision of society which outdoes reality. Leonora's mother was in her own way a supreme fantasist. 'She claimed to be descended from Maria Edgeworth, who wrote those Gothic novels. She probably invented that; she was capable of anything. She bought an awful portrait of the Empress Elisabeth of Austria at a jumble sale – just a photograph painted over – and put it up in the billiard room to pose as one of our ancestors. She used to say to me "She does look a bit like you, you know." I made my peace with the absurdity of it all after I left England. There's nothing like not seeing people to calm things down.'

The affair with Ernst was a liberation, yet in another sense an imprisonment. 'Dear Max', Leonora now purrs with quiet, clawed malice. Introducing her first volume of stories, Ernst patronized her as instinctual and illiterate; he used her pictures as spare canvas, over which he painted his own works. 'At that time, I still accepted a lot of shit. Being a muse! All it means is that you're someone's object. I was totally in love with him, fascinated by him, but I was so young.' Her portrait of Ernst is a kind of reckoning. She depicts him as a frosty merman in a landscape of ice, with a shock of gelid, snowy hair; a monster, perhaps, of predatory, deathly ego. I asked about the fish tail he sports in the painting. 'Maybe', she said, 'there was something fishy about him.'

By the time they met again in Lisbon and New York, Ernst had been collected by Peggy Guggenheim; it was in Mexico that Leonora acquired personal and artistic independence. André Breton described Mexico as 'the surrealist place par excellence', a land where bad dreams erupted through the level floor of reality: the seismic earth, the volcanoes, the sacrificial pyramids, the spectral cults which still had not been annexed by Christianity, the hallucenogenic juice of the cacti. 'It's a frightening place', said Leonora with a delicious shiver. 'Not only because of the government, though one hates all governments on principle. In 1985, after the earthquake in Mexico City, they sent in the army to keep the peace. Instead the soldiers looted and vandalized everything. A rescue party arrived from France with dogs to sniff out people buried in the rubble; they even stole the dogs. The whole Mexican Scotland Yard tumbled down, and they discovered all kinds of horrific dungeons. But the really dangerous cultures are the ones which deny the dark side. Mexicans have a tremendous death wish. They're so aware that people die; you see them being buried. I've never seen a funeral in Chicago. For Mexicans, the dead are all around.'

As well as painting, she prosecuted her grudge against the real world and its proprieties with a series of surreal pranks. She and her sister in crime, the painter Remedios Varo, fired off anonymous letters to unsuspecting strangers all over the world, professing love or offering recondite services. 'Breton pontificated against the letters we wrote. "Ah, quelle honte!" he used to say. I suppose it was a bit sneaky. But it's so liberating to pretend you're someone else!' During her madness, what she calls her 'sub-personas' invaded and possessed her, turning her character upside down. Now these alternative egos playfully came when called.

She also cooked surreally. The paintings bubble over from an internal cauldron; she has likened their creation to making jam, and for a while she worked in egg tempera because the medium – as well as reminding her of the ovulating White Goddess – had the raw fluency to which surrealism wants to reduce all phenomena. One guest found that his hair had been clipped while he slept, and used as filling for an omelette. On another occasion, she and Remedios dished up buckets of caviare (or 'couviar' as they smuttily called it) which was actually tapioca, coloured with the ink of squids and immaculately presented on a silver tray. 'Buñuel was at the party. I took him into the bathroom and showed him the pails of it we had. I said I'd had this windfall from England. He thought it was the most immoral thing he'd ever seen – the excess! He suggested calling the fanciest funeral parlour in Mexico City, laying it out and giving it a proper burial. That was very Mexican. I'm afraid my days of surreal cooking are over. Now it's mostly frozen dinners for one from the supermarket.'

The campaign of dissent and provocation, however, continues by other means. Leonora has not grown old graciously. She admires bag ladies, the eschatological harridans of the American street, who pursue their private visions through the crowd, grappling with invisible demons as they push their shopping trolleys. 'It's one of the things I'd like to be, a bag lady. They're always exploring, they're outside the rules. But a Tibetan Buddhist friend of mine who lives with them in the tunnels under Grand Central Station warned me off. Besides, I wouldn't like to be dirty.'

Like the geriatric revolutionary in her novel *The Hearing Trumpet*, Leonora prides herself on being a holy terror, intimidating authority. 'A policeman in New York once laughed at my English accent, and I demanded his number. The way to control the police is to point a video camera at them. I'd always carry one if I lived in New York; of course it wouldn't need to have any film in it. I go back to Mexico by railway – I won't fly – and those Amtrak trains are like moving concentration camps. All the way down through Texas there's nothing to see but dead motor cars, so I pass the time by threatening the conductors with law suits. We're brought up to be so inhibited. I'm glad I've got over being British and long-suffering. America has given me that. Americans are such great complainers! The magic formula here is to say you'll sue. That's my technique with my landlady in this building. She's a great big busty blonde called Mary Sue (or something like that). I say to her "Mary Sue, there's no light bulb on the stairs again, and if I fall down you'll be *liable*...." That pushes her panic button. I haven't been able to figure out yet how those driers in the laundry room which don't work could be life-threatening. But I will! Wait, perhaps I could say I caught pneumonia from having to wear a damp nightie. I know they won't do anything, but at least I have the satisfaction of being a nuisance.' Inside the senior citizen, the naughty child is still alive.

Having completed her reading from the prophetically obscurantist notebook and brought up to date the story of her irregular life, Leonora next gave me a demonstration of the surrealist imagination at its alarming, estranging work. She did not paint a picture or write a story; she took me for a walk down the street, supposedly so we could eat lunch at a delicatessen. As we walked, each item in the inventory of suburban normality vanished as she looked at it, almost as if she had waved a wand or uttered some hocus-pocus, and was replaced by a warped or freaky facsimile of itself.

In readiness for Halloween, pumpkins with fiendish, razory rins carved in their rind grinned on verandas, and inflatable plastic skeletons grimaced and capered in shop windows. The pavements were thick with blood-coloured leaves. 'Ah,' said Leonora, remembering the Mexican festival of spooks, '*Los Muertos*....' America might seem to have demystified the commemoration of All Souls' Day, but Leonora is aware of hidden terrors. 'My grandsons dress up in white sheets to go trick-or-treating. You have to be careful: people give children sweets with razor blades in them, or strychnine. By the way, isn't this architecture odd? Look at that house.' I glanced up at a gabled cone wearing a coat of shingles. 'It looks like fish scales', said Leonora. In *The Hearing Trumpet* she argues that 'houses are really bodies. We connect ourselves with walls, roofs and objects just as we hang on to our livers, skeletons, flesh and bloodstream.' She had, with the aid of a metaphor, alchemically changed this middle-class dwelling into an amphibious organism.

On the porch of the house in question hung a dripping yellow wreath. 'For the boys in the Gulf', snorted Leonora. 'These people love war. What a bastard Bush is! I went to the protests in Chicago, of course.' Now she had darted off diagonally across a lawn, and was kneeling in the shrubbery. 'Do you know what that is? I'm sure it's hemlock. Look at those sinister berries. I bet the people in the house don't suspect.'

We arrived at the deli, which was, she explained, a wishful reincarnation of a bohemian haunt she frequented in her youth. 'It likes to think it's the local *Café des deux magots*. Unfortunately they've got the Left Bank confused with Cannes: see those beach umbrellas over the tables indoors? They also think it's ethnic. There's a row of books up there under the ceiling, just to show it's artistic, but you can't reach them.'

The flowers were plastic, the waiters likewise. 'Everything in America is an imitation of something else. Why did they suppose that New York was a new York? What an idea! You know, when I first arrived in New York during the war, I thought there'd be cowboys. I wasn't so very wrong. They're all cowboys at heart, Americans, when they're not policemen. Or psychotherapists. I feel such insecurity in this country, as if it were all about to blow. To me, this is much more surreal than Mexico. There's no reality in America at all. Realism was a dirty word in the 1930s, but I have a deep respect for it, because I don't know what reality means. I'll have a sandwich, a Mother Nature's Threat it's called. No, Mother Nature's Treat, with alfalfa sprouts. On second thoughts, Mother Nature's Threat is nearer the truth....' I recalled her description of the floor heaving beneath her feet during the Mexico City earthquake, and also her account, in a memoir of her madness, of the voluntary vomitings which – as her emetic response to social iniquities – 'tore at my stomach like earthquakes'.

On the way back, we passed a hotel converted into a retirement community, with the upbeat slogan ActiveLife™. Several inactive residents were parked in a window, drooling. 'I'm rather tempted by that place', said Leonora with morbid glee. 'I've often thought of checking myself in. But no, I can imagine what it would be like: childhood all over again, with nanny criticizing your table manners. "Eat up dear, don't put it on the cloth." Not just yet, perhaps.'

The beached worms were still flexing on the tiles at her front door. 'I know what I'll do', said Leonora. 'I'm going to call Mary Sue. I'll say, "Mary Sue, I'm afraid I have some bad news for you. I've had a distinguished gentleman from England here to visit me, and he was *appalled* to see worms in the lobby. And I'm afraid, on the way out, he slipped on one of them, and hurt himself quite badly. I think I heard a bone break. Anyway, the paramedics have taken him away. Oh, I gave him your number. Mary Sue, I think you're going to be LI-A-BLE.... Can I make a suggestion? Mary Sue, please hire yourself a duck, and bring it straight over here to eat these worms.'" Giggling, she scampered back upstairs.

Another surrealist muse – Magouche Fielding, the wife of the painter Arshile Gorky – once remarked that 'surrealism wasn't good for your health', which is certainly true when you remember Leonora's insanity in 1939. But her career also demonstrates that surrealism, impenitent and impertinent in its attack on the powers that be and its jesting anarchism, could be a lot of laughs.

DAVID HOCKNEY AND REPRODUCTION

DAVID HOCKNEY IS THE LUCKY INHABITANT OF AN ARTIFICIAL paradise – or rather of several, snugly cocooned one inside another. First is the city of Los Angeles, whose unofficial iconographer he has become: a jungle of pampered greenery charmed from the desert with stolen water and kept alive by wetback labour. The next inset is the cleft of the Hollywood hills where his house perches: a romantic chasm choked with palms, banana trees and the blue fallen sky of his swimming pool. Then there is the house itself, painted, like its iridiscent owner, all the colours of the Rimbaud. Its wooden veranda is scarlet, the carpets are midnight blue, and yellow shelves glow like a grove of lemons; outside the windows, ornamental fish suspended on strings swim in the wind, as if the garden were underwater. And inside the house, on the day in the summer of 1992 when I visited him, Hockney switched on a magic box and revealed the lushest and most lavish of his imaginary Edens so far: his designs for Richard Strauss's fairy-tale opera *Die Frau ohne Schatten*, which opened later in the year at Covent Garden.

He had been working on the sets for seven months, in a labour of contagious love. 'I suppose I'm subsidizing the show. It's not a very economical way to do it – you have to be a fairly rich, middle-aged artist who likes to indulge himself – but we've only ten days in the theatre itself, so I built everything in miniature here, rigged up the lighting, then made a film of the whole opera. That way I know how it should look. You can do amazing things with a little video camera!' He proceeded to amaze me. His magic box was a television screen large enough to sleep two people comfortably, flanked by stereo speakers the approximate size of Portaloos. He had synchronized events in his puppet theatre – where stick figures, prodded into action by assistants, deputized for the more voluminous sopranos Gwyneth Jones and Anna Tomowa-Sintow who would flesh out the roles at Covent Garden – with a recording of the volcanic score. Fiddling with zappers, he settled down on a sofa for a run-through of the noisy, portentous four-hour parable. His dachshunds Stanley and

Boodgie snored at his feet, oblivious to the orchestral tumult.

Die Frau ohne Schatten commutes between two worlds: the starry realm of the Emperor and his childless Empress, the woman without a shadow of the title, and the soiled subterranean hovel of Barak the dyer and his discontented wife, who barters her own fertility (symbolized by the tricksy shadow). Both couples undergo purgative torments before they are reunited for a lung-busting, throat-tearing quartet in praise of procreation. Strauss and his librettist Hofmannsthal intended the work as their supplement to the initiatic trials of Mozart's *Magic Flute*, which concludes with the avian couple Papageno and Papagena numbering their offspring, and Hockney was enticed into the project by the director John Cox, for whom he designed a charming and touching *Magic Flute* at Glyndebourne in 1977. 'I'd seen *Die Frau ohne Schatten* a few times', he said, 'but the productions never took you to all those different, fantastic places where it's supposed to happen. So I thought, this is an opera I can help a bit.'

He helped it, with his usual generosity, by turning these notional settings into luminous reality. He flicked through a succession of vistas on the video monitor. A river of liquid gold twisted through fields whose crops were a crimson hallucination. The Emperor hunted in a forest of purple saplings. Barak's den was a mud hut of dripping ochres and squelchy earth tones, the grubby source of the pigment which makes Hockney's own art possible. Dyes dripped down the walls, swelling into amniotic puddles on the floor. During the ecstatic final quartet, Hockney – shouting down Strauss and briefly disturbing the dachshunds, who thought it must be dinner time – said, 'Now there's a scene change, and the whole opera ends in the future with their unborn children. Hofmannsthal said you ought to see the most wonderful landscape ever....' Hockney's version of the future was exactly that: a biomorphic carnival, conjured up by the flicking, writhing brushstrokes he made when the score first dinned into his head.

He warned me not to gasp too soon. 'Wait, wait, in a minute you'll see the river stand upright and turn into the tree of life. It can do that because it's a negative shape, a hole. There's only ever light inside it, not water. I love the way the eye can be fooled into seeing something that's not there. Notice all those wiggly spermy lines, like fish? The colours pulse in time to the music, as if they were alive – which they are. They send out waves, like sound does, directly into your body.' The production's climax was a conflagration of paint electrified by light – a blazing answer to what Hockney calls the 'transcendental dawn' of the final scene he designed for Wagner's *Tristan und Isolde* at the Los Angeles Opera in 1987 when, during the heroine's dying transfiguration, a mossy cliff suddenly changed into a white gulf, mystically blank: 'That was a different kind of future. *Tristan* is all about sex and death. This one's about sex and life!'

Strauss and Hofmannsthal concentrated on the symbiotic relationship of the two women in the opera, the lofty, crystalline Empress and the downtrodden, resentful wife of the dyer; but for Hockney the central figure was his fellow-artisan Barak. 'They could have given him any trade at all, couldn't they, so why a dyer? Colour's his business. He's a simple working man who just wants to make the world a brighter place.' His cheeky grin said the rest. Barak's mission is also Hockney's: he is a walking advertisement for the cheering agency of colour, with his tawny skin and yellow hair, his lime-green shirt and burgundy polka-dot belt, and the red and blue concentric whirls of the hearing aid he wears as if it were jewellery. Colour is an exercise in optimism. Blondes, as Hockney declared when he first dyed his hair, have more fun. Drab, sad reality, repainted by him, is better as well as brighter. In 1978, sending out a printed card to sympathisers after his father's funeral, he decided to scatter some fluorescent spots across the message. This was both a homage to his father's way of adding emphases to his letters and a smiling defiance of death: 'Everybody else underlines, but he'd put Dayglo spots so it dazzled your eyes. I remembered what he'd said: "Don't mourn."'

Hockney treated the Covent Garden stage as a gigantic canvas, on which he could celebrate the constituents of his art: the intoxication of colour, the quickening intensity of light. The stage also freed him to enjoy the exhilaration of space, on a scale beyond that of the most distended canvas. He explained the white abyss at the end of his *Tristan* by saying, 'I got this incredibly spacey feeling from the music'. 'Spacey' is a Californian adjective, favoured by those who have mush for brains and a mouth full of chewing gum, but Hockney used it with an intelligent precision which is probably unique in the state. It announced his desire to reach outside the frame of a painting or even the proscenium of a theatre. He dispensed with drawings for *Die Frau*: 'Everything was done in three dimensions. It's space you're making. You can't draw it, you've to build it.'

This construction of a world-theatre follows logically from the open-armed expansion of Hockney's work over the last fifteen years. Soon after moving to Los Angeles, he began work on a painting of Santa Monica Boulevard which was to be twenty feet long, unravelling endlessly like the street itself. He could not make the picture work. Perhaps the problem was its concentration on a frieze of pedestrians, most of them (including some loitering adolescent hustlers) arrested in profile – a point of view too static for a city which sees things at a blurry speed of forty miles an hour, and fundamentally unAngeleno in its concentration on passers-by, not traffic. But after abandoning the attempt, Hockney transferred its ambition to his great painting of Mulholland Drive, the ribbon of road along the top of the Hollywood hills which skirts his house. Here, by seeing it as a driver rather than a walker, he managed to rope in the whole of the random, centreless city, and to send the eye on a skidding, looping automotive journey through it. Similarly, his Polaroid 'joiners' rescued photographs from their frozen, deadened condition. These collages of snaps, all taken from different angles, found a way of containing both the enormity of American spaces – the gaping Grand Canyon or the rigmarole-like thoroughfares of Los Angeles – and the actual, extended time necessary to explore them.

A painting is propped up in space, but has no existence in time, just as a snapshot is confined to the single second when the shutter clicked; music moves ceaselessly in time but, being made of thin, vibrant air, occupies no space. Hockney's operatic work has encouraged him to dream of merging the two, rescuing each art from its own limitation.

'When I was working on *Tristan*, I bought a house on the beach down in Malibu, so I could get away from all the drop-ins I have up here, and I began to explore the Santa Monica Mountains behind the beach. I had all that spacey music in my head and a new CD player installed in my car, and I finished up choreographing a drive through the mountains with *Parsifal* on the sound track. It takes an hour and a half, and on the route I go, what you see matches what you hear. Isn't the Grail temple in *Parsifal* supposed to be in the hills outside Barcelona? Well, the landscape here's not unlike that. I'd take you on the drive, but it has to be at 6.30. It's all geared to the sun: nature does my lighting!' Like the veering voyage of the eye through the length and depth of Hockney's 'Mulholland Drive', or the view from his car window as Wagner's restless, chromatic score charts the ups and down of the parched Californian highlands, the stage at Covent Garden became a motion picture: the metamorphoses between ether and earth, beneath the pinnacles of the spirits and the caverns of men, happened in full view; the curtain never dropped. Hockney's designs were paintings which jutted out into a bold third dimension, and which were animated as well, growing and altering as we watched.

I wondered why he had been attracted to this particular opera. His previous theatrical assignments coincided with his own pictorial obsessions. His first opera – Stravinsky's *The Rake's Progress*, which John Cox directed at Glyndebourne in 1975 – was a sequel to Hockney's early series of etchings with himself as Hogarth's rake, going happily astray in the fleshpots of New York. The French triple bill which he designed for John Dexter at the Metropolitan Opera in 1980 – Satie's *Parade*, Poulenc's *Les mamelles de Tirésias* and Ravel's *L'enfant et les sortilèges* – counted as a tribute to Picasso, who provided the decor for the first performance of Satie's mechanistic ballet. But *Die Frau ohne Schatten*, with its top-heavy allegory and its propaganda for reproduction?

'I think', said Hockney, 'it's about creativity. But not just my level of it, with Barak and his paint pots. It's about my mother's level of it as well, which may be more important.' And to illustrate what he meant, he picked up the dormant dachshund Stanley – named after his father's hero Stan Laurel – and gave the dog a positively maternal hug.

Hockney's parents, the ground of his being, are an obligatory reference point in his art. His spry, dapper, ingeniously dotty father was the source of his talent and of his impish persona; his mother, whose creased skin and look of suffering solicitude he has drawn so often and with such love, is his best subject. Despite the rakish homosexuality of his early work, he has always needed an extended family, composed of the lovers, helpers and hangers-on and droppers-in who beleaguer him in Jack Hazan's film *A Bigger Splash*. An extra reason for his identification with Barak in *Die Frau ohne Schatten* is the dyer's irrepressible hospitality. Denied children of his own, Barak invites a mob of ragamuffins home for an impromptu banquet, to his wife's dismay. Now, however, Hockney is a family man in earnest: the single parent of two dachshunds.

Hockney replaced Stanley on the floor and watched contentedly as Boodgie, now awake since there was no more opera to sleep through, set about medicinally licking his soulmate's eye. 'Stanley's a bit bunged up, and Boodgie is putting him right. They're great healers, dogs. Remember the one in the Bible that cured Job's boils and sores with his tongue?'

Chopping up a roast chicken (never intended to be pet food) for their dinner, he measured exactly equivalent portions on to plates set far enough apart to prevent disputes. He is just as careful in his apportioning of affection. 'You've to be very careful you pet them equally. They watch each other, and keep notes. They live for love. Oh, and for food I suppose; that's the only material interest they have. I got Stanley first, then his brother, who was run over when I was away in England – I rushed straight back, and replaced him with Boodgie. The name doesn't mean anything, it was just baby talk when I first had him. I suppose you could say that the two of them are an item now.'

Like all the objects of Hockney's adoration, from his mother on through a succession of lanky lads, the dogs have had their devotion repaid with immortality. In one painting, Stanley's tapering snout has been smashed into cubistic facets; redesigned as a harlequin, he romps through the prints Hockney has created on a photocopier. A terracotta dachshund guards the grate in his sitting-room, and above it a *trompe-l'oeil* fireplace painted on to the wall is decorated with pretended snapshots of the same small tubular companion.

'They're not LA dogs', Hockney insisted. 'They haven't had nose jobs, or done commercials.' All the New York dogs I know are in analysis, but LA dogs are more concerned with their image than their psychic health: on Venice Beach, during this visit, I saw a labrador strutting in Raybans, and in Culver City I passed an establishment calling itself a Dogromat ('We wash cats too!'). Hockney's dogs have supplied him, perhaps for the first time, with a love which is unconditional and disinterested, not dependent on his celebrity. They are also a stabilizing influence. 'I used to think I couldn't have dogs because I travelled so much. Now I have them, I don't feel the need to travel. As a matter of fact, I never go away for longer than three weeks now.' Hockney proved his selfless fondness later when, while he was dandling them, I noticed a dollop of what President Bush used to call doggie doo-doo on his natty, expensive trouser leg. He swabbed it off without fuss or revulsion. These are the proudly worn badges of parenthood, like the nursing mother's epaulette of sick.

Perhaps Hockney has not entirely outgrown his sexual fears, currently concentrated on the operatic sopranos with whom he is obliged to have professional dealings. 'Ooh, those big ladies', he said with a nervous shudder. 'They all frighten me.' At the opening of *Turandot*, which he designed for the Chicago Lyric Opera the previous winter, he had endured a tongue-lashing from the paprika-tempered Hungarian prima donna Eva Marton, who – unable to cast off the persona of Puccini's castrating princess – berated him in broken English for not having sent the proper quantity of compliments and floral tributes to her dressing room.

Nevertheless, Hockney reveres the female principle. He has earned the right to his remark about creativity, and by his own indirect means has worked his way round to sympathy with *Die Frau ohne Schatten* and its enthusiasm for breeding. As his deference to his mother implies, every male artist envies the fertility which is a woman's by right. But Hockney has no need to fear such comparisons. He is a factory of ideas; more than a painter, he belongs to a tradition which – extending from Leonardo to Duchamp – sees the artist as a projector, an inventor, a conjurer with ideas.

His autodidactic reading list includes Euclid and Einstein. In recent years, as well as disassembling photography and experimenting with the fusion of music and painting, he has analysed the pictorial narratives of Chinese scrolls, investigated computer technology, and tested the creative potential of each new electronic appliance to come onto the market.

The fax machine, a medium of communication, suits his irrepressible gregariousness. He regards it as a charitable offering, specifically designed to compensate him for the gradual loss of his hearing: the fax, he says, is a telephone for the deaf. Hence his hobby of disseminating serial faxes throughout the world with instructions on how they could be collated into pictures. 'I learned how to get very subtle greys on a fax, a texture a bit like linen. It can make a beautiful object. Then I got a new machine that would bend them or make them go negative, so I'd send a message saying MIND-BENDING FAX COMING SOON.'

There was a further conceptual agenda: his faxes and the vividly inky prints made on his Xerox copier were Hockney's reproof to Walter Benjamin's haughtily modernist prejudice against mechanical reproduction, which – according to Benjamin – cheapened the charisma of the artistic image. Copied in miniature for sale to tourists, the *Mona Lisa* is desanctified. Losing her uniqueness, she congests the world with postcard-sized facsimiles of herself; her indignity is confirmed when Duchamp attaches a moustache and an obscene caption to her. Benjamin's theory offends Hockney's folksy, gregarious wish that the lives of all people should be cheered by art. He therefore set out to show that a reproduction could be a new and different picture, not merely a discounted version of some priceless, untouchable original. This project began with an installation at the National Gallery in London in 1981, when Hockney compared the experience of piously studying Piero della Francesca while you stand to attention inside the museum with the more relaxed connoisseurship of a postcard pinned up next to your bed. It advanced towards Hockney's 'home-made prints', composed directly on the glass of his Xerox machine, and his use of an electronic paintbox, drawing on a television screen with a computer: in both cases, he had abolished the notion of an original.

He was next obliged to dispense with the originating artist. This he was happy to do. In the age of Madonna and Jeff Koons, when exhibitionism has become an art form and creative work is a species of self-advertisement, the fax enabled Hockney to modestly experiment with his own cancellation. In 1989 he faxed the constituent squares of a gigantic picture to Brazil, where assistants he had never met assembled it in his absence: 'The work had been dematerialized somewhere and materialized somewhere else, and I thought it would make it more interesting if I didn't appear.'

Another of his playthings was a still video camera, one of only a few hundred manufactured. 'I thought I'd get it', he says, 'because I already had the printer.' With it he photographed an assortment of picture dealers, plumbers, opera impresarios and delivery boys who just happened to turn up at his house. He was curious to see how the images – flattened and depthless, the bodies merging with the squiggly landscapes which he used as a backdrop – would look when printed.

The results dangled from a high wall of his studio, built on the remains of a tennis court in a corner of his compound, where he chucklingly read the characters of his subjects in the postures they had adopted. A still of an LA beach bum, exuding attitude from every pumped-up muscle, stood near that of a pimply English youth on holiday, clad despite his round-shouldered sallowness in what Hockney called 'a Bradford Hawaiian shirt'. Further along, Dennis Hopper glowered as satanically as his brimstone-breathing sadist in *Blue Velvet* and clasped a new-born baby, which he might have been about to eat. 'I took the dogs with me once when I visited Dennis', said Hockney. 'Stanley went in and peed straight away in the middle of the carpet. You could see from the look on Dennis's face why he didn't make his career in musical comedy.' Stanley Donen, the director of *Singin' in the Rain*, leaned in a corner with his ankles crossed at an effortlessly debonair angle: 'Just look at that; you can tell he was a dancer'. Every artistic enterprise must have some human benefit. Our obsession with replicas derives from our instinctive need to reproduce ourselves, and the camera is the machine with which we trap the coveted likenesses of friends, relatives, loved ones. Hockney had taken the opportunity, in this series of life-sized portraits, to call the roll of his current extended family.

He knows that art is play, and is unembarrassed by his infantile enthusiasm for gadgetry. The cameras and printers are the train sets he probably never had as a boy in Bradford. His games, however, are grown-up – conceptual adventures, enquiring into our assumptions about time and its exclusion from the stilled life of a picture, about space and the false fixity of Renaissance perspective, about the integrity of the image and its fate when reproduced.

Even so, the result of these abstruse researches is his triumphant vindication of a child's world-view. *L'enfant et les sortilèges*, which he designed for the Met in 1981, concerns the rampages of an enfant terrible and his chastening by a troop of domestic devils. Colette's libretto begins with the child's uproarious refusal to do his homework; he is punished by a battalion of humanoid numerals which escape from his maths book and dance around him, screeching nonsensical sums – '*Deux fois six trente et un!*' A decade after the Met production, Hockney was following up a hunch about the delusion of visual order by reading texts on fractal geometry. In one of these he came across a reference to a meeting hastily convened in the nineteenth century by mathematicians who had discovered a flaw in arithmetic. In his book *That's the Way I See It*, Hockney reports that 'I was as delighted as the little boy in the Ravel opera who shouts, "Two and two is sixteen!" I thought, maybe it is.' The fact that the child shouts no such thing – the crazed equations are dreamed up to taunt him, by numbers running amok – is precisely the point: Hockney with typical generosity has attributed to the unworthy infant his own elastic mental conjecture.

The factory works at all hours: Hockney never stops creating, cogitating, chattering. He has a ravenous eagerness to learn, and an equal compulsion to teach. The most trivial observation can wind him up for an associative trip around the world.

The dozy indifference of his dogs to the television monitor prompted a dissertation on technology and perception: 'I've learned a lot from Stanley and Boodgie. They can't read the television picture. It's an abstract to them – which is exactly what it is to us, except that we've forgotten that. We assume it's reality, whereas it's as artificial as a painting. And another thing – why aren't we allowed to see high-definition television, like they have in Japan? I suppose it's for political reasons. With a better image, the long shot becomes possible. Then we might see more than they want us to. I never watch television myself, there's fuck-all to look at in a TV picture, I don't even think it's visual, it's just radio with the picture added as an afterthought. With the movies it was the other way round: they worked out the visual grammar before 1929, then sound came and that was the afterthought. But the people who make movies have also forgotten that they're dealing with a picture on a flat screen. They think if you aim the camera you get reality. I haven't seen a movie I liked since *Who Framed Roger Rabbit?* That's a master-piece, I've watched it twenty times. It works on many levels, like *Die Frau ohne Schatten.* No, I mean it, it's full of subtle jokes about the flatness of the picture plane. At least it's aware of its own medium: the acid bath they want to dip Roger in would also destroy the film, because of its acetate.'

Hockney scoffed, in the course of this spoken essay, that film-makers 'don't even understand colour any more. You remember the old *Adventures of Robin Hood* with Errol Flynn? I've got a video disc of that, and it looks as if they painted the forest green! Then compare that to the new one with Kevin Costner: it could have been shot in monochrome. Anyway, I suppose movies are more about light than colour, which has to come from a pigment.'

This is the kind of simple but revelatory observation which only a genius would make. Films are a shadow-play of wraiths and chimerae, a dance of ghosts switched on by electricity. Painting, for Hockney, is more substantial and nutritious because its colours, like Barak's dyes, were once exuded by living things: pigment is sap, blood, vital juice. Justifying his decision to give a tree in *L'enfant et les sortilèges* a red trunk and foliage of midnight blue, he said, 'A physical colour is a physical thrill.' One possible objection to his opera designs is that the proper correlative of music is light (or, more often, invisible darkness) rather than colour. The visual shocks of his *Tristan und Isolde* – orange sails on the ship, a blue garden and a yellow cliff – seemed garish in a work where the hero, far from delighting in the visible, sensual world as Hockney does, begs for oblivious blindness.

'You know,' he said, not waiting for me to catch up with him, 'I could make a movie, I think....' He went on to denounce Los Angeles as a city which is obsessed by images but does not understand them. For that reason, he considered the riots of the previous spring a phony war.

'No one here thinks seriously about what a picture is, even though images are omnipresent: it doesn't occur to them that the way you make a picture affects the picture you make. The trial was about an image, which everyone in the world had seen – the beating of Rodney King – but of course when they played it frame by frame in court they destroyed the tempo of it and made it something quite different. A smart lawyer would have picked that up, but no one noticed. Then when the riots started, it was really television that incited them. I was at Malibu, and I could hear the helicopters with the news crews in them, trying to find something to film. Fire looks so good on television! That's why those scenes of the guy being pulled from the truck and beaten on Normandie Avenue were so different from the tape of Rodney King being bashed. The cops didn't know someone was filming them, but the rioters did. It was a performance for the cameras in the helicopter above. The whole thing was the exact opposite of the way they covered the Gulf war on TV. Then there was no action, it was all experts showing off their maps. During the riots it was all action, with no experts and no maps to explain it and put it at a distance. That's why people got so panicked. Actually the looting was pathetic. I saw a woman run out of a shop with six ginger wigs. What would she want with *six*? In some areas, the only shops that burned looked as if they couldn't pay the rent and needed the insurance. And look at what *didn't* happen on Hollywood Boulevard. You'd think, if they were really serious, they'd have torched the Chinese Theater, wouldn't you? My brother who lives in Sydney called me while it was going on, to see if I was all right. I told him, "Don't worry, the city's only the size of Yorkshire." LA is all cardboard anyhow, it's not meant to last. You throw a burning rag in and it goes up, then you build it all over again tomorrow.'

A gallery of mementos is tacked or taped to the wall in Hockney's studio: pin-ups of his mother and (in a different photograph) of two louche youths grabbing each others' groins; the severed, shrunken heads of suitors decapitated by Eva Marton in the Chicago *Turandot*; a cryptic text from Schopenhauer about music and 'the true nature of all things'; a scroll awarding him an honorary doctorate from the Royal College of Art;

and a summons for speeding issued by the local highway patrol. In the course of my browsing I noticed a fax from the commissar charged with the reconstruction of Los Angeles after the fires had burned out. It requested Hockney's 'input'. He said he had no intention of replying.

This blitheness implies no lessening of his love for the precarious paradise he has adopted. His early Los Angeles images, sleek but anaesthetic, showed a city of collapsible pastel boxes with cool, ruffled pools and ironically weary palms. Then he took to representing the place in more ardent tones: 'Mulholland Drive' is a patchwork of scorching red, ripe orange and glossy tropical green. He also began to concentrate on warm domestic interiors, as in the painting which folds all of Santa Monica Canyon into the elongated house shared by Christopher Isherwood and Don Bachardy.

Hockney's current work, which developed alongside the alternative universe of the *Frau ohne Schatten* scenarios, treats the terrain around the city even more lovingly. 'A friend of mine', he said, 'called them abstract paintings with stories in them. Every line turns into something else as you watch. If you sit and look for a while, you realize you can make many spaces.' It is characteristic of him to emphasize the creativity of the viewer's eye. We decipher his doodles and twirls – a fallopian tube from which flowers are sprouting; an expanse of thick violet which might be the ocean, pushing against a web of yellow which might be the lighted grid of Los Angeles – and rearrange them into landscapes: he permits us to take the credit for inventing them.

This is a consequence of his experiments in reversing traditional perspective, with its single angle of vision which tapers to a vanishing point. Alberti's science immobilized the spectator and trained his eyes on a pin-prick of infinity where God, whom we will never see, presumably resides. In his collaged photographs, Hockney allows for a multiplicity of possible perspectives (and for the maladjustments between them, measured by the white strips which separate the Polaroids); in a painting like 'A Walk around the Hotel Courtyard, Acatlán', he does not superciliously study the place from outside, as if he had personally created it, but wanders through it and shares it with his fellow creatures. Hockney is a source of forgotten home truths about why we need an art like his. In finding a new way to depict the world or for us to re-envision it, he has made that world more habitable.

One of the new paintings, explicitly representational, imagines Malibu from mid-air: the mountains extend like cradling arms to embrace the bay. Near it in the studio hung a canvas which appeared entirely abstract, with a succession of protective curves guarding a secretive hollow. What story did it tell? 'I often come up to the studio to watch the dusk. The light goes very fast here, not like in northern England where it fades so gradually; and as it goes, it alters the colours and changes the paintings. One night I was looking at that one, and I suddenly realized what it was – a mother and a child. Can you see that?'

Yes: the curves were a tender, swelling body, like arid Los Angeles made fertile by irrigation; the hollow harboured the sea from which all life is spawned. Hockney had painted one more unconscious tribute to his mother's creativity, one more footnote to Strauss's metabiological opera, and – I suppose – one more love letter to his dachshunds.

These days, he is less concerned with swimming pools than with the ocean from which they are only a tame, waveless extract. In Malibu, his view of the Pacific suggests the soothing pantheistic sensation which Jung called 'the oceanic feeling': a sense of our common immersion in nature. He does not look out to sea towards a vanishing point or a hazy, equivocal infinity. 'Down there, it's not the horizon that dominates, it's the living edge of the Pacific – the waves on the shore. And they're always moving and changing.' As for the upturned male bottoms which used to twinkle in the pools he painted, he remarked, when talking about the end of *Tristan,* that 'spirit is everything, body's nothing.'

Though apocalypse rumbles under the surface in Los Angeles, Hockney – having dismissed the riots as an epidemic of imagery – is also unafraid of mud slides and tidal waves. 'My house at the beach was built by the old lady I bought it from, and she lived in it for fifty years. We don't get many storms around here. It's aptly named, the Pacific.' Secure for the time being in his paradise, he puffed on one of the mood-altering weeds which he calls his 'vegetarian cigarettes', and he smiled – I beg your pardon, but it's the only possible word – pacifically.

BARRY HUMPHRIES ON THE COUCH

I HAVE KEPT MY DISTANCE FROM BARRY HUMPHRIES FOR TWENTY-FIVE years, ever since, at a theatre in Tasmania, I sat next to a woman who was foolhardy enough to arrive late for his show. I forget who Humphries was being at the time – probably Sandy Stone, whose geriatric monologues were even then the equivalent of soil erosion, or the chirpy Edna Everage, still a housewife and not yet a self-appointed Dame brandishing a bunch of gladioli as her insignia of office; the flatulent, slobbering Sir Les Patterson – with his compulsory beer can and matching belly – had not been born. Whichever character it was stopped in his or her tracks to greet the latecomer, asked about her parking problems, enquired if her seat was comfortable, waited for her to get out her box of chocs, complimented her perm, wondered if that was a new outfit she had on.... The woman chortled sportily enough. Inches away, I sat rigid with terror, prayed for invisibility, and inwardly raged against this breach of the rules. Wasn't this billed as a nice night's entertainment, not a session in the stocks for the paying customers? Shouldn't actors have the decency to behave as if we were not present?

After that, I always made sure I saw Humphries from a seat in the middle of a row in the back of the theatre. When Edna took to prowling the aisles to press-gang recruits, I booked seats in the gallery. I did not mind being patronized by her as a pauper (she was becoming exponentially richer and snootier as the years passed); at least I was safe from observation, or conscription. Then Humphries commissioned a crane which could raise Edna aloft in a screeching, gladdy-raining levitation and bring her perilously close to my hide-out upstairs. Reading about this in the reviews, I decided that it might be prudent not to see his last London show at all. He is a comic genius, but he can be a fiend when he allows Edna's unedited, uncensored consciousness to blurt out all the truths we are supposed to bite our tongues at. Comedy like this exults in a freedom which is both reckless and ruthless. Taking no hostages, it can be very bad for your sense of self-possession.

When I finally met Humphries in 1992, I arrived early and waited for him in the street, telling myself that if he sent the rampant Edna or the lewd Les to represent him, as he tends to do when invited on to the genteeler television talk shows, I would be within my rights to bolt. But he had recently written a memoir, *More Please*, as himself – well, almost, because a great actor never stops acting, and Humphries' style in the book richly compounds the aestheticism of Pater, the fustiness of Betjeman, and the disingenuous disgust of an autobiographer who forestalls accusations of egomania by claiming to be 'a dissolute, guilt-ridden, self-obsessed boozer' – and he also arrived in his own person. A suit of strict charcoal stripes was his gesture towards anonymity: less sincere than my own desire to be invisible in the darkness of the theatre, because its message was contradicted by an orchidaceously florid tie. His hair, famously lank and dandified in his Wildean youth in Melbourne, was as well-behaved as a banker's. But surely those irrepressible characters of his were holed up inside his besuited body, ready to spring across the footlights at any moment? Edna was there in a flicker of suggestiveness around the pursed corners of his mouth. If he relaxed the line of his lips and flattened his jaw against his neck to push out a hanging garden of jowls, he would become Les.

His monsters travel with him, and one of them, flourishing her spangly handbag, soon threw off the constricting uniform of pin stripes. Our rendezvous was at the Freud Museum in north London, the house where Freud lived for a year between his escape from the Nazis and his death in 1939. Inside is an authentically gloomy recreation of his Vienna apartment; outside it is still lush suburban London, and over the fence a two-pronged gladioli, shemelessly scarlet, poked its pistil at Freud's front door. I pointed this out to Humphries, but it was Edna who appraised it with a smirk. 'Probably planted by Sigmund himself. I don't think the symbolism would have been lost on him, do you?'

Life was already rearranging itself into a semblance of the artist's fantasy. Having thrust a welcoming bouquet over the fence, it handed the comedian material for jokes as soon as we were through the front door of the museum. Humphries began by flicking through the visitors' book. During the week when Saddam Hussein was denying United Nations investigators access to the Agriculture Ministry in Baghdad, a psychiatric pilgrim from Iraq had come to visit the shrine. 'They should have told him,' said Humphries instantly, ' "You can only inspect half this house." '

Edna resurfaced on our tour of Freud's antiquities, a populace of unearthed totems – Egyptian funerary guardians, Roman matrons, Chinese sages, angels with chipped wings – displayed on the sideboards. Her hand lingered over the bristling head of a goat, horned and impish, no doubt suffering, in its absent nether parts, from satyriasis. 'Isn't it lucky', she said with a vocal swoop concluding in a stifled snigger, 'that we can't see the *rest* of him?' She spotted a terracotta statuette with an elephantine schnozzle: 'Look, it's little Barry Manilow!' Humphries added an aside: 'My client, Dame Edna Everage, invited Barry to be a guest on her television show last season in Los Angeles. When he came on, he kissed her a little stiffly. I think he might have been nervous. I'm afraid she behaved atrociously to him. She offered him a drink, and of course Barry wanted orange juice in order to be healthy. Edna didn't have any in her mansion, so she drove off to the supermarket to get some in the middle of the taping, and took the cameras with her. Barry stayed behind with Cesar Romero, who was Edna's butler. They had the most *boring* conversation you ever heard, but Cesar smiled brilliantly throughout it all. The dental work in America is superb.'

Edna was reined in when we came to Freud's confessional couch, blanketed with oriental rugs and piled with soothing pillows: a day bed impregnated with bad dreams like dust mites, where the Rat Man and the Wolf Man had confided their phobias, and where Gustav Mahler had extended himself when his wife, the man-eating Alma, was giving him a more than usually gruesome time. Humphries, who claims to have benefited from psychotherapy but is sceptical about psychoanalysis, studied the couch with a cocked eyebrow. 'Did you know', he said, 'that Edna believes she is the reincarnation of Alma Mahler? Oh, and of Anne Hathaway. That woman needs help urgently.'

But he had not brought Edna to Freud's house to have her brain ironed: he chose it as a meeting place because he enjoys and sympathizes with its sense of geographical dislocation. Just as Freud transplanted Vienna to London, reconstituting his forfeited world in NW3, so Humphries grew up in an Australia which thought of itself as the Home Counties adrift in the South Pacific, with a desert just beyond its trimmed privet hedges. The Melbourne suburb of sweating Tudor villas in which his parents lived was called Camberwell, in homage to an irrelevant English prototype. Like Freud, the young Humphries behaved as if he were a pining exile, although his cultural longings attached themselves to a home he had never seen and about which he had scant information.

'I used to read comics like *Film Fun* or *Knockabout*, which were shipped out to Australia during the blitz and arrived three months late. The Christmas issues turned up somewhere near Easter. There were other bits and pieces that dropped off America too. Gene Autry was one of my heroes, and I had a little pair of cowboy chaps that I paraded around in. I also fancied Ribbentrop, mainly because I thought his name had something to do with ribbons. My mother didn't like me looking at photographs of him, she used to say, "But he's not on our side, Barry!" I was never sure what our side was. The war was so far away, and I couldn't tell the difference between Mussolini and Tojo.'

As a schoolboy, he lived inside a wistful colonial fiction, trying to align Australia with an unseen, unattainably remote Europe. He moped with his easel along the surf-lashed beaches of the Mornington Peninsula south of Melbourne, on the lookout for some local equivalent of Cézanne's Mont Ste Victoire which he could paint. He played records of Beecham conducting Delius, aware that 'this most English of music' was resounding through a steamy night in south-east Asia. At a bohemian encampment which he visited in the bush, the Welsh lilt of Dylan Thomas and the Berlin growl of Lotte Lenya – also recorded, since everything in Australia then was an import and an ersatz – 'frightened the wallabies and traumatized the kookaburras'.

In time, having made his escape, Humphries has come to relish the mutations of that misplaced culture. He mentions the vogue for silver birches, planted to snub the straggly indigenous eucalypts. 'They were considered a very sissy tree when they were introduced. Now you can see how they've taken advantage of so much sun. They grow enormously tall and thick; they look quite Australian!' But no one ever quite lives down the agonies of childhood, even at a distance of several decades and twelve thousand merciful miles. Humphries still rails against the mind-rotting tedium of that suburban existence – drives on Sunday afternoon around the tracts of mock-Elizabethan or Spanish Mission bungalows his father's firm was building; at home, a police state of compulsory neatness and niceness ruled by his mother.

'She was a deeply inhibited woman, with a fetish about respectability. Behind it all was the memory of some fearful thing they referred to in hushed tones as The Depression, which in those days was not yet a mental illness. She had got to this new suburb, and was determined never to look back. She positively hated the past. The second-hand was banned from our house. No fork had ever touched another's lips, no book had ever been perused by another owner – remember how books were "perused" in those days? Once I came home from schools and found all my books were gone, she'd given them to the church. When I protested, she said, "But you've already read them!" '

His earliest comic routines emerged from the deathly gentility and slumbering smugness of this world, whose amenities were drearily enumerated by Sandy Stone and hymned by Edna in a song about the newly fashionable colour which she called 'maroan'. Humphries the amateur social historian subsequently established that the vogue for maroon in the early 1950s had a lot to do with the need to off-load the army's surplus of dye: 'They made beige a popular colour after the 1914–18 war for the same reason, because they were still trying to get rid of all the left-over khaki. Beige got paler and paler until about 1925, when it faded away altogether. Of course my mother thought our furnishings should support the war effort. We had burlap curtains – that was the polite name for hessian – and some lamps made from acid bottles, to show that we were suffering just a little.'

His mother was even unsentimentally up-to-date in her gardening. 'I once asked her why we had no roses, and she said, "They're a bit old-fashioned, Barry." She hated Morning Glory. The poor people who lived behind us had it trained over their outside lavatory, and some of it crept across our fence. She soon grubbed it up, she thought it was common. She went in for snap dragons, phlox, ranunculi, and that flower Australians insist on pronouncing as hy-der-angeas. I liked hydrangeas. You could get inside them, there was actually a cave in there, and the china-blue ones exuded a faint scent. That all came back to me one night through Edna. She was questioning some housewife from Pinner about her garden. This woman grew hydrangeas, and Edna asked her what they smelled like. "Oh no, Dame Edna," the woman said, "they have no perfume." But suddenly Edna got hold of this childhood memory of mine and she said "Yes they do! If you press your face right into them – and you look like a woman who's pressed her face into quite a few things in her time...." I suppose I had a Proustian rush. As a matter of fact, the hydrangea was the favourite flower of Proust, and of the Comte de Montesquieu [the homosexual exquisite on whom Proust modelled Baron Charlus].' The impasto of nostalgia and grossness, of respectable

Melbourne and decadent Paris, sums up the eclecticism of Humphries and the contradictions within his comedy.

In a culture as stranded and estranged as Australia then was, Humphries relied on fraying lineal connections and remittances from elsewhere. As a boy, he accosted the composer Percy Grainger, woebegone after his return from expatriation, and shook a hand which had shaken Grieg's which in turn had shaken Liszt's which had shaken Beethoven's which had shaken Haydn's which once, long ago and far away, had clasped Mozart's. He felt, for as long as the contact lasted, a link to paradise. Later he began sending off to Collectors' Corner in London for recordings of Stravinsky, Milhaud and Weill, unheard and unheard of in the lucky country. 'There was a Communist bookstore in Melbourne, where I got *Ulysses*. I don't know why they had it, I suppose it counted as seditious. Another source of supply was the Continental Book Room. I'd go into town on the tram after school, travel upstairs in a small lift, and there was this shop run by two stern European women with extremely short hair. The place smelled of very strange cigarettes. That's where I tracked down Kafka.'

Having reassembled the history of European music, art and literature on his desert island, Humphries set about belatedly subjecting staid Melbourne to modernism and all its shocking novelties. In his adolescence he was a one-man modern movement. The nightmares of German expressionist cinema gave him a sadistic delight in the aesthetics of terror. This he has not outgrown. When he told me that he hoped to take Edna's stage show to America, I remarked that Americans were less likely to be embarrassed than her shrinking English victims when she hauled them into the lights and quizzed them about their bathrooms: they all think themselves stars awaiting discovery. 'Then', Humphries quietly vowed, 'I'll just have to frighten them a good deal more!'

He also experimented with the nauseous concoctions of surrealism, exhibiting a 'shoescape' entitled *Pus in Boots* which consisted of two shoes retrieved from a rubbish dump, abrim with glutinous custard. Eventually he decided to be an exponent of down-under dada, an art consisting of antics calculated to outrage bourgeois bystanders. One of his dadaist stunts involved gobbling a puddle of Heinz Russian salad, which looks beguilingly like human vomit, direct from the pavement. He later repeated the trick with an airline sick bag, and was banned for a time from all Qantas flights. The dingbat Edna, crazily acting out her dream of celebrity and bludgeoning reality into submission with the blunt instrument of a gladdy, might have been invented by the first dadaist, Tristan Tzara: she is a walking jest, fanatically in earnest.

As he demonstrated with Freud's knick-knacks, Humphries has the absurdist ability to turn any of life's leavings into props, and to use them in a performance which conjures a character out of thin air. He described to me a journey through Tasmania with the film director Bruce Beresford, after they had been in retreat to write a script for *The Adventures of Barry McKenzie*. The film was based on another Humphries creature, an Ocker oaf with eyes so close together that they almost merged and a jaw like a fork-lift truck, an amalgam of the boatloads of young Barrys who used to spend two years in Earls Court bed-sits complaining about warm English beer before returning gratefully to Australia. 'We got to this bleak lowland in the middle of Tasmania – ragged-looking, sere, full of bracken and tarns – and we happened to drive past a broken-down timber lavatory. I said to Bruce, "I think I'll just get out and shed a tear."' (This is one of the multiple circumlocutions for peeing – an activity never referred to in nice Melbourne – which Humphries, through the character of the incontinent Bazza, has added to the Australian slangwidge. Using a variant, Humphries remembers that he scandalised his mother by saying that he had to go out and 'strain the potatoes'.) 'Well, what did I find there, hanging up outside the dunny, but a top hat, a cane and a pair of gloves? Can you believe it? I wondered if there might be a dress code in this lavatory. Maybe an attendant was lurking behind a gum tree, about to tell me "Sorry sir, but you can't go in dressed like that. But I can hire you a top hat...."'

And so the improvisation continued, witnessed only by Beresford, some stringy gums and a flock of passing crows. Here, however, was dadaism in operation, incidentally uniting Humphries' two worlds by imagining a London clubman who had bumped to ground in the empty, abraded, wind-scoured centre of Tasmania, where he abandoned his costume before going bush.

The anecdote also illustrates the wistful poetry which battles with raucous offensiveness in Humphries' act. 'I suppose I've lyricized the sadness or ghostliness I feel in a place like that, or in Melbourne. That's why I wrote the sketch about Sandy Stone wandering round after his own death spying on the Greeks who live in his house now or the Vietnamese in the Californian bungalow next door. I walk those streets feeling as out of place as I remember Percy Grainger being when I ran into him that day. My hand's pressed not on my heart but on the return ticket to London in my inside pocket, lest a gust of wind should blow it away!'

Great clowns are often temperamentally morose. They grin in order to bear it: comedy is their compensation for weakness or handicap, enabling them to control the reactions of those by whom they would otherwise be threatened. The same debility, according to Freud, creates artists, who have to award themselves in fantasy the satisfactions which reality withholds from them. Humphries is pensive and almost dejected when considering the sources of his own life-saving art. All comic careers begin with the tormenting recognition that others are laughing at you. The comedian accepts this shame and, shaking his fist, converts it into pride.

'It was a gift I found by accident I had. I mean that I was ridiculous. I found out at school that I had it. I made people laugh at athletics. I flapped when I ran – there's a name for it, dyspraxia – so they called me Granny Humphries. That was mortifying. But I learned how to use this talent to protect myself, and to get my own back. Comedy is largely about revenge.' In *More Please* Humphries understandably gloats over the distresses suffered in later life (sometimes with his personal connivance) by the teachers and playground bullies who persecuted him. His comedy also provided release from his mother's asphyxiating propriety. 'My sister Barbara rang me up from Melbourne a while ago and said "I hope you're going to be nice about our parents in this book of yours." But humour is a way of telling the truth, it can't be bothered with the politics of niceness. In Australia now they have a sort of neo-niceness: you have to have politically correct opinions about the aborigines or becoming a republic or whatever. It's all cant. That's why they're so paranoid about Les Patterson and his drinking. They can't admit that we're an alcoholic country, like Russia or Ireland.'

Like any satirist, Humphries exults in what he calls 'the illusion of power', bestowed by his ribald, disrespectful truth-telling. But *More Please* shyly admits another, less blood-hungry motive for his comedy, when he refers to 'the forgiveness of laughter'. I asked him about the tell-tale phrase. Forgiveness for what, and from whom?

'I suppose', he said, 'it's a kind of acceptance I'm looking for. A feeling that I'm part of the human race. I only have that with an audience, otherwise I'm a rather isolated person. I'm sure that's why I began talking to them and hauling them up on to the stage – because I felt lonely. The first thing I see is the audience. I was offered Jimmy Porter in the revival of *Look Back in Anger* recently, but I couldn't go back to doing drama: I can't bear the idea of that fourth wall. And there's also the need for reassurance. To be funny is a fugitive gift. I'm never sure I still have it until I get to the first laugh in a show. After that, there's a kind of bonding with the audience.' He squints into the future nervously: 'I would like to do another stage show. That is, if I'm still funny.'

People say that Edna is vicious, a holy terror. But Humphries believes that her onslaughts are a means of forcing timid, cringing individuals – the poor souls who hide from her in the cheap seats – into intimacy with others: a ritual murder of the ego, which is what theatre at its most infectiously joyous achieves.

'You should see it from my point of view. When you get them laughing, an audience changes colour. It's a social thing, so people turn to each other to share it, and as they do it's like a shutter swinging open – you get a flash of blue or pink from their clothes as their bodies swivel. Sometimes I overrun by forty minutes, and have people in the wings pointing at their wrist watches or slashing their throats with their index fingers. I always have to pay the firemen extra! The problem is that I simply hate to stop. That's why I had Edna start taking wide-angle Polaroids of the audience. I loved the absurdity of it, the way she motioned them to bunch up together as if they were a hockey team of two thousand people. But I also meant it. I wanted to take the audience home with me. I can't remember who was at the last cocktail party I went to, but I do remember people in my audience. I remember them by name, because Edna christens them – Thelma from Uxbridge, Marge from Cricklewood...'

Of course, together with cowards who decamp upstairs, there are those who refuse to lower the guard we construct around ourselves. 'I had one in the front row once. I'll never forget. She was studying a mandala in the carpet on the floor all evening, she wouldn't catch Edna's eye. I thought, has she just been told she's terminal? Is she recently bereaved? Eventually I concentrated *all* my efforts on her. I called her Heidi, because I thought she might just have been Swiss. I couldn't crack her. She was my Eiger sanction, my one that got away. But I photographed her, and kept the Polaroid on my desk for along while. As a terrible warning.'

Few others have resisted Edna, or failed to forgive her after she ravages them with a gladdy. Humphries acknowledges the primitive mystery of the proceedings. 'Well, it is a fairly filthy act, I must say. And I think it's the Dionysian thing, especially when Edna waves those gladdies – that's what gets to the audience in the dark. It's a steamy rite. I felt that when I heard my first blue comedians at the music hall in Melbourne as a boy. The laughter was like a baptism, and the esoteric dirty jokes were funny to me even though I had no idea why.'

At its most epidemic, this comic mayhem can kill, as it was reputed to have done at the ancient Dionysian orgies. Humphries recalls at least one casualty. 'Yes, I've had a man die. He had a stroke. They took him out to the foyer and put screens around him. He died clutching his gladdy. A happy end, I suppose.'

Patrick White once commented on the despair underlying Humphries' festive craziness. In *More Please*, describing his sojourns in psychiatric wards during his years as an alcoholic, Humphries himself refers to 'my daemons'. The classical spelling, learnedly typical of him, allows him to temporize between Christian devils and the attendant spirits, divinities of inspiration, whom the Greeks called by that word. His characters, the children of his brain who in being born take over his body, are also dae-mons, and perhaps have saved him from insanity by playfully licensing desires which would otherwise have destroyed or at least deranged him. 'I no longer drink', he says, 'but Les has a glass on my behalf.' The account in *More Please* of his most demented binge – which occured in Sydney in 1970 after a Melbourne newspaper cancelled his column because of what Edna would term 'uncalled-for' jokes about rich Jews celebrating Christmas – is written in the third person, as if Humphries even at this dried-out distance can only contemplate it by attributing it to someone else.

Edna's service to him is more complicated. He acknowledges having inherited a little of his mother's snobbery, 'though I think for me it's a sense of intellectual superiority.' Nevertheless, the little boy who insisted on shaking Grainger's hand has become an intimate of the great and famous. At a dinner to raise funds for AIDS charities in Whitehall in 1991, he shared a table with Princess Margaret, Elizabeth Taylor and her ringleted consort Larry Fortensky, and Stephen Spender (who is Humphries' current father-in-law). I was at a nearby table, closer to him than I had ever permitted myself to be since the incident in Tasmania – but, I told myself, he wouldn't try anything here, in the presence of royalty, would he? The dinner passed off without incident, except for Elizabeth Taylor's junketings to the ladies' room between courses:

apparently her male hairdresser, flown in from Los Angeles for the occasion, was waiting there to freshen her raven frizz. Grumpy at having been outranked, Princess Margaret resembled a thundercloud. Taylor – a little bowed by the years, although the beauticians had ensured that she looked sixteen – made a speech of three whole sentences in a croaky elderly voice, borrowing Spender's bifocals to help her read it.

Humphries then got up to open an auction, to which Dame Edna had contributed a pair of rhinestone-crusted specs. I winced a little as I heard him compliment 'the divine Mrs Fortensky' and remark that the Rubens ceiling of Inigo Jones's Banqueting House had for once been upstaged. Was he being ironic, or not? For the answer, you would have to consult Edna, who mocks celebrities – binning Jeffrey Archer, slapping a badge on Edward Heath so she will remember who he is – while promoting herself as the most vainglorious celebrity of all. She allows Humphries, deplorably well-mannered on this occasion, to jeer at high society while not jeopardising his membership of it.

She also permits him to indulge in prolonged spells of transvestism (which is, of course, the most venerable theatrical tradition of all, the initial incentive to dressing up) with complete sexual impunity. Perhaps that needs to be qualified: more or less complete. An admirer of the precious literary perfectionist Ronald Firbank, Humphries possesses not only all of the novelist's first editions but a pair of initialled knickers once worn by Firbank's sister Heather. To hear him describe how he tantalized Patrick White with a glimpse of these gusseted Edwardian scanties would have riveted Freud, if he had still been present in the house where Humphries told the story. 'I have never seen a man's eyes light up like Patrick's did when I produced those knickers! I could see him trying to size up whether Heather Firbank's hips were narrower than his...'

By way of Edna, Humphries has made posthumous peace with his neurotically prim mother. *More Please* ends with her death in 1985. In the next paragraph, Humphries reports – not coincidentally, although he is writing about his recovery from alcoholism – 'I realized I was happy'. Yet in the course of time Edna, who after all is Humphries, has grown as we all do into the physical image of the once-despised elder. 'When I see photographs of Edna, I notice expressions only my mother could have worn. My Auntie Frances told me recently that her hairdresser called her Edna behind her back. I said I was sorry, but she said, "No, no, it's a compliment!"'

How could Humphries have fended off his mother's progressive invasion of him? It is a biological destiny. I put it to him that, like Anthony Perkins in *Psycho*, he was an exception to Wilde's aphorism which claims that 'Every woman becomes like her mother. That is her tragedy. No man becomes like his. That is his tragedy.'

'Hmm', Humphries murmured and gave me a sharpish look, as if regretting a choice of venue which had prompted me to Freudian thoughts. Then he adroitly changed the subject by retrieving the bibliophile self of whom his mother, the enemy of the second-hand, so disapproved: 'I have some manuscripts of Wilde's aphorisms. He wrote them down before he went out to parties, and rehearsed them while he dressed.' In this respect, the free-associating Edna is Wilde's superior. Dispensing with scripts, she relies on the proddings of her unconscious.

Late in the afternoon, as tactfully as possible, I suggested to Humphries that his life-long satiric vendetta had been a failure. Despite his campaign to break through Melbourne's sanitary cordon of niceness, the suburbs have retaliated and patched up their indomitably bland, imperturbably boring self-image in the soap opera *Neighbours*. The anodyne theme tune of the series, with its homily about how we ought to be nice to the people next door, is even sung by Barry Crocker, who played Bazza in Beresford's film of Humphries' *Private Eye* comic strip. 'Ah yes', smiled Humphries sadly. 'My father-in-law is an addict. His eyes glaze over sometimes, and we say, "What is it, Stephen? Got a poem coming on?"' "No," he says, "it's time for *Neighbours*", and off he pads to watch it.'

But if *Neighbours* is Melbourne's revenge on the filial ingratitude of Humphries, he is already planning his own revenge on *Neighbours*. 'You know the street where they make it is jammed every day with Japanese tour buses? It's become an open-air museum. That's persuaded me that I should actually do something I've often thought about – open a museum which would be filled with totally nondescript, uninteresting suburban kitsch, all roped off and protected by National Trust volunteers. I intend to buy a house in Moonee Ponds – a suburb I hardly know, although they've now got an Everage Street there – and turn it into the Edna Museum. Come to think of it', he said, looking around the cave of ancient deities and modern diseases in which we sat, 'it will be exactly like the Freud Museum.'

There and then, he began to plan the decor. On Freud's walls are Pompeian frescoes of priapic man, centaurs and a galloping Pan. Above the couch is a print of the painting by Ingres in which Oedipus balefully questions the Sphinx about the source of his complex. All this was too old-fashioned for Edna's monument. In Moonee Ponds, pride of place will go to Tretchikoff's much-loved portrait of the Chinese girl with the green face – 'though Edna's favourite picture is Munch's "Scream". When she did her television show in Hollywood last year, she had it hanging over the mantelpiece. She cut a hole in the mouth for a camera to poke through. Of course there was an outcry about that, but you know Edna – she said "Why *can't* I cut a hole in it? It's *mine!* I bought it!"'

Upstairs in the bedroom, the Edna Museum will have one of those triptych-shaped mirrors which, with their plywood backs exposed to the passing traffic, obstruct the view in all the nicest Australian and British homes. Here, rather than on the couch, is where Freudian scruti- nies occur in Edna's household. 'Edna loves those three-piece mirrors. She once asked a woman who admitted to owning one of them if she'd ever given herself an all-over examination in it. "You know", she told this poor creature, "if you take everything off and then clamber up on to the vanity table in front and get the angle of the glass right and if you can do the splits without slipping off that varnished wood – well, you can see your intimate nooks multiplied to infinity!" Of course we'll have to have warders standing by in the museum. We wouldn't want the visitors undressing to try it out.' Edna the matriarchal hypocrite was at work again, elaborating an obscene little scenario to be performed in the privacy of the home, then prudishly intervening to make sure no one did as she suggested.

As I left, Humphries was stretched out on Freud's couch, not to discuss his daemons but to have his photograph taken. He settled comfily into the hollow, which might still have been warm, occupied before him by the Rat Man (who thought rodents were gnawing his fundament) and the Wolf Man (who dreamed he was being eaten by albino wolves, explained in Freud's diagnosis as a guilt-induced punishment for his homosexuality). Humphries, for whom his book is a 'self-memorializing', laid himself out as a peaceful effigy, ready for the cosmetic attentions of the undertaker.

Suddenly he awoke from rigor mortis and, remembering Edna's pet name for her audience, cried 'You can call me the Possum Man!' Then he slumped back to play possum, which in Australian lingo means to sham death. His art is a madness which he, needing the collaboration of an audience but not the solicitude of a psychiatrist, has under perfect control.

Joan Sutherland: High Priestess, Houswife

'Sometimes I wonder', said Joan Sutherland, pulling one of her self-deprecating funny faces, 'whether I can possibly be the person all the fuss is about.'

What she dismissed as 'the fuss' – the roar of the crowds, the bombardment of bouquets and the choral chatter of cash registers as out-of-this-world Cs, Ds, Es and Fs poured from her – had by then been going on for thirty years. Sutherland's record company once claimed that she possessed 'the voice of the century', and she probably did: who else ever combined such power with such agility, and preserved both for so long?

But at the age of 63, Sutherland signalled for the fuss to end, and in 1990 in Sydney gave her last operatic performance as Queen Marguérite de Valois in Meyerbeer's *Les Huguenots*, trying to forestall the St Bartholemew's Day massacre with starbursts of sovereign coloratura. She withdrew from a valedictory production of *Die Fledermaus* later that year at Covent Garden, not because her voice had gone but because her legs could not be trusted. She is persecuted by arthritis, and her knees have been battered by three decades of collapsing at the end of mad scenes; she was terrified that she might stumble and fall during one of Strauss's waltzes. Nevertheless she turned up as a guest at Orlofsky's party during the New Year's Eve performance of the operetta, to share some reminiscential duets with her favourite partners Marilyn Horne and Luciano Pavarotti, to warble 'Home, Sweet Home', and to be fussed over – screamed at, pelted with unseasonal blooms, loaded with trophies – one last time. No doubt still wondering whether she could be the person it was all about, she then removed the battleship-sized green gown which her husband Richard Bonynge had commissioned for the festivity, returned to her chalet in Switzerland, and definitively put her feet up.

The renunciation which saddened everyone else was a relief to her, because it freed her from the obligation to astonish the world two or three nights a week. She had been dropping hints about this for a very long

time. 'Joan just wants to look after the garden', I remember Bonynge saying in 1974. 'But I tell her, if you've got the voice, you've got to sing.'
That, I take it, was a marital order. Towards the end, there were signs that
she found it all something of a drag. At a New York recital in 1989 – unof-
ficially a farewell to the Metropolitan Opera – she toiled through the
pages stacked on her music stand (Victorian ballads and Massenet
mélodies by the quire) with many a sigh and quite a few scowls, like a secretary submerged in paper work or a housewife ironing a cruel and
unusual quantity of shirts. After the customary ovation and the customary verse of 'Home, Sweet Home', she traipsed gratefully home to the
flower beds. Her mind was already on her gardening in the speech she
made after her Sydney farewell in October 1990, when she thanked
Bonynge – her coach and conductor, who first goaded her into developing those high-wire skills – for his 'forty years of spadework'. She regards
herself as a hardy perennial, in need of mulching.

Despite Sutherland's conviction of being planted in the soil, her
singing was unearthly. Grimacing sceptically, she plodded for most of her
career through operatic plots whose main purpose was to justify the
supernaturalism of song. In Offenbach's *Les Contes d'Hoffmann* she played
a doll, cranked up to dispense cascades of deranged vocal frippery; in
Lakmé by Delibes she gamely masqueraded as an Indian temple girl,
whose bell song both narrates and enacts an enchantment as the magician's silvery tintinnabulations are recreated inside her throat. Lakmé is
described as a 'deified priestess' inspired by Brahma, just as Bellini's
Norma is the oracular high priestess of the Druids. The real divinity in
both cases belongs to the operatic diva, whose voice – if she can sing these
exalted roles at all – must be a gift from the beyond.

Sutherland embodied the sheer joy of singing. Listen, for instance, to
the ticklish scales of enraptured anticipation she added to Zerlina's aria
from Auber's *Fra Diavolo*, which she often sang in concerts. The miracle
could happen in her utterance of a single word: 'Gioir!', Violetta's
command to rejoice in *La Traviata*, made a sound like a chandelier,
fracturing light into innumerable facets. Nothing lifted the heart or made
the pulses race quite so hectically as her negotiation of an *allegro* passage
like the polonaise in Bellini's *I Puritani*, where she skipped and soared
along the vocal line, darting above and below to scatter decorations which
were never the tinsel of smaller-voiced coloraturas but always blazed out
with solar radiance.

Speeding through such thickets of minims, she reminded us that one of the emotional thrills of music comes from tempo and the acceleration of time. But she could also slow time down with her celebrated trill. While she temporized between two notes, time paused in its tracks and only resumed when she released the quaver and resolved the tension. The feat, in her performances of Donizetti's *Lucrezia Borgia* and *Maria Stuarda*, was emotional as well as technical. Lucrezia's trill over her sleeping son is the gentle beating of an angel's wings as it hovers in mid-air, and Maria's trill, as she recalls a smile of happiness she once enjoyed, contains all the pathos of our search for lost time and vanished youth.

Ending her career, Sutherland bluffly disavowed such pathos. 'Everyone retires from their jobs at some time or another', she told me, as if she were an office worker about to be freed from the typing pool. She has always deflected compliments with an Australian horror of seeming presumptuous, or countered praise with a blunt 'Come off it'. In her own view she is an ordinary woman with an unaccountably extraordinary set of vocal cords (and with a diaphragm that was Pavarotti's envy: he taught himself breath control by gripping Sutherland around the waist and studying the muscular manoeuvres within).

I spoke to her in Sydney three days before her farewell performance, when she was tensing herself for a last bout of what she wryly called 'being adulated – if there is such a word'. Being adulated entailed (as well as a final self-vindication in her singing of Meyerbeer's preposterously difficult music) being looped with streamers like an outgoing ocean liner, and battered by a firework display inside the Sydney Opera House. Then an escort of admirers chanting 'Auld Lang Syne' mournfully walked her car across Circular Quay to the Regent Hotel, where she tucked into a banquet in her honour and was eulogized by the Prime Minister, Bob Hawke, who with pardonable hyperbole described the occasion as 'one of the great arts events of the century'. Next day a tabloid columnist solemnly proposed Sutherland's inclusion in the ultimate Ocker pantheon as an honorary sports star, along with the cricketers Jack Brabham and Don Bradman, the swimmer Dawn Fraser, and the.immortal race horse Phar Lap (stuffed and still upright in a Melbourne museum). In Australia, she is simply 'our Joan', admired for her accomplishments but beloved for her embodiment of the national virtues: good humour, modesty, ordinariness or perhaps Everageness.

The previous weekend, she was diligently signing her way through the boxes of programmes and mementoes fans had sent in, trying hard not to get them mixed up. 'And then', she sighed, 'there are all the letters I've had from paraplegics....' It was a line worthy of Dame Joan's sister-superstar Dame Edna. Both of them are suburban girls who awoke to find themselves world-famous – except that Edna the megalomaniac relishes the self-generated publicity, while the placid Sutherland, unshakeably sane despite being the great interpreter of operatic insanity, could not wait to escape from it.

'At a certain point the career took over', she said. 'Now I've decided that the career has had enough of my time. Besides, it's such a strain to get into those costumes, with the steel bones and the lace-up backs. They're so heavy to wear. And having to put on all the war-paint!' In readiness for retirement, Sutherland had pensioned off the image-doctors. Her photographs were once finessed into glamour for record covers by discreet airbrushing; bunches of strategically placed flowers sometimes concealed her assertive chin. She laughed happily about these impostures. 'What is it they say my jaw is like – a ski jump? Or is that my nose?' Now returned to its owner, the face was gently creased, softened by time and elasticized by her self-mocking smirks. Her hair, formerly spun into a gravity-defying red bouffant, relaxed into sandy waves. She resembled everyone's Platonic idea of an auntie.

Yet her casual, comfortable manner could never entirely suppress the nervous strain of the highly strung virtuoso. 'All my life, I've been trying to do better. I've set my own standards. Now I can't find anything I can do better. I'll only do worse. And what more do I have to *prove*?' This emerged as a heartfelt, almost desperate plea: a great performer's life is spent defending a reputation which depends on physical powers, and these steadily decline as they are used. A soprano's high Cs are counted; her stock of E-flats is even more strictly rationed. Sutherland, who did not ask to possess the voice of the century in the first place, thought it unfair of us to expect that she should possess it indefinitely. 'I never dreamed of a career like I've had. When I went to England in 1951, I'd have been happy if I'd sung just one season at Covent Garden. Oh well,' she chuckled, 'maybe I wouldn't have been *all* that happy if they'd chucked me out after a year. . . . But I've always been fairly matter-of-fact. What you've got can be taken away tomorrow. You're only as good as your next performance; you're not even as good as your last one.' She shrugged, exemplifying the nonchalant fatalism which is the national mood of Australia.

I once saw Sutherland cope, as unflappably as the Aussie battler she is, with a national emergency. In April 1974 she sang *La Traviata* in Lisbon, an engagement off the beaten track which she accepted because, on the night their son was born in London in 1956, she and Bonynge had been to the cinema to see a dreary Cold War thriller called *Lisbon*. She was curious to visit the city, and thought the weather might be nice. The film, significantly, was Hollywood's pat on the back to Portuguese Fascism: Ray Milland battles communism, and converts a girl to capitalist values by promising to buy her as many dresses as she desires. By 1974 the regime was foundering, and a few hours after Sutherland's Violetta had died for the final time a folk song on the radio gave the cue for a revolution. Tanks rolled out of the barracks, politicians were rounded up, and the army took control. The airport was closed for several days. When it reopened, thousands of delayed foreigners and alarmed locals converged on the car park to queue for hours in the hope of being shovelled on to any plane going anywhere.

I was in Lisbon on holiday, and had met Sutherland once or twice at the theatre. Arriving at the airport, I found her ahead of me in the queue, cheerily waving. In her wake she dragged a personal baggage train: hampers of costumes and wigs; boxes of Portuguese rugs and tiles for the house in Switzerland; a basket stitched with coloured figures to keep her needle-point in. Her only helper was her all-purpose major domo Chester Carone, a one-time chorus boy and cinema manager. Bonynge, having jumped the queue with the connivance of British Airways, was already on a plane to London, where he was due to conduct at a recording session. She spurned the offer of help with her bags: 'I'm a big strong girl.' The revolution had not distressed her, although she did object to the hammers and sickles painted in red on Lisbon's baroque monuments and the political posters which had begun to paper the city's ceramic walls. Her hand, I felt, was itching for the mop and scrubbing brush.

The liberating army kept us under surveillance with its guns as the queue shuffled round in circles. It began to rain. The dye from Violetta's flouncy gowns seeped along the gutter. 'I don't suppose I'll be wearing those again', said their owner with little remorse. The basket for the embroidery developed a snagged tooth, ripping her stockings and tearing holes in her coat. Her wet hat drooped like a cabbage leaf around her ears.

She indulged herself in a single complaint: she was dying for the loo. Then, buffetted by wind, with waterfalls trickling down her shoulders, she grinned like a rainbow and said, 'Maybe I'll catch pneumonia. Then I won't have to go to Detroit on Wednesday for the Met tour!'

At the time, although I marvelled at her refusal to demand special attention for herself, I did not understand the true extent of her moral composure – or perhaps, since she is after all a creature of the theatre, I did not guage the true valour of the act she was putting on. For when I mentioned the incident in Sydney sixteen years later, she rolled her eyes and wailed, 'I was *terrified!*'

'I know they had machine guns, but they weren't going to shoot us. What were you afraid of?'

'MONEY!!!' cried Sutherland, with an urgency which merited an E-flat. 'I was sure they were going to search me, and I had cash stashed *everywhere.* We'd asked to have some of our fee paid in cash, so we could buy those tiles and have the carpets woven. But everything was cheaper than we thought, so Chester and I were stuffed with what we hadn't spent, all in small notes. Don't you remember the soldiers were searching people in the terminal, because the Portuguese were running away to Brazil with their jewels? But luckily they got tired of it before our turn came, and they let us through.' The incongruities of the scene sum Sutherland up. The diva for whom a draught ought to be a catastrophe quietly queues in the rain and merges with the crowd. Scratch the skin, however, and you find that she is not so ordinary: for a start, she is dressed in dollars.

Sutherland could disparage her fame and ignore what she called the 'hoohah' of acclaim because she saw her career as an accident. She was never powered, like Callas, by fierce ambition (although she had Bonynge to be ambitious for her). Fearful of claiming to be anything so pretentious as an artist, she said of singing, 'It's me job'. When I badgered her to explain how all this could have happened without her craving it or clawing her way towards it, she answered, 'It's a matter of luck, dear boy.'

She has retrospectively transformed her life into a charmingly humdrum moral fable, a tale less of genius imperiously ascending than of virtue and hard work fortuitously rewarded. 'Both Richard and I grew up out of the Depression. We had simple backgrounds – I won't say we were rock-bottom poor. Then came the war, a very troubling time, because we didn't know whether our relations would survive it. And afterwards there were all those post-war opportunities. We just grasped the opportunities: that was our luck. When I got to England, Covent Garden was rebuilding an opera company, and I became part of that. We worked and we learned. We lived frugally and were happy. My rent in London was £3 a week. Richard lived on the same, plus Mum's dinners.' (Mrs Sutherland, her daughter's first teacher before Bonynge assumed control, accompanied Joan to London as coach and chaperone.)

'That's why none of it could happen now. London today is so expensive. And besides that, it's all instant gratification. Young singers don't have time to sit and perfect their professions and learn by watching others, as I did all through the 1950s. They push their voices, they ruin themselves because they're in a hurry. Or else they shouldn't be singing at all. My spouse says I'd be no good as a teacher: I'd chuck my students out and tell them to be secretaries.' (Sutherland prudently trained herself as a stenographer in Sydney before setting off for London.) 'I don't approve of deluding people when they have no talent. Still, I can see why their teachers do it. I suppose singing teachers also have to earn a living!'

The homiletic version of Sutherland's early years includes a respite from the lowly, dutiful regime of work: the flight into cinematic fantasy which Australians during the Depression called 'Saddy arvo at the pitchers'. 'What else was there to do then?' she moaned. 'We were allowed to go for walks in Centennial Park – accompanied, of course. But for entertainment, we went to childrens' matinées. We didn't have so much ourselves, and we just gawped at those beautiful creatures up there on the silver screen – Myrna Loy, William Powell, all of them. They had such fabulous clothes, while we were sitting there in our simple cotton dresses. Poor Richard grew up in a Methodist family, and he wasn't allowed to go to the movies – at least not until *The Great Mr Handel* came out. His parents made an exception for that, because of the *Messiah*! He's made up for it by now, he has orgies at the video shop – "Look, look, there's a new Jean Harlow release!" '

Sutherland's shy adolescent dream of beauty was eventually transferred to opera: permissible so long as you don't believe in it, or confuse it with the stringencies of real life. Sutherland never abandoned herself to a role as Callas did, because to do so would have seemed almost morally reprehensible. Nor, unlike Callas, did she live her life as the continuation of an opera, a spectacle of blow-ups, breakdowns and walk-outs. Callas's idea of a holiday was an adulterous cruise on Onassis's yacht. Sutherland prefers something more mundane: 'I love getting in the car and tootling along. Of course one flies, but you don't *see* anything.' Shortly before we spoke she had treated herself to a trip down the Nile, politely listening to lectures about the Coptic monasteries by scholars from the British Museum. 'Some friends of ours had made the booking, and they couldn't go. When they told me, I said, "Hang on, when did you say that was?" Ricky was working, so I took our housekeeper with me. It was lovely.'

She refers to the loopy ladies or dippy dames of her repertory as 'rather fey creatures', cautionary instances of what happens when you cannot tell the difference between illusion and truth. Bellini's Amina in *La sonnambula*, who symbolizes all the vertiginous dangers of a vocal art like Sutherland's, tends to sleep-walk on parapets or across collapsing bridges. Elvira in *I puritani* wanders in and out of madness. Although Sutherland is anything but fey, she surely found somewhere inside herself an affinity with the anguish of characters like Donizetti's Lucia di Lammermoor. The version of her youth which she gave me staunchly omitted its tragedies. On her sixth birthday, her father died before her eyes, suffering a heart attack on their way back from the beach; in 1950 one of her sisters, emotionally distressed, calmly caught a bus to the Gap, where Sydney harbour opens into the Pacific, and jumped to her death. Then in 1961, forced to control her grief, she gave her first concert in New York shortly after being told of her mother's death in London. Her own medical tribulations – a painful back, that stiffening arthritis – were borne with the same bravery, not used as excuses for cancellation. 'Oh, often I wasn't comfortable. But I had to go on. There was never anyone else who could *do* it!'

Singing is self-revelation, even when the self reluctantly revealed is that of the convivial but reticent Sutherland. Her unique sound, when not insanely exceeding the speed limit, often had a drooping, lunar melancholy, heard in the lament of Handel's bereft enchantress Alcina or the wistful elegies of Amina. But her emotional sources have always remained secret. She nimbly dodged any compliments about her acting: 'Ah, you know Noël Coward's joke about me – he used to say [and she imitates Coward's epicene, ironic purr exactly] "You're always so *sincere*, dear."' I caught her leafing through a magazine which contained a full-page photograph of Plácido Domingo, glaring with saturnine passion in order to sell a new record. 'Ooh I say', murmured Sutherland to her colleague's overly operatic image, 'do you mind? Aren't you looking a bit intense?' And she burst into lilting, incredulous giggles. It is not that she herself lacked intensity: she merely considered it bad manners to confuse the private and the public, or the artistic and the actual, by exhibiting that intensity in the wrong place.

'I have my feet on the ground', she often declared. Praising the Australian Opera's production of *Turandot* in 1990, she pitied the soprano who had to sing while perched on a facsimile of the Eiffel Tower – 'Me, I like a good surface to stand on.' A level head and two steady feet saw her through three decades in the tantrum-prone, crisis-fuelled environment of opera. Engrossed by her soothing hobby of needlepoint, she remained calm while temperaments fizzed around her like Etnas.

I asked her about a previous production of *Les Huguenots*, at La Scala in 1962, which teamed her with three volatile partners: the dilatory tenor Franco Corelli, the applause-hungry, competitively loud mezzo Fiorenza Cossotto, and an elderly horse called George, on whose back Sutherland as the queen had to make an imposing entrance while laced, for the sake of her bad back, into a steel corselet. 'Well, in the first place Corelli – shall we say – rather underestimated his role, and didn't manage to learn the duet he has with me. They suggested cutting it altogether, but I wouldn't agree to that. Marguérite has such a short part – all I have after that first scene is a cough and a spit, then I'm off again – and I didn't want to lose any of it. So I more or less did the duet on my own. I ended up singing a good deal of nonsense, which Richard and the conductor made up between them; no one noticed. Poor old George wasn't much trouble. He was rather aged, and the groom had to give him a slap on the rump to get him on stage. He also had wind. Cossotto was playing my page, and at one point she had to go round behind him. He let fly right in her face. I was sitting up there on top and felt something go. "Is that *only* wind?" I thought. Cossotto came back round the front again looking quite green.'

'It couldn't have happened to a nicer person, could it?' I asked. Cossotto is known in the business as an unscrupulous upstager.

'Now', said Sutherland, snorting and pointing a finger, 'remember *you* said that! Don't you attribute that to me!'

At the Met in 1987 I watched her rehearsing for a concert with Pavarotti which comprised staged excerpts from *Lucia di Lammermoor*, *Rigoletto* and *La traviata*. The programme, one act from each opera, required her to die three times. Lucia collapses in dementia after slaughtering her husband on their wedding night. Gilda in *Rigoletto* sacrifices herself to save the man who has seduced her, but is carried out in a sack by the assassin Sparafucile so she can sing a final duet with her father. The sack on this occasion was very large, and the Met – in recognition of the diva's bulk – hired a contingent of extras to help Sparafucile transport it. Finally, the reformed courtesan Violetta expires of consumption. Sutherland met these serial fates with the same squared, stoical jaw and the same reliably transcendent high notes.

The rehearsal contained one moment of high drama when Pavarotti – possibly miffed because he was only allowed to die once, whereas Sutherland did so in triplicate – halted the proceedings. It happened during the final scene of *Lucia di Lammermoor*, among the Ravenswood tombs, after he plunged a rubber dagger into his plump chest on receiving the news that Sutherland's madness had proved to be fatal. The men of the Met chorus, immunised against tragedy by long exposure, were pretending to commiserate with his last melodious gasps. Pavarotti, who had been supporting himself against a specially reinforced Celtic cross, bounced upright, crossed the stage with unaccustomed speed, and buttonholed a member of the chorus.

'My friend', he said, 'are you 'appy?'

'I guess so', grinned the man.

'But you must *not* be 'appy!' roared Pavarotti. 'Why you smile when I am dying? Is this not sad for you?'

The man quaked. Behind him, his colleagues in the chorus suddenly looked as if a personal calamity had befallen each and every one of them.

Pavarotti, still not appeased, rotated to the front of the stage and called down into the pit: 'Maestro, I am right, no?'

Lost for words, Bonynge nodded. Pavarotti then settled back against his cross and resumed his exquisite exit, checking every few bars to make sure that the chorus was not enjoying itself.

When the rehearsal got to *Traviata*, Sutherland in a sensible Victorian nightie installed herself in a chair beside Violetta's sick-bed and forgave the sobbing Pavarotti. In the bitter New York winter, her coughing fits were not acted: she was suffering from a heavy cold, although her voice streamed out with its accustomed shining strength. At one point Bonynge stopped her to correct a musical error. She cupped her ear, woefully elongated her face as if it was made of plasticine, and honked through her phlegm and mucus, 'Oh Ricky, I can't hear a word you're saying, I'm *that* stuffed up.' He repeated himself. She blew her nose, recomposed her clown's features, and got back to the melodious business of dying. For Sutherland, the sublime and the banal overlapped, like the singing and speaking registers of her voice.

Doubtful about the propriety of taking opera too seriously, she tended to think of something else while directors explained their concepts and analysed whichever character she was – for the duration – serenely pretending to be. 'I can't bear it when they ask what the motivation is behind this or that. Eventually I work out why I'm supposed to be doing what I'm doing. By that time the director has usually gone off to Timbuktu or Bullamakanka [a mythological Australian destination, also known as Wop Wop, which signifies nowhere].' The Australian Opera was rightly proud of the gauzes abstractly designed by Sidney Nolan for its production of Verdi's *Il trovatore*. Sutherland, striding on-stage to sing Leonora, wondered aloud what one lofty blur was meant to represent.

'That's the moon, Dame Joan', someone helpfully ventured.

'Looks like a fried egg to me', muttered the domestic diva, and began to produce a constellation of sounds every bit as luminous and inexplicable as Nolan's planet.

Although Sutherland genially grumbled about the war paint and the weight of the dresses and the chore of learning the moves, her real work probably always began when the singing was over. Wherever in the world she sang, she was attended at the stage door at midnight by hordes of autograph hunters, jostling to get their programmes and record covers and photographs and scraps of grubby paper within reach of her pen. She was always endlessly gracious, ignoring her hunger pangs: this may have been her finest performance of all. She groaned at the thought of all those signatures doled out over the years. 'I've signed posters and special copies of books in limited editions, and then they bring what I've already signed to have it signed again – they don't believe I've done it myself!' I looked down and noticed that her hand, for once free of a pen, was automatically drawing the curlicues which make up her name (always underlined with a flourish, no matter how long the large the crowd was, and accompanied with 'Best wishes') on the boardroom table of the Australian Opera. She must have trained herself to do it in her sleep.

Despite her compliance, the obsessiveness of her admirers worried one who was so unimpressed by the phenomenon of La Stupenda (the honorific nickname bestowed on her after her first appearance at La Scala). 'The fans live only for opera. It upsets me to think that they spend so much money and end up with – what? All those signatures!' But the autographs are mystical relics, fragments chipped from a cult figure. Sutherland is burdened with the dreams of thousands, who plaintively see her living and achieving on their behalf.

It amused her that the signature no one seemed to want was hers on a cheque. 'In shops they don't like my cheques at all. I don't approve of credit cards – I'm Scots, you know – and since I can't drive I don't have a licence, so I can never identify myself. The only card I have in my purse has Mrs R. Bonynge on it. Anyway, why should a shop assistant recognise me? But it is inconvenient sometimes.' All the same, she beamed with relief at her evasion of the hoohah and her safe escape into nonentity: to any girl behind an Australian shop counter, she is much less famous than Kylie Minogue or her latest lookalike replacement on *Neighbours*. Somehow I can't imagine Sutherland vocalizing one of Lucia's crazy cadences in order to validate a cheque.

The paradox of the situation is that, with those interminable signatures, the celebrity is signing away her own existence, donating herself to others. No wonder Sutherland saw retirement as the chance to save the rest of her life for herself and her family. But even after she had absented herself from the scene, the fuss raged on unabated. Sydney in October 1990 buzzed with schemes, half jocular and half in earnest (since mockery in Australia is the matey apex of admiration), for monuments to its favourite daughter. She is already commemorated, in the Sydney Town Hall, by a gigantic ear of white marble with veins the colour of blue cheese: a beautiful metaphor for music, although the lady herself was a little suspicious when they unveiled it. The Australian Opera does a brisk trade in her image, appropriately homely, on tea towels and pot handlers. 'We should have her cast in bronze', said a radio interviewer to me. A journalist I met, thinking of the cantilevered jaw, said, 'She'd make a good Toby jug.' The *Sydney Morning Herald*'s gardening corespondent proposed a celebratory pergola entwined with red roses, 'vigorous, scented and mildew-resistant.'

For myself, I can attest that, on the night she retired, I ate Joan Sutherland. The dinner at the Regent ended with a confection called La Stupenda, intended to oust Peach Melba and the ubiquitous Pavlova (a meringue with the shape and consistency of Ayer's Rock) from fancy Australian menus. A mousse of passion fruit and white chocolate balanced on a plinth of hazelnut biscuit. Its outer skin was darker chocolate, and the entire structure floated on a lake of mango and strawberry coulis.

We live off cult figures, we feed on them; this was an edible monument. Patrick White, who died on the day before the stupendous one retired, once cattily described her as a 'soft sculpture, the colour of a jujube.' As the sweet slipped deliciously down, I thought of all the happiness she had given me in the twenty years since I first heard her, and of my dual reverence for her stratospheric art and her personal artlessness. No, she is wrong to think that we end up with nothing but those dusty programmes and their faded signatures. Memories are sweeter even than passion-fruit mousse and mango coulis.